The International ARMS REVIEW

The International ARMS REVIEW 2

A Jolex PUBLICATION

THE INTERNATIONAL
ARMS REVIEW
is published by Jolex, Inc.,
294 West Oakland Ave.
Oakland, New Jersey 07436,
in cooperation with
the John Olson Company.
All rights are reserved.
Reproduction of this work,
in whole or in part,
is strictly prohibited.
Telephone: (201) 265–7509

ISBN: 0-89 149-029-9 paper

Managing Editor

Roger Barlow

Associate Editors

R. Horlacher
R. A. Steindler
G. Wirnsberger
K. Schinmeyer
H. Schankliss

Contributing Editor & Translator

Lionel Seaton

Layout & Design

M. Hofmann

Printed in West Germany

Dear Reader,

Your enthusiastic interest in Volume I of the "INTERNATIONAL ARMS REVIEW" has encouraged our team of firearms writers to produce this second volume of the series. And, in an effort to make this edition even more interesting, our staff has conscientiously sought to cover only the most unique facets of the arms world. If a revolver was to be considered for a feature article, for example, it had to have some unusual quality that would separate it from the run-of-the-mill: a strange or untold background story covering its development or its inventor, or it had to be a rare specimen . . . a collector's piece . . . a model that possessed some unusual design characteristics, or one employing unusual ammunition or, finally, a specific piece that played an important role in a noteworthy historical event.

You can find technical descriptions of contemporary arms in any one of a dozen different arms magazines so there would be little point in having us simply mirror their format. Instead, we strive to tell our readers who, what, when, where and why a particular piece of armament came into existence. Often, it is the "why" that makes the tale worth telling.

In short, we've tried to produce a work that would provide hours of reading enjoyment to those interested in weaponry, whether he be a student, or collector, or someone whose occupation is based largely on the use of firearms.

We sincerely hope you'll find this second effort even more interesting than our first.

Sincerely,

John Olson

JOHN OLSON, PUBLISHER

TABLE OF CONTENTS

ANSCHÜTZ SUPER

The Olympic Games at Tokyo now belong to the past. The moment the Olympic Flame snuffed out above the stadium, yet another sporting event sank into history.

Gone are the efforts and achievements of the participants, brief were the scenes of the finals, and transient the disappointed faces of those who landed somewhere mid-field.

The pan-German Rifle Team did not even manage to win a single medal, they were unfortunate in competing against other marksmen who were a shade better. It really was only a hair's breadth that made the difference. In three-position small-bore matches, each contestant must fire 40 shots in the prone, in the kneeling and in the standing positions. The best German marksman was Harry Köcher from Plauen, who missed winning the Bronze Medal by only 3 points, and the Gold one by only 16. The American contestant, Lones W. Wigger, won the Gold Medal with 1164 from 1200 possible points. In the prone position, the German, Karl Wenk, broke the Olympic Record of 1960 — and was placed 7th! Karl Wenk achieved 594/600 points. A further 18 marksmen beat the record set up at the previous games in Rome. The Olympic champion was Lazlo Hammerl from Hungary with 597 points. Let it be re-

Model 1413
Calibre
.22 Long
Rifle

MATCH

peated here that both Gold Medalists established new world records in these events, and higher, achievements didn't seem possible.

*

We have recalled the days of Tokyo, for at those Olympic Games German gun and ammunition manufacturers achieved their greatest international success.

At the small-bore shoots all medals, without exception, were won with Anschütz rifles. The RWS rimfire cartridges of Dynamit Nobel Genschow were likewise invincible.

Not only the match-winners, but some 70% of the participants of 57 nations were armed with Anschütz rifles. The Medalists, with only one exception, competed with the Anschütz Super Match, Model 1413 .22 l.r.

Here we are going to report on the manufacture of this weapon. But before we start, a word about the exception. L. W. Wigger, the American, contested with

◄ *Barrel tubing waiting to be cut to length on the sawing machine.*

the Anschütz Model 1411 with standard US stocking and a Super Match barrel.

*

The technicians at the Anschütz plant know the high demands expected of them. Guns have been made there since 1856, and the grandfather of the present owner – Julius Gottfried Anschütz – started up with 10,000 thalers at Mehlis. His grandchildren have continued his work in Ulm-Donautal.

The new home was found in Ulm (West Germany), after the allies had handed Thüringen (East Germany) to the Russians.

Ulm, the famed cathedral city on the banks of the Danube, had also been badly ravaged and some 54% of this city had crumbled under bombs of the Allied Forces, between December, 1944, and April, 1945.

In Ulm industrial plants were few and far between. Since 1842 the city has had barracks and a fortress. After 1945 the aldermen had to think anew and entice industry to the city. The firm of J. G. Anschütz GmbH settled down in Ulm in 1950, in the empty halls of the Danube bastion. Today's owners, Rudolf and Max Anschütz, started again after the war more or less as their grandfather had done almost a hundred years before – they tooled up for a Flobert rifle and a simple air pistol.

The factory in the bastion was a makeshift arrangement and everyone was relieved when the plant was transferred to an industrial area at Ulm-Donautal in 1953. This great expanse of land is situated on the right bank of the Danube, adjacent to the Ulm-Friedrichshafen artery. Many big concerns are domiciled there, including H.

Krieghoff KG, that celebrated sporting-weapon manufacturer. The astonishing thing about this industrial area is that it is extremely difficult to find. For there are no signposts pointing the way!

Anschütz's lucky shot was their small-bore match rifles, which, over a relatively short period, won not only national, but international fame. If one asks the marksmen who use these rifles, and the men who make them, why this is so, the laconic reply is: "Anschütz rifles are quite good!" If the interviewee is cornered, you might get out of him: "Well, the ignition time is short, trigger release is light, ballistics are good," but nothing more. A small-bore rifle isn't a car".

*

The manufacture of highgrade rifles still requires a high degree of handicraft, despite au-

The barrel blanks, ▶ two at a time, being drilled.

Right: The barrel truer checks for alignment. Occasionally, he "lends a helping hand" with his hook. The human eye is still better than any straightening machine.

Part No.	Description	Retail price (1965:1 $=4,20) DM
1	Barrel	155,—
2	Receiver	42,—
3	Barrel retaining pin	0,30
6	Breech bolt	74,—
7	Bolt handle	27,—
8	Spring guide (extractor)	0,30
9	Ectractor	3,15
10	Extractor spring	0,30
11	Safety catch	9,50
12	Thrust bolt	3,—
13	Thrust-bolt spring	0,30
14	Firing pin	12,40
15	Firing-pin spring	0,75
16	Rear stay	2,10
17	Front stay	0,90
18	Cover sleeve	0,90
19	Sear spring	0,30
20	Trigger	4,75
21	Adjusting plate	0,90
22	Stop pin	0,30
23	Sear	3,60
24	Trigger-lever spring	0,40
25	Setscrew for adjusting plate	0,40
26	Axle pin for trigger, sear and trigger lever	0,25
27	Trigger lever	4,15
28	Setscrew for trigger spring	0,40
29	Trigger spring	0,40
30	Frame for trigger mechanism, complete	26,—
31	Frame for trigger mechanism (empty)	5,60
32	Bolt stop	3,50
33	Pin for bolt stop	0,25
34	Coil spring for bolt stop	0,30
35	Front receiver screw	0,30
36	Rear receiver screw	0,30
37	Toothed spring washer J 3,7	0,20
38	Toothed spring washer J 5,3	0,20
39	Loading ramp	2,95
40	Ejector	0,45
41	Ejector retaining spring	0,30
50	Globe sight, body	10,25

Part No.	Description	Retail price DM
51	Clamp collar	1,15
52	Screw hook	1,10
53	Nut	0,40
54	Interchangeable inserts	0,50
	Posts, width of – 1.7, 2, 2.3 and 2.6 mm	
	Rings, widths of aperture – 2.2 – 4.5 mm	
	(increments of 0.1 mm)	
60	Adj. swivel	4,25
62	Swivel screw	0,60
63	Baseplate	8,50
64	Countersunk screw for base plate	0,25
65	Schutzen hook	41,—
66	Baseplate for Schutzen hook, axially adj.	79,—
70	Stock, complete	296,—
71	Stock, without fittings	143,—
72	Schutzen hook, complete	120,—
73	Buttplate screws	0,25
74	Sleeve for adj. trigger	0,35
75	Abutment plate	0,60
76	Steel trigger guard	9,75
81	Bushing for front stock screw	0,35
82	Rear stock screw	0,65
83	Front stock screw	0,50
85	Palm rest	12,80
86	Baseplate for palm rest	1,95
87	Allen key, 6 mm	1,15
88	Allen-key screw for palm rest	0,40
89	Countersunk screws for palm-rest baseplate	0,25
6702	Special peep-sight eyepiece with scale	68,—
101	Rubber eye shade	2,70
	Sighting disc, aperatures 1 – 1.5 mm	
	(increments of 0.1 mm)	2,70
	Supermatch - conversion system	315,—
4721	Hand rest, adj. all sides	97,50
4722	Hand rest with flattened wooden grip	45,—
4723	Hand rest with cork sphere	45,—
4720	Retainer for hand rest (for a do-it-yourself special grip)	32,50
4730	Hand stop	14,75
4713	Interchangeable rubber butt caps for prone-position shooting	45,—

An example for ordering spare parts
Trigger guard (steel) No. 76 for small-bore rifle, model 1413

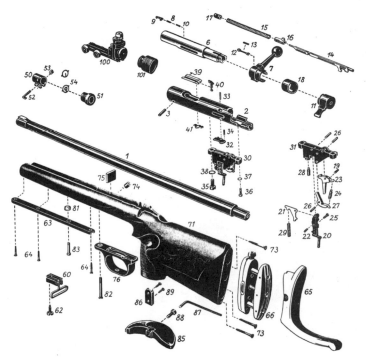

SPARE-PARTS LIST FOR

ANSCHÜTZ

SMALL-BORE RIFLE
MODEL 54
SUPER MATCH (1413)
Calibre .22 Long Rifle

The barrel ▲ receives its external shape on the special copying lathe, as the turning tool runs parallel to the workpiece sample.

used. Six different steels are needed to produce a Super Match. These are special steels for various special functions.

The raw material for the barrels is cut to length in the sawing machine before it passes to the driller. These long drilling machines bore two blanks at a time and oil is pressed through the tubes to remove the steel turnings. After barrel drilling, the first inspection falls due. The borehole is then reamed to an exact drawing pass. The grooves and lands are not cut with a broaching machine, a swage or die is forced down the barrel which in effect forms the rifling and at the same time hardens the inner surface.

tomatic machines and electronics. The gunsmith, not the machine, is in the forefront when producing a Super Match. Each part must fit without tolerances, and only the gun technician can supervise. The machine is valuable as a servant to the man who operates it, since the machine cannot take over the command itself. It is a long process before the various materials are formed into a gun that the marksman can point at the target.

Barrel steel is housed in the east wing of the spacious production hall. Nextdoor is the warehouse for all other types of steel

Now comes the second inspection, for even today there does not exist a machine that can replace the expert eye of the barrel truer who peers up the bore against the light to check the reflections of the rifling. If it isn't as it should be, the barrel truer makes the

Left: Milling the bolt way, which requires 64 different passes before entering the casehardening furnace.

necessary corrections before passing the piece on to the copying lathe.

In the copying lathe the turning tool runs parallel to a "master" barrel, hence the new barrels take on externally the same appearance.

After this stage, the barrels are sent to the chamber reamer.

*

Although the barrels are machined with utmost precision, as indeed are all parts, barrel making seems but a simple matter when compared with the operations for the bolt way.

For 64 different milling jobs are required for the bolt housing alone! Of course, this is accomplished with automatic machines; still, master craftsmen have to check each piece with slide calipers, gages, micrometers, etc. For specific parts, an accuracy of up to 100th millimetre is a must.

The bolt housings or receivers are then deposited in the casehardening furnace. After this process, the receivers are joined to the barrels, cleaned and polished. Then they are blued.

The finished barrels then go into store, until they are required by the men in the production halls who shape them, with other parts, to a functional entity.

Let us now turn our attention to the bolt which requires 13 different operations. First, the firing pin, which is of special hardened, dropforged steel, is tried for size, then the firing-pin spring is inserted and locked in position with a stay. The thrust bolt and spring are slipped into the bolt handle and the bolt handle itself is then mounted on to the bolt body, followed by the cover sleeve and safety lock. However, producing a Match trigger mechanism is even more intricate, as here 25 different parts have to be brought together. The trigger, of course, is adjusted for weight of pull and overtravel, etc. When barrel, bolt and trigger mechanism have been completed, the loading ramp is embedded in the receiver with the ejector, which is locked by a spring clip. Once the bolt has been mounted in the bolt way, the trigger-assembly frame (which carries the complete mechanism) can be screwed into place. Now come the last touches. Headspacing is important, and the trigger lever must be 1.5 mm away from the sear when the safety catch is applied.

During the next phase of testing, the German state has a word to say. For the state-appointed proof master of the City of Ulm discharges the duties of his office at the Anschütz testing range. Once the proof master has given his blessing with the appropriate proof marks, the rifles are test fired at 50 metres. Three series of 10 shots are fired, and if the rifle prints extreme tight-knit groupings it can be offered for sale.

However, in spite of the 30 shots, there are sometimes surprises in store. Only best quality ammunition is used, but every now and again a bullet will go astray, although the rifles are firmly clamped in position. There is no true explanation for these "fliers" — and there probaly never will be.

*

When buying a match rifle, a paper target with the original grouping is included in the price. This is a certificate of warranty for the performance of the gun. Again, it is interesting to know that German sharpshooters have their

Checking the receiver sights for optimal efficiency. Every third operation is a check at the Anschütz plant!

13

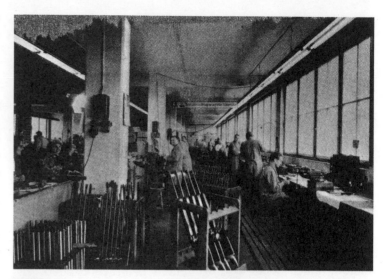

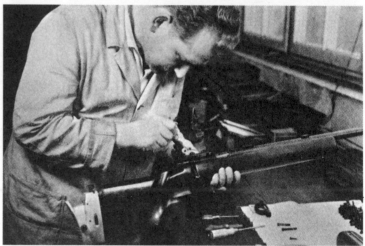

weapons re-checked before important competitions, either by the gun manufacturer or ammunition manufacturer, if there is reason for doubt.

Stocking is just as important as an accurate barrel. The stock is a link between the marksman and the fired bullet. Good shooting goes hand in hand with a thoroughly trained physique, and only when rifle and body are one can professional proficiency be expected.

The Super Match is stocked with well-seasoned French walnut, which is stored in drying rooms to maintain uniformity. There is no need to mention that the humidity of the drying rooms is controlled by electric modulator units.

The outline of the stock is pre-marked on the blank with a template, then the pre-shaped centre piece is cut out with a band saw. This, in turn, passes through the profiling through the thicknessing machine to give it uniform dimensions. The blank then goes into the single-spindle pre-copying machine, and ends up on the double-spindle finishing copying machine. The shaping machine – with six spindles – can mill out complicated palm rests or ream thumb holes behind the pistol grips, automatically.

After the various milling and reaming operations, the women of the sanding department step into action. Once the stocks are glass smooth, the stockers with their checkering tools go to work on forearm and pistol grip. Thereafter the stocks are stained.

*

The Super Match is now virtually ready. The stained stocks are polished, the receivers and barrels let in. The barrel must not have contact with the forearm, it must float freely.

The rifle is then tested again, this time with a receiver sight. These peep sights have micrometer click adjustments for windage and elevation. Each click changes the impact position by about 2.5 mm at 50 metres, and by about 5 mm at 100 metres. These click stops cannot be inadvertently knocked out of position, as with some makes! A screw-driver is needed.

The Super Match of today has changed since its first appearance. Over the years the experience gained at

competitions has been passed on to the gun designer. Improvements are forever being included. Although small, every little innovation helps! However, the Anschütz people do not intend to rest on their Tokyo laurels. What was learnt there will be exploited on the drawing board and in the workshops.

Competition is hard, and every gun manufacturer wants to claim that it was his design that was mechanically perfect, and which spurred his marksman on to victory.

Photos: By courtesy of Anschütz (10), dpa (1), Conti (1).

▲ *Chief Engineer Rud. Anschütz with Sales Manager Max Anschütz, during a company briefing.*

ENTOMBED IN ANTIQUITY

A life entombed in antiquity ... this is mindlessly said without realizing just how multifarious a pursuit of this kind can be. The gentleman, on whom we are reporting, has been an antiquarian since early youth. Mr Wendel is one of those professionals who has really devoted a lifetime to antique arms and armour. There used to be a number of antique-dealers specializing in the arms business, but a combination of circumstances has thinned out their ranks. Young Wendel entered his trade at a time when antique weapons were selling at a premium. He started his career as an unpaid assistant at Ernst Schmidt's, in Munich, an enterprise noted for its great assortment of weaponry. A part of the apprenticeship period was spent in the workshops, where Wendel gained first-hand experience in the fine art of gunsmithing and armour-plate repair. More important, though, he acquired a broad knowledge of intrinsic values so important for an assessor of antique arms and armour. Today we speak of forgery when referring to suits of armour and guns made during Wendel's early life. But can we honestly call these objects a "forgery"? These artisans followed their vocation openly for all to see. They created their products in conformance with old traditions, hence they kept within the boundary lines of legality. Lotze used to make halberds out of old butcher-axes, and Fanderl carved stands and faces for suits of armour, or built model ships and gun carriages. Zwerschina worked with leather and velvet: caparison and trappings, etc. Kilian and Heinrich hammered together suits of armour; and Hugel, the coppersmith, did beautiful embossings. Schneider was a genious at fabricating swords, halberds and pig-stickers, which were the prizes of the day. Wilk chased armour plating and halberds, and Wolf copied wheel-lock muskets. And then there was Berger, a fireman, who spent the whole of his spare time making antique handguns and ivory-embellished wheel- and flintlock smoothbores. All these artists would have been indignant at the accusation that they were forgers. They practised what they had learnt when young, nothing more. Scarcely 50 years before, flintlocks had been in regular use and had been, so to say, modern weapons. Moreover, these artisans were producing weapons for decorative purposes; there was a tremendous demand for replicas ...

Then came the First World War. Young Wendel was sent to the front, and was the

17

first soldier of the 1st Bavarian Infantry Regiment "König" to be reported dead. His comrades found him after the inaugural battle with a punctured lung and a grazed heart. How he managed to survive is unknown.

Once the doctors had patched him up, Wendel became an instructor in one of the few machine-gun companies. Later he was machine-gun officer on the West Front. What Wendel experienced during the war caused him to hate the machine gun. For the rest of his life, only antique weapons were of interest to him.

When the war ended, Wendel returned to his old firm. The business lay in ruins, there was no demand

An exquisite 18th century flintlock pistol. It was made in Turkey for the European market.

for old guns, or copies of such. The world had other problems. The manor-houses of East Prussia had been separated from the German reich, the castles on the Rhine lay fallow; and important clientele, such as Grand Duchess Kantakuzene, the Queen of Rumania, the King of Portugal, Count Swetschin – who bought up many antiques for the Russian czars – the King of Spain, the Grand Duke of Baden, or the newspaper magnate William Randolph Hearst, were no longer in Germany, or did not visit Germany.

Clients from other social classes were not forthcoming, so business seemed to be doomed. However, a fresh breeze began to circulate when leading families were forced to break up their century-old collections. Huge quantities of quality weapons that had never been seen in such numbers before flooded the market. Wendel took his chance and went into business on his own. Not only were the ruling families of Germany in dire need of ready money, the upper class of Austria and Hungary found themselves in the same awkward predicament. Wendel's business flourished and flopped alternately. He tried his fortunes with a partner, but that did not work out. Later he was nominated treasurer of the Associ-

A so-called left-hand dagger used in conjunction with the sword during the 16th century. A blow-up of the hilt ist shown on the foregoing page.

Arms decoration at the turn of the century. This page from a catalogue shows a full suit of armour with close-helmet, round shield and a hand-and-a-half sword. It is a copy made at the beginning of the 20th century. On closer inspection, two cannon halberds, partisans, wheel-lock muskets, tschinkes, flintlock pistols, and two twohanded swords, one with a crenulated, the other with a straight-edged blade, may be discerned.

Another page from a catalogue. Cannon, halberds, daggers, gauntlets, horns, wheel-locks, flintlocks, powder flasks, etc. The shield is of cast iron.

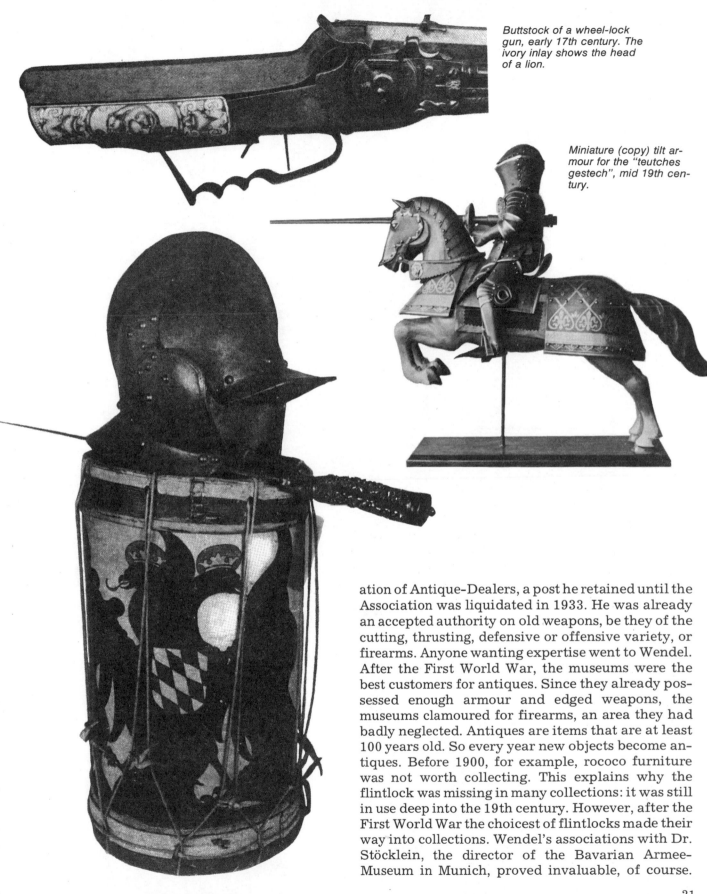

Buttstock of a wheel-lock gun, early 17th century. The ivory inlay shows the head of a lion.

Miniature (copy) tilt armour for the "teutches gestech", mid 19th century.

ation of Antique-Dealers, a post he retained until the Association was liquidated in 1933. He was already an accepted authority on old weapons, be they of the cutting, thrusting, defensive or offensive variety, or firearms. Anyone wanting expertise went to Wendel. After the First World War, the museums were the best customers for antiques. Since they already possessed enough armour and edged weapons, the museums clamoured for firearms, an area they had badly neglected. Antiques are items that are at least 100 years old. So every year new objects become antiques. Before 1900, for example, rococo furniture was not worth collecting. This explains why the flintlock was missing in many collections: it was still in use deep into the 19th century. However, after the First World War the choicest of flintlocks made their way into collections. Wendel's associations with Dr. Stöcklein, the director of the Bavarian Armee-Museum in Munich, proved invaluable, of course.

21

A copy of etched Maximilian armour with close-helmet, round shield and halberd. In the background can be seen various halberds and spontoons, flintlocks, wheel-locks, pistolettes, two cross-bows and model cannon.

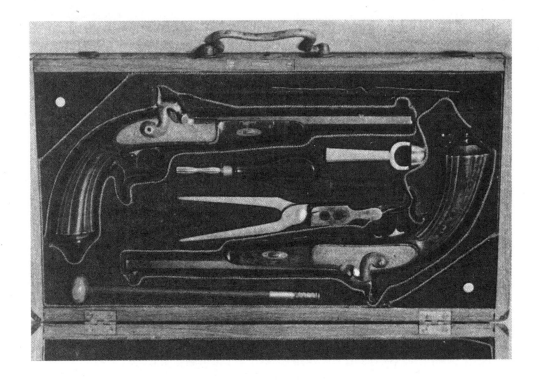

After 1933, the new people of importance (Nazis) furnished giant reception rooms, and gun rooms, with costly antiques. And by then the percussion arms had become of interest to the serious collector. Wendel says percussion arms are a good investment, since a goodly portion of them are converted flintlocks.

Since usually only high-quality flintlocks were thought worth while to convert, such weapons can be extremely valuable.

Just prior to World War II, Mr Wendel introduced his son to the business, so as to have someone to take the helm one day. As his son was an art student, he could combine his studies with practical experience in the shop.

But war broke out in the autumn of 1939, Wendel jr. was called up; the shop and apartment in Munich were eventually bombed out. Mr Wendel was homeless, and he only managed to salvage a small part of his arms library. As shoes are more important than antiques during a war, the authorities decided to let Wendel's shop to a cobbler. The antiques were thrown out on the street. Wendel, of course, tried to save what he could, but his fate was sealed. He smashed most of the objects against the house wall, and what remained lay exposed to the elements for someone to kick around or pick up and take home. It is not difficult to understand how Mr Wendel felt.

Even today, he has not managed to get this episode out of his system.

After Nazi Germany collapsed, Wendel jr. devoted all his energies to building up his father's business again. Dr. Schülein, the first lawyer admitted to practise law in Munich by the American Military Government, managed through the good offices of influential friends, to acquire a licence for Wendel to sell antique arms. Of course, at that period Wendel's only customers were members of the Allied armed forces. The Americans were great collectors and interested in anything steeped in history. Many of them were artists in their own right. One colonel, for exemple, brought back a pair of rococo pistols he had refurbished. One could not imagine anything more beautiful! However, he had worked on them for more than 120 hours. The cleansing agent? Old rags and cigarette ash!

Another American colonel, a crack restorer, used to come along and repair this or that. This was a very useful connection to have. Well, the hurly-burly period of post-war Germany now belongs to the past, and business life, and life in general, have settled back to normal. Mr. Wendel, sr., is no longer active in the shop, but he still has an open ear for anyone seeking information or advice. We hope collectors of antique weapons will be able to pick his brains for many years to come.   S-s.

Text and photos Hugo Burger

The SG 510 Assault Rifle of Switzerland

The SG 510 (also known as the AM 55 and StGw 57) is provided with a geared-up, delayed blowback locking system that utilizes twin bolthead pivoting cylinders, along the lines of the rollers used in the German G3 and the Spanish CETME. The transmission ratio is 1:4. This weapon is designed for mass production, so the emphasis lies on pressed sheet-metal components. It delivers both semi-automatic and full-automatic fire.

The large sidelever can be rotated to S (safe), E (semiautomatic) or M (full-automatic). The SG 510 always fires from a closed bolt. Ammunition is fed vertically into the breech from a 24-cartridge magazine. The spent cases are ejected to the right, at a right angle to the receiver. Grenades can be launched without adding a special provision. The integral muzzle brake reduces recoil by about 25 per cent. Both the front square blade sight, laterally adjustable, and the peep receiver sight fold down when not in use. A hinged carrying handle is located at the balance point, at the front of the receiver. For safety's sake a floating pin indicates whether or not a cartridge is in the firing chamber. The handguard and buttstock are of acid-proof rubber. The buttstock can be propped against a hard surface when the rifle is firing grenades. The SG 510 can be field stripped quickly without tools. No provision has been made for a riflescope, as the Swiss army makes use of a special sniper's rifle equipped with a stronger muzzle brake and a bipod. Here refernce is being made to a short-stocked, heavy barrelled repeater that is fitted with the K 31 action.

The three illustrations on the left show AM 55, a prototype.

7.5 mm Swiss Ammunition

The Swiss themselves call these cartridges "Modell 11",
and six specials exist alongside the standard rifle round.

1. Tracer with a 765 yard trail. Colour code: case head, red.
2. Light armour piercer, steel cored. Colour code: case head, violet.
3. Light armour piercer/tracer. Colour code: case head, red primer, violet.
4. Proof-house load. Colour code: case head, black case, coppered.
5. Grenade cartridge 44. For launching grenade 58.
6. Blank load. Used on manoeuvres. Plastic cased.

This version was presented to the
Swiss Kriegstechnische Abteilung for trials

The Swiss assault rifle as accepted by the military

Main Component Parts of SG 510

1 Rubber buttstock
2 Rear receiver compartment
3 Clasp lugs
4 Recoil spring/damper
5 Peep sight
6 Receiver proper
7 Carrying handle
8 Breechring
9 Removable caps for locking recesses
10 Spring clip
11 Barrel cowling
12 Front sight
13 Forward end of barrel designed as cup discharger
14 Muzzle brake
15 Bipod
16 Magazine
17 Charging handle
18 Crossbolt for trigger unit
19 Pistol grip with trigger unit
20 Bolt assembly
21 Passageway for sling

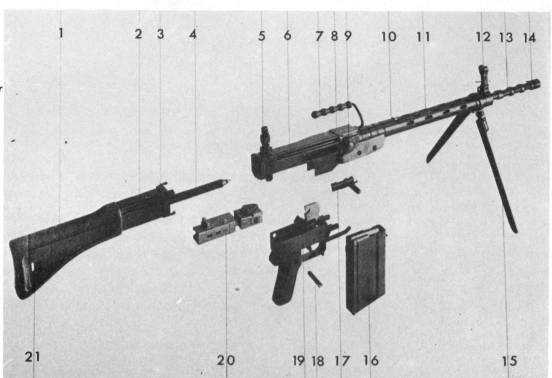

8

Cutaway of firing chamber and barrel

9

Parts Legend for Illustration 10

Bolt Assembly

1 Extractor
2 Cylinder check
3 Cylinders
4 Bolthead
5 Ejector
6 Cotter
7 Ejector spring
8 Retainer
9 Boltbody
10 Firing-lever pin
11 Firing lever
12 Firing pin
13 Firing-pin spring

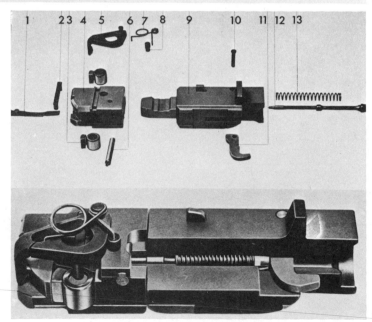

10

1. Receiver

This consists of three sections: the centre housing (6), the breechring (8), which is welded to (6), and the rear compartment (2). Element (2) is bayonet locked to the centre housing or receiver proper (6) by means of clasp lugs (3). The buttstock (1) is also secured to the rear compartment (2). The latter accommodates the recoil spring and special dampers (4), whereas the receiver proper (6) guides the bolt assembly (20). Ejection port and guide slot for the charging handle (17) are right of the receiver. The peep sight (5) is mounted on the roof of (6). The forged breechring (8) contains the recesses, sealed outwardly by removable metal caps, into which the locking cylinders of the bolt assembly (20) engage. Element (8) is also the base for the hinged carrying handle (7), the screw-in barrel (13) and the cartridge indicator pin.

2. Barrel cowling

A ventilated cowling or casing (11) extends as far as the front sight (12) and bayonet lug. The collapsible bipod (15) can be moved up and down the barrel cowling (11), and locked in position by a sprung clip (10). The right leg of the bipod (15) has a graduated scale for the rainbow (high-angle) trajectory described by a rifle grenade when ignited by a standard grenade cartridge, whereas the left leg is graduated for a grenade which is launched with a booster load.

The barrel cowling (11) is bridged to the breechring (8). The handquard wraps around the lower section of this junction.

3. Barrel

The muzzle serves as a muzzle brake (14) and grenade launcher, where by the bulbous section of the barrel supports the grenade. A spring clip mounted in the bulb nearest the front sight prevents a grenade from slipping off the muzzle if the rifle were inadvertently pointed downwards.

The longitudinal flutes in the firing chamber permit some gas to flow around the cartridge case, for balancing internal pressure. Furthermore, the case cannot stick to the wall of the chamber. However, in order to avert a massive escape of gas, these flutes stop about 13 mm (.512 in.) before the face of the chamber. For uniform cycling, the main force of the gas must slam the cartridge case against the bolthead, not by-pass the case.

4. Bolt assembly

This consists of the bolthead (4) with locking cylinders (3), cylinder check (2), ejector and spring (5), and extractor (1). The bolthead is pinned to the wedge-like protrusion of the boltbody (9), but can slide to and fro over a short distance. The boltbody contains the firing pin (12) with spring (13), plus the firing lever (11). The bolt assembly can be dismantled without tools.

5. Recoil spring

This consists of two long coil springs that are telescoped into each other (4). This unit is anchored in the buttstock.

6. Trigger mechanism

This is grouped in the trigger housing (19). The housing itself is hooked into the receiver (6) and held by a crossbolt (18).

The trigger housing contains the pistol grip, safety lever, magazine cutoff, and swing-out winter trigger guard. The pistol grip is hollow to accept the night sight.

The letters E (semi-automatic) and S (safe) are stamped on to the receiver (6), whereas the letter M (full-automatic) is stamped on the trigger housing (19).

How trigger functions

Semi-automatic fire.
For single shots, switch safety lever over to E. Pull trigger and release.

1 Safety lever
2 Trigger
3 Trigger spring
4 Axle for trigger and sear
5 Sear
6 Hammer
7 Fly
8 Sear spring

The fly connects trigger and sear. Hammer is held by tip of sear.

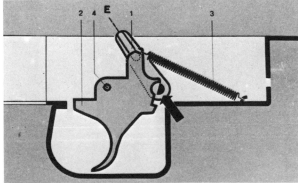

11

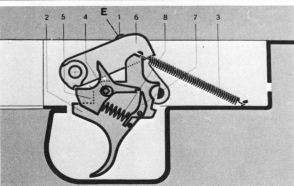

12

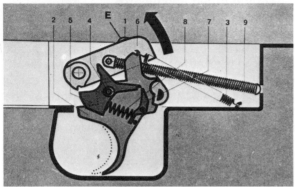

13

Since trigger and sear share a common axle, trigger and sear rotate together. When the sear slips out of the hammer notch, the mainspring (9) catapults the hammer forward.

A component in the trigger housing (19) can be installed in two different ways. When white is showing, the SG 510 will fire single shots only.

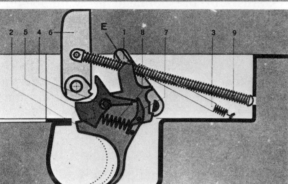

14

1 Safety lever	7 Fly
2 Trigger	8 Sear spring
3 Trigger spring	9 Mainspring
4 Axle	10 Bell crank
5 Sear	11 Bell crank head
6 Hammer	12 Automatic dog

The eccentrically positioned sear spring presses the sear, mounted in an oversized hole in the trigger blade, forwards/upwards. Once fly disengages, the tip of the sear is readied to slip into hammer notch again.

When black is showing, full-automatic fire is possible. After military training, Swiss citizens keep their guns (and other service equipment) at home, and practise marksmanship at civilian ranges. It is at these local ranges that white must show . . .

Irrespective of whether the SG 510 is set at semi- or full-automatic fire, the trigger remains two-stage. Trigger pull is also adjustable.

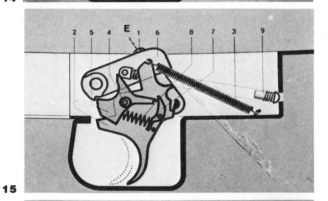

15

When the hammer has been re-cocked, the stay of the mainspring, anchored to one side of the hammer, forces the sear round its axle to re-engage in the hammer notch. The trigger must be released before the hammer can be catapulted forward again for the next shot. Once the trigger has returned to battery, the fly will re-mesh with the sear. This cycle is repeated as long as shots are fired singly.

Note: If the bolt assembly does not return to its forward (battery) postition, that is, the cylinders do not engage in recesses in the breechring, the firing pin, housed in the boltbody, lacks sufficient reach to ignite a cartridge.

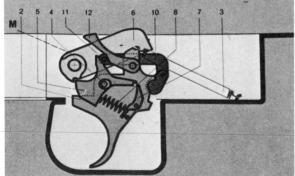

16

Full-automatic fire
By setting the lever at M, the head of the bell crank (11) is thrust between the sear (5) and the automatic dog (12).

When the trigger is pulled, the head of the bell crank lifts the automatic dog into the path of the bolt.

2 Trigger
3 Trigger spring
4 Axle
5 Sear
6 Hammer
7 Fly
8 Sear spring
10 Bell crank
11 Bell crank head
12 Automatic dog
13 Bolt

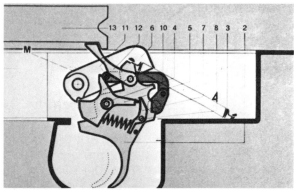

17

As long as the trigger is kept squeezed, the reciprocating bolt, on its home journey, depresses the automatic dog far enough to knock the sear out of the hammer notch. Everything is timed, and so once the bolt assembly has returned to battery, the hammer drops. Shots continue to be fired in rapid succession, until the magazine is empty, or until the trigger is released.

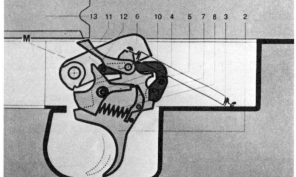

18

Safe
When the safety lever is rotated to S, the axle of the lever (arrow) prevents the trigger being pulled.

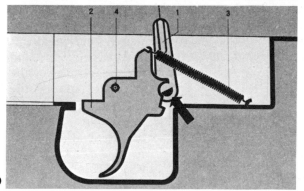

19

The SG 510 Assault Rifle of Switzerland

7. Sights

Micrometer Peep Sight (20) (21)

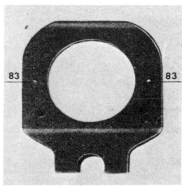

20

21

73 Base
74 Eyepiece
75 Insert
76 Lateral adjustment
77 Adjustment ring
78 Thimble
79 Button

Front Sight
21 Blade
80 Night sight
   filled with
   phosporescent
   substance
81 Hood
82 Post

Both front sight (12) and rear micrometer peep sight (5) are folded down when not required. The hooded front sight is mounted in a T-groove on an upright post, and is adjustable for windage. For night operations the hole (80) at the apex of the hood (81), filled with phosphorescent substance, is aligned whith a special insert that is placed in the peep sight. This sight is graduated from 110 to 700 yards. Each division of adjustment corresponds to 0.26‰ of the range, and change in point of impact (vertically) reads as follows:

approx. 1.2 in. at 110 yards
approx. 2   in. at 220 yards
approx. 3.2 in. at 330 yards
approx. 4.4 in. at 440 yards
approx. 5.2 in. at 550 yards
approx. 6.3 in. at 660 yards

The figure 3 appears twice on the scale, in red and white. Division marks and numbers in white are used when aligning tip of front sight with centre of bullseye. The red 3 allows a six-o'clock-hold (that is: front sight aligned with bottom of bullseye) at 300 metres (330 yards).

8. Magazine (illustration 23)

This (16) is made of sheet metal and is designed for 24 cartridges. The inspection holes in the sideplate allows cartridges to be counted. Loading is accomplished without a filler. A white magazine charged with six type-44 cartridges (Fig. 23) is used when launching grenades. Normal live rounds cannot be loaded into these white magazines. A slide on the magazine and a groove in the boltbody (20) prevent grenade cartridges being chambered automatically.

90 Follower
91 Front lug
92 Magazine
93 Rear lug
94 Button
95 Spring

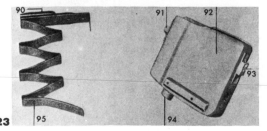

9. Operation (illus. 24–27)

Assuming the SG 510 has been readied to fire, with safety off, the operation is as follows:

By pulling the trigger, the hammer (14) is freed from the sear (5). The hammer (14) is catapulted against the firing lever (11), through thrust pressure generated by the mainspring (9). The firing lever (11) in turn impacts the firing pin, igniting the cartridge in the chamber. Gas pressure forces the brass cartridge case firmly against the walls of the firing chamber, slowing up extraction in older guns. For this reason, the SG 510 has its firing chamber fitted with longitudinal flutes, to allow some gas to flow around the outside of the cartridge case, thus tending to equalize internal pressure. Gas drives the bullet down the barrel, but also presses the spent case against the boltface, in the other direction. As seen in Fig. 24, at the moment of firing the two cylinders (3) are engaged in the recesses of the breechring (8), and are kept there by the force of the recoil spring (4) which bears against the bolt assembly (20).

At a specific pressure level, when the bullet has left the muzzle, the cylinders cave inwards and by doing so strike against the wedgelike protrusion of the boltbody (9). The boltbody thus suddenly accelerates to the rear, and when the link is taut, that is, as soon as the slack between boltbody (9) and bolthead (4) has been taken up, the bolthead is trailed along behind. This scheme accords an initial slow-motion opening of the breech, yet momentum builds up rapidly once the boltbody gets under way. During this opening phase, the heavy boltbody re-cocks the hammer (6); and the ejector (5), as it runs over a slope built into the receiver wall, flips out the empty cartridge case. This is clearly illustrated in Figs. 26 and 27. The compressed recoil spring and the damper unit in the buttstock brake the reward movement of the bolt assembly and then drives the assembly forward again, stripping the top cartridge from the magazine and chambering it. During this closing phase, the boltbody, which in a sense is now the trailing member, comes up behind the bolthead and cams the pivoted cylinders outward into engagement with the recesses in the breechring. The gun is ready to fire.

A difficult problem in this type of actions is to prevent the bolt assembly jarring against the face of the firing chamber. Picture how a hammer smartly rebounds when it strikes an anvil! As this phenomenon causes stoppages, weights and claws, etc. have been incorporated into bolt systems as a counter-measure. However, the SG 510 solved this problem by giving the firing chamber a peculiar shape. Its diameter narrows just before the shoulder (Fig. 9), which means that the cartridge sticks out of the mouth of the chamber, and buffers the blow of the returning bolt assembly. This cushioning cuts bolt chatter down to a minimum.

10. Field stripping

1. Grasp the pistol grip with your left hand and support magazine with your right hand. Depress release catch and swing out magazine in a forward direction.

2. Hold the rear section of receiver with your right hand, then activate bolt catch with index finger. Rotate buttstock counter-clockwise about one-eigth turn and withdraw stock from receiver. Remove charging handle by pulling it out of guide slot.

3. Draw bolt assembly out of receiver.

4. Depress clip and knock out crossbolt of trigger housing to the right. Pull down on pistol grip, then lift unit off to the rear. No further disassembly is necessary for cleaning purposes. Make sure that hammer does not drop after trigger mechanism has been removed.

5. The SG 510 is reassembled by reversing these steps.

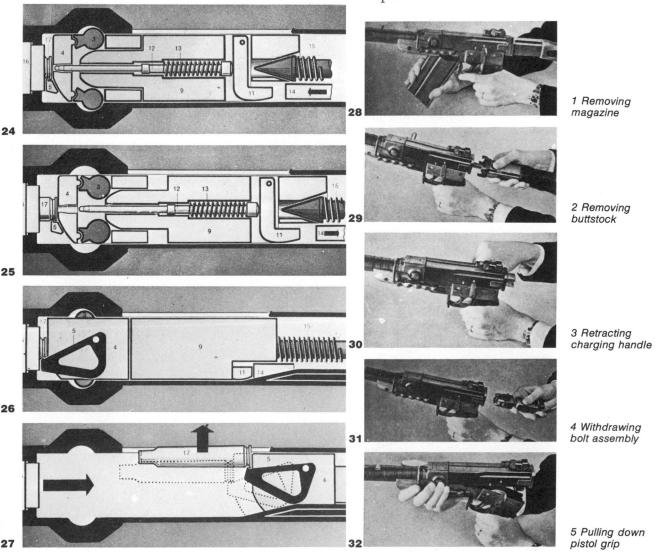

24

25

26

27

28   1 Removing magazine

29   2 Removing buttstock

30   3 Retracting charging handle

31   4 Withdrawing bolt assembly

32   5 Pulling down pistol grip

11. Rifle grenade 58

Weight 2 lb 7 oz
Muzzle vel.
normal charge 131 ft/sec.
booster charge 230 ft/sec.
Max. range
normal charge 186 yards
booster charge 470 yards

The rifle grenade 58 may be fitted with the following warheads:

1. Hollow charge for heavy armour. Modern hollow charge rifle grenades can penetrate 12 to 20 inches of "best quality" armour plating.
2. Antipersonnel with impact detonator.
3. Smoke canister for reducing visibility.
4. Dummy.

All Swiss rifle grenades contain a booster charge. If not required, it is deactivated by forcing a plastic plug down the muzzle, before the grenade is mounted. Hollow charge grenades are fired with a booster charge at all times.

3

12. Firing the rifle grenade 58

Figs. 34 and 35 show method of taking aim when target is in view. If the target is not in view the rifleman uses the scales on the legs of the bipod, together with a plumb line (33). A second soldier stands behind the first to check side rake. When launching a grenade, the rifle should on no account be pressed against one's shoulder. Recoil is particularly fierce!

However, if the rifleman has no hard surface to support the buttstock, he is recommended to clamp the buttstock under his right arm and hold it there as best he can, either in a standing or kneeling position.
Fig. 36 shows the dampening mechanism in the buttstock, as well as the deforming zones of the buttstock when it is propped against a hard surface, and pressed into service as a launching pad.

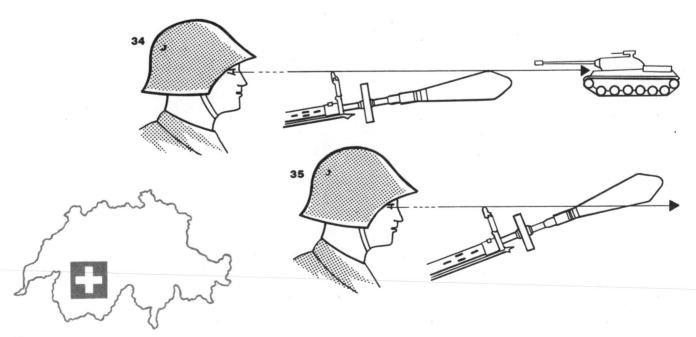

34

35

13. SG 510-1 to SG 510-4 Models for export

These four commercialized models (37–40) are basically identical with the SG 510, or, as some people prefer, StGw 57.

The SG 510-1 being the standard export model, the SG 510-2 a lightweight model, the SG 510-3 a model chambered for the East bloc 7.62 x 39 mm (intermediate) cartridge, and the SG 510-4 a model chambered for the NATO 7.62 x 51 mm cartridge. Chile purchased the SG 510-4 for her armed forces.

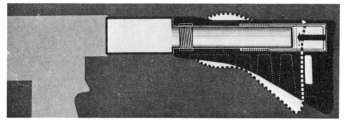

36

SG 510-1

37

SG 510-2

38

SG 510-3

39

SG 510/4

40

SG510/4

41

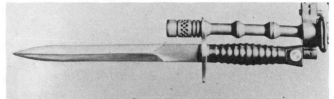

42

43

**Penetration ratings for
7.5 Swiss standard round**

Distance (yards)	5.5	328	656
Pine boards	24 in.	20 in.	16 in.
Sand	12 in.	16 in.	16 in.
Farmland soil	24 in.	28 in.	24 in.
Packed snow	47 in.	51 in.	51 in.
Steel plating	0.4 in.	0.2 in.	—

44

SPECIFICATIONS

Delayed blowback action (pivoted cylinders)	SG 510	SG 510-1	SG 510-2	SG 510-3	SG 510-4	Explanations
Calibre	7.5 Swiss	7.62 NATO	7.62 NATO	7.62 East Bloc	7.62 NATO	(7.62x51 NATO = .308 Win.)
Overall length of rifle	43.3 in.	41.3 in.	41.3 in.	36.2 in.	40 in.	
Length of barrel with muzzle brake	27.2 in.	21.5 in.	21.5 in.	17.7 in.	19.9 in.	
Number of rifling grooves	4	4	4	4	4	
Weight of rifle without magazine	12 lb 9 oz	10 lb 15 oz	8 lb 9 oz*	8 lb 14 oz*	9 lb 6 oz*	*)Wooden buttstock, no bipod
Weight of						
24-round magazine	8.8 oz					
20-round magazine		8.5 oz	8.5 oz			
20-round magazine, steel		10.8 oz	10.8 oz		10.06 oz	
30-round magazine, steel				11.8 oz		
Weight of barrel	3 lb	2 lb 3 oz	1 lb 15 oz	1 lb 11 oz	1 lb 11 oz	
Rear-sight graduation	100–640 m*	100–650 m*	100–650 m*	100–650 m*	100–600 m*	*) 1 m = 1.0936 yds. Each click represents 25 m, 100 m for sight of SG 510-4
Sight radius	25 in.	22.7 in.	22.7 in.	20.5 in.	21.3 in.	
Rate of automatic fire (depending on ammunition used)	450–600 pm	450–500 pm	450–500 pm	450–600 pm	450–620 pm	pm = per minute
Muzzle velocity (approx.)	2460 ft/sec.	2690 ft/sec.	2690 ft/sec.	2362 ft/sec.	2559 ft/sec.	These figures depend on charge, bullet weight and shape, etc.
Muzzle energy (approx.)	2688 ft. pds	2651 ft. pds	2651 ft. pds	2705 ft. pds	2476 ft. pds	

E. O. Rose

Roth-Steyr
Auto Pistol Model 1907

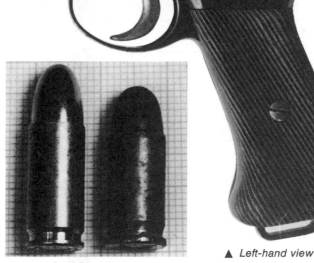

This pistol was officially adopted by the Austro-Hungarian cavalry in 1907. Compared with pistols adopted by other states, the Roth-Steyr and its cartridge were rather unusual. It was designed by Karel Krnka, a Czech, while he was employed by the Roth'sche Patronenfabrik (cartridge factory). Steyr and the Budapest Gun Factory produced this pistol under licence. That is the reason why the Roth-Steyr is sometimes encountered bearing the legend, "Fegyveryar," which signifies that that particular model was made in Hungary.

This is one of the earliest forms of successful locked-breech pistols. It has a turning barrel lock, the barrel being revolved through 90 degrees rotation by camming action of a stud as the slide recoils. When the breechblock is drawn forward by the compressed recoil spring, a fresh cartridge is chambered. This type of turning barrel lock was retained in the 9 mm Steyr of 1911. Although the striker is cocked by recoil, it must be pushed further back by trigger action before it disengages from the sear. Of course, this is a hinderance to accurate shooting, but, on the other hand, a striker of this design is also a safety precaution. A pistol with lighter trigger pull can be dangerous for a cavalry man on a charging horse. The 10-shot magazine is built into the handle. A special charger was used to provide leverage to strip the 8 mm cartridges easily into the magazine. The bullet fired in this pistol weighed 115 grains and measured .733 inches. Overall length of the cartridge was 1. 13 inches.

▲ 8 mm Roth-Steyr (l),
7.65 Browning (r).

▲ Left-hand view

The Roth-Steyr Auto Pistol 1907 was designed by Karel Krnka, a Czech. This is one of the earliest forms of successful locked-breech pistols.

An Infantry

**Text and illustrations
Gerhard Seifert**

Overall length	28 inches
Weight	1 lb 11 oz
Blade	Length: 23 inch Max. width: 1 ²/₅ inch Camber: ³/₄ inches
Hilt	Iron, consisting of quillons, knuckle-guard tierce knuckle-guard, tierce and carte bows, pierced ports on both sides, thumb loop, swollen grip bound with interlaced brass-wire cord.
Scabbard	Missing

**Zurich ▶
infantry
sabre, dated
1755**

Following the Prussian example, other European states also began to arm the infantry with short sabres. Of course, this change-over did not materialize over night. Sabres for the foot troops began to appear in the first third of the 18th century. However, not until about 1780 was the reformation truly completed. On account of the high costs involved, many a small state was confronted with a weighty alternative: Either the infantry would have to wait a number of decades for the new sabres, or sabre blades would be fitted to the hilts of swords already available. The Zurich sabre, illustrated on these pages, is characteristic of the second alternative. Sword experts see at a glance that the grip does not tilt forward, so this specimen cannot be a genuine sabre. Nor does the general impression of the hilt somehow fit in with the short, curved blade. We might say that there is no "affectionate" bond in this second-hand marriage! The hilt is the type used on continental broadswords between the middle of the 17th and beginning of the 18th century. The quillon, turned down at the rear, flows up into the knuckle guard that is bolted to the pommel. Counter-guard ports branch out of the quillons, as well as tierce and carte bows. The ports are of pierced design, and the tierce and carte bows are welded. Like the knuckle guard, the top of the tierce bow is fastened to the pommel, and the carte bow joins up with the thump loop. The grip is tightly wound with an interlaced brass-wire cord, the ends of which are anchored by brass ferrules.

The blade ends in a Groot-type point and has a 2³/₄ inch false edge. Fuller grooves on both sides of the blade go all the way up to the hilt. This specimen is nicely decorated with gilding and etchings, though, regrettably, much of the gilding has worn off. One side of the blade shows an etched Z under a crown, a group of arms and the date of 1755. This is undoubtedly the date of the blade, and its unison with the hilt. The reverse view also shows a crown, together with a scimitar-wielding lion. The motto, "für Gott und das Vatterland" of course means, "for God and the

Sabre Made in Zurich

Father-Land." Sayings of this nature were common on the blades of Swiss swords during the 18th century. The Z indicates that the blades was forged in the canton of Zurich. The date is also typical in this context. To be sure, it would not be right to exclude any other interpretation, but as far as I am concerned, the characteristics of this sabre wholeheartedly verify what I have said.

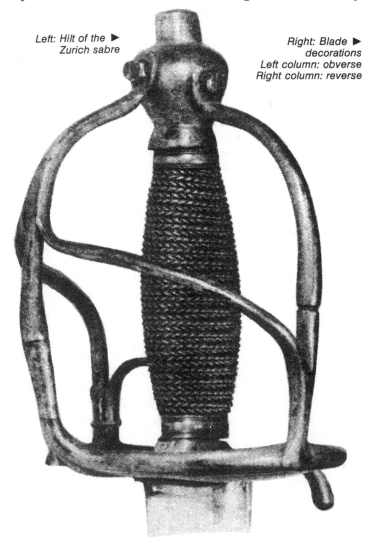

Left: Hilt of the ▶ Zurich sabre

Right: Blade ▶ decorations
Left column: obverse
Right column: reverse

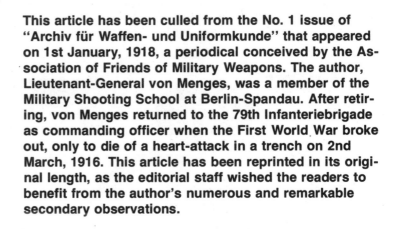

Prussian Longarms from 1809 to the Present

Courbiere Regiment (58), 1806

This article has been culled from the No. 1 issue of "Archiv für Waffen- und Uniformkunde" that appeared on 1st January, 1918, a periodical conceived by the Association of Friends of Military Weapons. The author, Lieutenant-General von Menges, was a member of the Military Shooting School at Berlin-Spandau. After retiring, von Menges returned to the 79th Infanteriebrigade as commanding officer when the First World War broke out, only to die of a heart-attack in a trench on 2nd March, 1916. This article has been reprinted in its original length, as the editorial staff wished the readers to benefit from the author's numerous and remarkable secondary observations.

During the Napoleonic Wars (1796–1815) Prussia's regular troops and militiamen were armed with the Infantry Musket Model 1809, the Jaegers and Fusiliers with the Rifle Model 1810. However, to begin with and during the 1812–1815 campaigns a general issuance of these arms remained wishful thinking; for one of Prussia's two gun factories, the one at Potsdam-Spandau, had closed in 1806/07, due to the vicissitudes of war. Though re-opened in 1810, this factory was compelled to shut down again during the French occupation of Berlin (1813–1814), just when the Prussians needed the weapons most. The second factory, inaugurated at the Neisse in 1809, could not make full-scale deliveries till 1812. Guns were salvaged from the battle fields and, if necessary, repaired by local smithies. Arms deliveries were obtained from England and Austria, etc., so that in a Prussian battalion English, French, Russian and Swedish guns, often different models from one and the same country, were represented.

The situation was even more maddening in refer-

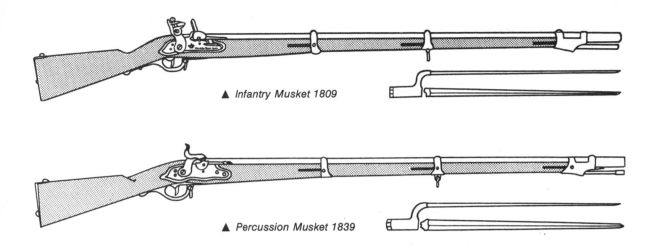

▲ Infantry Musket 1809

▲ Percussion Musket 1839

ence to rifles. Weapons with burnt-out barrels had to be pressed into service, purchases had to be made abroad, even many types of sporting arms were utilized. The voluntary Jaegers, who were earmarked for rifles, had to make do with carbines or sawn-off muskets.

The 1809 Infantry Musket, calibre 18.83 mm (.741 in.), measured 75.2 in. with permanently fixed bayonet, and weighed 10 lb 6 oz. Accurate aiming was impossible as no sights were fitted; the performance being too poor to warrant sights anyway. Barrel bands were used for the first time in Prussia, and the flintlocks sported a large "umbrella" to shelter the pan from wind and rain, a device that was copied by no other army. This broaches the subject of a flintlock's principal shortcoming: malfunctioning. Due to the Prussian funnel-shaped touchhole, the powder reached the pan when it was poured down the muzzle, so in wet weather the musket refused to fire. If rainy weather prevailed, the tactical sig-

nificance of the infantry in battle dwindled, contrary to that of the cavalry and artillery detachments. Then again, even on sun-blessed battlefields, a new flint would be only good for a maximum of 30 ignitions. The poor-quality powder of that period heavily fouled barrel and touchhole, eventually making the weapons useless. During training, under ideal conditions, the soldiers could deliver an amazingly high rate of firepower, but under the strain of a full-fledged battle they could, on average fire only 1 shot a minute. Effective range was also very restricted.

Better, but much slower, was the Rifle Model 1810, chambered for a 14.65 mm (.577 in.) ball. It measured 44 in. without bayonet and weighed 9 lb 8 oz.

The patched ball was started with a small hammer and poked a short distance down the barrel with the handle of the hammer. From then on the ball was pushed down on top of the charge with the ramrod, a difficult undertaking when the barrel had become

The Helmut-Gerhard-Schulz Publishing House, Hamburg, kindly provided us with pertinent documents for the drawings.

Brandenburg Hussars Voluntary Jaegers, 1st West Prussian Infantry Regiment, 1803

pared with the performance of the muskets. Of course, performance in those days was rather modest. A rifle with patched ball hit a target measuring 74x48 inches at a distance of 164 yards on average 49 times, and a musket 21 times out of a 100. Today a recruit is expected to place 3 shots within a 10 inch circle at the same distance!

After the Napoleonic Wars, native Prussian arms gradually replaced foreign ones, largely on account of cost. The rifles, however, continued to differ in respect of the number of rifling grooves, the rate of twist, weight, length and sighting arrangements, etc., till about 1850. At Saarn and Dantzing new gun factories were founded and new techniques developed. New regulations and measurements were drawn up by the War Ministry in 1820 and 1823, which contained but few improvements, at least when compared with those of 1809 and 1810.

In 1820 the first percussion caps were used on sporting rifles; the Army, though, treated the idea with contempt. Still, even the ardent defenders of the new system were plagued with headaches, since the caps often deteriorated during storage. However, when this problem was resolved Prussia had her muskets and rifles converted to caplocks.

Once the percussion system had proved itself under all types of weather, and it became generally known that these cap firers improved firepower, Prussia

fouled. By the way, the rifles were not provided with that conical touchhole. To begin with a fine priming powder was poured into the pan and the pan cover closed before the main charge was tipped down the barrel. Great care had to be taken that the ball engaged in and followed the rifling grooves.

The barrel was octagonal, the traditional shape for German rifles, and the lockwork was provided with a double set trigger. The rear sight was of the folding type. The effective range was less than 400 paces.

A hirschfänger or hunting-knife was hooked over a projection of the nose cap, a method that proved to be unreliable. Still, not until two decades later was the bayonet hook placed on the barrel itself.

The first person to write in detail about guns and their use was that indefatigable genius of the name of Scharnhorst. In his treatise, "Wirkung des Feuergewehrs," Berlin 1813, he compared the firearms of the great powers in tests conducted between 1808 and 1809. He noted the accuracy and rate of fire of the rifles, com-

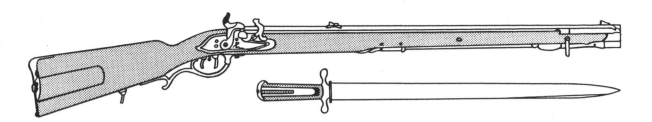

introduced the Jaeger Rifle Model 1835 and Infantry Musket Model 1839. Apart from the ignition system, the latter differed from Model 1809 in that it fired a smaller calibre ball, had an iron instead of a brass buttplate, and a fullered bayonet. An important improvement was a tail screw which obviated drilling an ignition passage in the barrel. Sights were now installed. Whereas the 1809 musket was charged with 148 grains of powder, the 1839 musket only required 106 grains. Accuracy and effective firing distance increased. However, due to the fact that the ball had to be smaller than the bore of the musket (bore diameter 18.05 mm/.711 in., ball 16.74 mm/.660 in., difference 1.31 mm/.051 in.), accuracy was still not as good as it might have been. As said before, a rifle shot better, but because of the rifling grooves it was harder to load and had to be loaded in the standing position. After 15 to 20 shots a rifle was no longer usable; for the barrel had to be thoroughly mopped out with water, oil and tow. In 1848 the muzzle loading problem was considerably facilitated by having a protrusion on the base of the breech plug sticking up through the gunpowder charge. Lieutenant-Colonel

Thouvenin of the French Army was the father of this invention. A cylindro-conical bullet was dropped down the barrel, without a lubed patch, and pounded with the ramrod until it expanded over the protrusion

and tightly fit the bore. This model was designated: Thouveninsche Jägerbüchse Modell 1835. The Jaegers were pleased with the change, for when properly loaded the rifle now fired more accurately over

▲ *Thouvenin*
Jaeger Rifle

1st West Prussian
Infantry Regiment No. 6,
1808

all ranges. The Infantry was not pleased, though. This stem or protrusion made cleaning more difficult than ever before. Henceforth, the stem was removed from all Infantry muskets.

In its stead, the Prussians used the Minié ball, designed by Captain Minié of the French Army. The barrel of the Infantry Musket received 5 shallow grooves, making it an Infantry Rifle. The Prussians called it: gezogenes Infanteriegewehr Modell 1839/55 (rifled Infantry Musket Model 1839/55), after the year of adoption. The 1.7 oz. heavy-weight, cone-shaped bullet had an iron cup (culot) in its hollow base. This cup was thrust ahead by the explosion of the powder charge, to expand the lead bullet into the rifling. Effective range rose to about 1000 paces, but a soldier could only pocket 48 instead of the traditionall 60 balls, because of the size and weight of the Minié ammunition. Recoil was also hefty.

Voices from a number of quarters raised themselves against the general adoption of rifled muskets, voices that grew even louder after a showdown battle fought in 1859. In this campaign the French, armed with smoothbore muskets and large-calibre rifles of inferior quality, beat the Austrians by concentrating assault tactics; although the Austrians were in possession of good-quality rifles. The French did not even make extensive use of their artillery. On behalf of the War Ministry, Caesar Rüstow challenged this opinion in a treatise. In 1861 this brilliant writer already assumed that closed formations could fire volleys at an enemy 300 paces away. At this point, it is of interest to note that very few people wrote about guns during this period. The few that did chiefly referred to tables of data issued by the Ministries, or gave long-winded descriptions of every hole and screw that could be found in a rifle. During the 40s the situation did not change, for those gun writers that had something to say had to keep quiet.

But a new invention was fighting its way to recognition, an invention that would exercise an unhoped-for influence on Prussia's destiny: the Dreyse breech-loading needle gun. Nikolaus Dreyse of Soemmerda was a circumspect gun designer, but more important for the success of this venture, a man of great energy and rare tenacity. His first draft proposals were presented to the authorities in 1827, but

Grenadier Regiment King Wilhelm 1st (West Prussian), 1870

▼ *Needle Musket 1841*

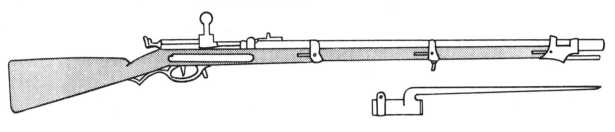

▼ *Pike Rifle 1854*

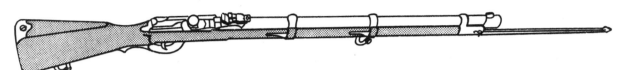

Prussian Longarms from 1809 to the Present

his invention was ignored until 4th December, 1840, when Friedrich Wilhelm IV placed an order for 60 000 of these rifles. The king saw in this invention a gift of special providence, and he hoped the secret would not be let out before history had lifted this gun to national fame. But, alas, history did not comply with such kingly wishes, for in 1848 a group of rebels stormed the Berlin arsenal. Some of the needle guns stolen were sold to foreign powers. Fortunately, (for the Germans) the revolutionary nature of the guns was not recognized by these other countries. Moreover, the Prussians misled the arms experts of the other countries by officially listing the Dreyse as a light percussion rifle. Not before 1855 was it desig-

nated the Needle Gun Model 41. During the first 8 years after adoption, the needle gun was not allowed to be "the subject of special lectures" at the division schools. Although Dreyse enlarged his factory, he was still not in a position to meet his contract. In 1851 the 3 Royal Gun Factories were licensed to assist in manufacture. Already in 1848 needle guns had been issued to the 3rd Battalion, at that time generally known as the Fusiliers, and a little later to the Guards. However, quite a bit of time elapsed before the entire Prussian Army was equipped with the Dreyse needle gun. Breech loading increased firepower considerably; loading could be conducted in a standing, kneeling or sitting position:

barrel swabbing was facilitated; and only one charge at a time could be loaded.

For the first time in history a self-contained cartridge was used, that is, a case containing a primer, propellent charge, and projectile. The bullet, originally cone shaped, attached to a semi-circular section, was mounted on a cardboard prop that contained the priming pellet and gripped the rifling grooves. After a time, a long lead bullet weighing 478 grains and having a maximum diameter of .536 in. was adopted which increased ballistic performance no end, although the weight of the cartridge had decreased to 596 grains. The folding sight, graduated up to 700 paces, was also modified
Overall length of needle gun = 56 in.
without bayonet
Diameter across bore = From .602 in. to .618 in.
Average .607 in.
Weight = 11 lb 3 oz.
Barrel = From the 1850s on produced from Berger-Witten steel, 4 shallow grooves.

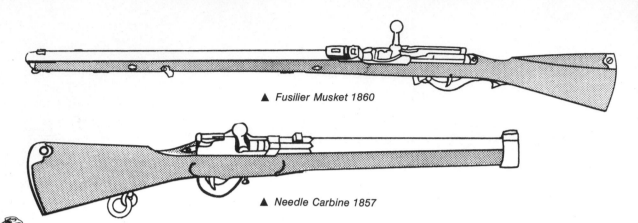

▲ Fusilier Musket 1860

▲ Needle Carbine 1857

While the regular troops had their triangular bayonets attached to the rifles all the time, and wore billhooks that dangled against the left leg, only the non-commissioned officers and army musicians of the militia detachments were provided with a sword-like weapon. The rank and file stowed their bayonets in a leather sheath that hung from the waistbelt. The militiamen also had to be content with Minié rifles. In the needle gun the Prussian Infantry possessed a weapon that was particularly accurate, and a lot of time and effort was invested in training the soldiers in its proper use. Unfortunately, simulated battle conditions and the art of estimating distance were badly neglected. The needle gun was extremely effective within 150 paces, against small targets. Officers on horseback who accompanied the infantry troops in 1866, and occasionally even after 1870, were sitting ducks at up to 400 paces.

At 600 paces the needle guns were still deadly if levelled at closed formations, and at 700 paces large objects could be "very much harassed" by skilled marksmen. Cassandras and Jeremiahs prophesied a terrible waste of ammunition if breechloaders were retained in service; but their jeerings and warnings were blown away by the wind after the battles of 1864, 1866 and 1870/71. Drilling and lecturing had incalcated into the brain of the dullest soldier that ammunition could on no account be wasted! On the contrary, the needle guns proved so successful when pitted against the muzzle loaders of the enemy in the battle of 1866 that even devoted supporters of the Dreyse system were surprised.

Before long, a number of different types of needle muskets and rifles were made, varying mainly in overall length and lockwork. Short and long buttstocks were produced in 1860, 1862 and 1865. Model 60 and subsequent models had straight-sided buttstocks, whereas the 1809 musket had a cheek cavity and models 39 and 41 a cheekpiece. Owing to lack of space it is impossible to describe every type of needle gun made, but the models can be listed:

Needle Musket Model 41
Needle Rifle Model 49
Needle Rifle Model 54 (also called "pike gun")
Needle Fusilier Musket Model 60
Needle Musket Model 62
Needle Artillery Musket Model 62
(presumably to arm the attendants of the ammunition trains)
Needle Rifle Model 65
Needle Pioneer Musket U/M (converted from Rifle 54)
Needle Pioneer Musket Model 69

The Pioneers were issued needle guns at a very late stage. In 1864 they were still armed with cut-down French muskets that had been converted to fire Minié projectiles. Indeed, before the Pioneers of 1858 had to rely upon booty muskets captured in 1815 that had been converted to caplocks!

Since the Prussian needle gun had proved successful in the battle of 1866, France also introduced a bolt-action rifle by the name of Chassepot in August of the same year, chambered for an 11 mm cartridge. The ballistic superiority of the French gun, which was rushed through in a great hurry, occasioned the Prussians to rearm. However, since full-scale rearming takes many years to accomplish, the order of the day was to quickly find a means of upgrading the performance of the Dreyse needle gun. One Herr Beck, the factory commissary, recommended that a buffer be fitted in front of the bolt, for better sealing.

Hence the charge was better utilized, the bullet made lighter, and the cartridge no longer had to be fed into the firing chamber. The bolt functioned better, too. The soldier was spared having to thump the bolt handle with the heel of his palm, to get the bolt open or closed. A tangent sight was also fitted that was graduated up to 1750 yards. When war broke out again in 1870, the German soldiers were still obliged to fight with a long-arm that was inferior to that of the French, since conversion work on the Dreyse needle gun had hardly begun. If the French had not been so hasty in manufacturing their new breechloader, fewer faults would have turned up in gun and ammunition, and if the German artillery had not assisted their own infantry so outstandingly, the French infantry might have won the day. After the war, the needle gun models 60, 62, 65 were converted, and issued to the troops by 1876. Still, the gun experts realized that the time had come for a more modern arm. For this reason, the Mauser 71 was finally adopted. If the Prussians

Cuirassier Regiment of the Grosser Kurfürst (Silesia) No. 1, 1910

had had more time a repeating arm would have been selected. Repeaters had already been thoroughly tested in the American wars of 1861–1865, and in 1870 tens of thousands of them were sold to the French by American and British firms. The Germans, therefore, experienced at first hand the superiority of American repeating arms.

The Mauser 71, a rugged rifle with massive operating parts, measured without bayonet 52.6 in. and with bayonet 71.1 in. It weighed 9 lb 15 oz, or 11 lb 12 oz with bayonet. The brown barrels were bored for an 11 mm cartridge, and the 4 rifling grooves were approximately as wide as the lands. The bolt had a reliable safety, and for the first time an extractor claw was fitted that hurled the empty case out of the action when the bolt was opened. The Mauser 71 was an immediate success, since it chambered a brass case in lieu of the old paper-covered needle-gun cartridge. The paper-wrapped bullet with lubricated nose weighed 432 grains, and the case was filled with 77 grains of New Rifle Powder Type 71. The cartridge, also containing a wax prop and two cardboard discs, weighed complete 664 grains. The soldier carried 80 rounds. A clip-on bayonet Model 71 replaced the fixed bayonet and the various sword-like weapons that hung from a soldier's waistbelt. A metal muzzle cap was issued, too. After a time a standard lanyard was introduced.

▲ *Chassepot rifle*

▼ *Infantry Rifle 71*

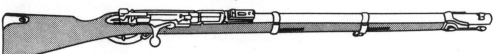

The short rifle or carbine 71 was likewise chambered for 11 mm rounds, but was nearly 4 inches shorter. Instead of 3 it had only 2 barrel bands (slightly different in shape) and its own type of trigger guard. This carbine was issued to the Jaegers, Pioneers, Railway Troops, Foot Artillery, the Sea-Battalions and the Navy Divisions. Today (1918!) the coloured colonial troops in East Africa and the Cameroons are armed with the short rifle 71. The Jaegers wore a hunting-knife with iron furniture.

The ballistic performance of the Mauser rifle was quite impressive: Muzzle velocity from 1411 to 1444 fps.
Total range 3280 yards.

Maximum height of trajectory over 765 yards: 24 ft. Maximum height of trajectory of converted Model 62: 28 ft. Maximum height of trajectory of Needle Gun, Model 41: 30.2 ft.

Under 330 yards, the Mauser could penetrate 8 inches of dry spruce wood and at 1800 yards these holes would still be about 3 inches deep.

At 1093 yards the 11 mm Mauser bullet penetrated 15 inches of sand, less at closer ranges on account of the higher speed at which the projectile is travelling; a factor which produces a mushrooming effect upon impact and reduces depth of penetration.

In 1861 Captain von Plönnies published his study on rifled firearms — an epoch-making work that wittily reported on the prerequisites for flat trajectory, high penetration and accuracy; a work that was couched in a most elegant style. Unfortunately, this founder of infantry ballistics died young, and Lieutenant Weygand had to fling himself into the breach. A fresh wind began to blow at the Officer Training Establishments and the use of the rifle was scientifically based on ballistic textbooks. The riflemen began to understand more about groupings, about the direction of fire under battle conditions, and about the simultaneous use of different sights, etc. The oldsters who during the 1860s laughed off dispersion as an untenable invention of the Army Training Establishments, suddenly became very quiet and a number of these high-ranking officers were obliged to brush up their knowledge by sweating through Captain Mieg's Green Book! At this juncture mention should be made of Captain Schön's History of Small Arms (Geschichte der Handfeuerwaffen) which appeared with excellent drawings in 1858. Colonel Thierbach followed suit in 1886 by describing the results of research carried out in more than 600 European gun collections. As Thierback was a precision mechanic himself, he was able to deal with all the parts of important weapons and he donated this unique work to the Armeemuseum at Dresden.

Infantry ballistics as a subject is nowadays presented much more vividly than in the past. One of the most diligent writers in this respect is General Rohne, whose survey results are not agreeable to read, but seldom disputed.

Increased use of repeaters persuaded the Prussian General Staff to remodel the Mauser 71 into the Mauser 71/84. As much as possible of the old Mauser was left untouched, unfortunately including the 11 mm cartridge which was already outdated in 1871. A tube magazine containing 8

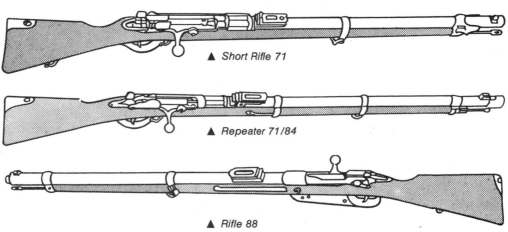

▲ *Short Rifle 71*

▲ *Repeater 71/84*

▲ *Rifle 88*

cartridges was mounted under the barrel. The 71/84 rifle could be fired as a single-shot or a repeating arm, though the magazine cutoff mechanism was not simple to operate and the loading of the magazine proved awkward. An ejector was included, as well as notches in the tangent sight for quicker setting.

The 71/84 repeater measured 51 inches (without bayonet) and weighed 10 lb 2 oz. This time the same model was issued to the In-fantry and the Jaegers. The tip of the bullet was flattened, but explosive charge and bullet weight were not changed. However, the overall length of the cartridge was whittled down from 3.07 to 3.01 in. The bayonet was likewise shortened, but the earlier M 71 was re-adopted later.

Accuracy proved unsatisfactory, as shots began to stray after changes in barrel temperature. Though this Mauser model had many faults, the news that flashed through the newspapers about the celebrations at the Spandau gun factory when the 100,000th repeater was made there, surprised the other European countries. It was claimed that the Mauser 71/84 changed Boulanger's intentions of getting his revenge on the Germans and thus prevented another Franco-German war! A committee convoked to troubleshoot the Mauser 71/84 had hardly rolled their sleeves up before the Mauser brothers at Oberndorf and Councillor of Commerce Duttenhofer-Rottweil presented a small-bore rifle with a new cartridge propellant.

Although the advantages of a sub 9 mm calibre were theoretically known, it was extremely difficult for the up and coming generation to by-pass the diehards and turn theory into practice. Light, long bullets of small calibre required a more rapid rotation around their longitudinal axis to keep them on course, that is, the rate of twist of the rifling had to be considerably faster. Of course, black powder fouling in this type of rifling enhanced the possibility of the bullet being driven out of the bore without following the grooves, an occurrence known as stripping. To obviate this danger a clean-burning propellant was needed, which was found in Duttenhofer's Rottweil Rifle Flake Powder, a nitrate compound. The shorter rate of twist, which means a longer rifling, increased the bullet's

Jaeger Battalion No. 11, 1902

*Foot Artillery
Regiment No. 11,
1914*

drag in the barrel, giving the new powder sufficient time to reach peak energy and drive the bullet out of the bore with maximum force. Black powder burned too slowly to be fully exploited in this way. Recoil was lighter and gas fumes became less, which resulted in a few changes in equipment and general tactics. As the storability of this new propellant was still unknown, the Army Authorities had bought a pig in a poke. This risk was entertained on the assumption that Duttenhofer's product was not a flash in the pan, and that it could be mass produced with consistent quality. Thereupon the Rifle 88 was officially adopted. Re-arming was conducted at all possible speed. Not only the regular troops, but the militiamen were also provided with the new Mauser. Money for the change-over quickly became available when Bismark proclaimed in the Reichstag: "For our home-guard, for our veterans, for the fathers of our children, only the best gun in the world can be good enough."

Over the years, teething problems cropped up in respect of the propellent powder and the jacket of the bullet. But in time these difficulties were all overcome.

The Rifle 88 is 49 in. long and weighs 8 lb 6 oz. Rifling is made up of 4 grooves measuring .173 in. in width, and rate of twist is 1 in 9.45 in. The 7.9 mm (.311 in.) cartridges are packed 5 to a clip, following the Mannlicher system, and loaded into the magazine complete. When the last cartridge is chambered the clip drops out through the bottom magazine opening. The barrel is encased by a steel tube that screws into the receiver ring at the rear end, and is partly enclosed at the front end. The inlying barrel, which protrudes through the front of this jacket, has a certain amount of play to allow for expansion due to heat. Another novelty is the bolt that lies vertically under the receiver ring and engages in a bearing in the stock to reduce recoil. The

Prussian Infantry advancing.

munition, wa so efficiently packed that each soldier could carry 150 rounds.

Ballistic performance was decidedly a step forward: Muzzle velocity approx. 2034 fps, total range 4,156 yards, penetrative energy 31.5 in. in dry pine at 110 yards and 9.85 in. at 875 yards. In freshly piled sand the depth of penetration was 35.5 in. at 110 yards and still 4 in. at 1,969 yards.

the same make. The Rifle 91 used by the Foot Artillery was nothing else but a Carbine 88 with a stacking rod, to hook the weapons together to stand like a pyramid.

According to what has been said, the Rifle 88 was considered to be a first-rate weapon and the shortcomings in bolt and sights to be insignificant. However the German general staff wanted to keep abreast of latest developments, as they were convinced that further progress would soon be made in gun technology. The outcome of their endeavours was the Mauser 98 which retained the 7.9 mm cartridges but discarded the barrel jacket of the Rifle 88. Furthermore, the bolt was given a third locking lug, gas vents deflected fumes away from the shooter's eyes, a receiver bridge was fitted, and the separate-piece bolt head was done away with. A hand-guard was provided for the shooter's left hand to shield it from burning, and the pistol grip facilitated a tight hold around the small of the stock. The rear sight was completely rehashed and the tangent sight that resulted was graduated up to 2187 yards. The bayonet was redesigned, too, and was fastened under the muzzle, not beside it.

sights are the same as those on the Mauser 71/84 and are graduated up to 2,242 yards. Two locking lugs were added to the bolt.

The bullet measured 1.22 in. and weighed 226.85 grains. Its core was of antimonial lead and the jacket of copper-nickel plated sheet steel or cupronickel metal.

The cartridge contained a charge of 42.44 grains later 40.59 grains, of Rottweil Rifle Flake Powder, weighed 421.30 grains and measured 3.25 in. This am-

A fresh wind also circulated in the textbook for the new rifle. It contained large and small print. Passages in small print were for officers only, not for the rank and file.

Emphasis was no longer laid on giving a name to every (unimportant) part of the gun, much to the regret of some NCO instructors! The importance of battle practice began to receive proper attention, and each and every battalion was provided with a range finder, although not always of

The Mauser 98 measures 49.25 in. and weighs 9 lb. The reinforced, 3-stage finished Krupp, Böhler or Bismarkhütte steel barrel has 4 grooves that are nigh twice as wide as the lands. Rate of twist remained at 1

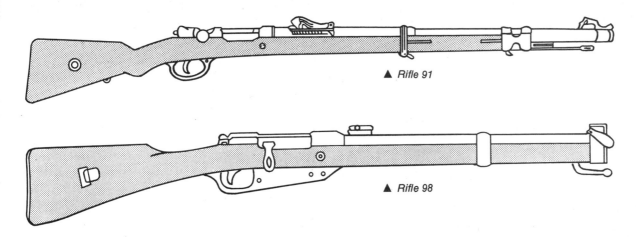

▲ Rifle 91

▲ Rifle 98

in 9.45 in. Though slightly changed, the safety catch engages when it is turned to the right, as was previously the case. The bolt can be disassembled without tools. Moreover, the packet loading system was dispensed with, and 5 cartridges were stagger-loaded via a clip that was inserted into the clip guide just ahead of the receiver bridge. The magazine floor was closed.

Issuance to the troops began in 1899 and ended about 1909. The branches equipped with the Mauser 98 were:
All infantry troops
NCO training schools
Sea-battalions
Navy divisions
Navy/Artillery detachments
Troops stationed in China
Cyclist detachments

In 1903 an "S" bullet was evolved with spitzer point and short groove-gripping sides that reduced friction. Together with a special fastburning "S" powder, performance was increased considerably. Maximum height of trajectory over 765 yards:
Rifle 88 = 12.5 ft
Mauser 98 S = 5.8 ft.
Maximum height of trajec-

tory over 1095 yards:
Rifle 88 = 33.8 ft.
Mauser 98 S = 17.9 ft.

Some military experts did not think that the "S" bullet would disable an enemy soldier for at least the length of a campaign. However, no complaints of this sort were heard from the Turks who fought two Balkan wars with 7.65 mm Mauser 98 rifles in 1912/13.

The "S" bullet measures 1.1 in. and weighs 154.3 grains. The hard lead core was later changed to a soft one. Furthermore, the cartridge measured 3.16 in., contained 49.4 grains of "S" powder, and weighed 366.5 grains. Average muzzle velocity was 2952 fps, and maximum range was 4,374 yards. Penetrative energy = 23.6 in. in strong pine at 110

German Infantrymen during WWI

yards and 4 in. at 2000 yards. Depth of penetration in sand or sand and earth mixed was 35.4 in. at most.

When firing at groups of men in the open, the Mauser 98 will inflict casualties even at extreme ranges. Of course, it is particularly effective at near and middle ranges. On the other hand, the Mauser rifle cannot penetrate the front shields of today's field guns. The soldier is advised to snipe at artillerists when they are engaged in limbering or de-limbering their cannon, or to try and by-pass the shields by getting a shot in at an angle.

Full recognition must be granted to the Royal Gun Factories for making such a quick change-over possible; our thanks should also be extended to the factories at Berlin, Suhl, Steyr, Solingen and Amberg.

In connection with this treatise we are including a list of the various muskets and rifles of this period, stating calibres, lengths and weights. This list has been borrowed from Lieutenant-General von Menges' book, "Die Bewaffnung der preußischen Fußtruppen mit Gewehren (Büchsen) von 1809 bis zur Gegenwart." *) It appeared in 1903, contains 70 pages, and details the rifles in large-scale drawings.

*) Arming The Prussian Infantrymen With Muskets (Rifles) From 1809 To The Present

Glossary
Gewehr = normally rifle, sometimes musket
Infanterie = infantry
Füsilier = fusilier
Schützen = rifleman
Karabiner = carbine
Büchse = rifle, sometimes short rifle
Pikenbüchse = pike rifle
glatt = smoothbore
aptiert = converted
Kürassier = cuirassier
Jäger = Jaeger (regiment)
Französisch = French
Russisch = Russian
Österreichisch = Austrian
Bayerisch = Bavarian
Zündnadelgewehr/büchse = needle gun
gezogen = rifled
U/M = converted
Stutzen = short rifle

List of longarms used by the Prussian (including calibre, overall length, weight) with German designations

		Calibre mm	Length mm without bayonet	with bayonet	Weight gram. without bayonet	with bayonet
1	Infanteriegewehr Modell 1871	20.4	1450	1810	5150	5575
2	Füsiliergewehr	20.4	1340	–	4300	–
3	Jägerbüchse (alte Korpsbüchse)	16.9	1250	1810	4350	5050
4	Schützengewehr (-büchse) 1787	18.5	1240	1580	–	–
5	Nothardtgewehr Modell 1805	15.69	1450	2165	4450	4820
6	Karabiner (Kürassiere u. Dragoner)	17.5	1330	–	–	–
7	Gewehr Modell 1809	18.57	1438	1935	4750	5200
8	Jägerbüchse Modell 1810	14.65	1119.4	1669	4320	5020
	Französisches Gewehr 1777/1802	17.52	1470	1934	4075	4474
	Russisches Gewehr 1809	17.78	1310	1720	–	–
	Österreichisches Gewehr	17.58	1500	1980	–	–
	Bayerisches Gewehr	17.84	1480	1940	–	–
	Bayerischer Stutzen	14.8	1240	1916	2780	3480
	Englisches Gewehr	20.5	1285	–	–	–
9	Jägerbüchse Modell 1835	14.65	1119.4	1669	4567	5267
10	Infanteriegewehr 1839 (glatt)	18.04	1440	1940	4450	4800
11	Infanteriegewehr 1839 (gezogen)	18.04	1440	1940	4500	4850
12	Zündnadelgewehr 1841	15.43	1425	1925	4900	5200
13	Zündnadelbüchse 1848	15.43	1250	1795	4583	–
14	Pikenbüchse 54	15.43	1245	1665	4500	–
15	Füsiliergewehr Modell 60	15.43	1305	1815	4700	5430
16	Zündnadelgewehr Modell 62	15.43	1340	1845	4750	5150
17	Zündnadelbüchse Modell 65	15.43	1245	1710	4550	5225
18	Zündnadelpioniergewehr U/M	15.43	1100	1620	3725	4860
19	Zündnadelpioniergewehr Modell 69	15.43	1105	1625	3875	5010
20	Aptiertes Füsiliergewehr 60					
21	Aptiertes Füsiliergewehr 62		same as 15, 16, 17 and 19			
22	Aptierte Zündnadelbüchse 65					
23	Aptiertes Zündnadelpioniergewehr 69					
24	Infanteriegewehr Modell 71	11	1345	1815	4550	5190
25	Büchse Modell 71	11	1240	1745	4510	5185
26	Infanteriegewehr 71/84	11	1300	1550	4600	4970
27	Gewehr 88	7.9	1245	1715	3800	4600
28	Gewehr 91	7.9	950	–	3100	3825
29	Gewehr 98	7.9	1250	1770	4100	4740
30	Karabiner 98	7.9	1100	–	3600	4300

1 mm = .0394 in.   1 gram. = .0022 lb or .0353 oz.

Frankenau's Shooting-Purse "System Lefaucheux"

**Text and Photos
E. Brunnthaler**

A curiosity among small arms is a pepperbox revolver camouflaged to look like a harmless purse. This instrument of death must have been contrived for wealthy citizens to incapacitate highwaymen and footpads, by offering the brigand a hail of bullets, instead of a well-stuffed purse. A Mr. Frankenau was granted letters patent for this bizarre shooting device on 5th September, 1877.

1

2

3

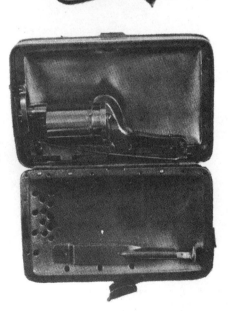

4

The example illustrated bears English proof marks, and is chambered for Lefaucheux cartridges. The purse consists of a strong sheet-metal frame that is sandwiched between two lids. Although missing in our specimen, leather folds and pockets for notes and coins lay under the top lid, whereas the cartridges and firing mechanism were tucked away under the second lid. In other words, the purse has two compartments. Figure 1 shows the purse closed for normal use, Figure 2 the purse closed ready for firing. Figure 4 reveals the firing mechanism, whereas Figure 5 exemplifies a patent drawing. The cover plate for the muzzle of the barrel (1), hinged to the side band, is joined to the bifurcated rod (2) which is pressed against the folded trigger (4) by a long curved spring (3). The straight trigger, on account of the oblong shape of the purse, is held, when inoperative, by the tongue (5). By depressing a screwhead just above the muzzle exit, the barrel cover plate swings out, the bifurcated rod (2) pushes the trigger out of engagement with the tongue (5), and the spring (3) snaps the trigger outwards into an operative position. This arrangement could prove perilous, however. For if the screw-head, which functions rather lightly anyway, were inadvertently depressed while the purse was still within one's pocket, the trigger would fly out and snag in the lining.

Most people are jittery if not terror-ridden when they come face to face with armed bandits. There is reason to suppose, therefore, that this sort of purse might go off in one's pocket. On the other hand, though, for steely nerved James Bonds this might be an ideal piece of equipment to have. The barrel (6) isn't really a barrel in reality; for its bore is larger than the 5.5 mm calibre of the bullets. It probably functioned as a flash inhibitor, to keep hot smoke and burning powder away from the other cartridges in the cylinder. Owing to design features, this purse gun can be grouped with pepperboxes. The 5 cartridges are loaded through a loading gate that is kept closed under spring pressure. As in other revolvers, the pawl (8) nudges the cylinder, one chamber at a time, around its axis. When a shot is fired, the pawl and the small claw (9) keep the chamber lined up with the exit hole. The trigger is designed to lift the hammer against the tension of the main spring (10) and drop it again, at one pull. The slits around the chambers accommodate the side pins of the Lefaucheux cartridges. The empty cases are removed with a thin extractor that is spring-mounted inside the lid. As seen in Figure 4, gas escape vents are bored into the lower lid. All parts are nickel plated, apart from the springs, and the box itself is covered with leather. The quality of the workmanship would lead us to believe that these shooting purses were entirely hand-made, and that not many of them were produced.

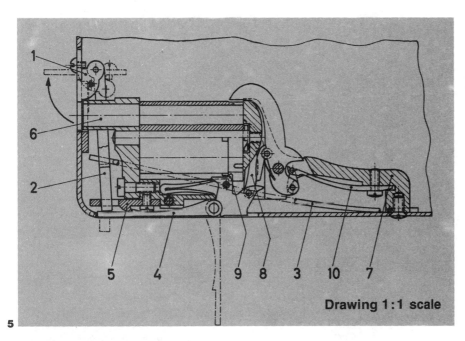

Technical data

External dimensions
4.14 x 2.56 x 1.10 inches
Calibre 5.5 mm
Cylinder length 1.13 inches
Cylinder diameter .78 inch
Number of chambers 5
Weight (no rounds, no money!) 10.24 oz.

Drawing 1:1 scale

5

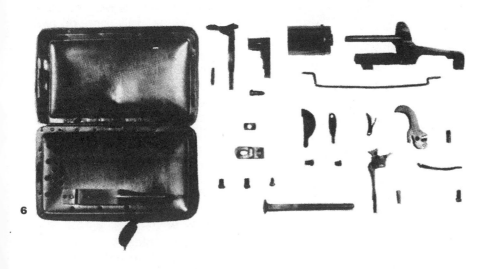

6

Text and Photos G. Freres

Manufrance

Slide-Action Shotgun Model "Rapide"

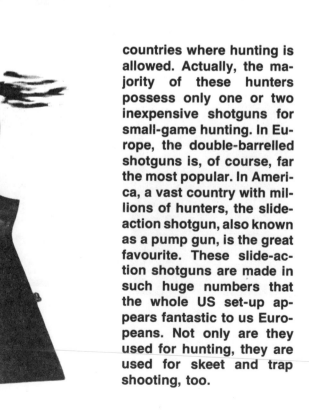

In the Federal Republic of Germany the lion's share of hunters is made up of small- and middle-income people, despite the exorbitant fees demanded by land owners advertising in some of the national papers. Naturally, the non-hunter thinks all these Nimrods must have pots of money if they can pay the land owners such princely sums for hunting rights. A similar situation probably prevails in most of the other European countries where hunting is allowed. Actually, the majority of these hunters possess only one or two inexpensive shotguns for small-game hunting. In Europe, the double-barrelled shotguns is, of course, far the most popular. In America, a vast country with millions of hunters, the slide-action shotgun, also known as a pump gun, is the great favourite. These slide-action shotguns are made in such huge numbers that the whole US set-up appears fantastic to us Europeans. Not only are they used for hunting, they are used for skeet and trap shooting, too.

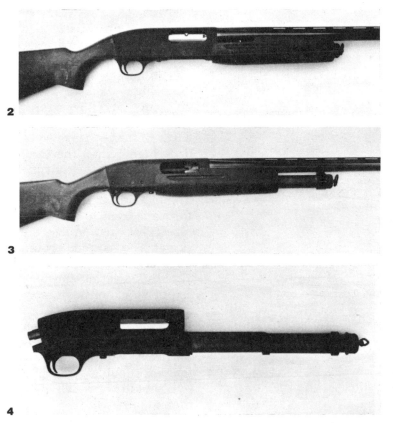

2

3

4

shotshells out of this Frenchman, and got a pattern percentage of 62.6%, on average. Although CHOKE CHASSE is boldly stamped on the barrel, which translates as "Hunting Choke", we would class this 0.50 mm constriction as "modified", possibly even "improved modified".

Buttstock and forearm (Illus. 6 and 7) consist of dark-stained walnut and the buttstock is provided with pistol grip, but no cheekpiece. To save money, apparently, checkering has gone by the board. The slide handle is fluted to give a better grip. However, with sweaty hands, it is often difficult to manage and checkering should definitely replace the fluting. For we soon discovered that the

The Manufrance "Rapide" is a slide-action shotgun, and as its name suggests, is comes from France. Is is a simple, inexpensive gun, showing good design and workmanship. The light alloy receiver (Illus. 5) is black finished and is fluted along its top as an extension for the ventilated rib. The barrel is made of special steel, also black, and is crowned with the aforementioned ventilated rib (Illus. 6). The bore is hard chromed. The choke is interesting for German hunters; for the CHOKE CHASSE (stamped on barrel) differs considerably from the German method of

5

making chokes. In Germany, about 6 cm before the muzzle the bore begins to taper inwards for a short distance, and then continues cylindrically to the muzzle with the same amount of constriction.

The barrel we inspected, on the other hand, was cylindrical up to 7.1 cm before the muzzle, whence the bore sloped off like a funnel right up to the muzzle. We pumped 6 different types of

"Rapide" only functioned properly when the slide handle was forcibly pushed to and fro. If the slide handle is laxly operated the disconnector won't disengage, and hence the gun refuses to fire. Operating the slide handle is something the hunter and trap shooter will have to practise. The buttstock is somewhat short for a 6ft man, the distance between buttplate and trigger being 35.1 cm.

6 *Barrel and forearm*

7 *Buttstock with buttplate and stock bolt*

8 *Rear of barrel, showing locking block engaged in recess*

9 *Locking block no longer engaged in recess*

10 *Breech bolt with extractor. Note locking-block guide at bottom, and erected locking block on top*

11 *Locking block flush with the breech bolt*

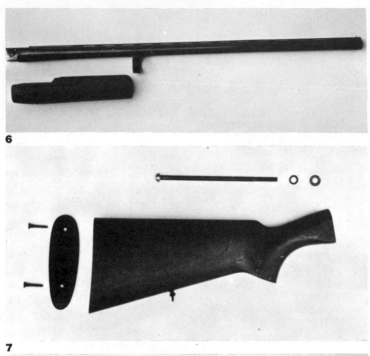

6

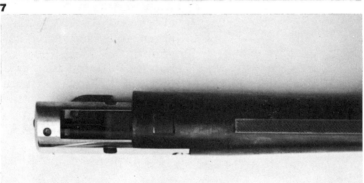

7

8

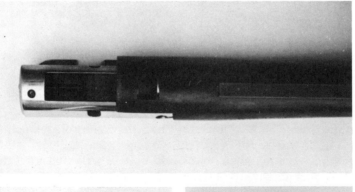

9

10

11

After slipping on a leather butt cap, the "Rapide" fitted well in the hand and against my face, in spite of the fact that the centre of mass was 17.5 cm ahead of the trigger and 18.3 cm when the gun was loaded with 4 shells. I could just see a bit of the top rib. And this sort of aiming should produce high shots of 10 to 20 cm at 35 metres The "Rapide" centered the paper. If the bead is raised a little higher than the flute in the receiver, the shots go high by about 20 cm. This is bad for the hunter, for he is used to lining up his sights just under the target. The "Rapide" could be adjusted either by slightly elevating the barrel, or by mounting a more straight buttstock.

Furthermore, a trigger pull of 3.34 kg is definitely too heavy. Where there is no fear of doubling, trigger pull should not weigh more than 2 kg.

However, all in all, the "Rapide" made quite a rugged impression. No troubles cropped up during the test. Once sighting and trigger have been adjusted, and the jerky slide movement has become part of your flesh and blood, the Manufrance "Rapide" might well become a fully fledged utility gun of interest to American and European hunters.

Operating the "Rapid"

To load, smartly pull back the slide handle as far as it will go. See Illus. 2 and 3. The action bar, which slides on the magazine tube

(Illus. 4 and 13), forces the breech bolt (Illus. 10, 11 and 12) back past the ejection port. The hammer is then automatically cocked (Illus. 14, 15 und 16). A shotshell can now be pushed onto the the ejection port, on to the carrier. Once the slide handle starts to move forward again, the bolt rides over the carrier dog and tips the carrier up in line with the chamber (Illus. 17). By pushing the slide handle the rest of the way forward, the bolt chambers the shotshell which is lying on the carrier. During the last closing phase the action bar activates the locking-block guide, which, in turn, nudges the locking block into a recess at the rear of the barrel. The action is now firmly locked (Illus. 8 and 9). A latch mounted on the trigger plate rises behind the action bar, preventing the bolt from opening. The action can only·be opened by firing the shell, or, in the case of an empty gun, by dropping the hammer or depressing the lock-release button that is just in front of the trigger guard.

Once a shell is in the chamber, a further 3 shotshells can be introduced into the magazine tube via the lower opening in the receiver. Loading can be accomplished whether or not the safety is applied.

The push-through safety button is mounted in the rear of the trigggger guard. It blocks only the trigger.

To unload the gun it is wise to apply the safety first. Then depress the lock release button and pull back the slide handle to

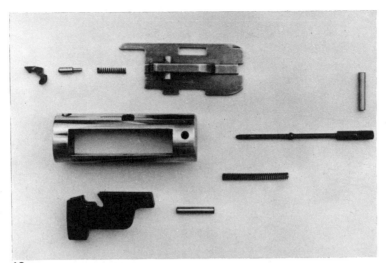

12

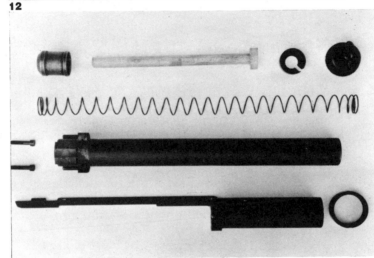

13

12 *Breech bolt dismantled. Top: extractor with plunger and spring, locking-block guide. Middle: bolt with firing pin and retainer. Bottom: locking block with axle pin*

13 *Magazine tube dismantled. Top: follower, hardwood plug, bushing, screw cap, spring. Middle: tube with mounting screws. Bottom: action bar, ring nut*

Manufacturer:	Manufacture Française d'Armes et Cycles de Saint-Etienne
Designation:	Model "Rapide"
Gauge:	12/70 or 16/70
Lockwork:	Slide action with locked bolt. Hammer mounted on trigger plate, firing pin in bolt
Safety:	Push-through button behind trigger
Trigger pull:	3.34
Receiver:	Light alloy, black finish
Barrel:	Special steel, length 71 cm (27.95 in.), hard chrome lining, ventilated rib, choke constriction .50 mm (0.196 in.). Interchangeable
Magazine:	Tube under barrel for 3 70 mm (2.75 in.) shotshells. Capacity for 1 shotshell with hardwood plug
Stock:	Stained walnut, pistol grip, no cheekpiece, no checkering, swivel
Measurements:	Trigger – buttplate: 35.1 cm (13.81 in.) Drop at comb: 3.8 cm (1.49 in.) Drop at heel: 5.6 cm (2.20 in.) Pitch: 3.6 cm (1.41 in.) No cast off
Weight:	2.94 kg (6.48 lbs)
Overall length:	123 cm (48.42 in.)
Price:	approximately $ 200.00 (U.S.)
Guarantee:	5 years

14

15

16

17

14 Trigger plate showing hammer and carrier in resting positions. Catch in "disengaged" position

15 Hammer cocked. Catch in "engaged" position

16 Trigger plate viewed from the right. Otherwise same as Illus. 14

17 Hammer cocked, carrier in up position

eject the shell in the chamber. The other shotshells in the magazine can be removed by working the slide handle or by pulling them out separately through the loading port. Here the carrier must be pushed up against the bolt and the shell stops in the receiver pressed apart. Where the law stipulates that not more than 3 shells shall be contained in a repeating or automatic shotgun, the manufacturer provides a hardwood plug for insertion in the end of the magazine to reduce its capacity. A chambered shotshell can easily be exchanged for another, i. e. if a different shot size is required. Activate the lock release button and pull the slide handle back about 1 cm. Then push inwards the shell that is protruding from the magazine, far enough for the right shell stop to

18

engage behind the shotshell's rim. By pulling back the slide handle the shell in the chamber will be ejected, but the shell in the magazine will not be transported by the carrier. A fresh shell is placed on the carrier and the action is closed.

Field stripping is simple indeed. After the action has been half opened, remove the magazine cap and the barrel can be lifted off to the front. Slide handle, action bar, and breech bolt can also be taken off to the front, once the left shell stop has been depressed.

When the two tapered pins have been pushed out, the trigger plate with hammer, carrier and catch can be drawn down out of the receiver. Of course, the gun can be dismantled still further but that is not necessary for cleaning.

Simply reverse the procedure to reassemble. However, please note that the hammer must be in cocked position before the trigger plate will fit in the receiver.

TABLE 1

Results obtained with 2.5 mm (No. 7) shot at 38.3 yds	Waidmannsheil 12/70 ga. 399 pellets 1.25 ozs Batch No. MS 5 K 17	Legia Star High Speed 12/70 ga *) 482 pellets (nickel plated) 1.26 ozs (No. 8 shot) Batch No. 25 R 78
Number of hits		
Inner circle *	87	107
Outer circle	153	206
Whole target	240	313
Density	1:1.7	1:1.56
Regularity (Mean deviation of a 5-shot series)	13.8 = good	23.4 = poor
Covered fields (Geared to number of hits)	11.6 = excellent	13.6 = good
Extreme variation of effective hits		
Diameter	25.6 in.	31.5 in.
At distance	32.8 yds	36.1 yds
Max. effective range	45.9 yds	49.2 yds
Rating	Excellent for normal purposes	Excellent for normal purposes
Pattern in percentage	60.2%	64.9%

*) With plastic cup wad
12/70 ga. = 12/ 2¾ in. cases

TABLE 2

Results obtained with 3 mm (No. 5) shot at 38.3 yds	Rottweil Stern 12/70 ga. 208 pellets / 1.21 ozs Batch No. MS 19 N 16	Eley Alphamax 12/70 ga. 209 pellets / 1.27 ozs Batch No. 58 K 3 Q
Number of hits		
Inner circle	52	50
Outer circle	84	83
Whole target	136	133
Density	1:1.86	1:1.81
Regularity (Mean deviation of a 5-shot series)	14.8 = poor	9.4 = satisfactory
Covered fields (Geared to number of hits)	10.0 = poor	9.4 = poor
Extreme variation of effective hits		
Diameter	–	–
At distance	–	–
Max. effective range	45.9 yds	44.8 yds
Rating	Excellent for normal purposes	Good for normal purposes
Pattern in percentage	65.4%	63.3%

12/70 ga = 12/ 2¾ in. case

TABLE 3

Results obtained with 2,5 mm (No. 7) shot at 38.3 yds	Waidmannsheil 12/70 ga. 399 pellets / 1.25 ozs Batch No. MS 5 K 17	Legia Star High Speed 12/70 ga. *) 482 pellets (nickel plated) 1.26 ozs (No. 8 shot) Batch No. 25 R 78
Number of hits		
Inner circle	87	107
Outer circle	153	206
Whole target	240	313
Density	1:1.7	1:1.56
Regularity (Mean deviation of a 5-shot series)	13.8 = good	23.4 = poor
Covered fields (Geared to number of hits)	11.6 = excellent	13.6 = good
Extreme variation of effective hits		
Diameter	25.6 in.	31.5 in.
At distance	32.8 yds	36.1 yds
Max. effective range	45.9 yds	49.2 yds
Rating	Excellent for normal purposes	Excellent for normal purposes
Pattern in percentage	60.2%	64.9%

*) With plastic cup wad

12/70 ga. = 12¾ in. cases

**Cross section
of the "Rapide"**

1 *Barrel;*
2 *Magazine cap;*
3 *Magazine tube;*
4 *Forearm;*
5 *Carrier;*

6 *Receiver;*
7 *Lock-release button;*
8 *Safety;*
9 *Breech bolt.*

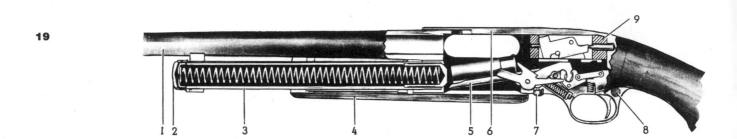

19

Manufrance Slide-Action Shotgun Model „Rapide"

Performance

We tested the "Rapide" with Waidmannsheil and Legia Star (2.5 mm shot), Rottweil Stern and Eley Alphamax (3 mm shot), as well as Rottweil Express and Remington Express (3.5 mm shot). See Illus. 18. The Waidmannsheil and Rottweil Express shotshells come with an O-S wad and roll crimp, whereas the other 4 makes have standard folded crimp. Furthermore, the Legia Star and the Remington had plastic wad columns, the three Germans made use of the traditional felt wads and the Eley had a wad of papier-mâché. The hulls also differed. While Remington and Rottweil Express use modern plastic hulls, the other makes still stick to sodia cellulose paper.

As pellet size in non-German shotshells differ from German DIN standards, the results of our tests are not comparable. The test can merely show how well the Manufrance

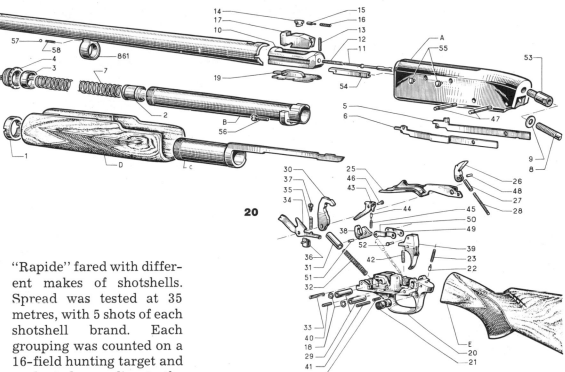

20

"Rapide" fared with different makes of shotshells. Spread was tested at 35 metres, with 5 shots of each shotshell brand. Each grouping was counted on a 16-field hunting target and evaluated according to the system described in, DER SCHROTSCHUSS *). The results are listed in Tables 1, 2 and 3.

The modified choke of the "Rapide" delivered a 60.2% pattern with 2.5 mm shot (also 64.9%), a 64.4% pattern with 3 mm shot (also 63.6%), and a 64.1% pattern with 3.5 mm shot (also 57.6%). The average then is 62.6%. Density ran between 1:1.52 and 1:1.86, 62.6%. Density ran between 1:1.52 and 1:1.86, which is not high, but ties in with the choke and the percentages obtained. Regularity and effective spread were unsatisfactory with 3 mm shot. The other two shot sizes were, by and large, satisfactory in this gun. We ascertained that the "Rapide" is choked for the hunter who takes a mixed bag, on account of the relatively wide-spread patterns.

*) DER SCHROTSCHUSS, by Herbert von Wissmann, is obtainable from Verlag Paul Parey, Hamburg and Berlin, West Germany.

Exploded view of the "Rapide"

1861 *Barrel;*
A. *Receiver;*
B. *Tube magazine;*
C. *Action bar;*
D. *Forearm;*
E. *Buttstock;*
1 *Ring nut;*
2 *Follower;*
3 *Bushing;*
4 *Mag. cap;*
5 *Right shell stop;*
6 *Left shell stop;*
7 *Mag. spring;*
8 *Stock bolt;*
9 *Washer;*
10 *Breech bolt;*
11 *Firing pin;*
12 *Firing-pin spring;*
13 *Retaining pin;*
14 *Extractor;*
15 *Plunger for 14;*
16 *Spring for 14;*
17 *Locking block;*
18 *Clips;*
19 *Locking-block guide;*
20 *Trigger assembly;*
21 *Safety button;*
22 *Plunger for 21;*
23 *Spring for 22;*
24 *Pin for 21;*
25 *Carrier;*
26 *Carrier dog;*
27 *Carrier dog plunger;*
28 *Spring for 27;*
29 *Hollow axles;*
30 *Hammer;*

31 *Thrust bolt for 30;*
32 *Hammer spring*
33 *Pin for hammer and latch;*
34 *Latch;*
35 *Latch spring;*
36 *Lock-release button;*
37 *Screw for 35;*
38 *Hammer catch;*
39 *Trigger;*
40 *Pin for 38;*
41 *Trigger pin;*
42 *Trigger spring;*
43 *Disconector;*
44 *Disconnector plunger;*
45 *Spring for 44;*
46 *Pin for 43;*
47 *Tapered pin for trigger plate;*
48 *Carrier dog pin;*
49 *Right trigger brace;*
50 *Left trigger brace;*
51 *Pin for 49 and 50;*
52 *Rear pin for 49 and 50;*
53 *Anchor screw;*
54 *Ejector;*
55 *Mounting studs for 54;*
56 *Screw for mag. tube;*
57 *Retaining ball;*
58 *Spring for 57.*

Dr. Manfred Rosenberger

THE DAKOTA

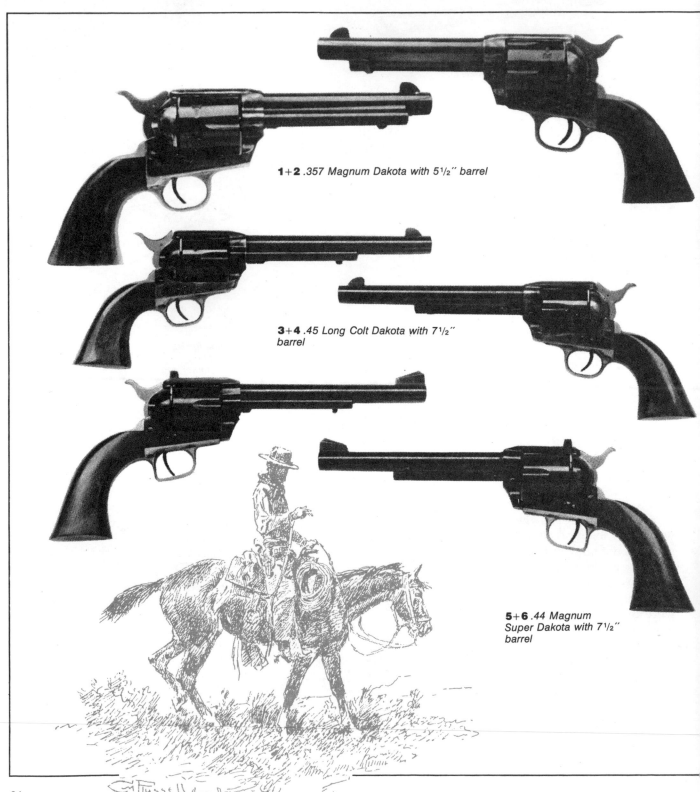

1+**2** .357 Magnum Dakota with 5½″ barrel

3+**4** .45 Long Colt Dakota with 7½″ barrel

5+**6** .44 Magnum Super Dakota with 7½″ barrel

REVOLVERS

The current boom in single action revolvers can be hardly ascribed to some sort of necessity for using this type of weapon, all the more so as the main body of single action enthusiasts stems from that non-influenceable group known as gun aficionados . . . And, as far as I'm concerned, a single action revolver lies exclusively in the domain of the gun nut. This shows up in actual shooting practice. Originally, the single action revolver was a quick-draw weapon, it was not designed for punching holes in paper targets, or for any form of precision shooting, for that matter. Whereas marksmanship shooting with a pistol or revolver might well be compared to handling a rifle, quick-draw tactics bear more similarity to scattergun practice: one shoots intuitively. No wonder, therefore, that a "true to style" handling of single action revolvers requires much practice, on the one hand, and that indefinable "something" on the other, that differentiates first-class shotgunners from all the others. However, here in Germany genuine quick-draw shooting is practised by a few specialists only, and as a rule they are ridiculed as Wild West nitwits. Although quick-draw shooting offers the best op-

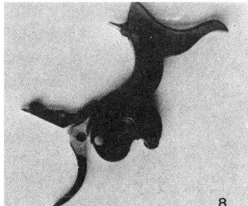
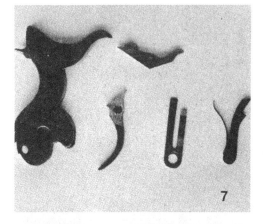
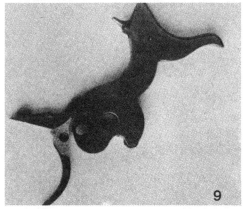
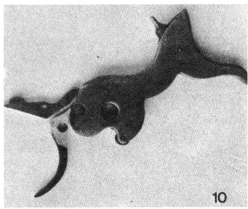

portunity for really learning how to master a handgun, this belittling attitude unfortunately still exists. Nonetheless, the popularity of single action revolvers, first and foremost, can be put down to the historical aura of these weapons. For their owners they bring about a "breeze from the old West."

Single action revolvers are being offered by a number of manufacturers these days. In the main, however, most models are more or less successful copies of the legendary "Peacemaker" of 1873, chambered for modern cartridges. Into this grouping we can include the Dakota and Super Dakota, which are imported by International Arms Corp., Los Angeles, Calif. Technically, these replicas hardly differ from the originals (illus. 1–6). Apart from the brass backstrap, the lacquered grips and the sights of the Super Dakotas, there are no differences externally. All the other parts are virtually identical.

7 From left to right Hammer with inserted firing pin, trigger, bolt (above), bifurcated flat spring for trigger and bolt, hand with spring.
8 Hammer in safety notch.

9 Hammer in loading notch. Note that the nose of the bolt is depressed. The cylinder can now rotate freely.

10 Hammer at full cock.

11 *Hammer down.*

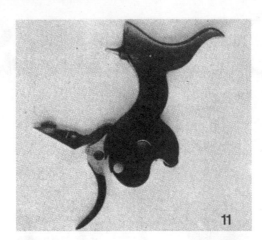

In the traditional manner, the Dakota sports a hammer, hand with spring, bolt, trigger, bifurcated flat spring for trigger and bolt, and a mainspring (illus. 7). Faithful to the prototype, the hammer has three under notches, into which the sear end of the trigger, under spring influence, engages. Starting from the top, the notches are: safety, loading and full-cock. The two first mentioned notches are so deep that the sear end cannot be drawn out by pulling the trigger. The hammer has to be fully cocked before the trigger will operate again. The hand is suspended on the left side of the hammer is such a way that it moves forward, through a slot in the breech face, against the ratchet near the centre of the cylinder, when the hammer is cocked. This upward movement of the hand rotates the cylinder 60 degrees to the right, the distance from fone chamber to the next. In this way the chambers of the cylinder are automatically aligned with the barrel. The rear projection of the bolt is pressed against a cam on the side of the hammer, via the bifurcated flat spring. If the hammer is not in the loading notch, the nose of the bolt protrudes through a cutaway in the frame into one of the arresting recesses of the cylinder, thus preventing rotation.

When the hammer is fully cocked, the nose of the bolt is drawn out of engagement with the cylinder recess, freeing the cylinder in the process. At the same time,

12 *The firing pin is held in the hammer face via a cross pin. The firing pin has a certain amount of free movement.*

13 *If the cylinder is to be removed from its frame, press the base pin to the right and pull cylinder pin forward ...*

14 *... when the gate has been opened, the cylinder can be slipped out of its frame. Note that the hammer must be engaged in the loading notch first.*

Faults: lacquered grip, springs slightly too hard, badly cut forcing cone in one test gun.
Note: The higher the number, the lower the rating.

Rating	Dakota		Super Dakota
	.357	.45	.44
Workmanship	2	2	1
Functional safety	1	1	1
Performance	3	2	2
Design	1	1	1
Finish	1	1	1
Sights	2	2	1
Balance	1	1	1
Pointing qualities	1	1	1
Hang	1	1	1
Total	13	12	10

the hand is drawn back into the breech face – the cylinder can now be freely rotated for pushing out the empty cartridge cases, and for reloading (cf. illus. 8–11). The hammer has the same shape as that of the Frontier SAA revolver. It has polished sides. Its hammer is relatively long, and somewhat goose-necked. The non-stationary firing pin, contrary to a stationary one, delivers rather a soft blow (illus. 12).

Like the SAA revolvers, the Dakotas don't have a swing-out cylinder either. If barrel or cylinder are to be cleaned, the hammer is thumbed into the loading position and the base pin on the side of the frame, in front of the cylinder, is pushed to the right (illus. 13) to permit the cylinder pin to be drawn out to the front. The cylinder itself can now be lifted out of the frame, to the right (illus. 14). The important thing is to remember to cock the hammer into the loading notch before attempting to remove the cylinder.

The same warning must be given when freely rotating the cylinder during loading or unloading. When the hammer is in the loading notch, the gate is opened on the right side (illus. 15) so that the empty cases can be poked out by means of the ejector rod, or fresh cartridges loaded (illus. 16). Backstrap and trigger guard of the Dakotas are made of highly polished brass. This bestows on them a distinct decorative appearance (illus. 17 and 18). On the other

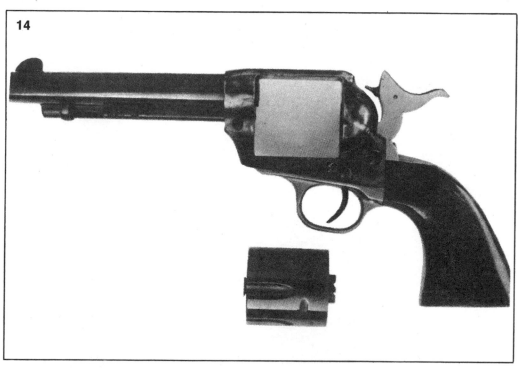

14

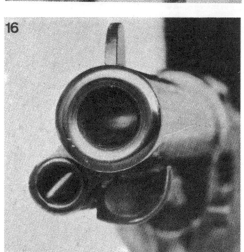

15 *When the gate is open, the cylinder can be rotated for loading, or unloading.*

16 *The ejector rod is manipulated for clearing the chambers of empty cases.*

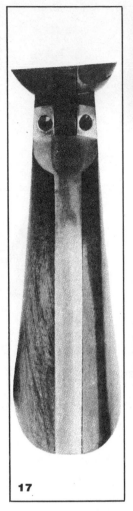

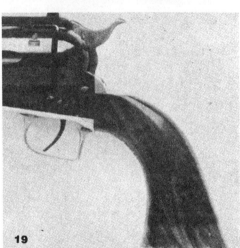

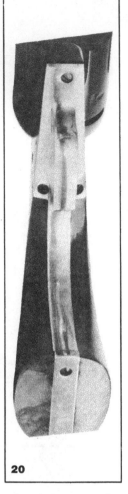

hand, though, the extra weight of brass makes this revolver slightly tail heavy. An interesting feature in this connection is that the grips are of one piece, i.e. not made up of two plates (illus. 26). This is an advantage, there's no doubt about that, for a one-piece grip cannot work loose or slant when worn.

The Dakotas come in two versions, the Dakota and Super Dakota. The Dakota is chambered for .22 L.R., .357 Mag. (and .38 Spec.) or .45 long Colt, whereas the Super Dakota can be had in .41 Mag. or .44 Mag. While the Dakota sports a casehardened frame, the Super Dakota is blued. Moreover, it has a reinforced topstrap. The handle of the Super Dakota is about 15 mm longer, and wider at the top. See illustrations 19 and 20. Furthermore, it has a square-back trigger guard – similar to that of the Ruger Super Blackhawk – to prevent the gun from slipping too far into the hand when recoiling (illus. 21). Paradoxically, the grips of both

17 Backstrap and trigger guard are made of brass . . .
18 . . . which bestows on the Dakotas a distinct decorative appearance.
19 The Dakota and the Super Dakota. The grips also differ slightly . . .
20 . . . they are longer and broader on the Super Dakota. Furthermore . . .
21 . . . the Super Dakota has a square-back trigger guard.

Dakotas are lacquered, which makes firm gripping difficult.

The sighting arrangement of the two Dakotas also differ somewhat. The Dakota has a sighting groove machined into its topstrap, whereas the Super Dakota is fitted with a rear sight proper that can be adjusted for windage by turning a support screw (illus. 22 and 23). The Dakota has a normal blade front sight. That of the Super Dakota is adjustable for elevation and its rear edge is cross serrated (illus. 24 and 25).

The Dakota is supplied with 4⅜″ (.22 L.R.), 5½″ and 7½″ (.357 Mag. and .45 Colt) barrels. The Super Dakota boasts 5½″ and 7½″ barrels.

For testing we were presented with three Dakotas, namely the Dakota with 5½″ barrel/.357 Mag. (serial No. 3153), the Dakota with 7½″ barrel/.45 Colt (serial No. 3556) and the Super Dakota with 7½″ barrel/.44 Mag. (serial No. 6140). See illustrations 1–6.

All three revolvers functioned superbly. However, the forcing cone of the .357 Mag. model had been badly drilled, which resulted in a one-sided spreading of lead and impairment in score groupings.

Furthermore, when using wadcutter bullets the imprints on the target sheets

22 Whereas the Super Dakota's rear sight has windage adjustment . . .
23 . . . the Dakota has the usual rear notch sight . . .
24 The broad ramp front blade of the Super Dakota can be elevated . . .
25 . . . the front sight of the Dakota, on the other hand, is soldered to the barrel.

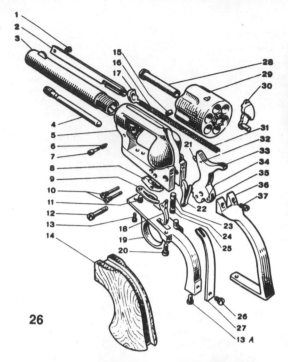

26

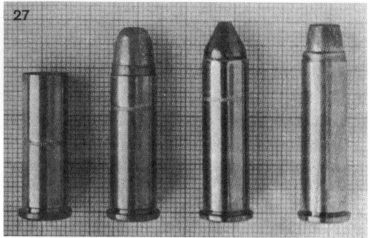

27

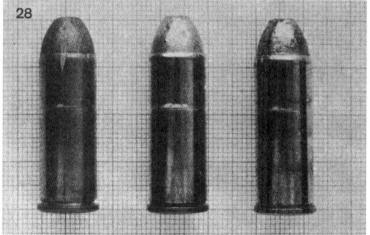

28

29

26 *An exploded view of the Dakota.*
27 *.38 Specials and .357 Mag. were used during testing. Left to right: 148 gr. wadcutter, 158 gr. lead round nose, 158 gr. armor piercing, 158 gr. semi-jacketed.*
28 *.45 long Colt. From left to right 250 gr. (Rem.), 255 gr. (Win.), and 255 gr. (HP).*
29 *.44 Special and 44 Mag. (right).*

were mostly not round. The lacquer on the grips of all three revolvers was exceedingly detrimental to good shooting. These polished grips slipped about badly in the hand while firing, and it wasn't until we removed all traces of lacquer that the guns nestled down nicely, despite recoil.

Different loads and makes of cartridges were fired from the three specimens, that is, 24 shots of each load (cf. illus. 27, 28, 29). All loads in the .45 Colt version virtually did equally well, although the different loads brands in the other two guns often differed considerably (cf. Table II). The discrepancy between the .44 Special and the .44 Mag. might well be ascribed to the fact that the .44 Special can only be a makeshift in a .44 Mag. revolver; owing to too great a length of twist and the considerably shorter cartridge case. As said earlier, the results of the .357 Mag. were influenced by the badly cut forcing cone. The scores, therefore, cannot be classed as characteristic. This is especially true of the wadcutter loads. Interesting indeed is the surprisingly good results obtained with the two .357 Mag.

loads, when compared with the .38 Special loads. This is probably due to the Tombac jacketing, which must take easier to the lands and grooves of the barrel. The wadcutters are particularly sensitive, and, if damaged within the barrel, often tumble end over end, and hence punch keyholes in the target. For this reason, the results obtained with the .357 Mag. version are quite interesting and instructive.

All in all, all three Dakota representatives made an excellent impression. This fact is all the more remarkable, as the prices are truly not exorbitant.

TABLE I

Ballistic data of the cartridges and loads tested

Cartridge Make	.38 Win.	Spec. Win.	.357 Mag. Win. Norma	.45 Colt Rem. Win. HP	.44 Spec. Fiocci	.44 Mag. Rem.
Bullet weight (gr.)	148	158	158 158	250 255 255	246	240
Bullet's shape	WC	Or	CS CF	OrF OrF OrF	Or	sWC
Bullet type	L	L	AP SJ	L L LG	L	GC
Velocity m.p.sec.	235	261	436 455	263 261 261	232	479
Energy mkg	27.0	35.6	99.0 112	562 57.0 57.0	29	159

Remarks
WC = wadcutter, Or = ogive, CS = conical, spitzer, CF = conical flattened, OrF = ogive flattened, sWC = semi wad cutter, L = lead, AP = armor piercing, LG = lead, galvanized (Lubaloy), GC = gas check.

Source
Das Magazin des Waffenfreundes 1965; HP-Hausmitteilung, Norma Technical Information, No. 63.

TABLE II

Average dispersion of the three Dakotas under test at 30 m
These results are based on an arithmetical mean of four 6-shot series apiece.

Calibre Barrel length (inch)			.357 5½	.45 7½	.44 7½
Cartridge	**Bullet**	**Make**			
.38 Spec.	148 WC	Win.	5.3 cm		
.38 Spec.	158 Or	Win.	4.0 cm		
.357 Mag.	158 CS	Win.	3.1 cm		
.357 Mag.	158 CF	Norma	3.3 cm		
.45 Colt	250 OrF	Rem.		2.8 cm	
.45 Colt	255 OrF	Win.		3.1 cm	
.45 Colt	255 OrF	HP		2.8 cm	
.44 Spec.	246 Or	Fiocchi			4.8 cm
.44 Mag.	240 sWC	Rem.			3.0 cm

AFRICAN WEAPONS

Christian Schenk

The missionaries were on the scene long before the industrialized nations dispatched foreign-aid personnel to the fledgling states of ·Africa. These missionaries not only propagated the Gospel in virgin forests, in the savannah, and in the mountains; they were also agriculturists, doctors, and consultants in all matters of life and death. It often took years before the trust of ·the various tribes could be won over. Obviously, the task of instructing people who whole-heartedly believed in demons was anything but simple. Every puff of wind, every ripple on the surface of a stream, and every imagined face in the swirls of the clouds symbolized the actions of a spirit. The missionaries partook of the native festivities and accompanied the warriors on their hunting trips. Here the whites soon realized that the weapons of the Africans possessed no prestige value, they were born of dire need. The weapons illustrated in this article were collected by Wilhelm Häberle, a missionary in the hills of Cameroon since 1934. He is now retired in his native Germany, and we inquired of him how the Africans in his region regarded their weapons. Whereupon he related a story about one of his bearers, a young man who was virtually still a boy. When I asked him if he had a rifle, he retorted in an injured tone: "Do you believe I'm not a man? Do you really believe I'm a woman?"

Figures 1—4 *Three bush knives. Positions 1 and 2 were made by the Banzos, position 3 by the Meta tribe. All bush knives measure just under 24 inches, and the blades are hammered by the village smithies. The sheath of the Meta knife is made of monkey skin. The sheath of the second Bonzo knife is plaited bamboo. The sheath of the other Banzo knife has been drawn from snake skin. Furthermore, the Kauri mussels used for adornment were officially legal tender 40 years ago. The ears on either side of the sheath accept a belt that crosses the shoulder. Bush knives are used for clearing a path through the jungle, as a kitchen utensil, and to gut slain animals. Nobody would dare leave his hut without his bush knife.*

Photos by Kubach, by courtesy of Wilhelm Häberle.

Figures 5 and 6
This in an 11-inch dagger, the handle and sheath of which are made of kid leather. These daggers are extremely popular with the Hausas of the Cameroon mountain districts. A high-quality dagger reflects its owner's wealth or station in life. The leather strap is wound around the warrior's left hand and the sheath rests against the inside of his left arm.

AFRICAN WEAPONS

Figure 7
Arrow heads. The arrow at far left is from northern Ghana, the others from the Cameroons. They are shot at birds, animals, and occasionally at members of other tribes. All arrow heads are dipped in a vegetable poison, the composition of which is a well-kept secret.

7

8

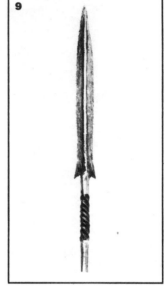

9

Figures 8–10
Spear heads. Two broad spears of the old Bali men. The etchings are to please the eye, they do not serve a ritual purpose. The Ghana spear sports two barbs, and the "walking-stick spear" might be compared to the Swiss alpine-stock. The tribesmen use them as a prop when toiling from one mountain slope to the next. Most African spears are beautifully balanced, and animals are often dispatched at distances up to 35 yards.

10

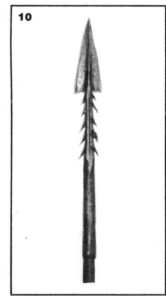

Figure 11
A sword-like bush knife. African smithies are experts in wood carving, too. Owing to these skills, the populace believes in magic powers that are transferred from the smithies to the weapons they make.

Figure 12
This is one of the ritual swords that were often put to use at the altar. A chieftain gave it to Wilhelm Haberle as a souvenir, an act replete in prestige value. The Wums carry the ritual sword when dancing at a wake (all-night watch over a corpse before burial), otherwise for dispatching a victim at the altar. The blades are made of iron smelted in bush blast furnaces. A head crowns the handle of the ritual sword.

Text and Photos G. Freres

THE ZIMMERMANN RIFLE MODEL Z 66

with hinge frame, shotgun-type action

The single barrelled rifle with break-open, shotgun-type action has always met with the approval of European hunters who want something special for their specific requirements. For the roebuck for instance, where the shot barrels of the drilling are not used, and the bolt-action rifle unwieldly and too heavy . . .

This is probably one of the reasons for the popularity of the hinge frame rifle in Europe. After all, normally only 1 shot is needed when hunting deer or boar. If a 2nd shot be necessary, a single-shot rifle can be speedily loaded again with a little practice, by holding the reserve cartridge in your left hand. Many big game hunters also use single shot rifles and are very successful.

Before the last war these break-open rifles were very common in Germany. Take, for example, the REMO by the firm Gebrüder Rempt in Suhl, or the COLLATH with its wayward breech system and wing safety catch that was produced by Teschner-Collath in Frankfurt/Oder. The calibres of yesteryear are also interesting. The range extended from the weak 6.5x27 P through the 6.5x40 G, 6.5x48 R and 6.5x58 R to the 9.3x72 R and 9.3x74 R cartridges. Cartridges with conical cases were popular, since the actions for these were less bulky, and the rifles themselves somewhat lighter.

When the war was over, a terrific demand for sporting weapons had to be met. The German bolt-action military Mauser 98 was easily sporterized, and offered at a reasonable price.

The Allied Armies of Occupation, however, forbade the manufacture of hinge frame rifles in Germany, at least during their first few years of office. Whether these rifles are now being made in East Germany, in Suhl or Zella-Mehlis, is not known. They are not being offered to West German

1 *Zimmermann hinge frame rifle, Mod. Z 66. Left view*

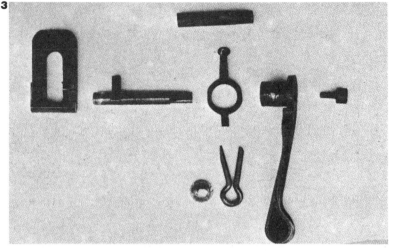

3 *Left: Flat bolt, eccentric shaft, top snap lever, crossbolt, top snap and screw, and top spring and screw*

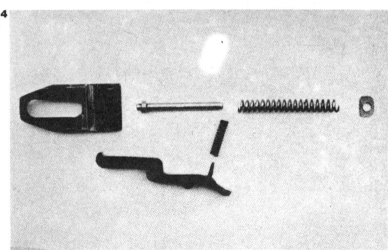

sportsmen, that's for certain. In West Germany, the first of J.P. Sauer & Sohn at Eckernförde produced a hinge frame rifle, Model IX, which, funnily enough, proved a failure. When first marketed after the war and today it is no longer available. Anyone who wants a hinge frame rifle should pay a visit to Austria. In Ferlach, at the foot of the Karawanken mountains, such rifles have been made for years by several gunmakers of good repute. These weapons are technically and aesthestically truly perfect. Price is their only disadvantage.

On account of the market situation, and reasonable price, the Zimmermann Model Z 66 hinge frame rifle should have a good chance of success. For German hunters it is surely of interest that this gun can be bought for the price of a good quality bolt-action rifle. Scope mounting is also inexpensive on hinge frame weapons.

4 *Left: hammer, guide, coil spring, stop plate, trigger bar and spring*
5 *The safety mechanism: Bearing bushing, recessed thrust bolt, nut, bearing bushing, spring and ball*

Description

The Z 66 is available in three versions. S means standard, SJ models have high-grade stocking and deep engraving, whereas the JPs come with high-grade stocking plus decorated side plates with deep engraving. We examined the standard version. Weighing only 2.8 kg (approx. 6.17 lbs), the Z 66 is one of the lightweights. However, this rifle is sturdy enough to dampen recoil, but not so heavy as to become a drag after a morning stalking session, even

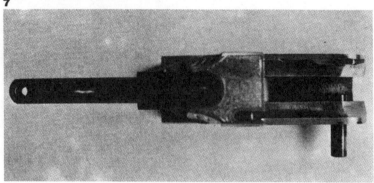

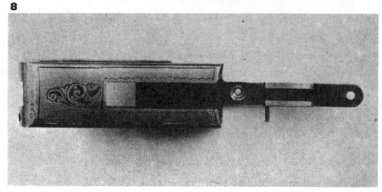

6 Trigger plate with German double set triggers and pusher arm; trigger guard and screws

7 Receiver viewed from above, showing half-withdrawn hinge pin

8 Receiver viewed from below, showing pin for trigger bar

9 Lateral view of receiver

with a scope. The Z 66 balances well and the pistol grip is just the right size for a normal hand. The comb is also set back far enough to avoid a collision with the ball of one's thumb. The forearm is nice and solid, though it could stand being a little longer, and ought to be more trapezoidal in cross section.

Centre of mass is 11.6 cm (approx. 4.56 in.) in front of the trigger. With scope mounted, centre of mass is 11.3 cm ahead of the trigger. When shouldering, the Z 66 nicely fits its owner's face. Length of buttstock, cast-off, drop and pitch harmonize so well that both sights align immediately the weapon is shouldered. But even when using the scope there is no need to strain your neck. This must be attributed to the stout buttstock with Bavarian cheekpiece and semi Monte Carlo effect. Another advantage is that this rifle is only 103 cm (approx. 3.4 ft) long with a normal barrel length of 60 cm (approx. 1.98 ft). All these features help to explain the excellent pointing qualities of hinge frame rifles.

How the Z 66 works

By thumbing over the top lever, which is tensioned by the hairpin spring, it withdraws the crossbolt from the openings in the barrel extensions. At the same instant, the eccentric shaft of the top snap turns the bottom flat bolt out of the recess of the under lug of the barrel. The breech will now open. Most hinge frame weapons are so designed that a cocking lever cocks the hammer when the breech is opened. For reasons of simplicity, and to reduce costs, the Z 66 does not operate with a barrel-activated cocking lever. As the flat bolt retracts from the under lug, it nudges a pusher arm, mounted on the trigger plate, back against the hammer. In normal fashion, the hammer is rotated around its axle pin until it is arrested in cocked position by the tip of the sear. The hammer is tensioned by a coil spring with guide rod, not by the usual double limb flat spring. It is interesting to note that the two limbs of the trigger bar are virtually equal in length. Usually, the jib arm is longer, so that the sear end smartly moves out of the hammer notch. However, we found weight of trigger pull and creep acceptable, without having to engage the double set trigger. Once the sear end of the trigger bar has left the bent of the hammer, the hammer drops on the firing pin which is mounted from behind the breech face of the receiver. The point of the

10

10 The complete receiver, lock-work uncocked
11 *The complete receiver, lock-work cocked and set trigger engaged*
12 *The barrel in monobloc*

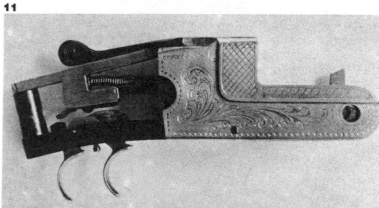

11

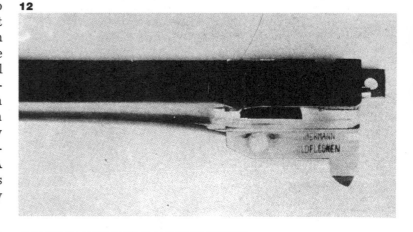

12

firing pin is nicely rounded and protrudes far enough to the front to always effect positive ignition. The trigger plate carries the aforementioned pusher arm and German double set triggers. This trigger plate is fastened to the receiver via two lateral socket-head cap screws, plus one that passes through the tang. A strong bushing runs between trigger plate and tang, which helps to steady the buttstock. A sliding button which is mounted in the stock is the safety. It blocks the trigger bar. Bearing bushings are screwed into both sides of the stock, in which a nutted thrust bolt can slide. This bolt has a recess which lines up with the trigger bar when the safety is disengaged. The trigger bar has room to lift, in other words. A small guide pin on the bolt can enter a slot in the left bushing. This is provided with two bore holes into which the ball and spring can engage when the safety catch is on "safe", or "fire". See illustration 5. This safety device works superbly, but the movement of the button does not conform to the anatomy of one's hand. A tang safety would be better. Constructionally, this is feasible, for the jib end of the trigger bar lies directly under the tang.

Manufacturer: Hans Zimmermann, Feinmechanik Waffen, 8789 Oberwildflecken (Röhn), West Germany

Designation: Hinge Frame Rifle, Model Z 66

Calibres: 5.6x57 R; 6.5x57 R; 7x57 R; 7x65 R; 8x57 IRS; 10.3x60 R (Switzerland). Other calibres available, too

Action: New type hammerless system. Greener crossbolt, single under lug and flat bolt

Safety: Mounted in stock, blocks the trigger bar

Receiver: C 45 steel, milled. Engraved, grey finish

Barrel: Special gun metal – 60 cm. Swaged rifling. Groove diameter – 7.26 mm, land diameter – 6.99 mm. Rate of twist – 215 mm

Sighting: Notch rear, post front

Stocking: Walnut lacquered with Bavarian cheekpiece and light Monte Carlo effect. Scotch checkering on pistol grip and forearm. Horn trigger guard

Stock measurements: Trigger – buttplate: 35.5 cm. Drop at comb 3.9 cm. Drop at heel: 6.7 cm. Pitch: 9.6 cm

Weight: 2.8 kg. With scope 3.4 kg

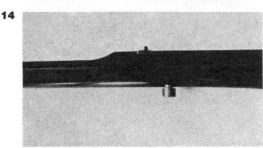

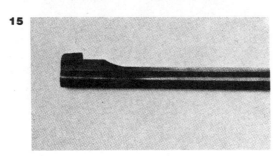

13 The Monobloc with scope rail
14 Barrel with forearm bushing.
Top rib elevated
15 Muzzle end showing front
sight and mount

The receiver is of carbon steel with the classification No. C 45. It is not forged, it is milled. The tang is brazed on the main body. All parts, such as top snap lever, crossbolt, eccentric shaft, flat bolt, pusher arm, hammer and trigger bar are finely made and hardened. The hinge pin is locked in place by a fillister-head screw. A tongue on the left leading edge of the receiver operates the extractor when the rifle is opened. The special steel barrel is mounted in Monobloc fashion, and brazed with silver solder. Contrary to brass solder, silver solder melts at 650 ° C. The thermal change point of steel is higher, so no risks are taken when silver soldering.

The Monobloc, also made of C 45 steel, carries the under lug and hinge pin locking lug, the crossbolt barrel extension and a scope rail. Furthermore, it contains a channel for the extractor. A ventilated rib is soft soldered along the top of the barrel. As seen in illustration 16, the forearm is screwed to the barrel. The buttstock is fastened with a stock bolt to the receiver. Buttplate and pistol grip cap are of plastic and are adorned with a white spacer. Stocking is good walnut and is Scotch checkered and lacquered. The trigger guard is made of horn.

Performance and finish

The weapon sent us by the manufacturers was chambered for the 7x57 R with 10.5 g (162 gr.) TIG bullet. Dispersion figures from the factory showed an average of 1.3 cm (.51 in.) over 100 m (109 yds) with three shots. Since testing dispersion with open sights has its problems, we mounted a 6 power scope, type Hensoldt Diasta D. We fired over 100 m with the rifle clamped in a Preuss gun rest. Using the same cartridges as the factory our dispersion averaged 2.9 cm (1.14 in.) with five shots. Let the facts speak for themselves . . .

Technical design and workmanship cannot, of course, be compared to that of high-class sideplate shotguns. For DM 850 (in Germany) one has to make compromises. The receiver, for example, showed machine tool marks, which mar general appearance but not functionability. After taking the Z 66 apart a couple of times, the top snap spring broke. This ought to be replaced with a forged cock spring.

THE ZIMMERMANN RIFLE MODEL Z 66

16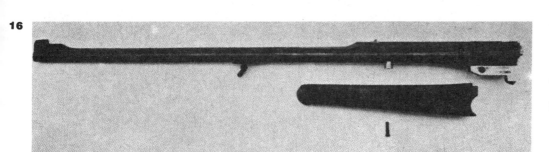

16 Barrel and forearm
17 Barrel with mounted scope
18 Hensoldt Diasta D scope
19 Buttstock with stockbolt and washer
20 Buttstock complete with receiver

17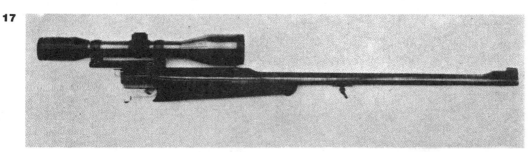

18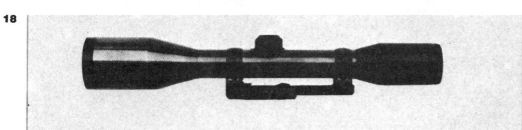

All in all, however, the Zimmermann Z66 made a rugged impression, probably on account of its new lock-up system. Performance is excellent.

19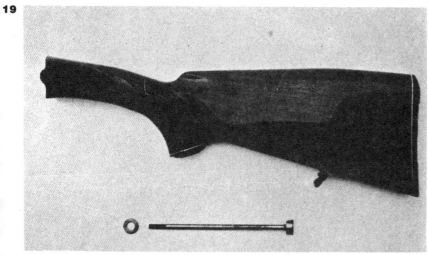

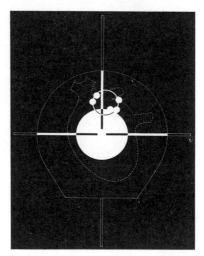

21 Grouping with calibre 7x57 R, 10.5 g TIG and 3.0 g R2, DWM, over 100 m with 5 shots. Dispersion: 2.9 cm.

20

The illustrations show the Master and Single CO2 Target Pistols produced by Hämmerli.

The Mechanics of Co² Energy

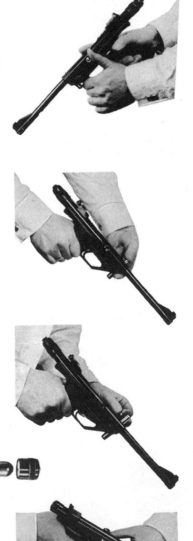

CO₂ weapons differ from air guns in that they operate with carbonic acid gas, and not with compressed air. That is what I read in the printed instructions. But how is it that you can shoot with CO₂? You all know how the normal air gun works. A spring is compressed; for that you require muscle energy. This mechanical energy is "stored" in the spring, and when the spring is released this energy is transferred to the piston head, which very rapidly reduces the space in the air chamber. Hence, pressure is created to drive the pellet out of the barrel. The amount of energy needed for each shot is measurable. It is easy to calculate the amount of energy a marksman needs, say, for 60 shots.

Very little energy is required by the shooter to operate CO₂ weapons, only a small spring is activated. However, the spring of CO₂ guns has nothing in common with that of the air gun. Well, if it isn't mechanical energy that provides power in CO₂ weapons, what is it? And where does it come from? The printed instructions say: The commercial CO₂ powerlets contain carbonic acid gas in liquid form. Once the powerlet is in the gun, however, a part of the liquid carbonic acid gas evaporates in the pressure chamber, whereby saturation pressure is reached. A minute portion of CO₂ gas is thus expended for each shot. Constant pressure is maintained; for the more the weapon is fired, the

Dr. Max Buschhoff

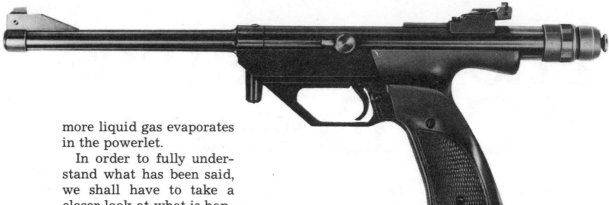

more liquid gas evaporates in the powerlet.

In order to fully understand what has been said, we shall have to take a closer look at what is happening in this microcosm. Only then can the questions be answered. Let us take a piece of iron and cut it up. First with coarse tools, then with finer and finer ones. Continue until no pieces remain that can be made smaller. At this point carry on in your mind's eye, beating and chopping to the point where only finest particles are left over. These would be the molecules of the substance iron. A cubic centimetre of a gas contains so many of these particles that all the people of this earth would need 300 years to count them, if they counted one a second. All these molecules leap-frog around with great intensity, and their kinetic energy increases with the rise of the gas temperature. Try and picture one of these particles in a vacuum, quite alone. We shall now bestow it with kinetic energy, and it begins to orbit. The particle ricochets off the one wall and bounces against the next, etc. The effect of these collisions is immeasurably small, as long as the particle is zipping around alone. If we, however, place myriads of these molecules in the vacuum, these collisions can be measured as pressure. Whereas the solitary particle could streak along in wide orbits, many particles together bark one another's shins before they ever reach the outer wall, which, however, does not influence measurable pressure. The unimpeded orbit of hydrogen molecules, for example, known as the mean free way, is .0000178 cm. A distance the human mind cannot imagine. If, on the other hand, the molecules were as large as tennis balls, the mean free way would be as long as the tennis court. Now, what could happen if we reduced the size of the vacuum in which all these particles are buzzing around? The collision rate increases, as does pressure. If the size of the vacuum were increased, pressure would drop. The same effect would be achieved by accelerating or decelerating the particles, all other things being equal. However, if the particles are accelerated, a temperature rise must be taken into account, and if decelerated, a fall in temperature. We now know three measurable quantities: volume, pressure and temperature, and a few of their relationships to one another. Scientists call them "variables of state."

If we continue to decrease the velocity of a particle of gas, that is, lowering the temperature, we shall suddenly reach a point where something strange happens. The molecules become so sluggish that they no longer rebound from one

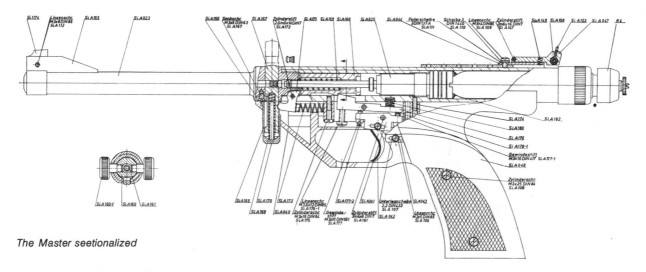

The Master sectionalized

another. On the contrary, they adhere in clusters, and wobble around. What was once gaseous has turned into a fluid. This new condition lacks the energy of the former. If we continue to cut down on temperature, we encounter a phenomenon that is even more odd. With uncanny precision, the particles begin to arrange themselves in cubes, parallelopipedons, tetrahedrons, etc. The substance has again changed its condition, it is now a solid. Conversely, a solid can be transformed into a fluid, and a fluid into gas, by raising the temperature.

Let us now observe a kettle on a stove. The water molecules bubble up and down, jog one another, strike the sides of the kettle – and force a passage to the surface. When a molecule, just below the water's surface, has gained an extra boost of kinetic energy by bumping into a galaxy of neighbours, it can free itself from the force of attraction

of these neighbours, and spring up into the air. If this extra boost was not explosive enough, the molecule will drop back into the pool. Sometimes, though, water molecules collide with air molecules, and are decelerated before they splash back into their own element. If, on the other hand, the extra boost of kinetic energy sufficed, the particle will not return. The fluid has not only lost a particle, but also the accompanying energy. We now appreciate that evaporation is a process which consumes energy. But what takes place if we clamp the lid down on the kettle, and keep the water at a specific temperature? After a while a state of equilibrium sets in. Within, say, a second, as many particles leave the water (within the kettle) as return. One speaks of the section filled with air as being saturated with water molecules, and pressure against the sides of the kettle is termed saturation pressure.

The higher the temperature, i. e. the greater is the kinetic energy, and the more intense is the saturation pressure. We should note that saturation pressure is only obtainable in a closed vessel over a fluid, and is controllable by temperature change only. Let us now turn our attention to the way in which air guns function. By compressing a spring a consistent pressure is created to fire the pellet. Consistent pressure is vitally important for target shooting. Looking for a means to create consistent pressure, we have found saturation pressure that exists over every fluid in a confined space. In other words, we could use the saturation pressure of water, alcohol or ether. Unfortunately, at room temperature (68–71° F) the pressures from these matter are too feeble to guarantee first-class shooting.

The Mechanics of Co² Energy

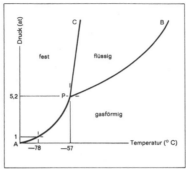

If we increased the temperature to produce the required saturation pressure, the gun would be too hot to handle. Searching for a substitute, we have discovered matter that is gaseous at room temperature. Carbonic acid gas (or carbon dioxide), CO_2, seems to fit the bill perfectly. But when is CO_2 a fluid? For only over a fluid in a closed chamber does a consistent saturation pressure arise. Where do the lowest and highest values of CO_2 lie? Its bottom limit can be plotted in the phase diagram of Fig. 1. The course of the curve A–P indicates vapor pressure from the solid substance, for solids also give off minute, but measurable vapor pressure. The curve P–B denotes vapor pressure of the fluid. The line P–C separates solid and liquid conditions. Here we become aware of the fact that in normal air pressure (1 atmosphere) CO_2 does not exist as a fluid. This, however, would be the prerequisite for employing saturation pressure as a

consistent pressure. Only after we increase pressure to 5.2 atmospheres excess pressure, do we reach stage P, the so-called triple point where solids, liquids and gas can co-exist side by side. At this pressure, which represents the lowest saturation pressure, liquification cannot be achieved under – 70.6° F.

Where, now, is the highest saturation point? Earlier on we mentioned that the three measurable quantities, volume, pressure and temperature, are known as the variables of state. This means, if we change any one of them, the others change, too. When, in Fig. 2, we illustrate the interdependence between pressure and volume at a constant temperature – such changes of condition are called isothermal changes, and the lines you can draw up in a diagram are isotherms – we ascertain a steady, nigh straight-line falling curve (e. g. Tl). At a specific temperature (TK), the curve begins to twist a bit. Over a longer stretch the curve runs horizontally. Here pressure remains consistent, i. e. liquid is present. The temperature at which this takes place is known as the critical temperature. With CO_2 it is 87.8° F, and the accompanying pressure is 73 atmospheres. For saturation pressure this is the ceiling. Over 87.8° F, CO_2 refuses to liquify, even under highest pressures. But,

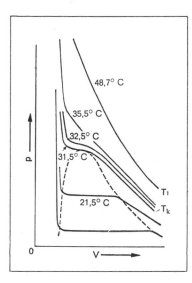

as said before, liquid CO_2 is a must to maintain consistent saturation pressure. Hence, we have at our disposal a range of temperature from $-70.6°$ F to $87.8°$ F.

Temperature °F	Saturation pressure (atm.)
- 69	5.3
- 58	7.0
- 40	10.3
- 22	14.6
- 4	20.1
+ 14	27.0
+ 32	35.5
+ 50	46.0
+ 68	58.5
+ 87.8	75.2

The above table shows the saturation pressures for various temperatures. In the meantime we have ample proof that saturation pressure is high enough with CO_2 to be used in a pellet gun at room temperature (between 50° and 86° F.).

Accurate shooting is then guaranteed. Still, the most important prerequisite must be stressed again. Saturation pressure (the propellant) can only remain consistent if the temperature does not change. Most CO_2 enthusiasts recollect experiencing different pressures during winter at the range.

However, the Hämmerli people have taken fluctuating pressure into account, by increasing CO_2 outflow when low pressure is in the chamber. Pellet velocity, therefore, remains virtually consistent in all weathers. You might raise objections to the fact that the "cushion of pressure" is withered down by each shot, that the liquid evaporates. Here heat is necessary, and by shooting fast enough we could reduce the temperature in the pressure chamber, and thus the saturation pressure, too. But for reasons already given, this would not impair accurate shooting. All this goes to prove that CO_2 weapons are reliable in function and performance. Not only that, by exploiting the laws of nature we can fire a pellet over a considerable distance without using our own muscle energy. Ambient temperature does the job for us. The principles of the steam engine have been rehashed to produce a CO_2 pellet gun . . .

Bibliography

1. H. R. Christen, Grundlagen der allgemeinen und anorganischen Chemie. Verlag Sauerländer Aarau; Salle Verlag Frankfurt (Main), 1968.
2. R. Brdicka. Grundlagen der physikalischen Chemie. VEB Deutscher Verlag der Wissenschaften, East Berlin, 1965.
3. Ullmanns Encyclopädie der technischen Chemie, Band 9, Urban & Schwarzenberg, Munich-Berlin, 1957.

INSERT BARRELS- A Makeshift?

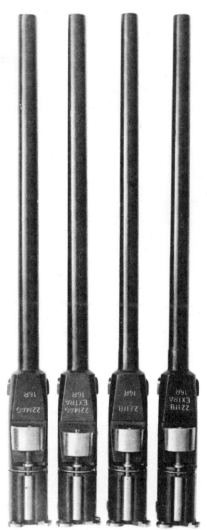

"If you want to convert your drilling into a truly universal gun, then you'll need an insert barrel!" So spoke many years ago a gunmaker to a young hunter, who, after some procrastination, followed the former's advice and bought himself a Krieghoff sub-calibre tube in .22 Winchester Mag. for the right barrel of his 16/70 ga. shotgun. Once the insert barrel had been fitted, this young huntsman sallied down to the range to put his "universal weapon" through its paces. His surprise was great: the gunmaker had not promised too much, performance was really excellent.

2

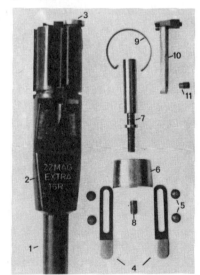

3

2 *Inserts can be installed in the left or right barrel of 16 ga. shotguns. But only in the right barrel of 12 and 20 ga. shotguns*
3 *Component parts of a Krieghoff insert barrel*
4 *Four bearing points are formed by support and regulating lugs (top view) Regulierwarzen = regulating lugs, Stützwarzen = suppoert lugs*

4

**Text and Photos:
Klaus Nocher**

"How is an insert barrel fitted?"

"Well, that's simple, press here into the groove and tighten with a spanner."

"How tight?"

"Well, tight it must be; you know, always the same, firm."

The first animal that hunter downed with his sub-calibre tube was a fox, oh what a joy! Crows, magpies, pigeons, and jays followed suit . . . until one day a check shot against a paper target showed a miss as wide as your hand, at 100 yards. That disillusioned hunter slowly made his way to the gunsmith who had sold him the unit, to complain bitterly.

His diagnosis was: "The insert is much too tight in the barrel, too much vibration to coincide with point of aim."

Year after year our hunter had to check that insert barrel if he removed it to clean the main barrel, for who knows in which direction it would shoot next?

What was needed was an abutment, something against which the setscrew would be limited — a counter screw! (By the way, at the time of this story Krieghoff was actually producing them.)

This simple contrivance resolved the problem of uniform fitting, and sportsmen put new faith in sub-calibre tubes.

Insert barrels have been made for decades for various purposes: for practice with inexpensive ammunition, for closed-season hunting, and for claybirding, etc.

Design

The 8.7 in. barrel that is slightly tapered (1) comes brazed into an eccentrically bored head-piece (Fig. 3). This head-piece, the diameter of which differs according to the calibre of the main barrel, accommodates what might be termed as the fixing and adjusting elements, as well as the extractor. The rim screw (3) acts as an abutment when the barrel is inserted, while the regulating lugs (4) are arranged to slide at the top of the head-piece by means of the fastening screws (5). See Fig. 4. The shim (6) is the lowest abutment point of the insert barrel (Fig. 5). By rotating the shim bolt (7), which is designed for an Allen

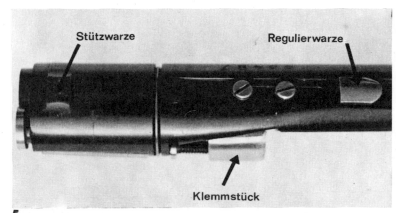

5 The shim forms the bearing point at the underside of the insert. Thanks to its shape, the shim always lies flat in the firing chamber of the shotgun barrel.
Regulierwarze = regulating lug
Stützwarze = support lug
Klemmstück = shim

 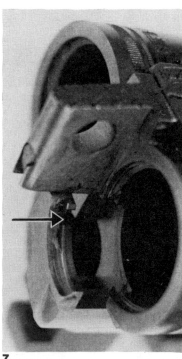

6 A heavy-duty tensioning pin is pressed into the shaft of the extractor, guaranteeing a constant depth for the insert barrel
7 Cutout in the shotgun extractor, to accommodate tensioning pin

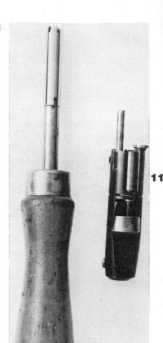

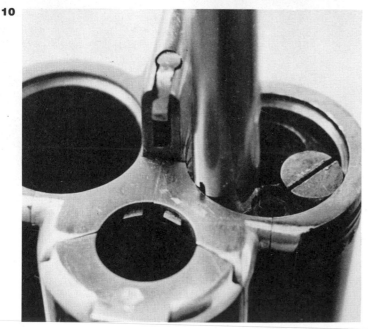

key, the shim is pressed against the walls of the chamber of the shotgun barrel to bring about a fit. The grub screw (8) arrests the movement of the shim bolt, preventing the insert barrel from working loose. The piece of wire (9) keeps shim and shim bolt together when the insert barrel is not in use, whereas the extractor helps considerably to exactly reposition the insert every time it is placed afresh in the barrel.

The extractor is guided in a tight-fitting V-groove (stop screw 11). A heavy-duty tensioning pin (Fig. 6) that fits into a cutout in the shotgun extractor (Fig. 7) is mounted on the extractor shaft. This cutout may on no account be V-shaped, its sides must run parallel to allow the tensioning pin to pass through under light pressure and rest against the extractor.

Fitting

The firm of Krieghoff prescribes explictly that its subcalibre barrels be fitted by a competent gunsmith or by its own factory. Nonetheless, for the sake of interest, the details of fitting shall be divulged here. By using the cutting tool (Fig. 8) delivered by Krieghoff, it is but a simple matter to mill out the cutouts for the rim screw (Fig. 9) and for the insert extractor (Fig. 10). Great care should be taken that the surfaces are smooth, and that the smaller extractor cannot slip off the larger one (Fig. 11).

If necessary, headspacing can be altered; for the action will not close, or only under great pressure will it close, if the insert is not seated deep enough. Conversely, if headspacing is oversized, split cartridge cases or blown primers are likely to be the consequence. This job cannot be accomplished with a screwdriver alone; for the screw must be flat filed along the bearing area, then counter sunk.

The insert barrel is then aligned by shunting the regulating lugs to and fro. Point of impact is shifted laterally by shunting one lug more than the other, or vertically by shifting both lugs. If the barrel has insufficient adjustment, higher or lower regulating lugs are obtainable, ranging from 2.8 mm (0.110 in.) to 4.2 mm (0.165 in.) in thickness.

Once the insert barrel has been bore sighted and the sights aligned, the heavy-duty tensioning pin is pressed into the extractor stem, and a corresponding cutout is filed in to the extractor of the shotgun barrel. The counter screw is screwed into the shim from the front, far enough to hold the insert barrel (Fig. 12).

Anyone wishing to fit this counter screw subsequently, ought, if possible, to use a self-locking grub screw. Otherwise, if the insert barrel is often re-

8 *Krieghoff cutting tool for installing insert*
9) *Half-moon cutout to accept rim screw*
10 *Milling the bearing surface for the extractor of the insert*
11 *A properly installed insert barrel*

moved, a normal grub screw tends to work itself loose. Shooting-in is best performed at a distance of 50 yards. Insert barrels chambered for .22 WRF Mag. should be sighted in to shoot about 1 to 1.5 in. high (cf. ballistic data).

Performance

Before we start passing judgement, we might first consider the demands an insert barrel should satisfy. It must shoot true, be light and pocketable, be easy to fit with (virtually) no tools, and the point of impact must never change, even if the main barrel has been used in the meantime. And an appliance fulfilling all these demands really does exist!

Of course, only an insert barrel that has been properly fitted in the first place, will produce the required results.

I tried out the insert barrels illustrated in Fig. 1, on a really cold day down at the range. Cold weather affects accuracy, so my experimenting was not in any way an official test. That is why I did not make use of all possible load/barrel combinations. In .22 WRF mag. (Fig. 13) I fired RWS full jacketed, RWS soft point, Win. Super Speed full jacketed, and Hirtenberg soft point bullets. And in .22 L.R. I used RWS Standard, Win. Super Speed, Rem. Standard Velocity, and Rem. High Velocity.

The grouping in Fig. 15 was achieved by using Hirtenberg soft point ammunition in a .22 Magnum EX-TRA insert barrel, over a distance of 109 yards. After each shot with the insert barrel, the left barrel was discharged with shotshell (No. 3). My insert barrel was fitted into the right shotgun barrel of a Krieghoff drilling 16/70 and .30-06 that was scoped with a Hertel and Reuss macro-variabel 2–7 x scope (Suhler claw mount). The barrels warmed up nicely, yet dispersion remained within a circle measuring only 2.36 in. Fig. 16 shows a beautiful grouping printed at 55 yards with RWS .22 L.R. standard. Maximum dispersion amounts to no more than 1.18 in. Other results can be gleaned from Table I.

EXTRA

Each insert barrel is machine-rest tested before it leaves the works, and graded as follows:
    Insert barrel .22 L.R.
    Maximum dispersion at 55 yards: 4 x 4 cm
    (1 4/7 x 1 4/7 in.)
    Insert barrel .22 L.R. EXTRA
    Maximum dispersion at 55 yards: 2 x 2 cm
    (7/9 x 7/9 in.)
    Insert barrel .22 WRF Mag.

12

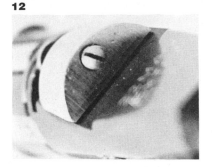

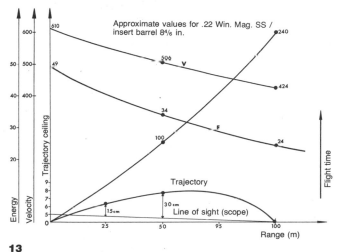

13

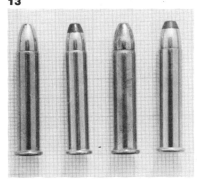

14

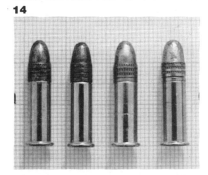

12 *This counter screw is most important for maintaining the point of impact should the sub-calibre tube be removed and re-installed*
13 *.22 WRF Mags. Left to right: RWS full jacketed, RWS soft point, Win. Super Speed full jacketed, Hirtenberg soft point*
14 *.22 L.R.s, Left to right: Rem. Standard, RWS Standard, Rem. Hi-Speed, Win. Super Speed*

15 *Grouping obtained with .22 Magnum EXTRA insert barrel, when firing Hirtenberg soft points over 110 yards. After each shot with the insert barrel, the left barrel was discharged with shotshell (No. 3). Dispersion: 2 3/8 in.*
16 *Grouping obtained with .22 L.R. insert barrel, when firing RWS standards over 55 yards. Dispersion: 1 3/16 in./5 shots*
17 *Insert barrel 1) has a cutout in the rim, to protect rim and firing pin against dry firing (new design). Insert barrel 2) shows a burred surface, as snap-caps were not used for practice firing*

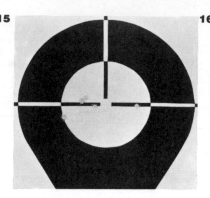
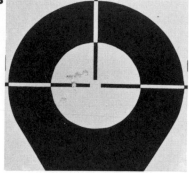

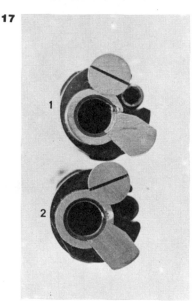

Maximum dispersion at 55 yards: 6 x 6 cm (2 3/8 x 2 3/8 in.)
Insert barrel .22 WRF Mag. EXTRA
Maximum dispersion at 55 yards: 3 x 3 cm (1 3/16 x 1 2/16 in.)

As seen from the groupings and the accompanying tables, my normal barrel, on average, produced better results than those stamped with EXTRA. Naturally, I don't want to gibe at the firm of Krieghoff — machine rests are more dependable than human beings – and I suspect the cause of this phenomenon to lie in my own inconsistent fitting of these barrels.

Ballistics

That the .22 L.R. is about the most accurate and highly developed of any rimfire cartridge available, is a well-known fact. Loss in performance with this cartridge (designed for a 25 in. rifle barrel), when fired through an 8 2/3 in. insert barrel is surprisingly low. This decrease only amounts to approx. 1.5 per cent for standard loads, and approx. 4 per cent for

high-velocity loads. In other words, the difference in performance between a normal barrel and an insert barrel when using .22 L.R. cartridges is negligible in practice. Hence, data provided by cartridge manufacturers for standard length barrels can be referred to for the ballistics of insert barrels as well.

However, according to RWS, drop in performance for their .22 WRF Mags. rates at approx. 13 per cent, when these rounds are fired in insert barrels. Here muzzle velocity differs appreciably from that obtained with the standard 22 in. barrel for this round. Table II compares the performance of three different cartridges when fired in Krieghoff subcalibre tubes.

General

Krieghoff makes insert barrels for 16 ga. shotguns (left and right barrels) and 12 ga. shotguns (right barrel only). On special order, insert barrels for 20 ga. shotguns are available, too. When using a drilling, I recommend that the sub-calibre tube be built into the right barrel; for the set or hair trigger can then be brought into play. Of course, insert barrels can be removed at will for cleaning the main barrel. On account of this interchangeability it is most important that the inserts be fitted properly. If a hammer must be de-cocked over an insert barrel for rimfire ammunition, make sure a dummy round is in the chamber.

The firing pin, as well as the rim of the firing chamber, can be badly damaged when dry firing rimfire guns. See Fig. 17.

If the sub-calibre tube is to be aligned with the target via open sights, the automatic rear sight of many combined guns must be blocked, that is, when the insert is in the right shotgun barrel.

Conclusion

The firm of Krieghoff prescribes 55 yards for the .22 L.R. insert, and 87 yards for the .22 WRF Mag. version. I think this distance is right for the .22 L.R.

Technical data

Manufacturer:	Krieghoff, Ulm, West Germany
System:	Insert barrel with tensioning device
Length:	8 4/6 in.
Direction of twist:	Right-hand
Rate of twist:	.22 L.R. insert: 1 in 15 3/4 in.
	.22 WRF Mag. insert: 1 in 14 31/32 in.
Grooves:	6
Diameter:	across grooves .22 L.R. insert: 0.216 in. (5.5 mm), .22 WRF Mag. insert: 0.219 in. (5.65 mm) across lands: .22 L.R. insert: 0.221 in. (5.62 mm), .22 WRF Mag. insert: 0.224 in. (5.69 mm)
Weight:	5.5 oz. approx.

insert barrel, for the point of impact would involve much guess work at greater distances. This problem would even apply to shorter distances if the insert was sighted in at 100 yards. At this zeroing-in range, the projectile would be about 4.33 in. above the line of sight at 55 yards, when using standard loads.

On the other hand, I advocate zeroing in the .22 WRF Mag. insert through the scope at 110 yards. For with this cartridge, the trajectory rises to only 1.18–1.60 in. As seen in Table I, a dispersion of only 1.89 in. was registered with the .22 WRF mag. insert (No. 46487) at 110 yards. Such results would be adjudged "excellent" by the German Wannsee Norms, for normal rifle barrels.

Considering the killing power of the .22 WRF Mag. cartridge on small animals, and the simplicity of installing such an insert, not to mention the reasonable price, I feel a sub-calibre tube is a commodity well worth having and that it can in no way be regarded as a makeshift contrivance.

A spare Allen key in the glove compartment of his car (as the main key always gets lost) will be a blessing for the owner of a sub-calibre tube . . .

TABLE 1 — DISPERSION BASED ON 5 SHOTS FOR EACH TEST

Barrel:	.22 WRF Mag. EXTRA No. 46400	.22 WRF Mag. NORMAL No. 46487	Barrel:	.22 L.R. EXTRA No. 45587	.22 L.R. NORMAL No. 45164
	Dispersion 110 yds.	Dispersion 110 yds.		Dispersion 55 yds.	Dispersion 55 yds.
Hirtenberg soft point	2.76 in.	1.89 in.	RWS standard Win.	1.70 in.	1.18 in.
RWS soft point	2.95 in	4.14 in.	super speed Rem.	1.77 in.	1.58 in.
RWS full jacketed Win. SS	4.14 in.	—	standard Rem.	2.28 in.	1.58 in.
full jacketed	—	2.48 in.	high vel.	2.08 in.	1.97 in.

TABLE 2 COMPARISONS FOR RWS LOADS WHEN FRIED THROUGH NORMAL LENGTH BARRELS AND KRIEGHOFF INSERT BARRELS "Semer" 8.66 in.

	Barrel length in.	Velocity (fps) muzzle	55 yds.	110 yds.	Energy (ft. lbs.) muzzle	55 yds.	110 yds.	Maximum ceiling in in. when gun is zeroed at 110 yds.
.22 WRF Mag.	22	2017	1673	1410	361	245	180	+ 1.18
	8.66	1755	1459	1246	275	188	137	+ 1.77
.22 L.R.	25.6	1082	984	885	101	87	65	+ 4.33
	8.66	1066	968	869	101	87	65	+ 4.33
.22 L.R. HV	25.6	1312	1099	967	151	108	79	+ 3.35
	8.66	1263	1066	951	137	101	79	+ 3.74

Source: DNG, Stadeln

Alfred Müller
Illustrations by the author.

Perfecting the Flintlock

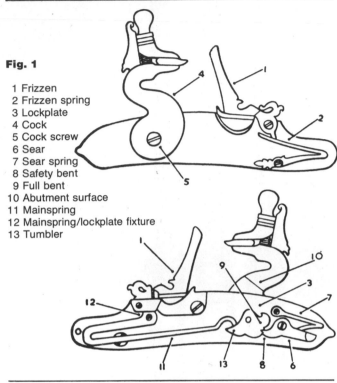

Fig. 1

1 Frizzen
2 Frizzen spring
3 Lockplate
4 Cock
5 Cock screw
6 Sear
7 Sear spring
8 Safety bent
9 Full bent
10 Abutment surface
11 Mainspring
12 Mainspring/lockplate fixture
13 Tumbler

Fig. 2

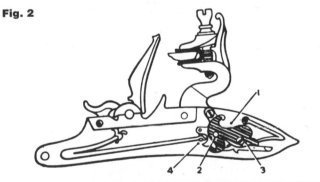

Fig. 3

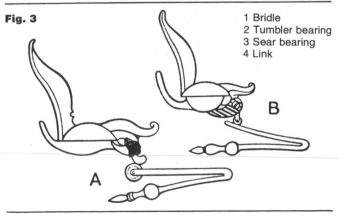

1 Bridle
2 Tumbler bearing
3 Sear bearing
4 Link

For many centuries, the flintlock remained the principal ignition system for small arms. This article outlines various approaches to improving the flintlock mechanism, as the system, of course, was not entirely satisfactory.

Just imagine you had to go out and get your meat, or shoot at clay pigeons, with a gun that fires the charge about a second after you had pulled the trigger! Putting your trust in such a stove-pipe would be a piece of folly, right?

Well, this is the sort of adventure a marksman let himself in for in the middle of the 18th century. He had to put up with it, or else go a-hunting with a bow and arrow . . .

Gunsmiths as well as shooters often put their heads together in study of that problem of hangfires. A French design represented the most modern lockwork of the time. Upon the cock falling, the contact between flint and frizzen created glowing sparks to ignite the priming charge in the pan. The flame in the pan then had to pass through a narrow vent to ignite the main powder charge in the chamber. Eternity passed between the pull on the trigger and the firing of the shot! In many instances, of course, the flint was worn, the movement of the cock feeble, the priming powder damp or ill-distributed in the pan, or the frizzen too sluggish, etc. All these foibles just had to be accepted in a day's shooting, and the gunsmith, to keep in business, had to think out better devices. Friction of the mechanical parts was a main cause for slow ignition time.

In early flintlocks (Fig. 1), the pin connecting cock and tumbler made use of the hole in the lockplate, through which it passed, for a (one-sided) bearing. Naturally, on account of the pressure from the mainspring, the cock-tumbler unit tilted in all directions, making a nice mess of the bearing-hole. The same sad tale applied to the sear, which was simply screwed to the lockplate. To overcome this headache, a so-called bridle was fitted (Fig. 2, hatched), providing the tumbler and sear with a two-sided bearing. This tilting problem also affected the (speedy) opening of the frizzen. The faster the frizzen opens, the quicker the priming charge is ignited, etc. So a sec-

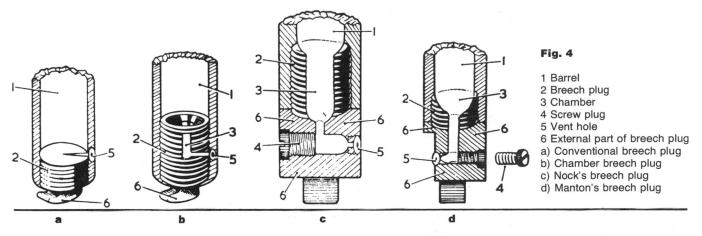

Fig. 4
1 Barrel
2 Breech plug
3 Chamber
4 Screw plug
5 Vent hole
6 External part of breech plug
a) Conventional breech plug
b) Chamber breech plug
c) Nock's breech plug
d) Manton's breech plug

a   b   c   d

ond bridle was incorporated, an integral part of the pan (Fig. 3, hatched section).

These two bridles can be inspected in any good English flintlock, starting about 1740. I emphasize English flintlocks, since the island inhabitants had an eye for technical innovation, whereas their colleagues on the Continent had more of an eye for ornamentation. I don't wish to belittle the Continental mentality, after al they produced the most beautifully decorated guns the world has ever seen!

About 1790, two other frictional problems were (largely) overcome. As seen in Fig. 1, the mainspring originally rested on the tumbler, causing considerable friction when the cock was thumbed back or released. The same situation occurred between frizzen and frizzen spring. A link was incorporated between tumbler and mainspring, and small rollers were inserted between frizzen spring and frizzen (Figs. 2 and 3).

Of course, firing time, long or short, is not only tied up with the friction caused by the movement of mechanical parts. What is known as internal ballistics is a highly important factor. Many experiments were aimed at evolving fast-burning gunpowder. All flint-operated weapons created a spark outside the barrel; the flame had to make its way through a constricted vent to reach the main charge. First only a "corner" if the main charge was ignited, the rest often smoldered or was left unburnt. Bullets could be propelled down the barrel with a quarter of the charge (what a waste of energy!), while a second later the remainder of the charge would burn. Other ways and means had to be discovered, that was obvious, and in time gunsmiths realized that a flame would have to enter the chamber from behind, to evenly burn the powder. The first step in this direction was the so-called chamber breech-plug (Fig. 4b).

This was longer than the standard breech plug (Fig. 4a), having a chamber that was filled with powder. This chamber was connected to the pan via a narrow vent. Although this device appeared ideal at first sight, it was a flop. Combustion was quick in the powder chamber, so the objective in that sense had been reached; but this time-saving element was neutralized by the slowness of the flame to pass through the narrow vent from the pan. Yet another promising invention that ended in smoke!

All the same, the idea was excellent. So before long Henry Nock, a famous London gunmaker, patented his own version of a breech plug (Fig. 4c) in 1787. Nock enlarged the chamber, and the vent, too. Since the vent was only separated by a thin plate of gold or platinum from the chamber, the priming powder ignited very quickly, and, owing to the constriction, flashed into the main charge with great intensity. Ignited with such force from behind, the combustion of the gunpowder charge was both rapid and cleaner.

Joseph Manton, another famous London gunsmith, modified Nock's system by placing the pan nearer to the axis of the bore of the barrel. This arrangement permitted the use of a smaller vent hole without encountering any disadvantages (Fig. 4 d). To cut out excessive friction, a small link was hooked in between tumbler and mainspring. Friction occurring between frizzen and frizzen spring was considerably reduced by employing rollers.

A final word about the disadvantages of the flintlock period. Nobody ever managed to waterproof the pan, so in rainy weather the hunter or soldier using flintlocks could stay at home. Still, for us moderns, flintlock arms exert a fascination that bewitches every gun fan sooner or later. It is great fun to fire one of these old-timers, and tension heightens after the trigger is pulled: Will it go off, or won't it? What a thrill when a white puff of smoke appears, and how wonderful the worlds is, if the target has been hit . . .

WALTHER'S NEW POCKET PISTOL TPH

"At last," sighed many a gun connoisseur when the new TPH (pocket pistol with external hammer) was first presented to the public.

At last, a small pocket pistol is available, sharing the advantages of the Walther PPK, but petite and light enough to be discreetly carried on one's person. See illus. 1.

Everyone knows how difficult it is to discreetly carry a gun when wearing evening-dress or casuals. If a pistol has to be carried, it is then better to take along a light-weight weapon, despite reduced stopping power and leave the big-calibre "rod" at home.

Moreover, a light-weight weapon is easier to handle than a large-calibre, heavy one. It is better to hit one's mark with a small pistol than to miss it with a big one . . .

Don't get me wrong, I am not singing the praises of mini-pistols, I'm just trying to emphasize their justification as a second gun. There are many small-calibre handguns on the market, but few that can compete with the new TPH. It sports a double-action trigger, is highly accurate, weighs only 11 ozs, measures 135 x 90 x 23 mm, and is beautifully finished (Illus. 2).

In Germany it is interesting to watch how a fresh gun-licence holder selects his first pistol. He fingers all the models the gun-dealer can show him, but 7 times out of 10 he settles for a Walther PPK. Over here, Walther has virtually the same reputation for precision as S & W and Colt in America. Hence the popularity of the new Walther TPH.

Siegfried F. Hübner

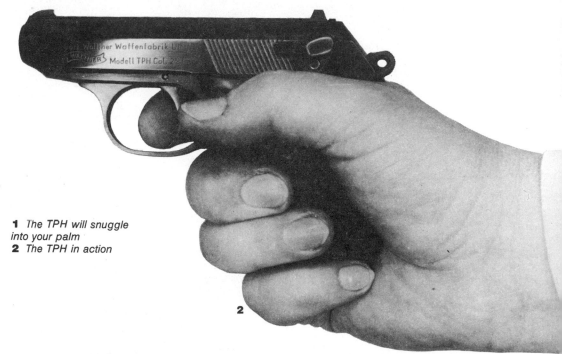

1 *The TPH will snuggle into your palm*
2 *The TPH in action*

Ammunition

The TPH is chambered for .25 ACP or .22 L.R. In this pistol, the .25 ACP cartridge has a muzzle velocity of 230 mps, and a muzzle energy of 8.8 mkg (approx. 754 ft/sec. and 63.6 ft.pds respectively), the bullet weighing 3.25 g (50 grains). The .22 L.R. Hi-Speed cartridge has a muzzle velocity of 340 mps, and a muzzle energy of 15 mkg (approx. 1115 ft./sec. and 108 ft.pds respectively), the bullet weighing 2.55 g (39.4 gr.). The muzzle energy of the .22 L.R. Hi-Speed cartridge is therefore approx. 44.4 ft.pds greater than that of the .25 ACP. And the plasticity of the lead bullet increases stopping power all the more. When using hollow-point .22 L.R. cartridges, which are banned in Germany, shock exceeds that of the .25 ACP round.

Illustration 3 compares the exit holes of a .22 L.R. Hi-Speed and a hollow-point .22 L.R. cartridge. In Germany, .22 L.R. ammunition is some 4 times cheaper than .25 ACP, and weak practice loads in .22 are also available.

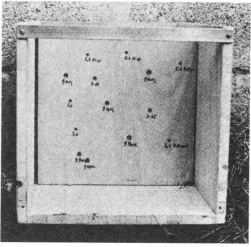

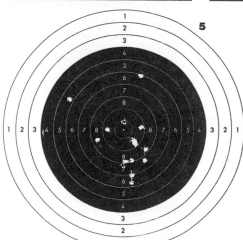

3 *Punching holes into a cake of soap. Left: Exit hole of .22 L.R. Hi-Speed. Right: Exit hole of .22 L. R. Hollow Point*
4 *Entrance holes of various calibres in plywood at a distance of 5.5 yards.*
5 *TPH groupings with .22 L.R. fired from 16.4 yards at 50 yd. smallbore target. Here reduced to approx. 1:2*

6 *TPH, PPK, PP – the pistols under test.*

7 *TPH .22 L.R.*
8 *PPK .32 ACP*

WALTHER'S NEW POCKET PISTOL TPH

TPH DATA

Calibre .22 L.R. or. 25 ACP

Capacity 6 rounds in magazine

Length of barrel 71 mm (approx. 2.8 in.)

Overall length 135 mm (approx. 5.3 in.)

Height 90 mm (approx. 3.54 in.)

Width 23 mm (approx. .905 in.)

Weight without cartridges 310 g (approx. 11 ozs.)

Receiver Light metal

Manufacturer Carl Walther, Jagd- und Sportwaffenfabrik, Ulm, West Germany

To test the two calibres, we set up sheets of plywood .78.7 in. in thickness at 5.5 yards, one behind the other. See illus. 4.

Illustration 5 shows the grouping of a TPH, fired from 16.4 yds at a 50 yard small-bore target (15 shots).

Penetration in plywood

.22 L.R. Normal R 4 cm (approx. 1.57 in.)
.22 L.R. Hi-Speed 6.5 cm (approx. 2.5 in.)
.22 L.R. Hollow point 4.5 cm (approx. 1.77 in.)
.25 ACP Geco 6 cm (approx. 2.36 in.)
.32 ACP Geco 8.5 cm approx. 3,35 in.)
.380 ACP Geco 8 cm (approx. 3.15 in.)

Illustration 6 shows the TPH, PPK and PP that were used for the test.

The TPH (illus. 7) has been patterned after the PPK. Illustrations 8 and 9 depict the PPK and PP versions.

Description

A double-action mechanism permits the safe carrying of a pistol with a round in the chamber. Like the revolver, this pistol can be fired by simply pulling through on the trigger, there is no need to cock the hammer first. Once the initial round has been fired, the hammer is cocked by the reciprocating slide, as in any other pistol. I am pleased to report that the weight of the double-action trigger pull of the TPH is by far lighter than that of the PP and PPK. When the safety catch is applied, as in all Walther pistols, the hammer automatically drops on a blocked firing pin; so there is no danger in de-cocking the hammer on a loaded chamber.

The barrel is permanently mounted on the receiver, and this probably accounts for the high accuracy of the pistol.

Illustrations 10 and 11 show the TPH field stripped. The take-down procedure is just as straightforward as that of the PPK. Pull down the front end of the trigger guard, pushing it to one side to rest against the frame. Then pull the slide to the rear as far as it will go, lift tail end and ease forward off the receiver. Unfortunately, the TPH does not posses a hold-open catch, for the slide.

The rear sight of the TPH has a white line, the front sight a white dot. We found this system to work very efficiently, especially during the twilight hours. The trigger is grooved in target-pistol fashion, and is not blocked when the safety is applied – the hammer simply falls on the firing-pin shroud.

The receiver is of light metal, the grips of black or brown plastic. The TPH fits nicely in the hand, but the little finger rests under the butt. An arrester blocks the hammer if the trigger hasn't been pulled, and a magazine safety is also incorporated.

As said earlier, this is the perfect gun to carry inconspicuously, and will doubtless become the favorite of the ladies, owing to elegant shape and simplicity . . .

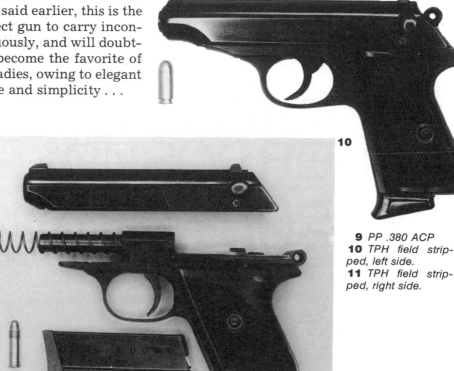

9 PP .380 ACP
10 TPH field stripped, left side.
11 TPH field stripped, right side.

Günter Frères

BROWNING SUPERPOSED SHOTGUN "SPEZIAL JAGD"

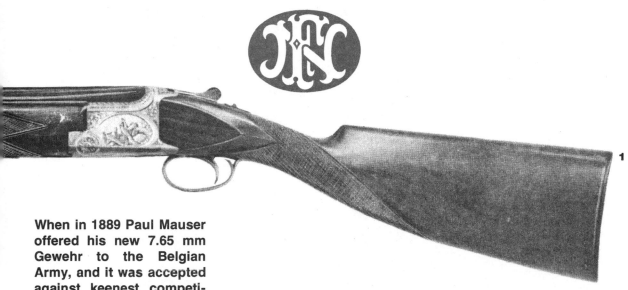

When in 1889 Paul Mauser offered his new 7.65 mm Gewehr to the Belgian Army, and it was accepted against keenest competition, it did not mean that the Mauser factory at Oberndorf had scooped another commission; for the Belgian government insisted that the new military rifle be made in Belgium, and nowhere else. However, the government members agreed to entrust the manufacture of these weapons to a Belgian factory that was to be newly founded for this purpose. Thus, the Fabrique Nationale d'Armes de Guerre S.A. was called into existence, one of the most famous gun producers in the world today. The German firm of Ludwig Loewe & Co. A. G. Berlin, who possessed all the Mauser shares, also had over 50 per cent of the shares of this new Belgian gun factory, that is, until Germany lost the 1914–18 war.

After the initial military orders had been effected, the Fabrique Nationale, generally known as FN, began tooling for an automatic shotgun, the first of its kind, designed by JOHN MOSES BROWNING, and marketed it in 1904. In the following 60 years, the Browning-FN team produced sporting, target and military weapons that have left their imprint around the world. But FN also manufactures commercial and military cartridges, field and anti-aircraft guns, military vehicles, engines, and component parts for rockets, etc.

After WW I, FN introduced their first superposed shotgun, which soon made a name for itself, for ruggedness and dependability. Skeet and trap shooters the world over use this gun. In the meantime, FN has presented an array of new o/u guns, including "Lightning Skeet", "Lightning Trap", "Broadway", etc.

For the German market, the "Spezial Jagd" (loose translation, "Hunter's Special"), the gun under review, was created. Heinrich Münch, the well-known gunsmith in Aix-la-Chapelle, recommended specific changes for German clientele.

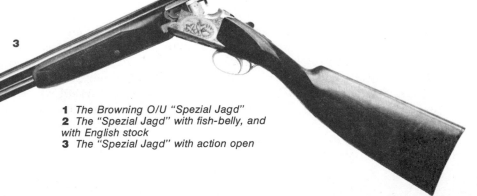

1 The Browning O/U "Spezial Jagd"
2 The "Spezial Jagd" with fish-belly, and with English stock
3 The "Spezial Jagd" with action open

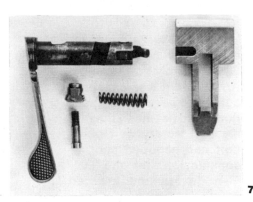

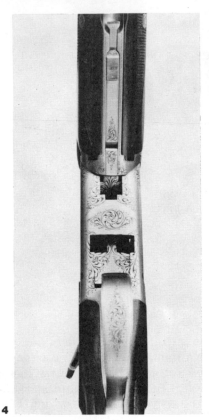

Description

The "Spezial Jagd" (Illus. 1 and 2) was developed for the German taste, but is available throughout Europe. The difference between the "Spezial Jagd" and the Browning "Standard" is that the receiver of the German model can be had in a deep black or silver grey finish. The black finished model is border engraved with decorated screws, while the silver version sports full hunting scenes. The "Standard" is only available with straightforward, blued receiver. The receiver of the German model differs also in shape. It is rounder, lighter, and the tang is narrower. Hence, the gun itself is somewhat lighter, too.

The buttstock of the "Spezial Jagd" has also been modified. Instead of the pistol-grip stock, the German model is fitted with an English-type straight grip, or, if preferred, with what we Germans call a fish-belly stock (Illus. 3). The fish-belly stock is proportionally thicker than the English straight-grip type and fits more anatomically to one's face. Basically, this fish-belly stock is the same as that used on the Merkel o/u shotgun, model 200, but has been streamlined to match the lines of the FN shotgun. Furthermore, instead of the usual ventilated rib, the German model has a solid one. Otherwise, the FN "Spezial Jagd" ties in with the other FN models, designed chiefly for the US market. However, the changes made for the German model have enhanced the appearance of the gun tremendously, plus improving pointing quality and balance. This gun lies well in the hand, mainly on account of the profusely checkered forearm and the stock that has been conceived for a 6ft man.

The centre of balance is only 4.53 in. in front of the trigger. The "Spezial Jagd" shoulders perfectly. Drop at comb, at heel, and pitch are so finely worked out that one automatically looks squarely along the top rib.

How the FN functions

By thumbing over the top lever, against the pressure of a spiral spring, the flat bolt is withdrawn from the dual barrel lumps via an eccentric shaft (Illus. 7). When the flat bolt has been fully retracted, its rear surface frees the cocking lever, allowing the barrels to be dropped (Illus. 10). The flat bolt also rides over the shoulder of the trigger, preventing activation thereof while the gun is open. A cam nose on the forearm bracket exerts pressure against the cocking lever (Illus. 4), which, in turn, cocks the hammers. During this cocking phase, the hammers force the ejector trip rods forward to cock the ejector

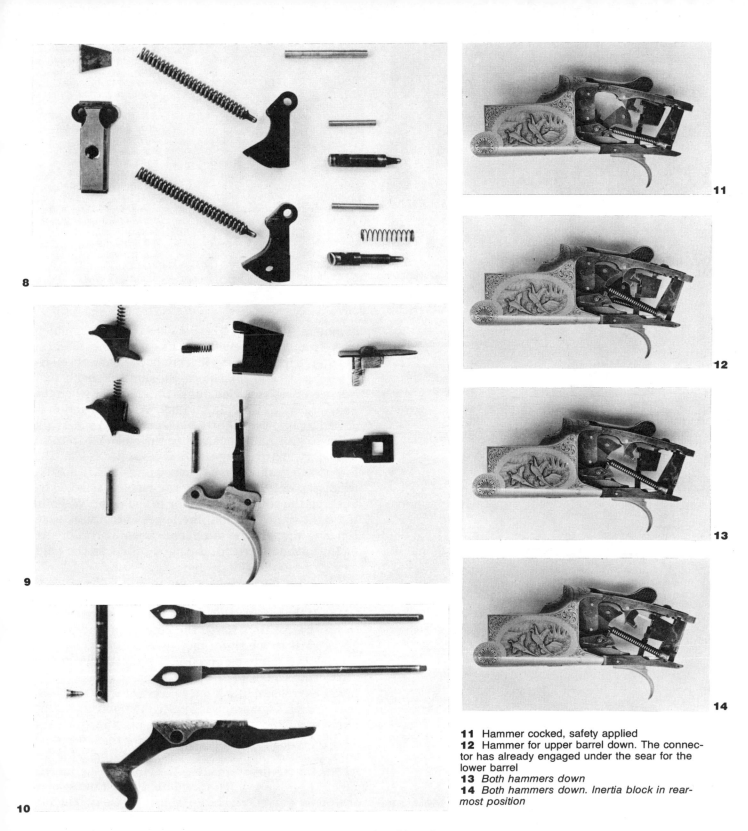

8 *Firing pin for lower barrel (with spring), for upper barrel without spring, firing-pin retaining pins, hammers, mainsprings with guides, hammer axle, tang piece, and flat spring*
9 *Sears with springs and pin; trigger, trigger pin and connector; inertia block with spring; safety slide and flat spring*
10 *Cocking lever with axle and retaining screw, the two ejector trip rods*

11 Hammer cocked, safety applied
12 Hammer for upper barrel down. The connector has already engaged under the sear for the lower barrel
13 *Both hammers down*
14 *Both hammers down. Inertia block in rear-most position*

103

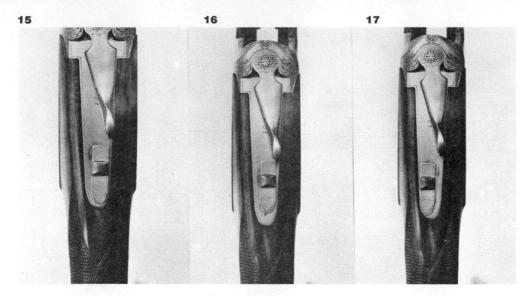

15 Tang seen from above. The selector/safety slide is on SAFE, and pressed to the right. Barrel sequence; lower/upper

16 The selector/safety slide pushed forward to FIRE

17 The selector/safety slide on SAFE, and pressed to the left. Barrel sequence: upper, lower

18 The buttstock with stock bolt, trigger guard, buttplate

19 Forearm with bracket assembly

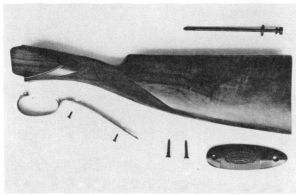

18

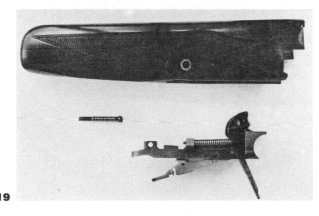

19

hammers (Illus. 10). These ejector trip rods, which pass from the receiver housing into the forearm bracket, trip the ejector sears once a shot has been fired (Illus. 19 and 20). Hence, the shell, or shells, that has been fired is hurled out of the chamber when the gun is opened (Illus. 22 and 23). When the action is closed again, the slightly over-cocked hammers (in order to give more leverage to the ejector trip rods) come forward to engage in their respective sears. The thumb safety slide can be pushed fore and aft, and laterally as well. Barrel firing sequence is selected by pushing the slide to the left or to the right. When in the right-hand position, the lower barrel fires first. When in the left, the top barrel. See illustrations 15 to 17. Pushed forward, the slide unblocks the triggers.

The connector, which is mounted on the trigger, can also move longitudinally or laterally (Illus. 9, 11 to 14). If the safety catch slide is thumbed to the right (lower barrel fires first), the connector and inertia block shift to the right, too.

Once the safety catch slide is pushed forward to "fire," the connector engages under the sear of the lower barrel and lifts it out of contact with the hammer as soon as pressure is applied to the trigger. The hammer can now fall on the firing pin and ignite the shell. Strange to say, the firing pin for the lower barrel has a rebound coil spring, the firing pin for the upper barrel does not. Recoil activates the inertia block (Illus. 14), which rebounds against the sear of the upper barrel. When the trigger is released before the next shot the connector then engages under the sear of the upper barrel to lift it out of contact with the hammer. The tang piece (Illus. 8), which is situated between top and bottom receiver tangs, serves as an abutment for the two mainsprings and as an anchor for the buttstock. The long stock bolt also

screws into the tang piece (Illus. 18). The trigger guard with its two screws also helps to fasten the buttstock to the receiver. The stock is fitted with a plastic buttplate.

The two barrel lumps are slotted to accept the flat bolt when the action is closed. The dual ejectors are mounted flat against the side of the barrels. A short rail is brazed to the under barrel, to which the forearm bracket is fixed (Illus. 21). In turn, the forearm is screwed to the bracket. Contrary to most other hinge-frame shotguns, the forearm of the Browning cannot be lifted off the barrels when the takedown latch has been activated. The forearm can only be moved approx. .5 in., but this suffices to allow the barrel assembly to be hooked out of the receiver. Between the two barrels, small pieces of wood have been screwed, on either side. These make for a better closure between barrels and forearm. The top rib is solid, not ventilated, and bears a silver bead (Illus. 24).

All in all, the technical aspects of the "Spezial Jagd" can be considered a great success. Barrels and lockwork are carefully made and finished, and in part polished. The barrels are deep black and the select walnut stocking is skillfully adorned with fine 20-line checkering.

Performance

For pattern testing we used WAIDMANNSHEIL and LEGIA STAR HIGH SPEED with 2.5 mm (No. 7) shot, ROTTWEIL STERN and ELEY ALPHAMAX with 3 mm (No. 5) shot and ROTTWEIL EXPRESS and REMINGTON EXPRESS with 3.5 mm (No. 3) shot (Illus. 25). The LEGIA STAR and REMINGTON shotshells had plastic cup columns, the three Germans had traditional felt wads and the English ELEY had a wad of papier-mâché.

Unfortunately, a standard shot chart for all countries does not exist. No. 7 shot is 2.5 mm in Germany, but 2.4 mm in Belgium. And then in actual practice, the size of the pellets does not conform with the size printed on the box! For example, a 2.5 mm pellet is in reality a 2.45 mm pellet in WAIDMANNSHEIL shotshells, and 2.31 mm in LEGIA STAR products. Weight and material of each pellet type differ, too. Hence, each shotshell manufacturer loads a different number of pellets per case. The reader will now appreciate that the results of Tables 1, 2 and 3 cannot be scientifically compared with each other. At best, they show how different shotshells fare in this Browning shotgun. We fired 5-shots with each brand from each barrel, at a target placed 38.3 yds away. The 16-field hunting target has an inner circle measuring 14.8 in. in diameter (4 fields), and an outer

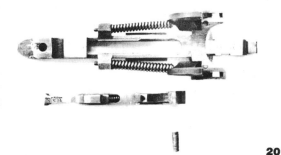

20

21

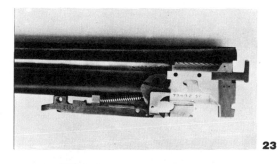

22

23

20 Bracket with ejector hammers
21 Position of parts when action is opened
22 Ejectors cocked
23 Ejectors fired
24 Muzzle crowned with bead

24

25 *Shotshells used for pattern testing*

TABLE 1

Results obtained with 2.5 mm (No. 7) shot at 38.3 yds

	Waidmannsheil 12/70 ga. (2.45 mm diameter) 399 pellets / 1.24 ozs Batch No. MS 5 K 17		Legia Star High Speed 12/70 ga. *) (2.31 mm diameter) 482 pellets (nickel plated) 1.26 ozs Batch No. 25 R 78	
	Lower Barrel	Upper Barrel	Lower Barrel	Upper Barrel
Number of hits				
Inner circle	79	103	112	140
Outer circle	135	161	208	213
Whole target	214	274	320	353
Density	1:1.76	1:1.92	1:1.62	1:1.97
Regularity (Mean devition of a 5-shot series)	29.8 = poor	22.6 = poor	16.4 = satisfactory	19.4 = poor
Covered fields (Geared to number of hits)	8.2 = poor	10.8 = poor	13.6 = good	13.6 = poor
Extreme variation of effective hits				
Diameter	22.5 in.	25.6 in.	29.6 in.	29.6 in.
At distance	31.7 yds	38.3 yds	39.4 yds	40.5 yds
Max. effective range	43.7 yds	49 yds	49 yds	49 yds
Rating	Satisfactory for normal purposes	Good for long range	Excellent for long range	Excellent for long range
Pattern in percentage	53.6%	68.7%	66.4%	73.3%

*) With plastic cup wad

12/70 ga. = 12/2³/₄ in. case

TABLE 2

Results obtained with 3 mm (No. 5) shot at 38.3 yds

	Rottweil Stern 12/70 ga. (3.02 mm diameter) 208 pellets / 1.21 ozs Batch No. MS 19 N 16		Eley Alphamax 12/70 ga. (3.06 mm diameter) 209 pellets / 1.27 ozs Batch No. 58 K 3 Q	
	Lower Barrel	Upper Barrel	Lower Barrel	Upper Barrel
Number of hits				
Inner circle	60	54	59	64
Outer circle	86	87	80	93
Whole target	146	141	139	157
Density	1:2.09	1:1.86	1:2.21	1:2.06
Regularity (Mean deviation of a 5-shot series)	7.8 = good	10.6 = satisfactory	8.2 = good	3.8 = excellent
Covered fields (Geared to number of hits)	9.4 = poor	9.8 = poor	9.8 = poor	10.2 = poor
Extreme variation of effective hits				
Diameter	–	–	–	–
At distance	–	–	–	–
Max. effective range	48 yds	47 yds	47 yds	50.3 yds
Rating	Satisfactory for long range	Excellent for normal purposes	Excellent for normal purposes	Good for long range
Pattern in percentage	70.2%	67.8%	66.5%	75.1%

12/70 ga. = 12/2 ³/₄ in. case

circle measuring 29.6 in. in diameter (12 fields). The method used for counting the number of hits is described in the booklet, "Der Schrotschuß" *). This procedure was developed before the last war (1939–45) in Berlin by the German Experimental Station For Small Arms, and it is still the only method for evaluating shotgun patterns used in Germany today. If the tester relies on information from gun catalogues he is not going to get reliable results. Shotshells must be opened and pellets counted before the test can begin.

*) "Der Schrotschuß" by Herbert von Wissmann, Verlag Paul Parey – Hamburg and Berlin

The lower modified choke barrel delivered 53.6 and 66.4 per cent patterns with 2.5 mm shot, in the

TABLE 3 **Results obtained with 3.5 mm (No. 3) shot at 38.3 yds**	Rottweil Express 12/70 ga. (plastic) (3.46 mm diameter) 145 pellets / 1.24 ozs Batch No. EW 20 E 14		Remington Express 12/70 ga. plastic) *) (3.27 mm diameter) 170 pellets / 1.20 ozs Batch No. AL 1106	
	Lower Barrel	Upper Barrel	Lower Barrel	Upper Barrel
Number of hits				
Inner circle	35	37	37	47
Outer circle	61	68	67	76
Whole target	96	105	104	123
Density	1:1.72	1:1.63	1:1.66	1:1.86
Regularity (Mean deviation of a 5-shot series)	6.0 = good	4.8 = good	11.4 = poor	10.8 = poor
Covered fields (Geared to number of hits)	13.6 = poor	14.0 = poor	14.8 = excellent	14.8 = satisfactory
Extreme variation of effective hits				
Diameter	28.8 in.	34.7 in.	34.7 in.	27.5 in.
At distance	42.6 yds	41.5 yds	41.5 yds	43.7 yds
Max. effective range	53.5 yds	54.7 yds	54.7 yds	59 yds
Rating	Satisfactory for long range	Good for long range	Good for long range	Excellent for long range
Pattern in percentage	66.2%	72.4%	61.2%	72.4%

*) With plastic cup wad

12/70 ga. = 12/2¾ in. case

outer circle. The 3 mm shot printed 70.2 and 66.5 per cent patterns, and the 3.5 mm shot produced 66.2 and 61.2 per cent patterns.

The upper full choke barrel came up with 68.7 and 73.3 per cent patterns with 2.5 mm shot, 67.8 and 75.1 with 3 mm shot, and 72.4 and 72.4 with 3.5 mm shot. The arithmetical mean for the lower barrel is, therefore, 64 per cent, and for the upper barrel 71.6 per cent. The conclusion here, of course, is that the "Spezial Jagd" has a relatively wide spread, and so is quite suitable for the normal hunter. Most hunters find that full chokes delivering between 75 and 85 per cent patterns are of no particular use to them. With such tight chokes, the average hunter will either have blown his game to smithereens at 20–30 yards, or missed the target completely.

Pattern regularity, while good, might have been more uniform. Maximum effective range with the various loads and the hits in the outer circle prove that this Browning is excellent for mixed hunting conditions. It should be particularly suitable for autumnal field or duck shooting at distances around 35 yards and over. When floating the bead just above the receiver, the lower barrel printed squarely on the target. The upper barrel shot 2–4 in. high. By and large, the point of impact was quite acceptable. For high shots, within reason, allow the hunter to use the six o'clock hold, to float the target above the bead, so that the animal is not concealed by the bead when aiming. Incidentally, both barrels showed signs of leading after 30 shots per barrel, especially in front of the forcing cones.

THE COMPONENT PARTS OF THE BROWNING "SPEZIAL JAGD" O/U SHOTGUN

Part No.		Description
5	1	Bead sight
6ad	1	Barrel plate wood, right
6ag	1	Barrel plate wood, left
7	2	Barrel plate screw
8	1	Ejector, right
9	1	Ejector, left
10	1	Ejector extension, right
11	1	Ejector extension, left
12	2	Ejector extension stop screw
12a	2	Ejector stop screw
13	1	Cocking lever release
14	1	Pin for No. 13
15	1	Forearm bracket
16	1	Forearm takedown lever
17	1	Pin for No. 16
18	1	Takedown lever latch
19	1	Spring for No. 18
20	1	Retaining pin for No. 18
21	1	Ejector hammer, right
22	1	Ejector hammer, left
23	1	Axle for the ejector hammers
24	2	Ejector hammer spring
25	2	Ejector hammer spring guide
26	2	Ejector hammer sear
27	2	Spring for No. 26
28	2	Pin for No. 26
29B	1	Forearm (see next illustration)
33	1	Hinge pin
34	1	Ejector trip rod, right
35	1	Ejector trip rod, left
36	1	Cocking lever
37	1	Cocking lever pin
38	1	Hammer, right
39	1	Hammer, left
40	1	Hammer axle
41	2	Mainspring
42	2	Mainspring guide
43	1	Upper firing pin
44	1	Lower firing pin
45	1	Rebound spring for No. 44
46	2	Pin
47	1	Flat bolt
48	1	Top snap
49	1	Top snap spring
50	1	Top snap spring retainer
51	1	Top snap dog
53	1	Screw for No. 50
56	1	Trigger pin
61	1	Sear pin
66	1	Tang piece
67	2	Tang piece screw
68	1	Stock bolt
STA 37	1	Lock washer
STA 5	1	Washer for stockbolt (12 gauge)
STA 46	1	Washer for stockbolt (20 gauge)
70	1	Trigger guard
71	2	Trigger guard screw
72	1	English or pistol grip buttstock (see next illustration)
73	1	Buttplate
STA 28	2	Buttplate screw
75t	1	Forearm screw
76d	1	Escutcheon, right
76g	1	Escutcheon, left
78	1	Top snap dog screw

COMPONENT PARTS FOR ONE-TRIGGER BROWNING O/U SHOTGUN

160u	2	Sear spring
111	1	Trigger
112	1	Support for connector (No. 118)
113	1	Pin for connector
114	1	Support pin for connector
115	1	Spring for connector
116	1	Sear, right
117	1	Sear, left
118	1	Connector
119	1	Inertia block
120	1	Safety slide

121	1	Spring for safety slide
122	1	Block for safety slide
123	1	Spring for inertia block
124	1	Guide pin for spring (No. 123)
125	1	Tang piece screw, top
126	1	Trigger spring

COMPONENT PARTS FOR TWO-TRIGGER BROWNING O/U SHOTGUN

32a	1	Partition for triggers
32b	1	Pin for partition (32a)
32c	1	Screw for pin (32b)
32d	1	Axle for 32b
54	1	Trigger, right
55	1	Trigger, left
57	1	Connector
58	1	Sear, right
59	1	Sear, left
60	2	Sear spring
62	1	Safety slide plate
63	1	Safety slide
63a	1	Washer for safety slide spring
64	1	Safety slide retaining pin
65	1	Safety slide spring

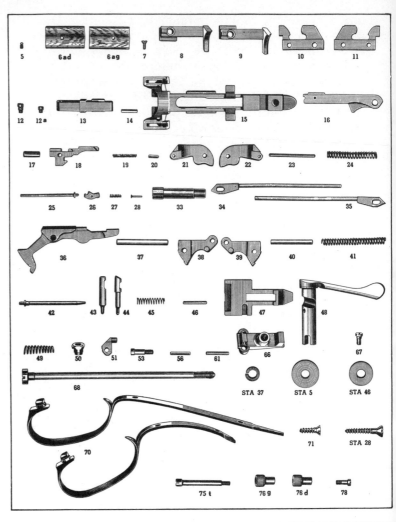

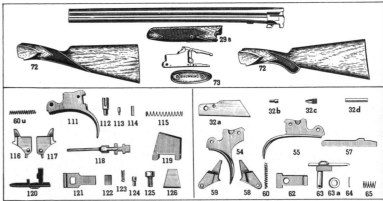

Manufacturer: Fabrique Nationale D'Armes des Guerre S. A., Herstal, Belgium

Designation: Browning "Spezial Jagd" Superposed Shotgun

Gauge: 12/65 or 12/70

Bolting: Dual barrel lumps, plus flat bolt

Lock: Box lock. Single trigger with barrel-sequence adjustment. Automatic ejectors. Also available with double triggers

Safety: Safety slide on tang is also used as selector for barrel sequence

Receiver: Forged steel. Black finish or silver grey tone with hunting scene, lacquered

Barrels: Special gun steel, 27.6 in. Solid, narrow rib and silver bead. Lower barrel: modified choke. Upper barrel: full choke. Other chokes available on request

Stock: Oil finished. In English or fish-belly. Fine select walnut with 20-line hand checkering. Trigger guard engraved

Measurements:
Length of pull .... 14.4 in.
Drop at comb .... 1.5 in.
Drop at heel .... 2.5 in.
Pitch .... 2.7 in.

Weight: 6 lbs. 15 oz.

Pictures of a Handgun Collection in Munich

1 *Flintlock blunderbuss with excessive muzzle ovalness (0.78 x 1.42 in.). Brass barrel, furniture of engraved iron. An H in a jagged escutcheon is stamped on inside surface of lockplate (mark unidentified). Frizzen spring is assisted by a roller. Assumed to be of English or French manufacture, c. 1750–1800. Overall length: 10.8 in.*

2 *Turkish pistol with so-called Spanish snaphaunce lock. The true meaning of the term "snaphaunce" is open to argument. This appellation is either used to describe a cock without a tumbler (that rested against an external sear arm), or a lock without the right angle pan cover, known today as the battery or frizzen.*

The barrel bears Oriental characters and the brass stock is finely chased. This type of pistol is frequently encountered, and distinguishing a copy from an original can be extremely difficult. Overall length: 20.7 in.

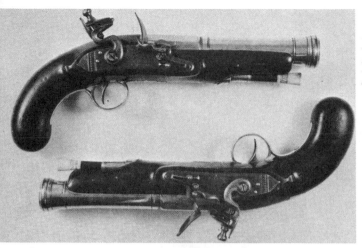

3a, 3b *Pair of English blunderbusses by Harrison-Manchester, c. 1800. Bronze barrel octagonal at rear, round at front. Muzzle also round, belled to about 0.827 in. Trigger guard of brass, engraved. Frizzen spring assisted by roller. Smooth stock. Overall length: 10.4 in.*

3a

3b

4 *Austrian Cavalry Pistol Model 1798. Brass furniture, black stock, probably delivered to the Prussian Army. Calibre 18.2 mm (0.717 in.). Overall length: 16.8 in.*

5 *French Cavalry Pistol model An. 9, Manufacture Royal St. Etienne 1810. Pan and furniture of brass. No sights. Calibre 17.7 mm (0.697 in.). Overall length: 13.9 in.*

6 *English flintlock by Prosser-London, c. 1800. Safety slide behind cock engages in tumbler when pistol is on half cock. Frizzen spring assisted by roller. Coarse diamond checkering around handle. Iron furniture. Calibre 16.5 mm (0.65 in.). Overall length: 15.5 in.*

4

5

6

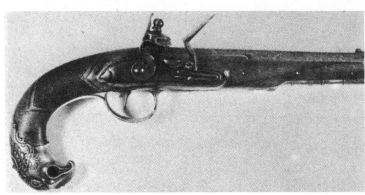

7 Duelling pistol by Caspar Lorenz, c. 1800. Smoothbore, Damascened barrel, engraved furniture of brass. Butt shaped as an eagle head. Calibre 13.5 mm (0.53 in.). Overall length: 13.6 in.

8 Double-barrelled flintlock, presumably of French origin with swing-over tap. According to the position of this tap, either top or bottom barrel, or both barrels together, could be fired. A safety slide locks cock and keeps pan cover down. Silver inlay work on handle. Calibre 11 mm (0.433 in.). Overal length: 8.4 in.

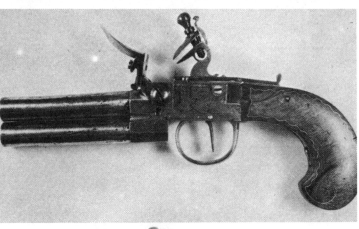

Pictures of a Handgun Collection in Munich

9+10 Two flintlock pocket pistols with detachable barrels. Safety slide blocks cock and pan cover. Overall length: 6.5 in. and 6.9 in.

11 Powder horn (chamois) with silver fittings and lion-head eyelets. Nipple or touch-hole pick in cap. Presumably Austrian or Bohemian piece of work, c. 1700. Can anyone give more information? Overall height: 8.3 in.

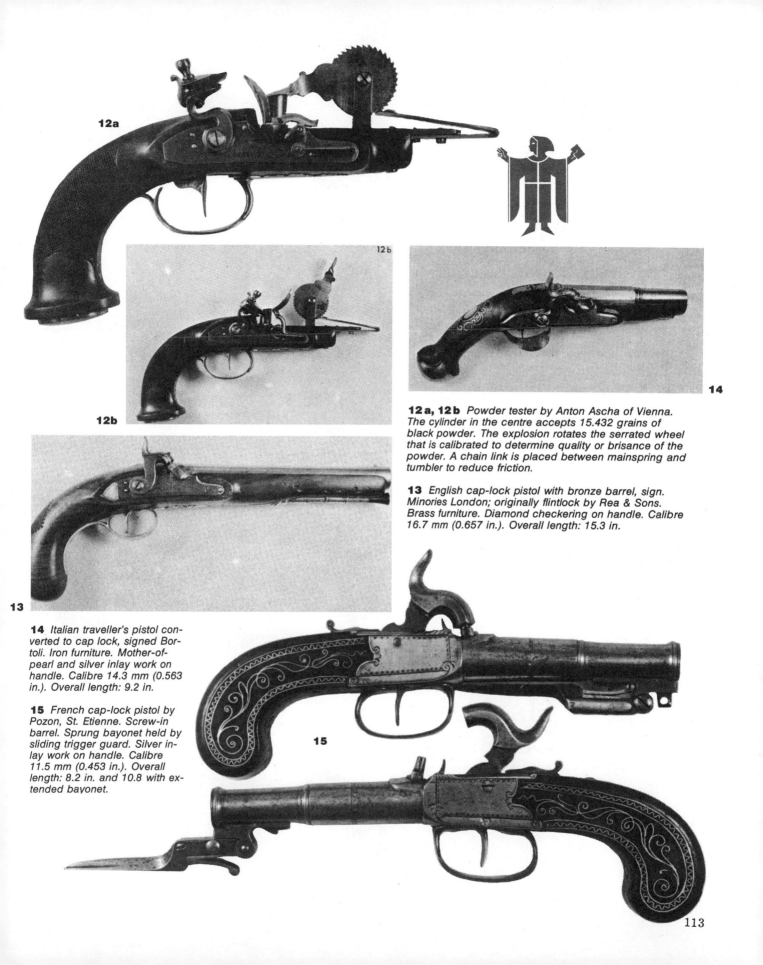

12 a, 12 b *Powder tester by Anton Ascha of Vienna. The cylinder in the centre accepts 15.432 grains of black powder. The explosion rotates the serrated wheel that is calibrated to determine quality or brisance of the powder. A chain link is placed between mainspring and tumbler to reduce friction.*

13 *English cap-lock pistol with bronze barrel, sign. Minories London; originally flintlock by Rea & Sons. Brass furniture. Diamond checkering on handle. Calibre 16.7 mm (0.657 in.). Overall length: 15.3 in.*

14 *Italian traveller's pistol converted to cap lock, signed Bortoli. Iron furniture. Mother-of-pearl and silver inlay work on handle. Calibre 14.3 mm (0.563 in.). Overall length: 9.2 in.*

15 *French cap-lock pistol by Pozon, St. Etienne. Screw-in barrel. Sprung bayonet held by sliding trigger guard. Silver inlay work on handle. Calibre 11.5 mm (0.453 in.). Overall length: 8.2 in. and 10.8 with extended bayonet.*

16 *Pocket pistol with brass barrel and inlay work. Strangely shaped handle. Origin unknown. Calibre 9 mm. Overall length: 7.8 in.*

17 *French police pistol Model 1842, Manufacture Royal de Mutzig. Back-action lock with link between mainspring and tumbler. Iron furniture. All parts numbered. Calibre 15.3 mm (0.60 in.). Overall lenght: 9.7 in.*

18 *French officer's pistols, Manufacture Chatellerault. 1848 and 1849 stamped on barrels. Back-action lock with link between mainspring and tumbler. Finger rest on trigger guards. Damascus barrels. Iron, brass plated ramrods. Calibre 17 mm (0.669 in.). Overall length: 14.7 in.*

19 *Bavarian Cavalry Pistol, c. 1845. Iron furniture. Barrel band held by spline. Smoothbore. Calibre 18.3 mm (0.721 in.). Overall length: 15.2 in.*

Pictures of a Handgun Collection in Munich

16

17

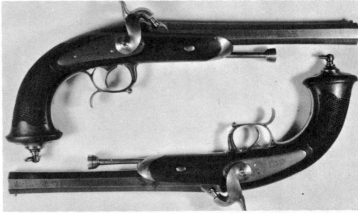

18

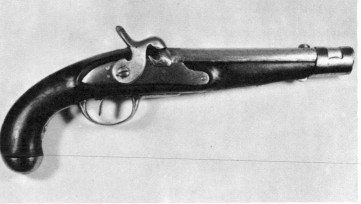

19

20 Austrian Cavalry Pistol, model 1859, constructed 1864. Rifled barrel. Calibre 13.8 mm (0.543 in.). Falling lever safety for half cock position. Iron furniture. Overall length: 16.1 in. Weight: 3.3 lb.

21 French pocket pistol. Damascus barrel lightly ornamented in gold. Iron furniture. Calibre 12.2 mm (0.48 in.). Overall length: 7.6 in.

20

21

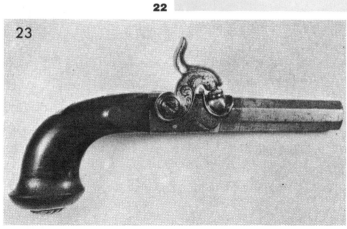

22 Double-barrelled pistol where barrels and receiver are of one piece. Calibre 10.7 mm (0.421 in.). Overall length: 11.2 in.

23 Belgian cap-lock pistol. Folding trigger. Spare caps are accommodated in the butt. Overall length: 7.6 in.

24 Belgian pistolette with screw-in octagonal barrel. Calibre 11.3 mm (0.445 in.). Overall length: 5.7 in.

22

23

23

24

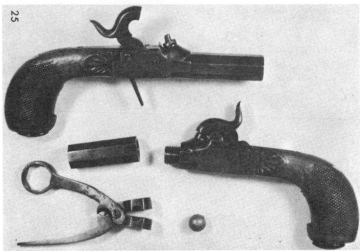

25 *Pair of Belgian pistolettes. Bullet mould combined with barrel wrench. Folding trigger. Spare caps in butt. Buttcap of German silver.*

26 *Belgian pistol with bar lock. Rifled barrel. Engraved furniture of iron. Finger rest on trigger guard. Calibre 15.7 mm (0.618 in.). Overall length: 12.25 in.*

27 *Pepperbox by Blissett-London, c. 1850. Six barrels in one block of metal. Pawl and additional arresting pin align and position each barrel in turn. Hammer cocked via the trigger. Calibre 9.7 mm (0.382 in.). Overall length: 8.75 in. Weight: 1.58 lb.*

25

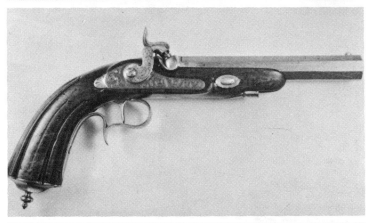

26

Pictures of a Handgun Collection in Munich

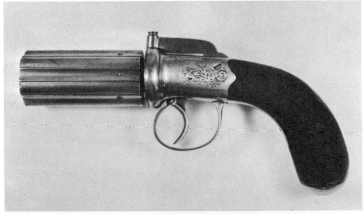

27

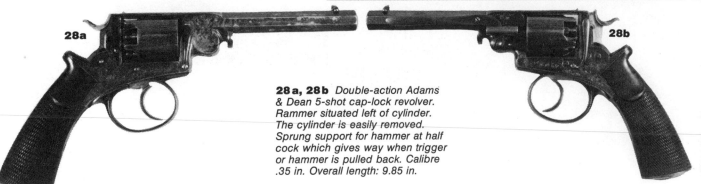

28a

28b

28a, 28b *Double-action Adams & Dean 5-shot cap-lock revolver. Rammer situated left of cylinder. The cylinder is easily removed. Sprung support for hammer at half cock which gives way when trigger or hammer is pulled back. Calibre .35 in. Overall length: 9.85 in.*

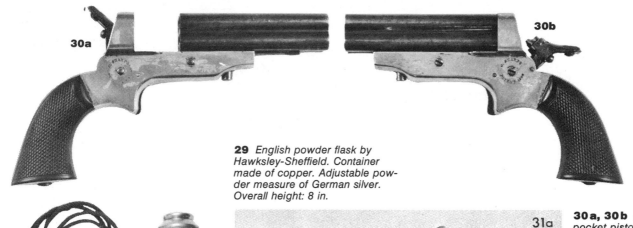

29 English powder flask by Hawksley-Sheffield. Container made of copper. Adjustable powder measure of German silver. Overall height: 8 in.

29

31a

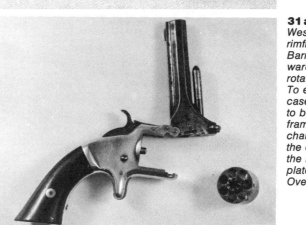

30a, 30b American pocket pistol by Sharps & Co., Philadelphia. Four barrels in one block. Barrel unit slides forward for loading. Firing pin turns 90 degrees each time hammer is cocked. Patented 25. 1. 1859. Bronze frame, originally silver plated. Calibre .28 (rimfire). Overall length: 5.4 in.

31a, 31b Smith & Wesson, model I, for rimfire .22 cartridges. Barrel swings upwards. 7-shot cylinder rotates on short pin. To extract spent cases, cylinder had to be removed from frame and each chamber slipped over the extractor rod under the barrel. Silver plated bronze frame. Overall length: 6.9 in.

32 Lefaucheux pin-fire revolver. Calibre 11 mm (0.433 in.). 6-shot cylinder, giant trigger. Extractor with built-in clamp spring. Presumably a French officer's revolver. Overall length: 10.5 in. Weight: 1.7 lb.

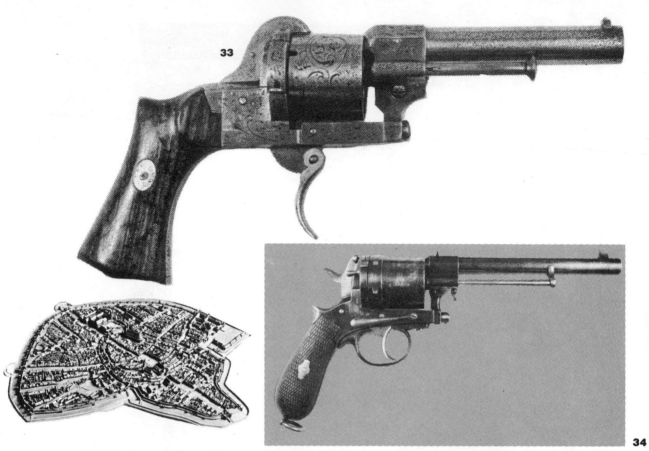

33 Lefaucheux pin-fire revolver with folding trigger. Hammer raised by trigger only. 6-shot cylinder. Extractor has built-in clamp spring. Calibre 7.65 mm. Overall length: 7.6 in.

34 Austrian Gasser heavy-duty revolver, model 1870. Calibre .44 in. Open frame, rigid cylinder mounting. Lateral extractor. Overall length: 12.7 in. Weight: 3 lb.

35 Smith & Wesson Russian Model .44 in. Single action only. Automatic extractor. Finger rest on trigger guard. Overall length: 12 in.

36 French Lebel Army Revolver, Model 1892, Manufacture St. Etienne. Constructed 1896. 6-shot cylinder cranes out to the right. When gate is open, cylinder can be rotated from chamber to chamber via the trigger . . . with hammer down. Calibre 8 mm. Overall length: 9.5 in.

Pictures of a Handgun Collection in Munich

37 German Mauser C 96 (Broomhandle). Locked action. Staggered magazine accepts 10 cartridges, loaded from clip. Sight graduated from 50–1000 metres. Calibre 7.63 mm. Overall length: 11.8 in.

38 English Webley Mark VI. Constructed 1915. Break-open action with automatic extraction of spent cartridge cases. Double action, 6-shot cylinder. Calibre .455 in. Overall length: 11.3 in.

39 Pair of Flobert pistols with rifled octagonal barrels. No real breech. The hammer therefore has two functions: breechface and igniter. Dual extractors are mounted on the sides of the hammer. Calibre 6 mm (0.236 in.). Overall length: 12 in.

Feinwerkbau LG 300 Match Air Rifle

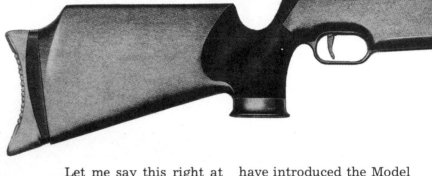

There are still people around, I am told, who equate shooting with air guns as "pea shooting." When these scorners are asked to explain themselves, they say shooting must have a bang and only sissies shoot at 10 metres. If you ever get an ear full of this, just push an air rifle into his hands and sacrifice a couple of pellets. It won't be long before he skulks off, never to return . . .

Let me say this right at the beginning: competition shooting with air guns is a sport that demands the greatest skill from a rifleman (or rifle woman), physical fitness and lots of training – that is, if the air gun marksman wants to draw a line between himself and the boy who shoots sparrows from a neighbour's window.

The firm of Feinwerkbau Westinger & Altenburger in Oberndorf, West Germany, have introduced the Model 300 Match Rifle, an improvement on the older Model 150.

"Single-stroke side lever, recoilless, stationary barrel, spring-operated piston, match trigger, aperture rear sight, and walnut stock," these are the brief specifications of the 300 model. However, for those readers interested in top-grade air guns, I shall have to go into more detail.

Text and Photos Klaus Nocher

System: In traditional manner, air pressure required for propulsion is engendered after the let-off. In other words, the piston is forced forward by its spring when released by the trigger mechanism, compressing the air column in the cylinder. This pressure suffices to expel the pellet from the barrel at a speed of between 485 and 575 ft./sec.

Power house: The parts that make up the pressure generating department (Fig. 3) are: sleeve (receiver housing), sidelever, cylinder, piston with cannelure for piston ring, double compression spring and column cap. The hardened, mirror polished piston is sealed in a honed cylinder by means of a circumferential steel joint. The principle here has been borrowed

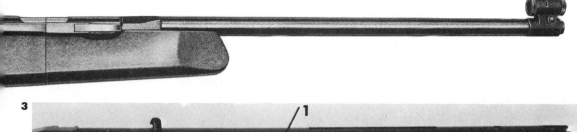

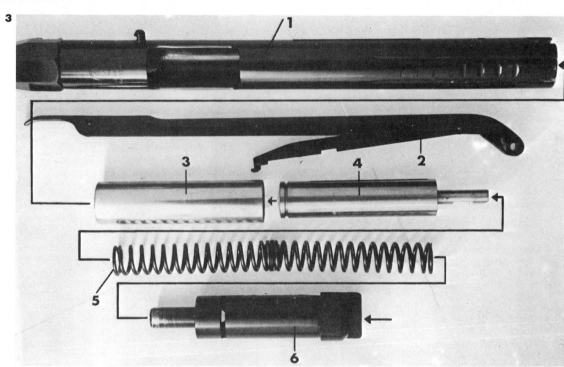

3 Power house: 1) sleeve (receiver housing), 2) sidelever, 3) cylinder, 4) piston with cannelure for piston ring, 5) double compression spring, 6) column cap.
4 Chamber nozzle for the waisted pellet.

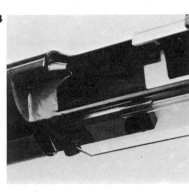

5

6

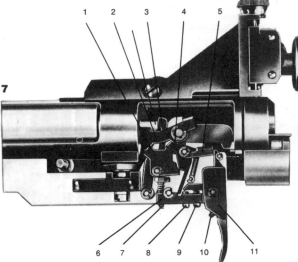

7

1 2 3 4 5

6 7 8 9 10 11

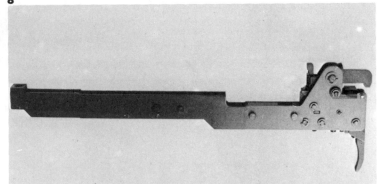

8

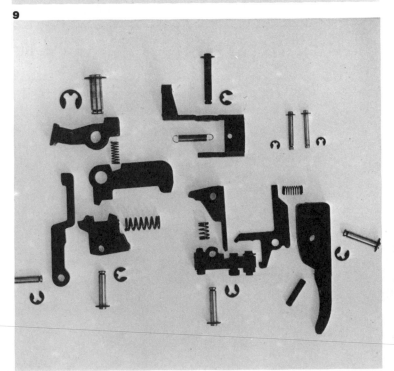

9

5 *Cylinder closed, piston cocked.*

6 *Plastic buffer on front end of piston for added protection. The arrow points to the two-point bearing of the recoil guide.*

7 *1) hammer, 2) sear, 3) cocking piece, 4) centre segment, 5) safety lever, 6) trigger bar, 7) adjusting screw for weight of trigger pull, 8) trigger stop screw, 9) pre-travel adjusting screw, 10) adjusting screw for trigger position, 11) trigger with take-up arm.*

8 *The complete trigger assembly.*

9 *The trigger mechanism as separate parts.*

from the automotive industry. Such an arrangement is very long lived and it keeps compression constant in all weathers (consistency for point of impact).

The manufacturer can have no fears, therefore, that someone will put forward a claim for spring and sealing replacement during the 2 year guarantee!

Fig. 4 shows the chamber opening into which the waisted pellet is seated, in a cutaway model. The cylinder in this photograph is ⅓rd closed. In Fig. 5 we see the sealing between cylinder and barrel, whereby the funnel-shaped seal is housed in the cylinder. This sealer is selfenergizing, for the greater the air pressure, the tighter the seal is at the chamber. Since the sealer is not exposed to friction, it should also enjoy a long service life. At worst, it might be attacked by chemicals.

The front end of the piston is provided with a plastic buffer (Fig. 6), which protects the cylinder when the piston flies forward. It also cuts out that front jerk, which is so often annoying in air guns.

Trigger: Feinwerkbau must have done a bit of brainstorming here. Match requirements dictate a hair let-off, despite the terrific spring power resting behind that trigger. So the piston had to be released by a round-about means. The various parts are illustrated in Fig. 7. The piston, with locking arm R, is subject to spring pressure, in the direction of the arrow. When the trigger is pulled, the

10

11

12

10 From top to bottom: Adjusting let-off, pre-travel and trigger position.
11 The globe is pinned to the barrel.
12 Receiver sight.

trigger bar (6) pivots over the trigger pre-travel adjusting screw (9) and abuts against the trigger stop screw (8). Weight of trigger pull can be adjusted by rotating screw (7). When the trigger bar (6) is depressed, via the screw (9), the centre lever (4) is freed. The hammer (1) flies backwards, knocking the sear (2) down out of engagement with the piston. Actual discharge is enacted within milliseconds. The various trigger parts are housed in an enclosed frame, as depicted in Fig. 8. However,

the separate parts are illustrated in Fig. 9.

Most readers could not have imagined how complicated the trigger is of a top-grade air gun. Pretravel, let-off, trigger position and weight of trigger pull are all very easily adjusted (Fig. 10). Trigger pull is adjustable from 100 to 300 gram. And with a special spring, to 1,500 gram. Fig. 13 shows the cocked piston in a cutaway model.

Recoil: Right from the start, I must say that felt recoil does not exist in the Feinbau 300. Rather unorthodox engineering has been applied to eliminate it. It is a known fact that a compressed spring flies out equally in both directions, when released. In the usual air weapon, however, the spring can only move with the piston, for its other end is firmly anchored to an abutment. When surmounting the moment of inertia in the mass of the piston, a recoil "slap" is therefore, experienced by the shooter.

Feinwerkbau have built the whole caboodle into the stock, parallel to the axis of the bore, viz. on a three-point bearing. Only the so-called recoil guide (sheet metal) is screwed to the stock, and the unit can recoil about 6 mm on highly polished, glass-hard supports. The operation is as follows: The hammer flies back and frees the sear from the piston, at the same time tipping up the hook arm (Fig. 13). The latter can no longer rest on the rear one-point bearing.

As just mentioned, a compressed spring also strikes out to the rear, and in this case it forces the entire unit backwards. This the barrel, and 2 female screws, front and back, facilitate a quick change of inserts or lenses (Fig. 15). These low-lying sights are matt black.

Stock: The standard version for the 300 is of walnut, and anatomically favourably shaped. Its steep pistol grip (Fig. 16) is hand-filling, and can be lengthened by 10 mm through an exten-

13 Trigger mechanism in a cutaway model: "A" hook arm, "S" safety disc for the piston.
14 The receiver sight is of aluminium pressure casting.
15 Looking down the front globe.
16 The steep pistol grip Is very hand-filling.
17 The buttstock cap is vertically adjustable.

double directional push arrangement is synchonized, hence recoil is not felt. The unit is pushed back to its home position when the sidelever is activated.

Barrel: The barrel and receiver are firmly joined together. Barrel length is 555 mm, and it has 12 right-twist grooves. The model I am describing has for extra weight a barrel mantle of .4 kp.

Sighting: The rear is a micro peep sight (Fig. 14), the front an aperture sight for various inserts (Fig. 11).

The receiver is grooved for the peep sight, to hold it in 4 positions. The globe of the front sight is pinned to

sion. An extension is also available for the buttstock, which is very handy for shooting in the standing position. The rubber butt cap (Fig. 17) is vertically adjustable. It can also be swung into the horizontal. Once the minor adjustments have been made, this is an air gun that delivers fine shooting.

Safety: Feinwerkbau have invested a lot of thought for the marksman's personal safety. So much so that three independent safeties have been incorporated. As soon as the sidelever is manipulated, the safety lever (Fig. 7) blocks the trigger. At the same time, the disc "S" (Fig. 13) sides out of its bearing to intercept the piston, should the latter for any reason not be checked by the trigger mechanism. And finally, a bevelled tooth rack prevents the sidelever from flying forward, should the marksman lose his grip on it during the cocking operation. Furthermore, this rack compels the marksman to go the whole hog when compressing the spring. If he does not, the sidelever will stick out of the flank of the gun, and not fold down.

General: The world records broken with Feinwerkbau air guns go to prove that design and construction of these weapons is just right. The test grouping delivered by the factory showed 5 shots printed into a circle measuring only 5.2 mm. Handling is truly simple, and women and youngsters can cock the piston without any difficulty (max. tension 4.5 kg). The author, disregarding one picayunish detail, could find absolutely no fault with the the Model 300.

The adjustable screw for finger length at trigger could not be reached through the appropriate hole in the trigger guard, at least not with the special screwdriver the factory provides. I had to poke at the slot of the screwhead from the side. However, the screwdriver hole in the trigger guard can easily be enlarged with a round file. Take the trigger guard down first, so that filings won't enter the gun.

The Model 300 is available with the heavy barrel, or

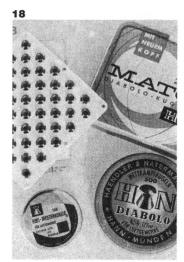

55642

18 *The arrow points to the original factory grouping.*
19 *Precision shooting depends greatly on individually packed pellets.*
20 *Various accessories: Globe inserts, pistol grip extension, buttstock extension, special screwdriver.*

with a normal barrel. The standard version has a built-in plate for swivels, specially for three-position match shooting.

Facit: I can wholeheartedly recommend the Feinwerkbau Model 300 air rifle. For serious air gunners, this rifle is a joy to use and own.

Technical data

Manufacturer: Feinwerkbau Westinger and Altenburger, Oberndorf, West Germany.

System: Compressed air, sidelever, spring-driven piston.

Calibre: .177

Barrel length: 555 mm

Rifling: 12 grooves, right-hand twist.

Sighting: Receiver and globe attachments, for inserts and lenses.

Distance between sights
Trigger: Stationary. 810–840 mm. Height 23 mm Fully adjustable. Weight of pull adj. between 100 and 300 gram.

Weight: Approx. 4.5 kg. With bbl. mantle 4.9 kg.

Stock: Choice offered. Walnut. Pistol grip and buttstock can be lengthened through extension pieces.

Text and Photos Klaus Nocher

THE TAURUS

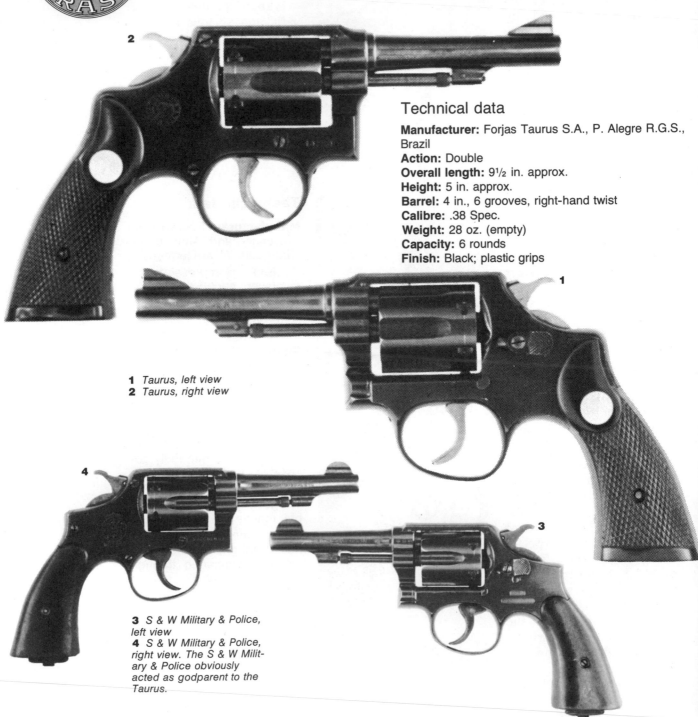

Technical data

Manufacturer: Forjas Taurus S.A., P. Alegre R.G.S., Brazil
Action: Double
Overall length: 9½ in. approx.
Height: 5 in. approx.
Barrel: 4 in., 6 grooves, right-hand twist
Calibre: .38 Spec.
Weight: 28 oz. (empty)
Capacity: 6 rounds
Finish: Black; plastic grips

1 Taurus, left view
2 Taurus, right view

3 S & W Military & Police, left view
4 S & W Military & Police, right view. The S & W Military & Police obviously acted as godparent to the Taurus.

FROM BRAZIL

5 *Sideplate and grips removed*
6 *The S & W for comparison*
7 *The double-action layout. The pawl spring is located in the sideplate*
8 *The firm's emblem (on sideplate)*
9 *The quick-draw type post sight is milled into the barrel.*

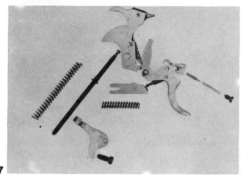

5 **6**

7 **8**

9

Forjas Taurus S.A. of Brazil is producing a revolver that very much resembles the S & W Military & Police .38 Special, both inside and out (Illus. 1, 2, 3 and 4). Nonetheless, once the stocks have been removed, one notes certain differences, after the sideplate has been lifted out, other differences also spring to light. The Taurus is chambered for the .38 Special and has a double-action trigger mechanism. It has a coiled mainspring and trigger spring. The latter, housed in the rebound slide, also exerts an arrest-ing pressure on the non-cocked hammer (Illus. 5 and 6). The 6-shot cylinder is mounted on a sprung centre pin, whereas the nose at the extractor end fits into a cutout in the breechface. The third anchoring point being the cylinder stop that operates with the trigger.

The firing pin is hollow riveted in the hammer, but can still move for self-adjustment. An eccentric arm, adjustable via the strain screw, forms the anchor for mainspring and hammer strut (Illus. 7). Contrary to S & W practice, the pawl spring is not situated in the trigger, but in the sideplate that bears the firm's name (Illus. 8). The front sight is a slanted quick draw type post, the rear sight an open notch.

Taken as a whole, it may be said that the Taurus is a reasonably well made, inexpensive revolver . . .

Christian Andsager

Beretta

the chamber, the hammer can be dropped to half cock for safety's sake. Nonetheless, lowering the hammer to half cock ought to be thoroughly practised on an empty chamber, since the mainspring is very powerful and the hammer might slip from under one's thumb. The swing-over safety catch blocks the trigger only. Furthermore, when the safety catch has been rotated to the safe position, the barrel can be freed from its receiver grooves.

Though trigger travel is short, it is also a little stiff. Still, for a military pistol, accuracy is not bad at all. Firing RWS ammunition in a 1942 war-time model, with one hand, I placed 5 shots within a 2.4 in. circle at 27 yards.

The 1934 pistol is available in .32 ACP and .380 ACP. Both quality of workmanship and appearance are praiseworthy, despite the simplicity of the design. The ring of the external hammer is well serrated, as in all single-action pistols the hammer must be thumbed back for the initial shot. If a cartridge is in

This handy little pistol was once the official side arm of the Italian army, and it was widely used by the Italian police before the end of WW 2. The firm of Pietro Beretta has been in the gunmaking business since 1680 and is noted for goodquality sporting, target and military weapons.

1 *Remove magazine and retract slide to clear chamber.*

2 *Push the safety catch over to safe, so that it will enter the hold-open notch when slide is jerked back. Free barrel from the receiver grooves by tapping muzzle.*

Military Pocket Pistol 1934

Rifling takes a right-hand twist (6 grooves), and the recoil spring and guide are housed under the barrel. The trigger bar has an arm that extends up into a slit in the slide. This neat arrangement prevents accidental discharge before the slide closes, as the linkage between firing pin and trigger is disrupted until the breech is properly closed; and for the same reason fully automatic fire will not ensue if the trigger is kept squeezed after a shot.

The front sight is integral with the receiver, the rear sight, however, can be adjusted in its slot by using a small brass hammer or punch. The firing pin is seated behind a small recoil spring, the function of which is to drive the firing pin away from the breech-face when hammer tension has been relieved. In Luger fashion, the extractor is mounted on top of the receiver, not at one side. The magazine of the .380 ACP model holds 7 cartridges. A spur on the floorplate acts as a finger rest.

1 Slide 2 Barrel 3 Recoil spring 4 Recoil spring guide 5 Receiver 6 Safety catch 7 Magazine 8 Left-hand grip

No further dismantling is necessary. To re-assemble the pistol, simply reverse procedure.

3 Push barrel through the top opening of the receiver. Then hold slide and release safety catch, easing slide assembly off front of receiver. Safety catch can be lifted away from receiver.

TECHNICAL DATA

Length 5.9 in.
Height 4.7 in.
Barrel length 3.4 in.
Weight 1 lb 8 oz
Weight loaded approx. 1 lb 11 oz
Capacity 7 .380 ACPs
Muzzle vel. 870 fps
Muzzle energy 156 ft. pds.
Penetration into dry pine at 27 yards: 3.5 in. The Beretta .380 ACP is a simple but reliable pistol for defense.

Text and Photos H. J. Stammel

Sauer & Sohn SR

In over 20 years I have shot virtually everything that Germany's revolver makers have made. Apart from the Korth and the Sauer Western Six Shooter (both built under licence), the others have caused tears of desperation to flow down my cheeks. I thought nothing could match the Americans. But the situation is beginning to change.

When I completed extensive testing of the SR 3 I could have cried with rage: Why didn't a revolver like this appear years ago . . .? I could have saved a lot of money by not buying those expensive, first-class American revolvers!

The Sauer & Sohn people at Eckernförde have been hatching their "egg" for a long time, and have been launching one prototype after another. Since the US market is the one that interests them most, and the

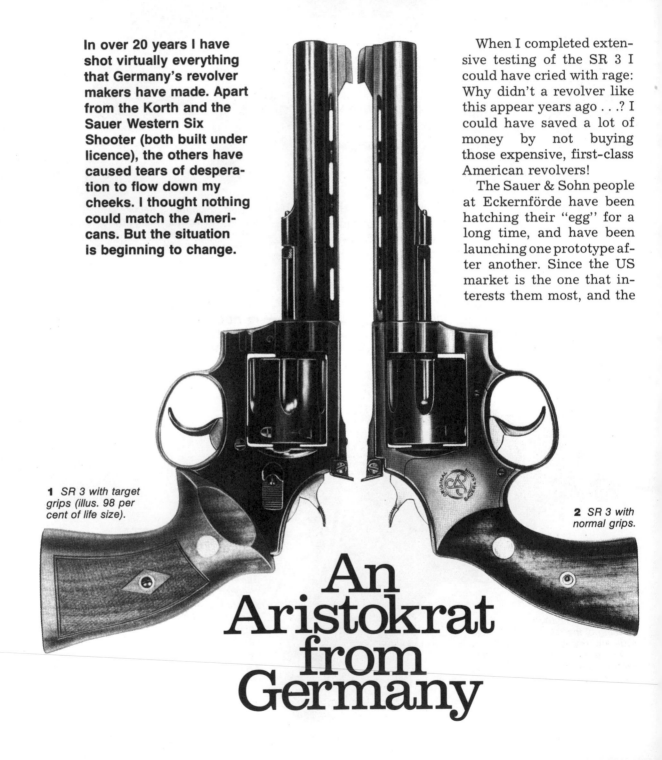

1 SR 3 with target grips (illus. 98 per cent of life size).

2 SR 3 with normal grips.

An Aristokrat from Germany

3 Revolver

Sauer & Sohn team know from reading the American gun journals, etc. how high the quality standards are in that country; that, for example, all other makes of handguns are critically compared with the truly superb Colts and S & W models. They seem to have been lured by some sort of fetishistic ambition to produce a German revolver that even the most nitpicking American would have to accept. Most of the European attempts to design and construct American quality handguns remind me of the US car combines who have been watching the victorious advance of European automobiles – and with glassy eyes have repeatedly bungled the counter attack with their "compact" vehicles. Nonetheless, the testers in the various car magazines are tired of sounding yet another US retreat! Advertised perfection is still not quite perfect, they report. But if one takes a hard look at American cars, perfection is missing all along the line.

However, when I see an American top quality revolver, when I hold it in my hand and feel the smoothness of precision-made lock parts, the balance and butt

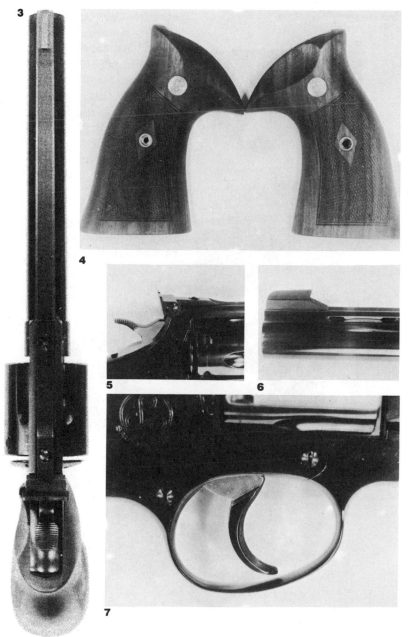

3 An aerial view of the SR 3. Note the fine proportions, the broad hammer spur and the wide rear sight.
4 Oiled walnut target grips, checkered. Note original "Sauer & Sohn" silver plaque.
5 Micrometer sight with set screw, elegant and practical.
6 Sand-blasted front sight with anti-reflection flutes.
7 Trigger and trigger bar, in shape and position ideal.

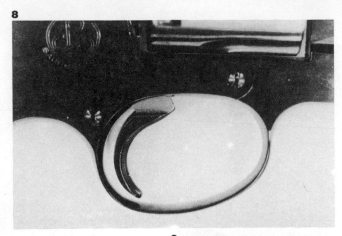

8 *Trigger, cocked.*
9 *The trigger is 9 mm wide. Superb for match shooting.*
10 *Breech face, showing hand and firing pin, and thumbpiece for cylinder swing out.*
11 *The yoke fits so perfectly into the frame that an interstice is difficult to detect even in an enlarged photo.*
12 *Cylinder thumbpiece does not wobble a millimetre, and does not rub the blueing off the frame.*
13 *Cylinder swung out 90 degrees, extractor activated.*

design, I breathe in its perfection before I even fire a shot.

Serious marksmen in Germany wouldn't dream of using anything else but Colts or S & Ws at competitions.

Of course, just as one can get around in American cars, so one can shoot with German revolvers. One even reaches one's destination in American cars, and so too are targets hit with German revolvers ... But American revolvers are in a class of their own. The quality blueing, the sights, the trigger, trigger pull, the eye-catching design, the velvety clicking of the lock parts, and so on. And the accuracy of American handguns gives one the feeling of accelerating in a racy Mercedes, BMW, Ferrari or Jaguar.

When I unpacked the SR 3 my eyes popped. In my mind's eye I began to compare its every line and curve with those of my beloved American models. Take a good look at shape, cylinder, sighting and handle (grip) – each element blends in with the next. Undoubtedly, the SR 3 has been based on the S & W medium frame. Still, is every revolver maker obliged to introduce new designs? The internal combustion engines of different cars are basically similar, too.

The workmanship of the SR 3 is excellent, and the high polish blue is reminiscent of top grade American work. Metallic high polish adorns the sides of the hammer and trigger shank – like the pearl tie pin of a gentleman. And the lock mechanism, believe it or not, is slightly more velvety and positive than that of the S & W Masterpiece or Colt Python, and as silent as the ticking of the most expensive Swiss watch. When thumbing back the hammer, the SR 3 has to be placed against one's ear to hear the full-cock notch engage.

And then the let-off! Trigger and falling hammer operate so smoothly that a kiss exchanged by two robins on a fence couldn't be more gentle. One thinks trigger pull is much too light, and is then surprised

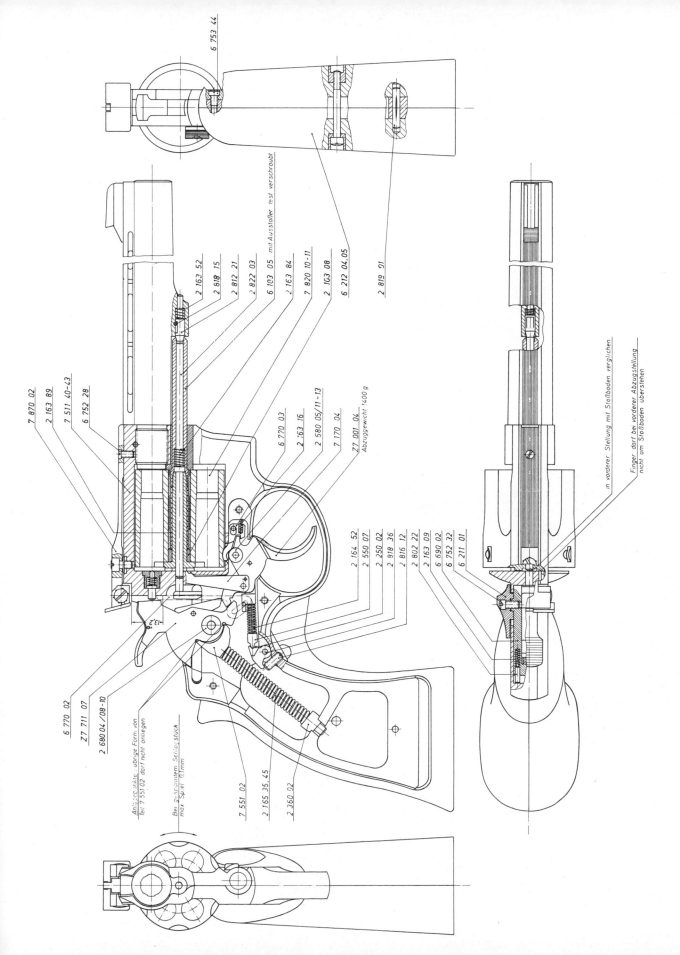

6 753 44

2 163 52
2 818 15
2 812 21
2 822 03
6 103 05   mit Ausstoßer fest verschraubt
2 163 84
7 820 10-11
2 163 08
6 212 04,05
2 819 91

7 870 02
2 163 89
7 511 40-43
6 752 28

6 770 03
2 163 16
2 580 05/11-13
7 170 04
Z7 001 04
Abzuggewicht 1400 g

2 164 52
2 550 07
2 250 02
2 818 36
2 816 12
2 802 22
2 163 09
6 690 02
6 752 32
6 211 01

6 770 02
Z7 711 07
2 680 04 /08 -10

Anlageflächte übrige Form: von
Teil 7 551 02 darf nicht anliegen

Bei gespanntem Schlagstück
max Spiel 0,1mm

7 551 02
2 165 35, 45
2 360 02

-13,2

in vorderer Stellung mit Stoßboden verglichen

Finger darf bei vorderer Abzugstellung
nicht am Stoßboden überstehen

133

to learn that the trigger has 1.400 g (just over 3 lbs) behind it. That's target quality! The secret not only lies in precision machining, the broad 9 mm trigger also plays a part.

A wedding ring of 9 mm would be ostentatious, but this width is the optimum for target revolver triggers. Anyone who does not appreciate this trigger has either drunk too many bourbons or needs a couple of weeks' sunshine at Torremolinos (Spain). The target grip of the SR 3 is oil impregnated and, contrary to the grips of the Colts and S & Ws, wraps completely around the backstrap. I personally find it a wee bit more grippy than the Python's.

When the SR 3 is dusted down with a cloth, it can be used as a mirror for shaving, the revolver, not the cloth, of course. The fitting of the side plate, the cylinder and the yoke is so masterly that even under a magnifying glass the work can be compared to that of Colt and S & W.

This is finest quality workmanship. The micrometer sight has a good rectangular notch which lies exactly 4 mm over the ventilated rib. The rear sight leaf, adjustable, of course, is broader than those of Colt and S & W. (Colt: 18 mm, S & W: 17 mm, SR 3: 20 mm). It is higher, too. (Colt: 8 mm, S & W: 9 mm, SR 3: 10 mm). The sprung ramp is 75 mm long (Colt: 38 mm, S & W: 72 mm) and has 12 fore and aft flutes to match those of the ventilated rib.

The firing pin of the SR 3 is bushed, as is that of the Colt Python, but otherwise the two systems differ. The SR 3 has a spring-loaded pin that is so short that it won't reach the primer when the hammer is down, yet when imparted a blow by the falling hammer the firing pin flies forward with sufficient momentum to fire the primer.

The yoke assembly and mechanism is based on the traditional Smith & Wesson design. The cylinder swings out 90 degrees, greatly facilitating ejecting and loading. A definite advantage over the Colt. The spacing between cylinder

14 *Swung out cylinder viewed from the rear, showing ratchet and extractor.*
15 *Extractor rod fastened under barrel in S & W fashion.*
16 *Cylinder, yoke and extractor.*
17 *Cylinder face.*

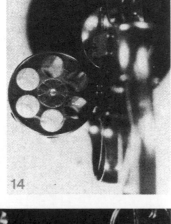
14

15

16

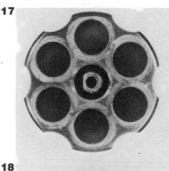
17

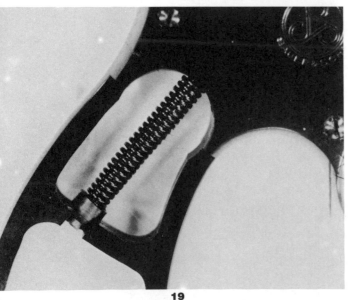
19

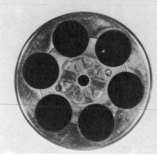
18

18 *Front of cylinder with centre pin guide. Note that the flame has not exceeded the edge of the cylinder, which proves extra tight spacing between cylinder and chamber end of barrel.*
19 *Mainspring of non-breakable steel. Short but powerful. Sectional views of the Sauer & Sohn SR 3 Revolver.*

and chamber end of barrel has been reduced to such a breathtaking tolerance that an interstice is barely visible. This tolerance is half that of Colt and S & W models.

When shooting the SR 3 I held a paper handkerchief on both sides of the cylinder/barrel interstice. Singeing and powder particles were reduced by more than half when compared with the two American revolvers. I even fired the SR 3 in the dark to see how much

with a medium frame for .38 Specials, the petite measurements of the latter are acceptable.

The SR 3 weighs 1010 g (2.22 lbs) which is ideal for a revolver with target grip that fires .38 wad cutters. The SR 3 sits as sure as fate in anyone's hand, big or small. Its 10 mm broad hammer spur has accurately milled cross serrations, just perfect for cocking the hammer without changing one's grip. If one takes a peep under the side-

made at 25 m in a machine rest, only three entry holes were identifiable as such; the other three must have gone through their predecessors. Dispersion from the machine rest was 19 mm (.75 in.) for 6 shots. Now, I was biting my under lip as I went down to the range, for I wanted to test fire the SR 3 at 35 m one handed, and at 50 m two handed. At 35 m I shot 200 cartridges (50 Sako Wad cutters 148 gr., 50 Remington Targetmaster wad cutters 148 gr., 50

20 *Hammer cocked. The wide spur facilitates thumbing back without changing one's grip.*
21 *Inside sideplate. Highly polished like a Swiss watch.*

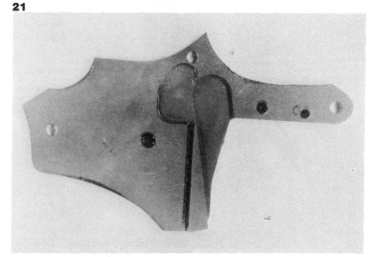

fire it spits out of its sides. Again, a definite edge over the Americans!

The ramped front post sight stands 7 mm high. It is sand blasted and has reflection – dampening cross flutes. Obviously a Masterpiece design. The ventilated top rib measures 8.25 mm, and is 1.75 mm narrower than that of the Python. This rib is 5 mm high, and hence 1 mm lower than that of the Python. Since the Python is equipped with a heavy frame for .357 Magnum, the SR 3, however,

plate, and under grip, we find coil springs doing all jobs, which is a pleasant surprise. As said before, hammer and trigger are highly polished and the frame is smooth to the last millimetre. So even taken apart, the SR 3 can be belted to match a dresscoat and lac – varnished shoes.

The 150 mm barrel (5.9 in.) is made of high quality chrome/molybdenum steel, the frame of drop forged special steel. In the target sheet supplied by the factory showing groupings

Hirtenberger wad cutters 148 gr., and 50 Geco wad cutters 148 gr.). Two 6-shot series were fired into the deer-heart target sheets. These target sheets are normally for rifles at 100 metres, but I prefer them to the life-size silhouettes on account of the white circle, despite the fact that the latter's bullseye is 5 x larger.

The grouping of the first 12-shot series with Sako cartridges was excellent.

The first shot went low, probably because the factory had sighted the gun in at 25 m. The second shot, after sight adjustment, was vertically exactly over the first one, but too high. After adjusting the sights again, the subsequent 10 shots snuggled close together in a 37 mm (1.47 in.) circle. This does honour to the SR 3, and to me too, I think. Dispersion at the factory with hand-held shots was 50 mm at 25 m. Once I had sighted in at 35 m I fired off 50 Sakos and 50 Remingtons in rapid succession. Fulfilling my greatest expectations, every bullet hole was exactly where I wanted it to be. The widest circle of dispersion of 8 target sheets was 39 mm (1.53 in.), the narrowest sion with Sakos was 69 mm (2.73 in.), with Hirtenberger 115 mm (4.53 in.), and with Geco 180 mm (7.1 in.)!

During test shooting I didn't drink a drop of anything, I was thinking about pleasant things only and concentrated on what I was doing – to get the "stove pipe" hot as quickly as possible.

22

23

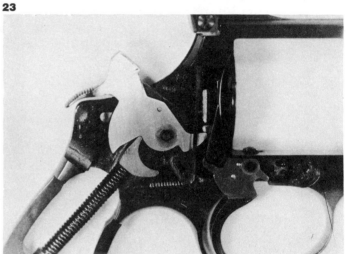

22 *The lockwork, consisting of hammer, trigger, pawl, bolt, springs. The workmanship here is truly something to admire.*
23 *Hammer cocked.*

27 mm (1.06 in.). The average totalled 34 mm (1.23 in.).

However, with the Hirtenberger ammunition the situation changed radically. After cleaning the barrel and letting it cool down, I shot off four 12-shot series. The average circle of dispersion was 85 mm (3.15 in.)! The Gecos were a tragedy. Average dispersion of 4 series was 120 mm (4.7 in.). At 50 m with the Remington Targetmasters accuracy was restored. Dispersion was cut down to 65 mm (2.55 in.) as an average of 4 series. Considering the weak load of this cartridge, the results were fantastic. The average disper-

The results: The SR 3 is marvellously accurate. My test proves that my pet aversion against German revolvers must now go up in smoke. The American testers are tops when it comes to knowing guns. I know most of their test reports, and some of the writers, too. Thirteen years ago in 1963, Hank C. Buchanan said to me in San Diego: "You know, Joe, you Vikings have been making for many decades damn good rifles, shotguns and automatic pistols. And we don't write much about your ammunition because it's also damn good. But one thing you guys will never be able to make – that's a revolver. One that I would lay on the same shelf with my Colts and S & Ws." I could not defend myself, so I poured some raspberry schnapps from the Black Forest down Hank's throat without saying a word, and we trundled off to the range with three of his long-barrelled favourites in my pocket.

Today I would unhesitantly compete with him – using the SR 3. I would shoot for house and home without taking too much of a risk. A whole family of these SRs is planned, with long and short barrels, with fat and thin grips, with and without ventilated ribs, with different types of sights, etc. They are to be available in .38 Special, in .22 L.R., and in .357 Magnum.

Pistol shooters all over the world will want to put the SRs through their paces, a sportsman-like challenge for the revolver makers at Eckernförde . . .

Technical Specifications of Sauer & Sohn SR 3 Revolver

Manufacturer: J. P. Sauer & Sohn GmbH, Eckernförde, West Germany (founded in 1751).

Designation: SR 3.

Type: Double action solid frame revolver, swing-out cylinder.

Ignition: Separate firing pin in breechblock.

Safety: Automatic hammer arrester.

Length of barrel: 150 mm.

Number of grooves: 6.

Rate of twist: 457 mm.

Direction of twist: right.

Diameter across lands: 8.79 (+ .03) mm.

Diameter across grooves: 9.04 (+ .03) mm.

Frame thickness: 15.2 mm.

Calibre: .38 Special (6 rounds).

Cylinder: Locked in frame via centre pin. Rotates to the left. 40 mm long. 37 mm in diameter.

Steel used: Barrel: Krupp Chrome/Molybdenum.

Frame: Drop forged special steel.

Cylinder: Krupp Chrome/Molybdenum.

Weight: 1010 gram.

Overall length: 290 mm.

Trigger pull: 1400 gram., adjustable.

Width of trigger: 9 mm, match type.

Handle frame: Steel.

Grips: Checkered walnut, sport grips with thumb rest; grips interchangeable with other types.

Sighting: Front post, rectangular rear notch, adjustable.

Distance between sights: 190 mm.

Ventilated rib: Length 132.5 mm, width 85 mm, height 5 mm.

Finish: Rich blueing.

Lockwork: Precision made parts, velvety operation.

Other models

SR 3: .22 L.R. Target and Competition Revolver.

VR 4: .38 Special Defense Weapon (3 and 6.4 in barrels).

VR 4: .22 L.R. Defense Weapons (4 and 6 in barrels).

TR 6: .38 Special with 2 in barrel.

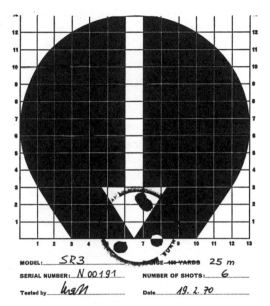

MODEL: SR3 RANGE 100 YARDS 25 m
SERIAL NUMBER: N 00191 NUMBER OF SHOTS: 6
Tested by _____ Date 19. 2. 70

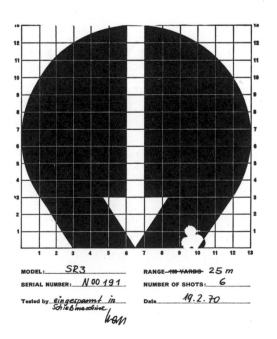

MODEL: SR3 RANGE 100 YARDS 25 m
SERIAL NUMBER: N 00191 NUMBER OF SHOTS: 6
Tested by eingespannt in Schießmaschine Date 19. 2. 70

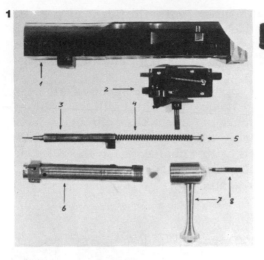

In the Federal Republic of Germany, shooting with the free rifle is a program that is backed only by a few supporters. Free rifles are used at 300 metres: 40 shots in the standing, in the kneeling, and in the prone positions. The weight of the rifle must not exceed 8 kg. Maximum calibre is 8 mm. J. Poignant of Sweden broke the world record in the prone position with 397's at the European Championships in 1963. However, this score was improved on by Kurt Johansson, a fellow Swede, when he shot 399 rings at the Swedish Championships.

THE FREE RIFLE MODEL VAP 65

His achievement was not recognized as a world record, though, for world records may only be set at European and World Championships, and at the Olympic Games. Compared with the rules of other types of sport, such as athletics and swimming, marksmen are at a definite disadvantage. Whereas other sportsmen can take advantage of best physical condition at relatively small events, and break records, the sharpshooter must pull his punches until that far-off, big day arrives. The two Swedes shot with rifles of the Vapen Specialists AB Stockholm.

1 *Receiver (1), Frame for trigger mechanism*

2 *Frame for trigger mechanism. Front setscrew (1), setscrew for adjusting weight of trigger.*

The Vapen Specialists AB Stockholm started constructing their free rifle in the mid-1950s. The first weapon was completed in 1957, and Kurt Johansson put it to trial at a contest in Switzerland. In the meantime, of course, this rifle was subjected to much development, and today the Scandinavian free-rifle marksmen use this model exclusively. VAP rifles were sent to Germany, Finland, and America. Earl Wright and J. Foster, members of the US National Team, received them, too.

Barrel and breech bolt are of high-grade Bofor steel.

This material has an ultimate tensile strength of approx. 130 kg/m². The receiver is fully enclosed, the only opening being a loading port on the right-hand side. According to the Mauser system, the bolt sports two locking lugs. The extractor is embedded in the bolt face. The shaft of the firing pin is hollow to accept the spring, and the pin itself is interchangeable. On account of the design, the firing-pin spring won't fatigue or shorten. The rear end of the breech bolt is plugged, and screwed, through which the bolt handle protrudes. The trigger mechanism is adjustable for various degrees of slack, or single stage. Trigger pull can be adjusted from 0.7 oz. to 1.1 lb. And the trigger itself can be lengthened or shortened to suit the marksman's finger. The bearings of the trigger are coated with hard metal to reduce wear and tear. When using copper or tombac jacketed bullets, the barrel of the VAP 65 would have a service life of approx. 10,000 rounds. Stocking is of normal Match design, with an adjustable Schutzen hook as well as palm rest and guide rail on the forearm. Hand and palm rests are available in many individual shapes.

Sighting is not central, it has been positioned 8 mm

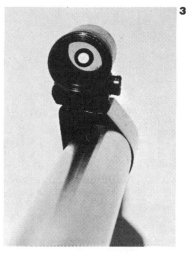

"into the marksman's face." An Anschütz receiver sight is standard equipment, but a Redfield model will be supplied if required. All set or fixing screws are of the Allen key type.

The VAP Model 65 is also deliverable in a southpaw version.

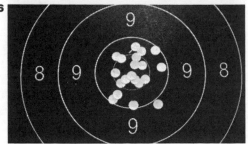

Free Rifle VAP Model 65

System	VAP single shot
Bolt	Mauser type
Firing-pin travel	7 mm
Ignition time	3/1000th sec.
Trigger	Slack or single stage
Calibres	6.5×55 (Swedish Mauser), .308 Win., .308 Nato, 7.62×53 R. Other calibres can be supplied.
Barrel	6 grooves, 1 in 10 inch twist
Barrel length	According to calibre 700–750 mm
Weight	7–7½ kg
Sights	Anschütz or Redfield
Dispersion	60 mm at 300 metres
Stocking	Walnut

5 and 6 *Two groupings by Kurt Johansson at the Swedish Championships in 1965 – prone shooting: 399 rings.*

Text W. Weiher
Drawings S. Berg

German Hollow Charges and Hollow Charge Ammunition of WW II

One of the most successful, best
remembered and cheapest of
the German weapons of World War II
was the panzerfaust. The term "weapon"
needs defining, as this anti-tank device was
part and parcel of its own explosive charge. For the
projector, a short tube, which served as a carrier
for the projectile, charge, discharge mechanism and
sighting attachment, was discarded after use.
Whether this singularity was good or bad will not
be dealt with here.

Fig. 1
Hollow charge grenade

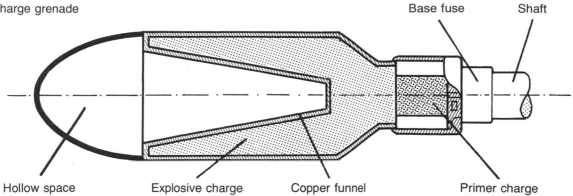

Base fuse Shaft

Hollow space Explosive charge Copper funnel Primer charge

The panzerfaust revolutionized tank fighting in that one man was in a position to knock out an iron giant single-handedly without overly exposing himself to danger. This was feasible by using a hollow charge grenade, and by exploiting the principles of recoilless discharge. The problem of anti-tank warfare arose for the Germans in the autumn of 1917 when the British sprung surprise attacks with such vehicles to restore mobility to trench-ridden battlefields in France. One famous battle took place in Cambrai, where the Germans had not reckoned with a tank invasion. The Germans stayed the course by concentrating machine-gun fire at the vision ports of those seemingly invulnerable war machines and by drawing upon their field artillery, etc. Of course, compared with today's armoured vehicles, the tanks of the 1st World War were virtually nothing more than farm tractors covered with boiler plating. The anti-tank rifle developed by Mauser was probably the first of its kind. It resembled an oversized infantry rifle, was single shot, chambered for a 13 mm round, and sported a bipod.
One should not underestimate the effect of even a small-calibre hard-core bullet that has made its way through armour plating; for once the bullet has flattened it explodes . . .

Recoil was so violent that only men with hearts of oak could handle the early anti-tank guns. A broken shoulder was a fairly common occurrence in those days! Before the era of hollow charge ammunition, the soldier fighting tanks had to rely on hard-core projectiles and high terminal velocities. Tank armour got thicker and heavier, so the calibres used for combating these tanks in turn became larger. When the Russians showed up with the T 34 tank during the last war, the armour was so heavy that the Ger-

mans could only reply with their cumbrous 7.5 cm Pak 40 field guns. Eventually, the Germans were obliged to train 8.8 cm anti-aircraft cannon (Flak 18 and 36) on the Russian tanks. With a muzzle velocity of 2953 fps, these long Toms certainly caused devastation among the enemy's tanks; but anti-aircraft guns are designed to shoot down planes not tanks, and owing to their immobility they proved to be sitting-duck targets themselves.

Tank grenades used to have thick, hard points that in some models were capped with soft iron to help prevent the grenade from slipping off sloping armour. Behind the point, the hardness of the projectile's jacket diminished, to obviate the danger of the grenade being smashed to pieces. On account of the stout walls of a tank grenade, the charge was relatively undersized. However, powder charges of high brisance were employed to make up for this deficiency. Other armies used solid shells. Base fuses in tank grenades (nose fuses smash before penetration) were hitched to a retarding mechanism so that the grenade might pass through the armour plate before the final explosion. When spaced armour was introduced, which aimed to explode the projectile against the outer plate (dissipating the blast harmlessly against the heavy inner one) tank grenades had to be redesigned to explode behind the second layer of shielding metal. Tracer composition was also packed into the base of the grenade, permitting the observers to follow the grenade's course. Shells began to decrease in size when they were built around tungsten carbide cores and launched from conically bored tubes, to increase velocity. These, however, ate up a lot of material, money, time and labour. Terrific quantities of propellent were necessary, and the guns firing these hard-core shells rapidly succumbed to

Fig. 2
Hollow charge grenade

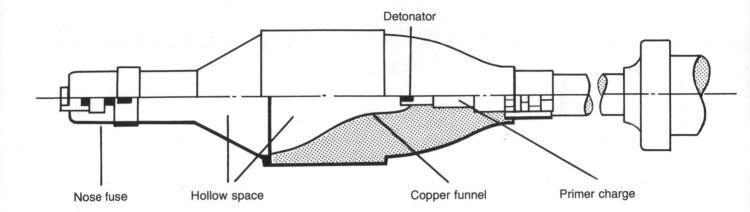

Detonator

Nose fuse   Hollow space   Copper funnel   Primer charge

wear and tear. A lot might be said on that score, but in this treatise there is not adequate space.

The principle of hollow charge explosives was known long before World War II. At this juncture, as a means of elucidation, I should like to describe a test I personally conducted during the war. If a blasting charge containing 3.53 oz. of cylindrically pressed TNT is stood up on a steel plate measuring 5/8 in. in thickness, that charge will only leave behind a star-shaped smudge on the plate when detonated. But if the base of the blasting charge is hollowed out, the explosion will punch a hole in the plate, even though some of the charge is lost due to the hollowing-out process. How is this possible? Detonation waves and a stream of hot gas are channeled down the hollow as though through a funnel and will focus at one small area of the armour plating. A parabolic mirror concentrates light or sound in the same way. Of course, my experimenting was crude. I used a pen-knife and made no attempt to calculate the exact constriction for the funnel. Nonetheless, the result was awe-inspiring! Normally, a bomb, shell or grenade is filled to the brim with an explosive charge. This, however, is not the case in a hollow charge or in hollow charge ammunition, since the striking end must be hollow.

For optimum results, the depth and shape of the partition that separates the hollow from the explosive must be pre-calculated for each type of missile and charge.

Hollow charges were used for the first time during the last war when the Germans captured the Belgian fortress Eben Emael. Entry was forced by having commandos and paratroopers place 110 lb hollow charges against the 16 inch walls.

Hollow charges of this type were made in various sizes. The H 3, which weighed just over 7 lb and was clamped on to tanks by means of three permanent magnets, was one of the more common models. It resembled a funnel, was made of sheet metal, and the powder train fuse was set for 7.5 seconds. Although this device exploded at all sides, the main force of energy was focused against the tank. The H 3 could drive through 8 inches of armour plating, and the only countermeasure left to the tank crew was to have the tank coated with cement, to thwart the magnets.

After further experimentation it was discovered that stout copper plating, when used as a housing for a hollow charge, increased performance considerably. The generation of intense heat melted a hole in the armour plating and transformed the grenade into a flying ramrod. Tanks knocked out by these hollow charges had holes measuring about 1 inch in diameter, the edges of which were puffed outwards, blue, and molten, as though someone had been using a cutting torch. This picture has often led observers to believe the process of making such a hole to be a slow one. In reality, though, the stream of gas and molten metal blasted against the tank travels at between 39,000 and 66,000 fps. Occasionally, the copper funnel of the charge is found sticking in the armour plate like a splinter.

Even the detonation of a hollow charge has its own distinctive ring, one hears a high whinging-whistling tone, which is very different from the bang of a normal explosive.

Hollow charge shells (HL-Geschosse) were also developed by the Germans for their light field howitzers, to combat tanks. The effect of the hollow

Fig. 3
Panzerfaust (armoured fist)

Projectile

Projector

Sighting

Fuse attachment   Firing button   Cocking lever

Hollow charge   Detonator

charge being important, not high velocity. Once the missile had reached the target it was the missile itself that released the knock-out blow. Sensitive nose fuses replaced the base fuses of the standard tank grenades. Knock-out efficiency remained constant at all distances. For the sake of simplicity and speed, the artillerists fired normal loads. As the nose fuse in these shells was separated from the main charge by the hollow and the copper funnel, which in itself jeopardized a flawless ignition, an open tube was passed from the middle of the funnel through the explosive charge down to the base of the shell, to connect with a second fuse. In other words, the nose fuse activated the one in the base, which, in turn, triggered off the main charge. The detonator of shorter shells was turned into the hollow so that both fuses lay opposite each other (Fig. 2). Shells equipped with only one fuse were not subjected to alteration, of course. Against tanks, spinning missiles proved to be less effective than the ones that were fin-stabilized.

The most famous of the German hollow charges is doubtless the panzerfaust, or armoured fist. It is not a rocket as was often supposed, for the panzerfaust lacked any sort of built-in propelling energy, and was launched from a recoilless hand projector. The impact head, measuring between 5 and 7 inches in diameter and weighing anything up to 7 lb, was mounted on a steel-finned shaft. This unit was inserted in a projector, a short tube of 1.5 inches in diameter, which contained powder charges in two separate compartments.

The charge in the forward compartment launched the "fist", whereas the charge in the rear compartment blew out astern, to neutralize the effect of recoil. Normally, recoil would have been much too

German Hollow Charges and Hollow Charge Ammunition of WW II

heavy for one man to handle. The projector, therefore, could never be placed against one's shoulder in rifle fashion. It was either to be laid **over** the soldier's shoulder, or tucked under his arm. Furthermore, it was most unwise for anyone to stand within several yards behind a panzerfaust that was about to be fired! Three sizes of panzerfaust were produced, for targets at 30, 60 and 100 yards. On no account were duds to be picked up and re-fired, as the base fuses of these "fists" were particulary treacherous, owing to the simple but over-sensitive design.

A genuine rocket launcher, on the other hand, was the so-called panzerschreck (tank terror), which in effect was an American bazooka. Its hollow charge projectile, 3.5 in. in calibre, was launched from a bazooka-type tube that the Germans nicknamed ofenrohr (stove-pipe). Unlike the projector of the panzerfaust, the launching tube of the panzerschreck could be used over and over again. The projectile was provided with a nose fuse, a long powder train with nozzle and stabilizing surfaces. A generator-fed electric igniter set off a powder tube that was fitted with radiating wheel spokes. The trajectory of the panzerschreck missile was considerably flatter than that of the panzerfaust, and hence was accurate up to about 150 yards; although maximum range was reputed to be 400 yards. Two men were needed to operate the panzerschreck, and yet another disadvantage must be mentioned. On hot, sunny days gas pressure within the powder train rose, the consequence of which made a fine mess of the gunners; that is, if the stove-pipe was resting against their faces. The missile fired in the panzerschreck was similar to the one illustrated in Fig. 2.

The Germans also introduced a hollow charge rifle grenade fired from a discharger cup that was mounted on the Karabiner 98 k. Here maximum range was about 280 yards. Also worth mentioning is the hollow charge projectile that was discharged form a Very pistol (Fig. 1) with attached shoulder stock. Strange to say, this contrivance was christened "kampfpistole", which means, in English, fighting pistol. Nonetheless, the 2 in. projectiles fired in these Very pistols could penetrate 3 inches of armour plating!

The panzerfaust has been adopted in modified form by today's Bundeswehr.

Although hollow charges are significantly effective against armour plating, they are not particularly successful against reinforced concrete. Other armies followed suit, the Americans with their bazooka, and the British with their bomb launcher PIAT (Projector, Infantry, Anti-Tank), for example. The Russians, on the other hand, introduced a hollow charge hand grenade that was steered by strips of cloth to obviate somersaulting. It was ignited by means of an impact detonator.

This article cannot claim to be complete. My goal was to make the reader familiar with this interesting type of explosive that was extensively pioneered during the Second World War by the Germans, not to write a complete textbook on the topic. However, today hollow charges and hollow charge ammunition are used by the armies of the whole world. The veil of secrecy has long been lifted.

G. Wirnsberger

MANNLICHER-SCHOENAUER RIFLE MODEL 1900

In 1900 the Steyr Gun Factory introduced a 5-shot bolt-action rifle with rotary magazine: the model Mannlicher-Schoenauer, an improvement on the rifle designed by Otto Schoenauer and J. Werndl in 1885. It has a dual lug turn bolt which cocks the striker when the action is opened. The magazine resembles that incorporated in the 87/88 model; it is rosette-shaped in cross section and its centre spool is driven to the right by a spring. This spool can be easily removed by rotating the magazine floorplate, and the cartridges are thrown out by depressing a button on the right side of the receiver. A fresh cartridge can be loaded after each shot fired.

The 6.5 x 54 mm cartridge for this rifle is rimless. In 1903 this Mannlicher was adopted by the Greek Army (Model 1903, later Model 1903/14), and during WWI Mannlicher-Schoenauer rechambered it for the Mauser 7.9 x 57 mm cartridge. From then on the Mannlicher was called the Modell 1915 and was provided with a bolt sleeve lock, as were the Mauser rifles. After the war the Steyr-produced Mannlicher-Schoenauer rifles fell into Italy's hands as booty, and so the Breda factory continued to manufacture them, usually stamped with the year 1927.

The 1903 model also became extremely popular as a sporting rifle. When Steyr first delivered to the commercial markets in 1904, the Mannlicher-Schoenauer rifles were chambered for 6.5 x 54 mm, later for 8.2, 9, 9.5 mm, and later still for 7 x 64, 8 x 60, 7.62 x 63 (.30–06), 4 x 57, 9.3 x 62 and 10.75 x 68.

In 1950 the first post-war replicas became available in a number of versions, chambered for 6.5 x 54 M.Sch., 6.5 x 57, 6.5 x 68, 7 x 57, 7 x 64, 8 x 57 IS, 8 x 60 S, 8 x 68 S, 9.3 x 62, .243 Win., .257 Roberts, .270 Win., .30–06 Spr., .358 Win., and .358 Win. Magnum.

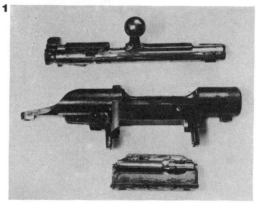

1 *The turn bolt and bolt housing of the 1900 model. Side view of rotary magazine (Mannlicher patent 1900).*

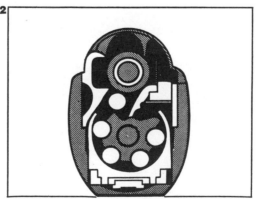

2 *Cross section of magazine, viewed from the front. The cartridges are stacked in a series of concave troughs in the rotary spool.*

Wolff Heinrich, Prince zu Stolber-Stolberg

Air Gun
in Flintlock Disguise

In an article entitled, "The Arms Collection at Baldern Castle," **International Arms Review** reported on a flintlock musket that in reality was an air gun, with a powerful pump in the buttstock. The caption read, "The lock and cock actually work, but there is no ignition passage between pan and breech."

Of course, a vent hole for an air gun would be superfluous. All the same, I feel the lockwork on the gun described had a practical as well as an aesthetical function. The design of the lock is particularly suitable, in a very ingenious way, for operating the valve mechanism of an air gun.

Among the few weapons I managed to salvage is an air gun of virtually the same design as that described in

the article above, and which stems from the first quarter of the 18th century.

It has an overall length of 51.4 inches, and the smooth brass barrel of 10 mm (.394 in.) in calibre measures 34.4 inches. The barrel is encased in a highly polished brass tube, measuring 37.4 inches, that becomes angular at the breech end, that is, over the forearm. It runs conically from breech to muzzle, and the top edge is beautifully engraved. In the barrel tang there is a screw hole which can only have served to hold the rear sight, possibly a peep-sight. The hollow case that surrounds the true barrel, but which looks like the actual barrel of a musket itself, is a chamber for storing the compressed air. A brass tube runs from the base of the air chamber down to the butt of the stock, with a piston stroke of 11.8 inches. A non-return valve joins air chamber and pumping system. The head-piece of the pumping rod juts out of the butt, to which a handle was probably fitted.

On the underside of the hollow tube, in line with the frizzen spring, is a pin that activates a valve for closing or opening the air chamber at the barrel end. Once the trigger is pulled, a connecting lever lifts the valve pin to release the air.

If you look carefully, you can see the connecting lever on the left of the lockplate, which is tipped by the hook-like nose of the tumbler. The collar of the lever lifts the valve pin. Atop this is the return spring that forces the sear into the bent of the tumbler. The cock serves as cocking lever only. Still, its jaws are so designed that a flat piece of metal, instead of a flint, can be held to strike the frizzen (just an ornament) thus preventing the cock from breaking.

Regrettably, there are no stamps or markings on this air gun. So there is no way of learning the maker. Furthermore, the shape of the slugs and the material they were made from remain unknown, too, as well as exterior ballistics. It would be interesting to learn whether or not the slugs were loaded with a patch, in the same manner that balls were rammed down muzzle loaders.

Although secret drawers, cane sticks, poisonous rings, fireplace emergency exits, etc. were all the rage in the 18th century, I am still not entirely convinced that this disguised air gun was intended to be a secret weapon.

Owing to the small number of air guns made, the gunsmiths probably used the locks of flint weapons that were available at that period of time. Special locks for air guns would have followed the style of the period anyway, only the frizzen and flashpan would have been omitted, and the cock perhaps slightly changed in its shape.

A Revolver from the Cutlery Town of Solingen

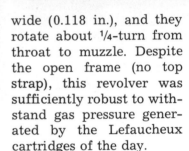

The town of Solingen in West Germany, not far from Cologne, was for centuries a famous centre for the edged-weapons industry. Even today Solingen is still the nucleus of Germany's cutlery trade. Still, it is not generally known that the Solingeners once also produced revolvers. Round about 1866 a few factories of this town started to include revolvers in their production programme, but only as a side line. The firm of Friedrich and Robert Höhmann, who made knives, sugar tongs and similar household articles, employed a gunmaker by the name of Gustav Böntgen to manufacture the revolver that is the subject of this report. Ill. 3 shows this firm's trade mark, an HB separated by a crown, stamped on the left-hand side of the barrel. Frame, cylinder and barrel are forged, and the lock mechanism, believe it or not, is a double action one. Of course, as might be expected, a tremendous amount of finger energy is required to lift and drop the hammer when bringing the double action trigger into use. But when the hammer has been thumb cocked in advance, trigger pull decreases to about 14 oz. The

gap between cylinder and rear barrel, measured with a slip gauge, is only 0.09 mm (0.00354 in.), which represents a wonderful achievement in engineering. The ejector rod, mounted on the right side of the frame, is used to poke out empty cases, rearwards through the gate. In order to remove the cylinder, the base-pin screw on the left side of the frame, plus a second screw just beneath the base-pin screw, must be removed. Barrel and cylinder can then be lifted away from the frame. The cylindrical barrel, having an outside diameter of 17 mm (0.669 in.), is integral with the leading strap of the frame. Apropos of rifling, the bore measures 11 mm (0.433 in.) across the lands, and 11.65 mm (0.459 in.) across the grooves.

The 4 grooves are 3 mm wide (0.118 in.), and they rotate about ¼-turn from throat to muzzle. Despite the open frame (no top strap), this revolver was sufficiently robust to withstand gas pressure generated by the Lefaucheux cartridges of the day.

On 10th September, 1866, the Town Fathers of Solingen resolved to establish a Revolver Proof House. In the following year, on 28th February, 1867, the "Probieranstalt für Schußwaffen" was inaugurated, after being ratified by the Prussian War Ministry and by the Minister for Industry and Trade. Revolvers that passed the tests were stamped on barrel and cylinder with an SP within a dotted oval (Solinger Probieranstalt) and the Prussian Crowned Eagle (Ill. 2). On the other hand, revolvers that did not stand up to the tests were stamped with an A (Ausschuß), which means scrap or reject.

The work at the Proof House was undertaken by an Inspection Unit of the Prussian Army, upon which quality control of edged

Technical data

Calibre	12 mm (.472 in.)
Chambers	6
Rifling	4 grooves, right-hand twist
Finish	Barrel and cylinder browned, frame blank, engraved and polished
Cartridge	Pin type (Lefaucheux)
Barrel length	155 mm (6 in.)
Overall length	290 mm (11.4 in.)
Grips	Ebony, checkered

weapons ordered by the Armed Forces was also incumbent. It is not known whether revolvers from Solingen were bought by the Army. However, by the end of 1868 some 2076 Solingen revolvers had been Proof House stamped. The model illustrated was sold

**Text and Photos
K. Jörgens**

commercially, and its first owner was a citizen of Solingen. His name is engraved across the top of the barrel. Again, it is not known just how many revolvers were produced in Solingen. The manufacture of revolvers seems to have dwindled enormously during the 1870/71 Franco-Prussian war, as edged weapons were of greater importance. After this war Solingen ceased to make revolvers...

4

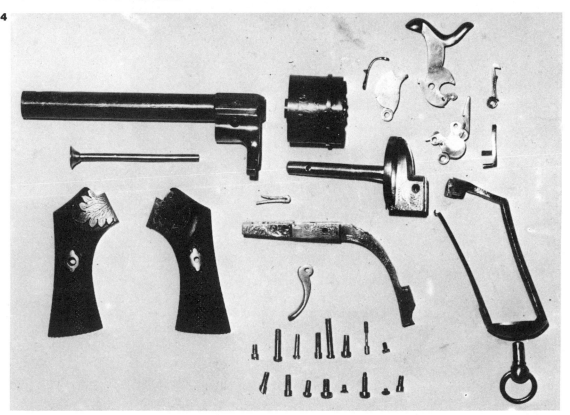

Hans Widhofner

CASELESS AMMUNITION

Some years ago the newspapers made quite a splash with the news that Smith & Wesson had bought out the rights for Austrian invented caseless' ammunition. We were told that this invention would probably revolutionize the arms and ammunition industry.

Ordinarily, a cartridge consists of the bullet, the powder charge, the primer, and the case (Fig. 1). Only the powder charge (propellant) and the primer are absolutely necessary to fire a bullet out of a gun. Just think of the muzzle loaders our grand-dads use to fire, and of today's grenade launchers, which are also muzzle loaders (Fig. 2). Then again, a number of breech-operated field guns exist that are loaded separately with shell, propellant, and primer. In many instances a huge cartridge would be too cumbersome to handle without hoisting equipment.

After this bit of information we must begin to wonder how the metallic cartridge as we know it today came into being.

Evolution of the cartridge

Originally, the rifleman carried his bullets in a pouch and his powder in a powderhorn or powderflask. However, to facilitate and speed up loading, bullet and a pre-measured amount of powder were wrapped in a paper envelope towards the end of the 17th century. The rifleman bit off the top of the envelope, poured the pow-

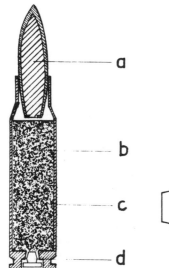

Fig. 1. 7.62 NATO cartridge a = bullet, b = propellant, c = case, d = primer

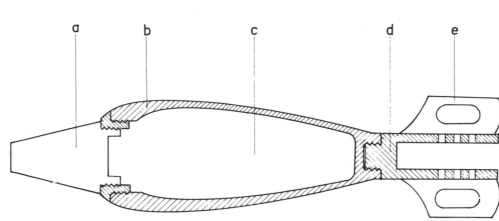

Fig. 2. 81 mm grenade, a = detonator, b = cowling, c = explosive charge, d = tailpiece with primer powder and propellant, e = stabilizing fins, mounted with metal clips.

der down the barrel, shoved the envelope down after the powder as a wad, and then crowned this duo by ramming down the bullet. With percussion guns, a cap was then pushed on to the nipple.

Malicious tongues assert that even today a recruit with missing front teeth will be turned down by the army ...

Another step forward was made when the Model 1841 needle gun, a breech loader, was introduced in Prussia. Bullet and powder were now wrapped up with a primer capsule, making a so-called fixed cartridge. The needle gun could be loaded and fired three times faster than the muzzle

loaders of the non-German armies. This fixed ammunition consisted of a cylindrical cardboard casing, a sabot (a prop for keeping the bullet in position) made of crushed paper, bullet and powder charge. The primer capsule was seated in the base of the sabot. A long needle, in lieu of today's firing pin, passed through the outer casing and the powder charge before igniting the capsule (Fig. 3).

Metallic cartridges

Progress was really under way when copper or brass cartridge cases, with primers in the case head, appeared. Breech loaders were now here to stay! Expanding brass cases sealed the breech at the moment of firing, making rubber rings and complex breech seals superfluous. Magazines were an obvious follow-up of the metallic cartridge. Furthermore, the metallic

cartridge paved the way for semi- and full-automatic weapons.

The case

We have emphasized the fact that a cartridge case is not absolutely necessary to fire a bullet out of a gun. Nevertheless, this case does perform a host of useful functions:

a) Metallic case for bullets

1. Medium for joining bullet, propellant and primer.
2. Protection for propellant and primer, i. e. against humidity, dirt and oil (automatic weapons are usually kept well oiled).
3. Protection against rough handling and blows.
4. Bullet is positioned by case, and case can be loaded and unloaded a number of times.

CASELESS AMMUNITION

5. The case expands when the shot is fired, forming a perfect seal for the breech. After the shot, the case contracts to its original diameter, or nearly so, allowing for easy extraction.

6. A cylindrical case withstands mechanical feeding, chambering and extraction in a machine gun. Some MGs fire 1200 rounds a minute, or faster in special aircraft guns. Deformed cases would cause fatal stoppages.

7. The case bears the brunt of the heat generated during the explosion, and, therefore, protects the firing chamber from burning out. By the same token, the case helps to keep the gun from overheating.

8. The case retains most of the powder residue, keeping firing chamber and barrel relatively free from corrosion and fauling.

b) Cardboard cases for shotgun pellets

The arguments propounded under a) generally hold good for b) too. Shotgun cases (or hulls) are made of non-metallic materials as they only have to withstand pressures of approximately 10,000 lb. per sq. inch, whereas metallic cases withstand pressures up to 55,000 lb. per sq. inch.

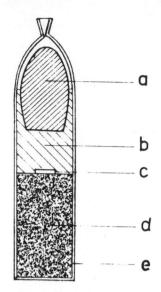

Fig. 3. *Self-contained cartridge for needle gun, a = bullet, b = sabot, c = primer capsule, d = propellant, e = envelope.*

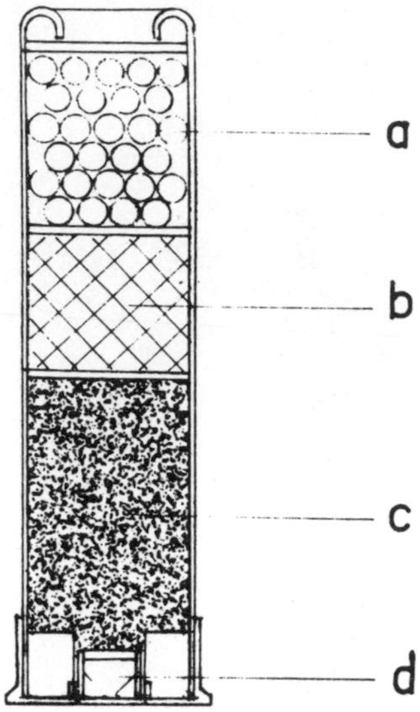

Fig. 4. *Shotgun shell, a = pellets, b = wad, c = propellant, d = primer.*

Of course, cardboard is not as robust and as weatherproof as brass; still, it is considerably cheaper than brass, and is all that is required for the huntsman.

The disadvantages of a case

Obviously, production costs are high for a case fulfilling so many prerequisites. So many demands have to be satisfied when designing and manufacturing a cartridge case that the cost of the case equals that of bullet, powder charge and primer.

The weight of a cartridge case also approximately equals the weight of bullet, powder charge and primer put together. For example, the bullet of the NATO 7.62 mm round weighs 150 grs., the powder charge 45 grs., and the case 185 grs. The Axis Powers ran out of

brass in both World Wars. Church bells were melted down to meet the need, or lacquered steel was used. For some purposes steel is better than brass, but steel cartridge cases are difficult, and even more expensive, to produce.

Arriving at a common denominator, we may claim that caseless ammunition can be manufactured in half the time, at half the weight and at half the price of fixed ammunition. Aspects of this nature would make caseless ammunition particularly interesting to the Armed Forces.

Caseless ammunition

Various groups have been experimenting along these lines. Örlikon, a famous Swiss arms and ammunition manufacturer, attempted to solve this problem about 40 years ago, before Hitler went to war. However, in 1939 experimentation was stopped,

Caseless and primerless ammunition

In 1964, the Amt für Wehrtechnik of the Austrian Army became aware of a powerful spark igniter developed by an Austrian for underwater blasting. The inventor also proposed that water should replace the powder charge for firing a projectile. The spark would evaporate the water and propel the bullet out of the gun. Of course, obtaining energy through evaporation is not new by any means.

The Austrian Army requested this spark-igniter inventor to focus his energies on an igniter system for caseless and primerless ammunition. By 1965 a condenser replaced the spark igniter. First the current from the mains was used, then a 12-volt accumulator, and finally two miniature batteries.

Herr Stoll, an army engineer, informed us that an electrically operated 9 mm submachine gun could fire full-automatic and single shots. Despite the fact that only about 30 hand-made caseless bullets had been made for the trials, feeding and ejection worked perfectly. At the moment, more detailed information is not obtainable.

What does the future hold?

The road is long and stony from successful tests to thoroughly fieldtested, militarily accepted equipment. Prof. Hanisch emphasized again and again the importance of inventing a pellet that leaves no residue behind. Pellets have no case to remove fouling. Storage of these pellets is yet another problem, but this seems to have been solved in the meantime.

Great things are also expected of the electric igniter and batteries, although size, service life and proper functioning under all weather conditions are problems in themselves. The firing chamber will have to be sealed by some other means, as there is no case to expand. The fact that Smith & Wesson has invested money and brains in further experiments, shows just how important this project for America is. Since the Americans have already gained a lot of experience in explosive pellets for the rocket industry, the outcome of the idea of caseless ammunition is a fair challenge.

We must assume other nations are also doing a bit of experimentation behind the scenes. So perhaps in the near future we shall be able to write more about the accomplishments of this ultra-modern ammunition. At the moment, progress is being subjected to military hush-hushery.

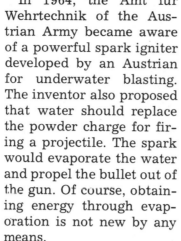
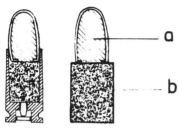

Fig. 5. *Left 9 mm round, right 9 mm caseless round, a = bullet, b = explosive pellet.*

as Switzerland feared an all-out German attack, and badly needed scientific personnel in other areas.

Needless to say, the Germans tried to find a solution to caseless ammunition during the war. Flake powder was compressed into hard pellets, on to which a lead bullet was pasted. As far as is known, this project flopped, as the primer, stuck to the other end of the pellet, usually fell into the raceway of the breechbolt, causing a serious stoppage. The introduction of "blow-out" slots to puff fired primer away from the gun also ended in failure. And although some genius then decided to have the spent primers follow the bullet down the barrel, this venture somehow bobbled too. The only alternative was to ignite a propellant direct by electric current.

"We shall compete
with cannon at
Eichenen near Tuttlingen,
and trust we shall
win the Hertzoglich
Württempergisch
Artillery-Companie
prize, awarded
by the Lord Mayor.**"**

Hans-Herbert Frank

THE HUBBUB OF CANNON

The announcement of a "cannon happening" at Steinbruch, West Germany, did not promise very much. However the Cannoneers and gunners soon secured recognition and respect, thanks to outstanding performance. Twelve miniature cannon bellowed away at targets, laid siege to a castle, and set two houses on fire. Match shooting with miniature copies of medieval cannon celebrated a loud and cheery debut, as this spectacle provided a welcome change for both the shooters, in black dress and top hats, and the onlookers. Members of the French, American and German army, and Swiss hobbyists, arranged this meeting. These fournations entered into a full-scale duel to win the "Hertzoglich Württempergisch Artillery-Compagnie" (sic.) prize, and the notice reading, "Attention! Keep Clear, Range Firing With Live Ammunition", was to be taken seriously. The cannon thundered and fired for all they were worth, and, believe it or not, they really did hit the target, bullseyes in many instances, about 33 yards away. Indeed, these toys for adults, replicas showing greatest detail of original cannon, were accurate enough to squarely knock down a target at up to about 70 yards. Proof enough that the metal-working apprentices of Messrs. Georg A. Henke, Tuttlingen, were on

"As ye all knoweth,
we have dedicated
ourselves to the art
of the artillerist."

the right path to become master craftsmen. The German boys had constructed these cannon entirely in their free time. In actual fact, the idea was conceived by Dr. Monauni, the manager of the metal works. Some years ago he had seen a miniature cannon used as a paper weight on someone's desk in Italy. The owner not being willing to sell, Dr. Monauni picked up tools and turned the cannon on a lathe. When the German apprentices saw this beautiful model they wanted to prove to him that they were just as talented.

The competition involving the four nations was divided into rapid – fire and slow-fire courses. Officers of the German Army refereed the match, putting the scoring under Teutonic surveillance! As in real life, the cannoneers had to await the order to fire. When the cannon besieged a castle and set fire to two houses, the onlookers really did begin to marvel at the fire-power of these little monsters. The prize, a clock presented by an American air line, was won by the hosts with a 30

cm cannon. Paradoxically, the German artillerists from Immendingen, the professionals, came last. All the same, Lieutenant-Colonel Stachwitz, commander of the 295th Feldartillerie-Bataillon, presented a regimental plate to the lord mayor, Herr Balz, patron of the event, as a memento of the glorious occasion. The German Army had not only acted as referee, they displayed a 10.5 cm howitzer, a target finder, and handed out free soup into the bargain. While the soldiers were busy ladling out thick, whole-pea soup, the lord mayor broached a big cask of beer, so nobody went home hungry or thirsty. The contestants enjoyed them-

selves so thoroughly that they have decided to do a repeat in the years to come.

Vom Hofe O/U

**Text and Photos
Dr. Manfred Rosenberger**

Ever since the inception of firearms, aesthetically made guns have held a place of honor. A rifle, for example, was not simply an instrument of death, it was also a work of art. It is not by accident that we speak of the Art of the Gunmaker.

Of course, today very few sporting weapons can be awarded the rating "magnificent." Mass produced run-of-the-mill specimens can hardly be individual or artistic. The crux of this dilemma is that the old-generation gunsmiths, craftsmen in the strictest sense, have virtually died out, without having passed their skills on to young blood.

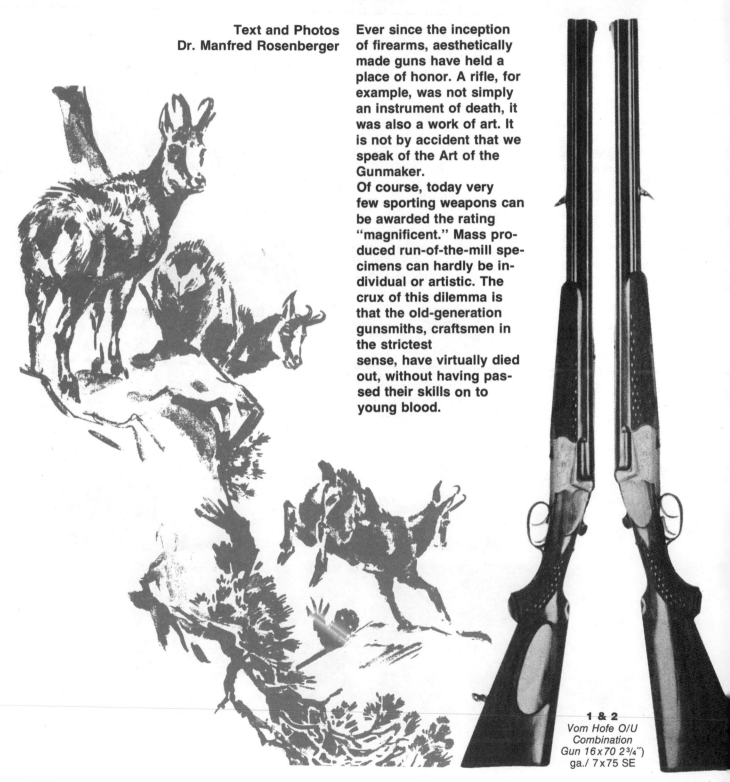

1 & 2
*Vom Hofe O/U
Combination
Gun 16x70 2¾")
ga./ 7x75 SE*

Combination Gun

The vom Hofe O/U combination gun comes with a Ferlach boxlock action with hammers, springs and sears mounted on the trigger plate in Blitz fashion, employing a Kersten locking system with double underlugs. This locking system consists of two underlugs, two barrel extensions, a double cross-bolt, a double flat-bolt, hinge pin, top snap, top snap lever, and top snap shaft (Fig. 3). The two barrel extensions mate with slots in the standing breech (Figs. 4 & 5), where the double cross-bolt passes through the holes in these extensions (Figs. 6, 7 & 8). Together with the twin underlugs, this cross-bolt system makes for the most durable lock-up available among top-break guns. All the same, an excellent bolting system is useless if the parts do not fit to perfection. For a long service life, surfaces must be mated to the closest tolerances, so that the chamber end of the barrels rests perfectly against the standing breech before the bolts are inserted. Close fitting is still

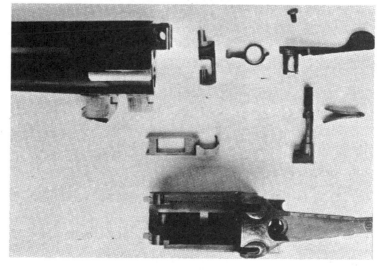

◀ **3** *The component parts of the Kersten locking system. Top: Barrel with extensions and underlugs, double cross-bolt, top snap lever, top snap. Centre: double flat-bolt, top snap shaft, top snap spring. Bottom: receiver.*

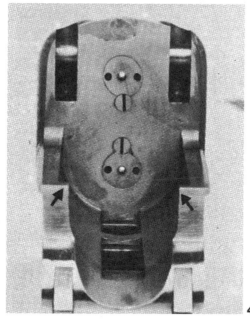

4

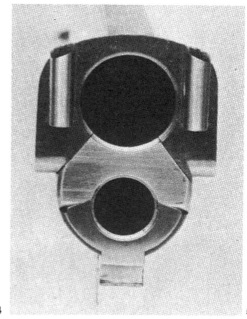

5

4 *The two barrel extensions mate with slots in the standing breech, and are arrested by the cross-bolt. Arrows point to abutments which activate the extractor when the gun is broken.*

5 *The chamber end of the barrels is stoutly proportioned to give extra stability along the breech joint.*

16 (2 ¾") ga.
7 x 75 SE

6 *The gun broken.*

Vom Hofe O/U Combination Gun

hand work and therefore a challange to every gunsmith worth his salt. On no account should the crossbolt rattle in the receiver; both ends must fit perfectly into the holes of the barrel extensions, no grating or looseness can be tolerated. If barrels and breechface do not match with hair-line precision, pitching and pulling will develop as the cartridge explodes and will destroy the union entirely, showing ugly gaps between the breechface and barrels.

The same must be said for the flat-bolt underlugs combination. The bolt slips into the cutouts at the rear of the lugs (Figs. 9, 10 & 11.)

The flat-bolt, like the cross-bolt, acts against the pitching movement. Pull-off movement, on the other hand, is countered by the bearing surfaces of the cross-bolt (and of the receiver) chiefly by the hinge

pin and the front underlug. The flat-bolt must not chatter in its guideway, and, of course, it must engage in the cutouts of the underlugs without a murmur of slack. Of the utmost importance is that the semi-circle of the front underlug must correspond with the circumference of the hinge pin exactly. The same holds true for the curvature of the other surfaces of the underlugs. Shoddy work will surely lead to rattling later on.

When the top snap is activated, the top snap lever pushes the crossbolt out of the side of the receiver. At the same time, the flat-bolt is withdrawn from the cutouts in the underlugs (Figs. 7, 9, 10 & 12.)

The chamber end of the barrels is stoutly proportioned (Figs. 5 & 8) in order to give extra stability along the breech joint.

In accordance with the Blitz system, both hammers are mounted on the trigger plate (Figs. 13 & 14.) Since the rear ends of the firing pins stick out to the left of the top snap shaft (Fig. 12,) the hammers are also placed one atop the other, on the left of the receiver (Fig. 14.) The hammers rotate in normal fashion around an axle pin, and are guide-assisted by the cam-face of the axle support (Figs. 15 & 16.)

When the action is broken, the two cocking levers are see-sawed about their axles as the forearm moves downwards; an action that pushes the hammers back to full cock. See

7

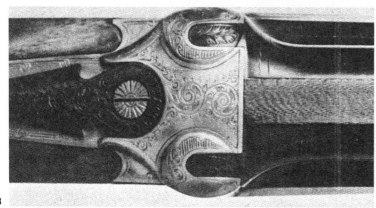

8

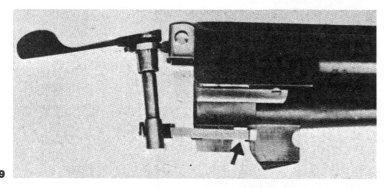

9

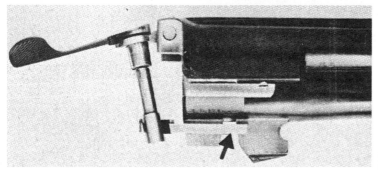

10

7 The top snap, via the top snap lever, pushes the cross-bolt away from the barrel extensions.

8 Top view of receiver. Notice how well the extensions fit into their slots.

9 & 10 The top snap shaft guides the flat-bolt into the cutouts of the underlugs.

Figs. 15, 16, 17 & 18. Once a trigger is pulled, its shoulder nudges the sear, which is holding the hammer in cocked position, out of the hammer notch. The mainspring then drives the hammer forward, against the firing pin (Figs. 17 & 18.)

The front trigger for the rifle barrel can be hair set, and finely adjusted. The trigger plate has a short screw at the front end and a long tang screw at the rear that holds the buttstock to the receiver (Fig. 19.)

The safety unit comprises the thumbpiece, operating rod, elbow lever, and spring (Fig. 20). The front end of the operating rod passes through a hole in the receiver (Fig. 12,) and comes to rest against the top snap shaft. When the top snap is thumbed to the right, to open the action, the operating rod is forced back, nudging the elbow lever over the upright posts of the triggers (Figs. 21 & 22.)

The undulating rear edge of the silver-grey receiver snuggles firmly into the buttstock, and makes for a stronger joint.

In conformity with the stoutly proportioned chamber end of the barrels, matched by the large-area facing the standing breech, the inside angle of the receiver has been heavily reinforced in the Ferlach style. See Figs. 23 & 24. Flanks, floor and scallops of the receiver, as well as top snap, trigger guard and the chamber end of the upper barrel, are scroll engraved, or beautifully deco-

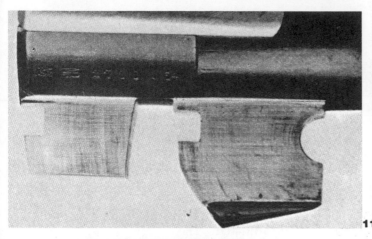

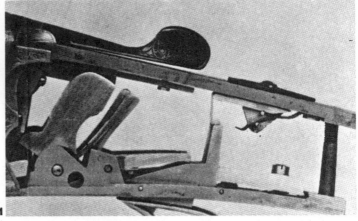

11

13

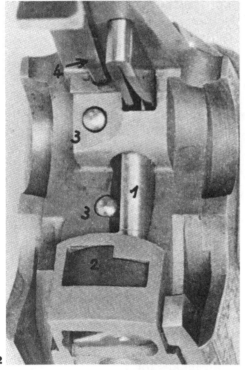

12

14

11 *Of utmost importance is that the semi-circle of the front underlug correspond with the circumference of the hinge pin. The flanks and other surfaces, of course, must tie in perfectly, too.*

12 *The inside of this vom Hofe combo is immaculately finished, and as the illustration shows, "nothing unsightly has been swept under the carpet." 1) top snap shaft, 2) flat-bolt, 3) firing pins, 4) safety operating rod.*

13 *The hammers are pivoted from the trigger plate, in traditional Blitz fashion.*

14 *Arrows indicate the striking surfaces of the over and under hammers.*

rated with hunting scenes. See Figs. 8, 23, 24 & 25.

In keeping with all fine modern top-break shotguns, or combination guns, the firing-pin bushings are screwed into the breechface from the front (Fig. 4.) Blown primers cannot propel a firing pin through the back of the receiver, whereby many an hunter has suffered an injured hand, nor is it a costly repair when the firing-pin orifice has increased in size because of wear and tear. It's simplicity itself to screw out a breechface bushing, if the bushing is faulty or the firing pin needs replacing.

The rifle barrel is of Böhler Antinit steel or Böhler Super Blitz steel, the shotgun barrel of Böhler Blitz steel.

They are pushed into each other at their rear ends, and silver soldered, measuring 25.6 in. in length. The side ribs and ventilated rib are soft soldered too. Extraction does not deviate from standard practice. The two limbs of the extractor run in guides along the rifle barrel (Figs. 5 & 6.) When the action is opened, an abutment on the receiver flanks (Fig. 4) causes the extractor to lift away from the chambers.

The front sight consists of a streamlined silver bead (Fig. 26) mounted on a ramp. The rear sight is a folding leaf with U notch (Fig. 27.) Eye-pleasing is the stock, as it has been shaped from high-quality

Rating

Workmanship	0
Functional safety	0
Performance	0
Finish	1
Design	0
Sights	1
Balance	1
Pointing qualities	1
Stocking	1
	5

Suggested changes: A spiral spring should be inserted to keep the safety operating rod permanently pressed against the elbow levers. Perhaps the cocking lever should be supported by soft springs, too. That would dampen arbitrary movement.
(The lower the number, the higher the rating)

15 & 16 *The hammers are guide-assisted by the cam-face of the axle support (arrow).*

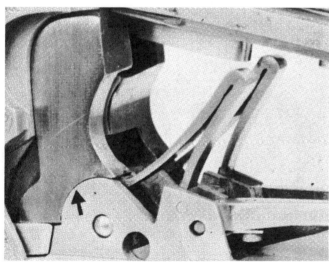

15

16

Manufacturer	W. Gehmann (Karlsruhe and Stuttgart, West Germany)
Type	O/U combination gun (rifle bbl. under)
Designation	Original vom Hofe Bockbüchsflinte
Grade	Standard
Action	Boxlock with Kersten double bolting system, hammerless, firing-pin bushings screwed into front of breechface
Trigger	Each barrel has separate trigger, rifle bbl. trigger may be hair set and finely adjusted
Pull	Rifle bbl. trigger: 3 lb. Shotgun bbl. trigger: 3 lb 5 oz.
Safety	Trigger blocking, automatic. Thumbpiece on stock wrist
Overall length	40.2 in.
Weight	7 lb 5 oz.
Receiver	Die-forged steel, silver grey finished, scalloped rear edge, decoratively reinforced inside angle
Barrels	Rifle: Böhler Antinit steel or Böhler Super Blitz steel Shotgun: Böhler Blitz steel. Barrels are fastened together at their rear ends and silver soldered. Side ribs soldered as far as the muzzle. Length: 25.6 in. Rate of rifling twist: 1 in 11 in. (right-hand). 6 grooves. Shotgun bbl.: full choke
Ammunition	16 x 70 (2¾'') ga. and 7 x 75 R SE (or 5.6 mm vH SE, rimmed)
Sights	Streamlined silver bead and U-notch folding leaf (Slight adjustment by moving mount)
Sight radius	16.9 in.
Stock	Selected walnut. German-type cheekpiece. Straight comb. Scotch checkering on forearm and pistol grip
Dimensions	Overall lenght: 27.9 in. Length of pull (front trigger): 14.2 in. Drop at comb: 1.6 in. Drop at heel: 2.95 in. Pitch: 2.75 in.
Finish	Barrels: black by brush application. Stock: matted. Receiver: Silver grey pickling, beautifully chased with hunting scenes Sling swivels, Plastic buttplate and pistol-grip cap
Extras	Dummy sideplates, richly engraved, Holland & Holland sidelocks, Stag horn trigger guard. Recoil pad, Cartridge trap
Price	ca. DM 4600.– – 4700.– (2,300.– – 2,350.– US $)

17 *Once a trigger is pulled, its shoulder nudges the sear out of the notch of the hammer. The mainspring then drives the hammer forward, against the firing pin.*

18 *When the action is broken, the two cocking levers are see-sawed about their axles as the forearm moves downwards, an action that cocks the hammers.*

19 *The trigger plate sports a short screw at the front and a long tang screw at the rear end. This holds the buttstock to the receiver.*

20 *The safety mechanism consists of thumbpiece, operating rod, elbow lever and spring.*

21 *When the top snap is thumped to the right, to open the action, the operating rod is forced back . . .*

22 *. . .and nudges the elbow lever over the upright posts of the triggers.*

17

18

19

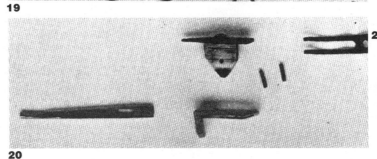

20

21

21

22

22

walnut. The buttstock sports a German-type cheekpiece and a straight comb (Fig. 28.) The wrist is of average length for this type of weapon, and flows into a relatively low pistol grip (Fig. 29.) The slender forearm and pistol grip are finely checkered (Fig. 30.)

We tested a gun bearing the serial No. 2736, which was chambered for the 16x70 (2¾") ga. shotshell and the 7x75 R Super Express vom Hofe. A total of 100 rounds of different brands of shotgun shells (Fig. 31) and 40 factory-loaded soft-nosed car-

Vom Hofe O/U Combination Gun

tridges of both available types (Fig. 32) functioned perfectly in our test gun. As far as finish is concerned, this vom Hofe combo was "immaculate" in every respect. All parts fitted gracefully, and there were no signs of burrs, furrows, or other tool marks, not even hidden away in the interior of the receiver (cf. Fig. 12.) The barrels swung up and down with a pronounced velvety feel, and the bolts took up their positions noiselessly. Indeed, the vom Hofe quality is seldom found these days.

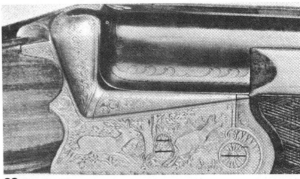

Table I — Averaged results from 10-shot groups

Distance (yards)	109	218
		Diameter of dispersion (inches)
Load		
7 x 75 R 124 grs SP/P/Sto	1.02	2.40
7 x 75 R 170 grs SP/FP/Sto	0.71	1.77

Abbreviations: SP = soft point, P = pointed, FP = flat point, Sto = stopring bullet

25

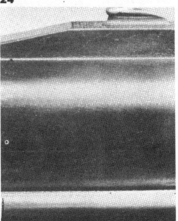

23

24

26

23 *The rear of the receiver is scalloped, making for a tougher union with the stock.*

24 *The inside angle of the receiver has been heavily reinforced in the Ferlach style.*

25 *Note the beautifully cut hunting scenes and artistic scrollwork.*

26 *The front sight is a streamlined silver bead mounted on a ramp . . .*

27 *. . . and the rear sight is a folding U-notch leaf.*

Table II — Ballistic data for 4   7 mm vom Hofe catridges (DWM)

Cartridge		7 mm SuperExpress		7 mm x 75 R Super Express	
Bullet's weight (grs)		124	170	124	170
Type		SP/Sto	SP/Sto	SP/Sto	SP/Sto
Shape		P	FP	P	FP
	Distance (yds)				
Velocity fps	0	3638	3294	3465	3068
	109	3291	3022	3117	2821
	218	2959	2789	2799	2595
	328	2641	2569	2500	2379
Energy ft. pds.	0	3631	4087	3298	3544
	109	2966	3436	2662	3001
	218	2401	2929	2141	2539
	328	1910	2503	1714	2134
Max. height of trajectory (inches)	109	0.985	1.06	1.14	1.06
	218	2.13	2.36	2.60	2.68
	328	4.80	5.48	5.04	5.99

Abbreviations: SP/Sto = soft point/stopring
P = pointed, FP = flat point
Source: Ballistische Leistungen der DWM-Jagdbüchen-Patronen, Ed. 63

The 7 mm SE and the 7x75 R SE are the most potent cartridges of their class (cf. Table II) and may be considered truly universal for hoofed game. The bullet used is known as the Torpedo Stopring, and it has a metal capped hollow point.

We found these two vom Hofe cartridges did exemplary work on small deer and towering moose, irrespective of range. Furthermore, it did not matter much whether we struck bone or flesh. A tough but soft nickel-plated Tombac jacket surrounds a lead core, which, itself, is partly surrounded by a steel ring (Figs. 33 and 34.) This ring, acting in unison with the Tombac jacket, prevents premature decomposition, on the one hand, though the degree of mushrooming is determined by the structure of the target animal, on the other. Traverse cuts around the bullet also help prevent an uncontrolled splattering of lead. Stopring bullets behave best at peak velocities, since they are aerodynamically balanced, and particularly resistant to cross winds.

The full choke shotgun barrel of the test gun easily handled the heaviest loads. Density at 38 yards: 1 = 1.85, regularity: excellent, coverage: 11.2 (excellent), max. effective range: 56 yards. Point of aim and centre of impact were virtually identical at 38 yards. In one case only the primer of an Alphamax shell refused to detonate.

After the trials we found the headspacing of the breech had in no way altered. Balance, pointing qualities and length of stock deserve the rating, "very good," as sights lined up as if by magic when rapidly shouldered.

28 *The stock is of selected walnut. Note straight comb and German-type cheekpiece.*

29 *The wrist flows into a relatively short pistol grip.*

30 *Pistol grip and forearm are adorned with Scotch checkering.*

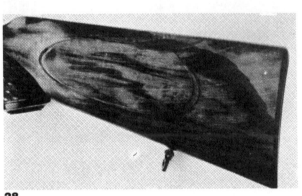
28

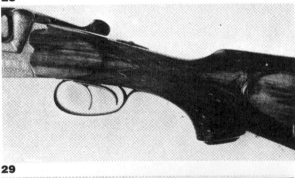
29

30

31

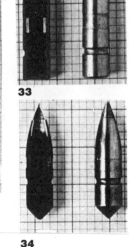
32

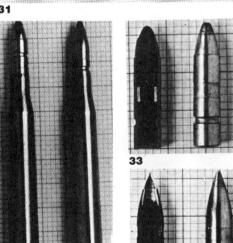
33

34

31 *The shotgun shells we used in our tests.*

32 *The 7x75 R Super Express vom Hofe. Left, 170 grs and right 124 grs. stopring bullet.*

33 *170 grs stopring (7 mm).*

34 *124 grs stopring (7 mm)*

Text and Photos J. B.

THE MP 61 "SKORPION"

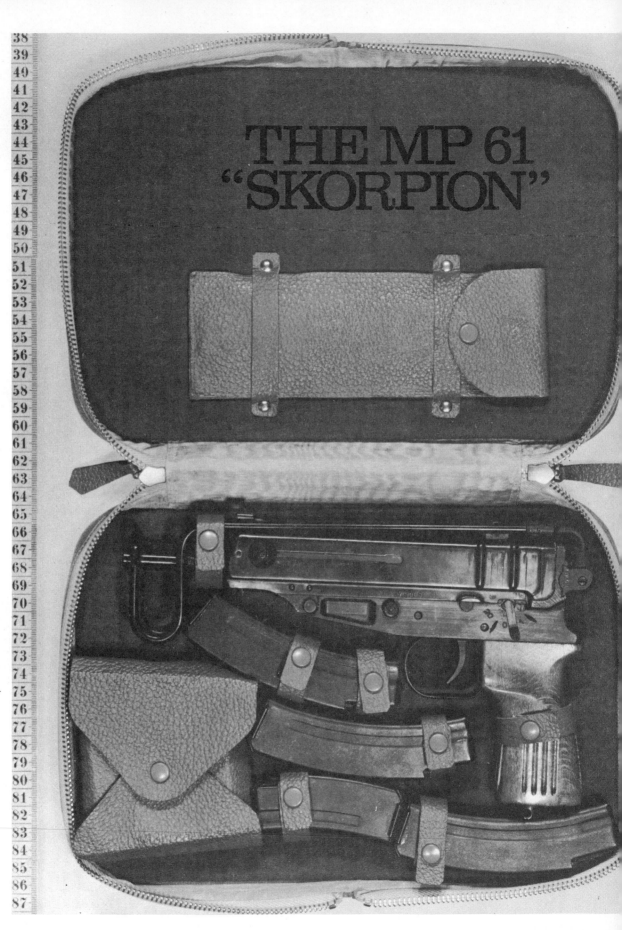

1 *Gun and accessories strapped into place.*

A 7.65 mm Czech (?) Machine Pistol

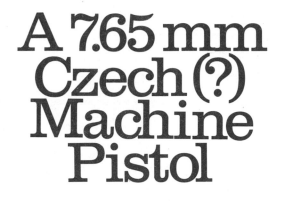

Barrel length 4.45 in.

Lands 6 (right-hand twist)

Fold-over sight for 75 and 150 metres
Blowback design

The MP "Skorpion" is considerably more petite than its predecessors, and is chambered for the 7.65 mm Browning (.32 Automatic) cartridge. This is certainly a unique feature, as all the other known machine pistols and submachine guns are chambered for 7.63 mm Mauser, 7.65 mm long, 7.65 mm Luger, 8 mm Nambu, 9 mm Bergmann, 9 mm Browning short and 9 mm Browning long, 9 mm Mauser, 9 mm Luger, 9 mm Steyr or the .45 ACP. The Czechs, up to now, have made submachine guns chambered for 7.62 mm Tokarev, 9 mm Browning short and 9 mm Luger. The "Skorpion" and its accessories (4 magazines, 3 for 20 cartridges, 1 for 10 cartridges, cleaning equipment, bottle of oil, tools) are packed in what might be mistaken for a gent's dressing case. It measures 12 x 9 x 2.5 in., and is provided with two zips. The label on the case reads: PRAGO EXPORT, MADE IN CZECHOSLOVAKIA.

When the shoulder stock is folded, the "Skorpion" measures 10¼ in., and can be fired as a normal pistol. By means of the selector lever this gun can be made to fire single shots or full-automatic bursts. The "Skorpion" measures 20 in. when stock is unfolded.

2 Carrying case of light-brown, pigskin leather, bearing label: Prago Export, Made in Czechoslovakia.

The selector gives the firer a choice between single shots and full-automatic fire, or "safe".

4 The "Skorpion" with shoulder stock folded forward. Twenty- and ten-shot magazines.

1

THE HEYM DETECTIVE

When looking over a firearm, performance and quality alone cannot serve as guidelines, the price is also an important aspect. Since revolvers are particulary expensive, in this instance we shall start with the pecuniary end first and see what the firm of HEYM in Münnerstadt, West Germany, is offering for the price.

In Germany this revolver costs only DM 154, which is exceedingly low even for this country. With this in mind, now let us see exactly what sort of product the DETECTIVE really is.

When handling this revolver for the first time, you have the feeling that "I have seen this handgun before." You are not far wrong either! For the DETECTIVE is a reasonably fair copy of Colt's Police Positive Special or Detective Special. Dimensions do not

2

**Text and Photos
Klaus Nocher**

quite tally, but the buildup most definitely is that of Colt. However, the HEYM revolvers have a die-cast receiver, yoke and barrel sleeve, the other parts being made of steel.

System: The DETECTIVE is a double-action revolver with a 6-shot swing-out cylinder. It is chambered for .22 L.R., .22 WRF Mag. and .38 Special; but here we are dealing with a .22 L.R. model. The revolver in hand has a 3'' barrel, but 2'' and 4'' barrels are also available.

The barrel has a die-cast sleeve that is pressed and pinned into the receiver. Inside, the barrel is rifled with 4 grooves (right-hand twist); on top it has an integral ventilated rib.

By activating the thumbpiece the cylinder swings out of the receiver to the left. The extractor is guided by a double groove in the body of the cylinder and the ratchet head is aligned by two pins (Fig. 5). In this way

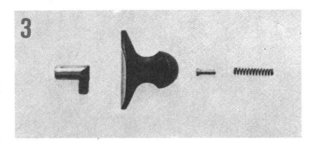

the extractor cannot twist out of position.

In the centre of the ratchet is a hollow into which the nose of the bolt fits when the cylinder is back in the receiver.

The sideplate is fastened by two screws. The entire lockwork is visible once

this sideplate has been removed. See Fig. 6. And by taking off the grips, the lockwork can be lifted out of the receiver (Fig. 7). Here, the similarity between Colt and Heym is again obvious.

Safety: Fig. 8 shows the interplay between trigger, safety bar and safety lever. When the trigger is pulled the safety bar is drawn down, making room for the hammer (Fig. 9). Upon releasing the trigger the rebound slide forces the safety bar over the safety lever; hence the hammer is lifted away from the primer, as is illustrated in Fig. 10. This system is very rugged.

Sights and grips: The DETECTIVE is provided with a square notched rear and a post front sight (too low). See Figs. 11 and 12. Top strap and rib are longitudinally fluted.

1 *The HEYM DETECTIVE, right view*
2 *The HEYM DETECTIVE, left view*
3 *Thumbpiece, spring, pin and bolt*
4 *The cylinder, swung out*
5 *The extractor is rigidly guided*
6 *Lockwork is reached by removing the sideplate*

THE HEYM DETECTIVE

The extra tough grips are of extruded plastic, are checkered and bear the HEYM emblem.

Performance: The revolver being described (No. 03099) was subjected to 200 shots. We used 50 each of RWS (normal and high velocity), 50 Remington (standard) and 50 Pobeda (Fig. 15). No trouble was experienced. However, at 25 meters range the DETECTIVE shot

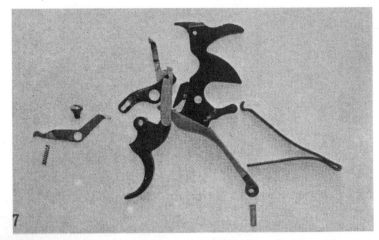

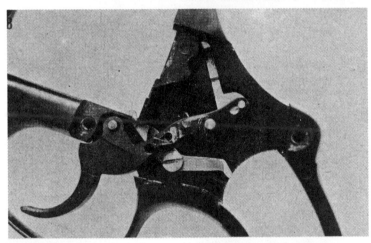

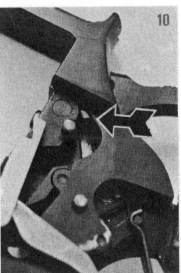

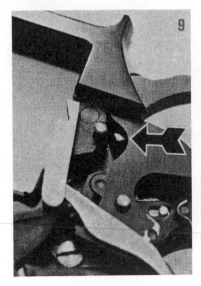

7 Parts of the lockwork
8 The safety rod is connected with the trigger via the safety lever
9 Arrow shows position of safety rod with trigger pulled back and hammer down
10 The safety rod pushes hammer away from primer
11 Square notched rear sight

approx. 25 cm too high. We aimed at 6 o'clock to get into the bullseye. Grouping with all ammunition was about the same (Fig. 14).

Nevertheless, after shooting we discovered that the barrel had loosened from the receiver, and could be turned about ²/₁₀th mm. The rear of the barrel had also collected a fair bit of lead. Still, the gun had not been cleaned during the whole session. Otherwise, no wear and tear was apparent (Fig. 16).

With a second DETECTIVE (No. 03639) we virtually did our own prooftesting to see if we could shoot the barrel loose . . . In rapid succession we fired off 100 RWS High Velocity and 100 Win. High Speed. The shooter did his best to guide the shots into the bullseye, with the bullseye "sitting atop" volver that in regard to price is remarkable. If only HEYM would decide to screw the barrels into the receiver and to line up the sights with point of impact the impression left would be considerably improved.

The German distributor is the firm of HEGE Jagd- und Sportwaffen, Schwäbisch Hall, West Germany.

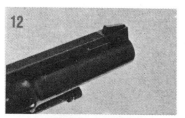

12 The front sight is a little too low
13 The plastic grips are particularly tough
14 Grouping at 25 m (Remington standard vel.)
15 Ammunition we used
16 Breech face after 200 shots: clean and flawless

the front sight. This he achieved, discounting a few strays. Although the DETECTIVE got very hot, the barrel refused to budge. However, after the 70th shot, the RWS cases could hardly be removed from the cylinder; whereas the Winchester cases slipped out without a hitch. The second DETECTIVE was not cleaned during the shooting session either.

The HEYM DETECTIVE is a practical-purpose re-

Technical data

Manufacturer: (Jagdwaffenfabrik Friedrich Wilhelm HEYM, Münnerstadt)
Model: DETECTIVE
System: Double-action revolver
Calibre: .22 L.R., .22 WRF Mag., .38 Special
Barrel lengths: 2, 3 and 4 inches
Twist: Right
Rifling: 4 grooves
Overall length: 170 mm, 200 mm, 230 mm
Weight: 700 gram., 740 gram., 780 gram.
Trigger pull: 2105 gram (measured)

This English flintlock took me two years to produce.

The Making of Small Arms a Century and more ago

Heinz Denig acquaints us with the mystique of master craftsmen of bygone days.

When eyeing a gun of the last century in a museum or an antique shop, we can quickly lose ourselves in contemplation if there is time to ponder. Firearms of yesteryear might be classified as "objects d'art," utilities dressed in the style of the period, or functional implements void of trimming. Still, all antique guns have one thing in common: an aura of mystery. In one way or another, these old-timers seem to evoke a spirit from another world. And when bringing to mind the fact that these guns were handmade throughout, our fantasy begins to wander even further.

There is a man standing in front of his work-bench engrossed in what he is doing. He is filing away at a small piece of metal which occasionally is held against a measuring gauge. Now he is fitting the finished tumbler link between tumbler and mainspring, making sure that the limb doesn't rub against the lockplate . . . Gunsmith, a magic word. A technician skilled in piecing together rifles, shotguns and pistols. The ability to construct a gun is dependent on engineering, physics and chemistry. An ancient master gunsmith was therefore more than a handmaid of the steel industry. He knew the secrets of mixing sulphur, saltpeter and finely ground charcoal with pestle and mortar. Early gunsmiths lived in a superstitious age, and were often decried wizards of black magic.

A firearm is a machine which, when loaded with gunpowder, is in a position to hurl a body, the projectile, with great force through the air. A chemical interaction, released by a mechanical function. That's a sober description of the workings of a firearm.

174

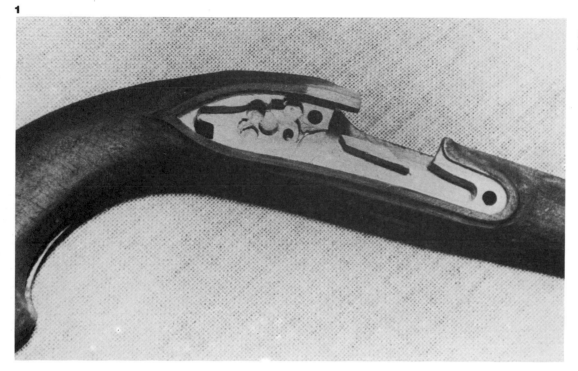

1 *The gouged-out bed for the lockplate.*

These gunmakers showed great dexterity in treating iron and steel, and when they twisted barrels from rods of metal or forged weldless barrels, the workpiece had remarkable elasticity. Even in its finished state, a barrel must remain "fluid," in contrast to the parts of the lockwork, which are as hard as glass but not brittle. The frizzen, the part of the flintlock mechanism that is struck by the flint, also had to be specially tempered. If it were too hard or too soft, or made of the wrong metal, the frizzen would quickly wear out, or not produce an ample quantity of sparks. Then again, the making of springs that will not tire, each designed for a specific function, requires of the gunsmith more than a superficial knowledge of metallurgy. The stock maker (stocker), of course, must be an expert on the usability and workability of many different kinds of wood, including those imported from Africa and other tropical countries. This branch uses a great number of tools – chisels, gouges, floats, shovels, wood files, saws, shaping and checkering tools, etc. The stocker must also be able to custom stock a rifle or shotgun to the requirements and/or anatomy of his client. Moreover, we must not forget the artists in the gun trade who inlay firearms with ivory, silver and gold, or the breath-taking work of the engraver.

Early gunsmiths not only conceived the general design of the weapon for a client, they made virtually all the parts right down to the last screw and pin, with their own hands. And yet many old guns have seen a hundred years and more of life, and shoot impeccably.

Although many an early experimenter was burned at the stake, especially during the 15th and 16th centuries, by the officers of the Inquisition on behalf of the Church of Rome to suppress heresy, gunsmiths were held in high esteem by those people who wielded power; despite the black magic, explosions and offensive smells of brimstone and forge-fires, etc. that were associated with the early gunmaker's profession. It was in the true interest of the Church, as well as of the government of a state, to help the growth and development of the gunmaking trade, since with gunpowder arms heretics and other nations could be more swiftly subdued!

At this point, before I work myself up over technicalities, I want to introduce myself to the reader by informing him that my first firearm was picked up in 1947, just after the war. Although the military government of the Allies strictly prohibited firearms ownership for German nationals, my love for that old gun was not impaired . . . In fact, I was so enamoured of everything pertaining to weaponry that I read avidly on the subject whenever I could.

Soon it was no longer an offense in Germany to collect muzzle loaders, so I sometimes managed to

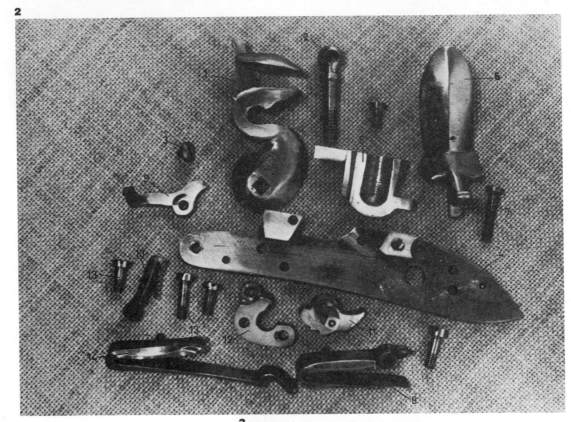

2 *Parts of the lockwork:*
1 *Cock*
2 *Jaw screw*
3 *Screw for cock*
4 *Lockplate*
5 *Pan*
6 *Frizzen*
7 *Screw for frizzen*
8 *Spring for frizzen*
9 *Sear*
10 *Sear spring*
11 *Tumbler*
12 *Bridle*
13 *Bridle screws*
14 *Mainspring*

3 *Complete lock and sideplate.*

4 *Close-up of lock*

procure a broken-down, rusty old specimen. In the meantime I had been apprenticed to an art metalworker, so naturally I experimented with my new knowledge to de-rust, clean and repair a couple of shabby-looking examples. Years later, after I had admired the impressive arms collection at the Berg-Isel musem (I had also read Thierbach's classic), I decided I wanted to make a gun of my own. Still later, I came across an old English flintlock military pistol, badly motheaten but not for sale. However, I did manage to get it on a loan basis. I applied rust remover to the lockplate and gingerly disassembled the whole thing to make exact drawings.

Guided by borrowed gun literature from the middle of the last century, I followed the path of retrogressive development. I chose carbon steel, which is quenched in water, as it is the nearest relative of the steel known to our grandfathers. Old chisels were hammered to form the lockplate. I was kept busy a whole winter before the cock, frizzen and other parts of the lock had been forged and filed down to match the specifications. Apart from a drill, the only machine tool I used was a lathe, to make tumbler and barrel. The circular base of the tumbler rotates in the large hole of the lockplate, whereas the cock is mounted on the four-sided post, on the far side. Furthermore, the bridle, which is screwed to the inside of the lockplate, acts as a second journal bear-

ing. The full-cock and half-cock bents must be most carefully positioned before they are cut into the tumbler. In my early attempts, I found the sear slipped into the half-cock bent when the trigger mechanism was released. Only files of AI quality were used; but the job of making every part fit like a glove, and to work like clockwork, demanded of me tears, sweat and blood. As I felt the using of screws with metric threads was inappropriate in an English pistol, even in replica, I turned my attention to original Whitworth threads. The jaw screw of the cock therefore received ¼ in. BSW thread, the retaining screw for the cock ⅛ in. BSW thread and the bridle screws ³/₁₆ in. BSW thread.

When I got around to fitting the flashpan into the lockplate, winter had passed by and the trees were in leaf again. It was not so much the shape but rather the resilience of the springs that now caused my headache. My colleagues at the workshop knew all about hardening, but a lot less about tempering springs. Of course, they were reluctant to admit their ignorance, thus they sent me on many a wild-goose chase. My books, in their own way, were quite knowledgeable about springs, but they contained nothing on how to make springs **springy.**

Every attempt at reaching the right temper ended in tragedy. I resorted to other types of steel, but when I heated V springs over a bunsen burner or on a hotplate they either turned to "rubber" or gave off a sharp ping, and split . . . The thinner of the two limbs was the first to heat up, so it became soft before the other limb had reached the required temperature.

Although I am a metalworker by trade, that seemingly dead stuff steel began to take on a new significance! I read all about steel, and the treatment thereof, at the city reference library; and I must confess

4

that this extra knowledge stood me in good stead in later years. One day I found what I was looking for without realizing what I had found, for the sentence was so short and simple. A few hours later I dashed back to the book realizing now that I had been rewarded, perhaps by special providence, for my diligence and patience. The sentence read: " . . . or quench the steel in liquid alloys, the melting point or temperature of which corresponds to the temper, then cool off . . ., etc. Liquid metal, uniform heat, irrespective of the various thicknesses of the work-

piece! Was this the solution? I immediately started experimenting with the melting points of lead and tin. The difference between the melting point and tempering heat of lead is only about 10° C.

While lead was melting in a crucible, I prepared 10 trial V springs made of various steels. Low grade steel turned bright red in the flame of the bunsen burner, better grades of alloy-treated steel cherry red. The springs were then hardened either in water or oil. Fleeting wisps of smoke began to ascend from the mouth of the crucible, the lead glowed silvery while blue oxidizing flame flitted across the surface. Into this "quagmire" I plunged the polished springs with the aid of a pair of tongs. The springs, once released from the tongs, bobbed up to the surface.

Within seconds the polished steel changed its colour to blue, and then to grey. I poked the springs under the surface again, in order that the molten lead permeate into the very heart of the metal. One hot spring after another passed through an oil bath, and lay smoking on my work-bench to cool off.

I picked up the first spring, and lightly squeezed it with a pair of pliers. Then I released my grip, and after a few seconds of deliberation I squeezed even harder. The fibres in the steel need time to adjust to their new structure. Gaining courage, I compressed the springs far enough to make both limbs meet. It was a joy to feel the resiliency in my closed hand. The second, the third, and all the others responded in the same way. This made me suspicious, everything was too perfect to be true.

Over night, I compressed all the springs in a couple of vices, to see how they would shape up the following day. Next morning, I discovered that a few of them had lost 1–3 mm in the distance between the two extended limbs. The others were in perfect shape! Strangely enough, the springs that underwent structural change were of carbon and alloy steel. Quenching time probably makes all the difference here; best results can only be achieved through trial and error. However, it must also be documented that the springs that had given way in the first instance kept their shape for the future, even after long-period fatigue tests. As long as the springs were pinched together, the limbs promptly returned to their idle position. However, these V springs just as promptly broke at the knee joint if I pulled the limbs **apart.**

After concluding a number of experiments, I forged, bent, filed and hardened three lockwork springs. The frizzen spring was provided with a tear-shaped extension in front of the retaining screw.

Initially, the sear spring was rather non-yielding; but filing introduced the right degree of flexibility.

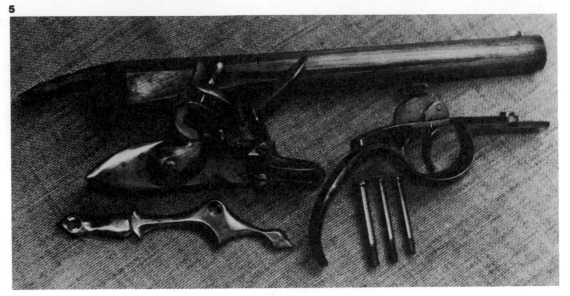

5 *Barrel, lock, support plate, trigger guard and trigger, screws.*

The mainspring, on the other hand, was too flexible, so it had to be re-made completely.

I must say the finished lock looked very new; still, most people would mistake it for the original article. I clamped a hard piece of wood between the jaws of the cock, and thumbed the cock back. The sear rode over the half-cock bent, and engaged in the full-cock bent with a crisp click. Then, when I released the hammer, the piece of wood landed with a wham against the frizzen, throwing it up in the process. I did not rehearse this too often, as the other lock parts had not been hardened. To harden the frizzen, I dipped it into oil before the colouring had passed its straw-yellow phase. Molten lead would have been an excellent quenching medium, too.

The lathe I used had seen a number of metalworkers come and go. The name of its manufacturer had not been listed in the Industrial Directory for more than 30 years. New and better machines are introduced each year, yet the most perfect machine of all remains one's hand.

The thickness of a barrel wall is based on the formula that regards powder charge, pressure and tensile strength of the material used. Though the calculation produced a thinner walled barrel than the one in the original pistol, I placed reliance on my figures. A 25 cm barrel sporting a 17 mm bore was turned and drilled on that old lathe. For the tang screw a thread of 11 intervals to an English inch was cut into the barrel extension. The rear third of the barrel was filed to an octagon, though no two sides were equal. And the front bead was soldered near the muzzle, likewise the escutcheon for the barrel wedge.

The broad, curved trigger was forged, filed and matched to the trigger guard. Trigger guards were usually cast in brass, but I got around this by welding

brass plating together. When finished, the guard resembled the original in all respects.

While scouting around for a nice piece of walnut for the stock, I encountered a hunk of handsome cherry wood. I cut out the contour with a strap saw and then chipped away with a magnificent set of tools lent me by a sculptor who specialized in wood figures. For the sake of accuracy, I coated the belly of the barrel with a mixture of soot and oil so black marks were left on the wood to be carefully shaved away. It took the best part of a week, working a couple of hours every evening, before the barrel fitted with nothing but a hairline to show. After that I started on the bedding for the lockplate. This also would try the patience of Job as blacking and scraping goes on for days on end. Then it happened! While boring the hole for the barrel wedge escutcheon I came out at the wrong place on the other side. Still, I managed to patch up this blunder, and everything fitted perfectly in the inletting.

I loaded my pistol with home-made gunpowder. The cock was thumbed back to half bent, the pan sprinkled with priming charge, the frizzen closed. Remembering old illustrations, I tipped the pistol slightly to the left and tapped it so that the priming charge was heaped against the vent hole. I pulled the trigger when the cock had been readied, but only a sparklet or two resulted. After replacing the flint I tried my luck again. This time the charge went off like an old magnesium flashgun and smoke billowed upward geyser-fashion. But the shot did not go off! I had omitted to drill the vent hole through to the barrel . . . and even today I have not taken the trouble to make good this omission . . .

Meanwhile, I have made a number of replicas of caplock pistols, and I have gained experience with them at the range. I am always thrilled when I fire a home-made pistol for the first time, and the explosion, fire and smoke hurl me back a couple of hundred years in history; at least for a few seconds.

The do-it-yourself gunsmith must not be surprised when I say it took me two years to produce my flintlock. Actually, one day I shall have to spend another week to apply the finishing touches. If everything is done conscientiously, old books on the model you have chosen will have to be found, read, and evaluated. Materials resembling those of the original pistol are not always easy to come by either. Then there is the problem of cutting old-type threads, nor is the rifling of the day simple to copy, etc., etc. I was obliged to design my own lever-action tool to cut appropriate rifling. Rate of twist, the width and depth of grooves and lands can be adjusted in this tool, and pistol barrel rifling takes about three hours of muscle-bracing work.

At the moment I am experimenting with the welding of Damascus barrels made from ribands of iron twisted around a mandrel. There are still a host of problems to be overcome.

Making antique pistols isn't a cheap hobby. Of course, when I started, it was cheaper to make one's own than buy the real McCoy. Since then, however, the gun market has been flooded with inexpensive but good replicas, especially from Italy.

A homeworker skilled in metal and wood working and having experience of model making should be able to create a simple flintlock without inlay-work or engraving in the following time limit, if he works 10 hours a day.

1 Cock complete with upper jaw and screw	2 days
2 Lockplate with all bore-holes and threads . . .	1 day
3 Tumbler, bridle, sear, sear spring and mainspring	3 days
4 Pan, frizzen and frizzen spring	3 days
5 Eight screws and assembly	2 days
Lockwork	11 days

6 Barrel boring, lathework, filing, tang screw . .	4 days
(cannot give time limit for welded barrels)	
7 Trigger and trigger plate, assembled	3 days
8 Trigger guard, cast or welded in brass	3 days
9 Sideplate, barrel wedge, tang screw, buttplate, assembly, etc.	4 days
	14 days

10 Stock, shaping and fitting	5 days

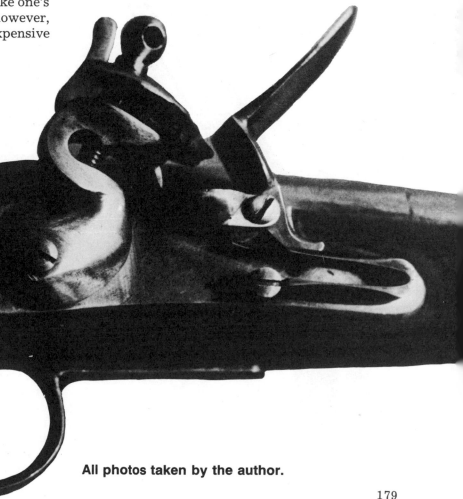

6 *Metal parts mated to wooden stock.*

6

All photos taken by the author.

◄ *Breda quick choke with ventilated rib*

1

BREDA AUTOMATIC SHOTGUN

When, about 75 years ago, the first automatic shotgun was presented to the hunting public, it caused a sensation. After all, at that period of history, some hunters were still shooting with pinfire Lefaucheux and hammer shotguns, as well as with black powder. However, the automatics soon became popular, especially in countries where small game is predominantly hunted. What the new shotguns were capable of was demonstrated in 1909 by Count Ivan Draskovich of Hungary when he downed 1212 cock pheasants in a day. Although he was escorted by gun bearers, and used three guns, his achievements were nonetheless outstanding . . . Still, in other countries, in Germany, for example, automatic shotguns did not gain such a firm footing. Not until after the war, after 1945, did they become more popular.

Since the early prototypes, a flood of new automatic shotguns – each lighter, better and more elegant than its predecessor – has reached the market. However, for the present a standstill in shotgun design seems to have been reached; for two main types of automatics, externally very similar to each other, have crystallized. The first, perhaps the more conventional of the two, is recoil operated and has a reciprocating barrel. The second is gas operated and has a stationary barrel. Nonetheless, both types have the following in common:

1. Barrel and breech are locked together at the moment of firing.

Quick Choke Model

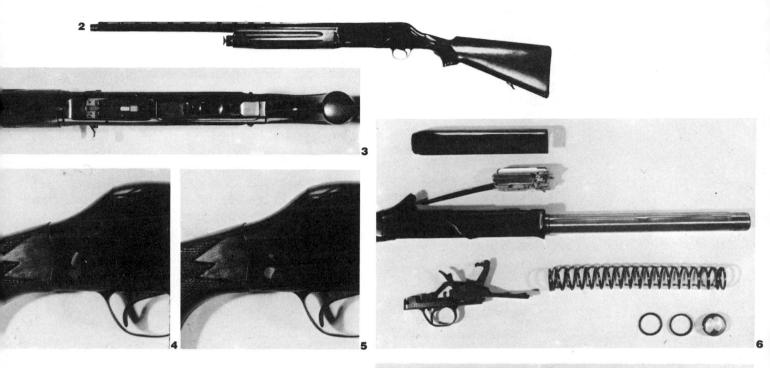

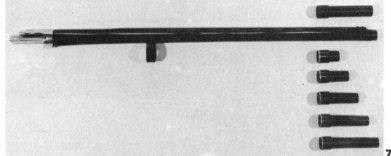

2. The lock does not open until the shot of the shell has left the barrel.

The Breda automatic shotgun is of the conventional recoil type with reciprocating barrel (illus. 1 and 2).

How the Breda works

The best way to load the gun is as follows. Apply the safety lever (illus. 4), then open breech by retracting operating handle to rear latched position. You can now either pop a shell in the open chamber, or lay it on the carrier (illus. 15). Press the carrier latch button on the right side of the receiver (illus. 9) to let the bolt close. During the closing phase of the bolt, the carrier tips up and aligns the shell with the open chamber. As the shell is being chambered, the two extractors ride over the base rim of the shell (illus. 13), and breech bolt and barrel lock together (illus. 19 and 20). The magazine tube (illus. 6), situated in the forearm (illus. 8), is loaded by depressing the carrier latch button again, and then pushing the carrier down to locked positon (illus. 3). The Breda magazine will accept 4 12/65 ga. shells or 3 12/70 ga. The magazine spring follower forces the shell towards the carrier. Once the carrier is activated again, by pressing the carrier latch button, the gun is ready to fire, providing the safety catch is released. On pulling the trigger, the hammer is released from the

1 (left) Breda quick choke with ventilated rib
2 Left view
3 Seen from below. Carrier in down position
4 Safety applied
5 Safety disengaged
6 Receiver cover, bolt assembly, magazine tube, trigger assembly, recoil spring, recoil spring washer, bevelled brake ring, and friction brake
7 Five chokes and amplifier, with barrel

AUTOMATIC SHOTGUN

sear post, and the flat hammer spring drives said hammer against the firing pin (illus. 13), which is housed in the breech bolt. Recoil propels barrel and bolt, both locked together, in a straight line to the rear, until the bolt strikes against an abutment in the receiver. This rearward motion is decelerated by the recoil spring around the magazine tube, the bevelled brake ring and the friction brake (illus. 17), as well as the action spring (illus. 7) in the buttstock. The recoil spring energizes the barrel, via the brake ring, whereas the action spring activates the breech bolt, here via the bolt link.

Once the bolt strikes against the abutment in the receiver, bolt and barrel move forward again a short distance, that is, until the carrier dog engages in the operating handle (illus. 15). The bolt itself, though, can run forward about another 5 mm. During this

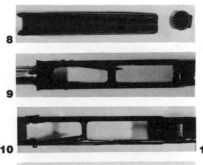

8 Forearm with magazine cap
9 Receiver viewed from above. Note carrier latch button, carrier latch lever, and cut-off lever
10 Receiver viewed from below, with action spring
11 Receiver cover
12 Bolt assembly
13 Parts of the bolt assembly: locking block, breech bolt with extractor claw, operating handle with firing pin and bolt link, bolt plate.
14 Safety lever and take-down pin
15 Trigger assembly: hammer, carrier in down position, carrier dog, and disconnector post on trigger
16 Hammer cocked, carrier in upright position
17 Recoil spring, washer, bevelled brake ring, brake

"second" return phase the lock-up between barrel and breech is disengaged (illus. 19) and the barrel is pulled forward by the recoil spring, extracting and ejecting the empty hull at the same time. A fresh shell slips on to the carrier, since the returning barrel momentarily released the shell catch levers. As the carrier tips upwards, the breech block closes and rams the shell into the chamber. However, the gun cannot fire until the trigger has been released from the previous shot, that is, the hammer must be freed from the disconnector (illus. 15). After the last shell has been fired, the breech block remains open for reloading.

To unload the Breda, depress carrier latch button and push carrier down to locked position. Now depress bolt pawl which will release all shells in the magazine. Clear the chamber by retracting the

operating handle. If, however, the shooter wishes to change the type of shell in the chamber, but not in the magazine, he need only activate the magazine cutoff lever on the left side of the receiver. The shells in the magazine can no longer feed into the chamber, and the shell in the chamber is removed by operating the bolt.

The friction brake requires adjustment for light and heavy loads. This is accomplished by rotating the bevelled brake ring away from the bronze friction brake for light loads, and towards it for heavy loads. The Breda cannot function properly unless correct adjustment is made for the type of shotshells you use.

This gun is easily field stripped. Commence by opening bolt, then unscrew magazine cap, pulling barrel and forearm forwards, off the magazine tube.

The receiver cover (illus. 11) can also be slid off the front. When the safety catch is placed at an in-between position, it can be lifted out of the receiver. By depressing the carrier latch button, the trigger plate assembly (illus. 15) can be pulled out of the receiver. On thumbing down the bolt pawl, the bolt can be pushed forward over the magazine tube. The action spring, housed in the buttstock, can only be removed by unscrewing the buttplate with an Allen wrench. The gun should not be dismantled further for ordinary cleaning purposes.

15

16

17

Workmanship is excellent. The barrel, receiver and bolt parts are finely machined and, in part, polished. Barrel, receiver and receiver cover are of a deep black. Forearm and buttstock are good quality walnut, and lacquered. However, lacquer does not do well when exposed to outdoor conditions. An oil-impregnated stock would weather better. The pistol grip is on the long side, but the stock (without cheekpiece) is fairly well proprotioned, although still too short for a 6 ft. man. The Breda shouldered perfectly after I slipped on a leather butt cap. Handling is facilitated by the "grippy" forearm. When using the special spanner, no difficulties arose when fitting the choke.

For a number of days, we put the Breda through its paces, and purposely did not clean it. After 1000 shots it was still going strong. The disconnector, however, refused to cooperate on three occasions. So the trigger had to be pushed forward by hand. It did not take us long to eliminate this stoppage, though. Even when the Breda was pointing skywards, the hulls ejected perfectly.

18 Rear section of barrel showing cutaway for locking block
19 Breech unlocked
20 Breech locked
21 Thread for quick chokes. Note arresting pin.
22 Special spanner for mounting chokes

18

21

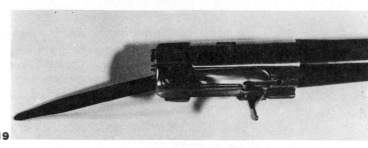

19

22

20

Manufacturer: Breda Meccanica Bresciana S.A., Brescia, Italy

Designation: Automatic Shotgun Model Quick Choke, with ventilated rib

Gauge: 12/70, 12/76, 20/70 and 20/76

Action: Locking, recoil operated

Safety: Lever on right side of receiver blocks trigger

Trigger pull: 2.3 kg

Receiver: Steel, black finish

Barrel: Cylinder, bore coated with hard chrome, ventilated rib, thread for screwing on chokes. Length without choke tube 62.2 cm, with full-choke tube 71.1 cm, black finish

Magazine: Tube magazine in forearm accepting 4 12/65s or 3 12/70s

Stocking: Lacquered walnut, pistol grip but no cheekpiece. Normal checkering on forearm and p.g.

Stock measurements:
Trigger – buttplate	= 36	cm
Drop at comb	= 3.5	cm
Drop at heel	= 6	cm
Pitch	= 6.3	cm

Weight: 3.13 kg

Performance

For these tests we used three different brands of shotshells, but for the sake of convenience stuck to one size of shot for each brand. The Rottweil-Stern, popular for hunting and clay-pigeon shooting, was filled with 2.5 mm (No. 7) shot.

And the black Waidmannsheil was loaded with 3 mm (No. 5). This shell does not have to be introduced, for it has been around for a number of decades. Finally, we chose the Legia Star red which is made at the FN plant in Belgium. It has made a name for itself in Germany, and is filled with 3.5 mm (No. 3).

We fired each brand 5 times through 6 different choke constrictions, and 5 times through a chokeless barrel. Hence, we let off 35 shells of each brand. At a distance of 35 metres we set up our 16-field hunting targets, the results of which can be gleaned from the three tables below. We used the German system of evaluating pellet distribution, as described in the brochure, "Der Schrotschuss".

Frequently, shotgun performance is tested by firing a shell at a 75 cm (29.5 in.) circle 35 m away. The hits within the circle are counted and multiplied by 100, the result then being divided by the number of pellets originally in the shotshell. This system can only be employed when the pellets of at least 5 shells are counted, and an average value calculated. The number of pellets per shotshell as indicated in catalogues, etc. is generally an unreliable source of information. There are considerable differences be-

TABLE 1

Results obtained with ROTTWEIL STERN 12/70 ga. shotshells, 2.5 mm (No. 7), 385 pellets. Range: 35 metres

	1 mm Constriction	0.75 mm Constriction	0.50 mm Constriction	0.25 mm Constriction	0.00 mm Constriction	without choke	1.40 mm amplifier
Number of hits							
Inner circle	100	88	90	87	50	41	40
Outer circle	158	161	156	162	101	99	97
Complete target	258	249	246	249	151	140	137
Density	1:1.90	1:1.64	1:1.73	1:1.61	1:1.49	1:1.27	1:1.24
Regularity	11.8 = good	17.2 = satisfactory	11.2 = good	17.2 = satisfactory	7 = excellent	6 = excellent	11 = good
Covered fields	11.2 = good	11 = excellent	10.6 = good	11 = excellent	3.6 = poor	2.6 = poor	3.6 = poor
Extreme variation of effective hits							
Diameter	60 cm	65 cm	60 cm	65 cm	—	—	—
At distance	35 m	30 m	33 m	30 m	—	—	—
Max. effective range	45 m	42 m	44 m	42 m	28 m	22 m	20 m
Rating	Satisfactory for long range	Excellent for normal range	Excellent for normal range	Excellent for normal range	Good for near range	Good for near range	Good for near range
Pattern in percentage	67 %	65 %	64 %	65 %	39 %	36 %	35 %

TABLE 2

Results obtained with WAIDMANNSHEIL 12/70 ga. shotshells, 3 mm (No. 5), 212 pellets. Range 35 metres

	1 mm Constriction	0.75 mm Constriction	0.50 mm Constriction	0.25 mm Constriction	0.00 mm Constriction	Without choke	1.40 mm Amplifier
Number of hits							
Inner circle	65	61	48	59	18	28	20
Outer circle	91	89	91	88	57	67	48
Complete target	156	150	139	147	75	95	68
Density	1:2.14	1:2.06	1:1.58	1:2.01	1:0.95	1:1.25	1:1.25
Regularity	9.6 = satisfactory	4.4 = excellent	8.0 = good	2.4 = excellent	16.4 = poor	9.4 = satisfactory	11.0 = satisfactory
Covered fields	10.2 = satisfactory	10.4 = poor	9.75 = poor	11.4 = good	4.8 = excellent	6.5 = oexcellent	2.8 = good
Extreme variation of effective hits							
Diameter	—	—	—	—	—	—	—
At distance	—	—	—	—	—	—	—
Max. effective range	46 m	44 m	43 m	44 m	22 m	30 m	20 m
Rating	Good for long range	Satisfactory for long range	Excellent for normal range	Satisfactory for long range	Satisfactory for near range	Good for near range	Satisfactory for near range
Pattern in percentage	74 %	71 %	66 %	69 %	35 %	45 %	32 %

TABLE 3

Results obtained with LEGIA STAR 12/70 ga. shotshells, 3.5 mm (No. 3), 154 pellets. Range: 35 metres

	1 mm Constriction	0.75 mm Constriction	0.50 mm Constriction	0.25 mm Constriction	0.00 mm Constriction	Without choke	1.40 mm Amplifier
Number of hits							
Inner circle	32	33	40	32	22	23	24
Outer circle	67	60	64	57	41	42	42
Complete target	99	93	104	89	63	65	66
Density	1:1.43	1:1.65	1:1.87	1:1.68	1:1.61	1:1.64	1:1.71
Regularity	10.2 = **poor**	7.2 = satisfactory	2.8 = **excellent**	8.4 = **poor**	5.6 = **good**	4.4 = **good**	7.6 = satisfactory
Covered fields	14.8 = **excellent**	14.4 = **excellent**	15.4 = **excellent**	14.8 = **excellent**	11.4 = **good**	11.8 = **excellent**	10.8 = **poor**
Extreme variation of effective hits							
Diameter	73 cm	73 cm	65 cm	63 cm	62 cm	62 cm	62 cm
At distance	39 m	39 m	40 m	40 m	33 m	33 m	33 m
Max. effective range	**Satisfactory** for long range	**Excellent** for normal range	**Good** for long range	**Excellent** for normal range	**Excellent** for near range	**Excellent** for near range	**Excellent** for near range
Pattern in percentage	64 %	60 %	68 %	58 %	41 %	42 %	43 %

tween each brand. We took the trouble of pre-counting the pellets before we fired the shells, so our results must be accurate.

The results with 2.5 mm shot remained pretty constant with the 1 mm, .75 mm, .50 mm and .25 mm choke constrictions. Results with chokeless barrel and with amplifier are likewise constant. We could not include extreme variation of effective hits, nor could we stipulate the distance at which greatest variation is achieved, since the number of pellets per shotshell are too few for our tables. This shotgun is designed for relatively close ranges.

The results of the 3 mm shot show a similar relationship. Choke constriction of 1 mm to .25 mm is constant, whereas chokeless and amplifier deviate more than with the 2.5 pellets.

The 3.5 mm pellets can also be divided into two groups. The first with the 1 mm to .25 mm constrictions, the second chokeless and with amplifier. If one considers regularity and coverage, the 1 mm and .50 mm chokes worked best with 2.5 mm pellets. The .25 mm constriction was the better choice for the 3 mm shot, and the .50 mm for the 3.5 mm. Point of impact was good with all choke constrictions. It can be said that even full choke did not deliver very narrow patterns, which is an advantage for the everyday hunter. The results showed that not only the degree of choke, but also the angle of the forcing cone influenced patterning. However, we found performance quite satisfactory in this gun. Still, the reader should be reminded that the same gun would produce other results with other shells and other shot sizes.

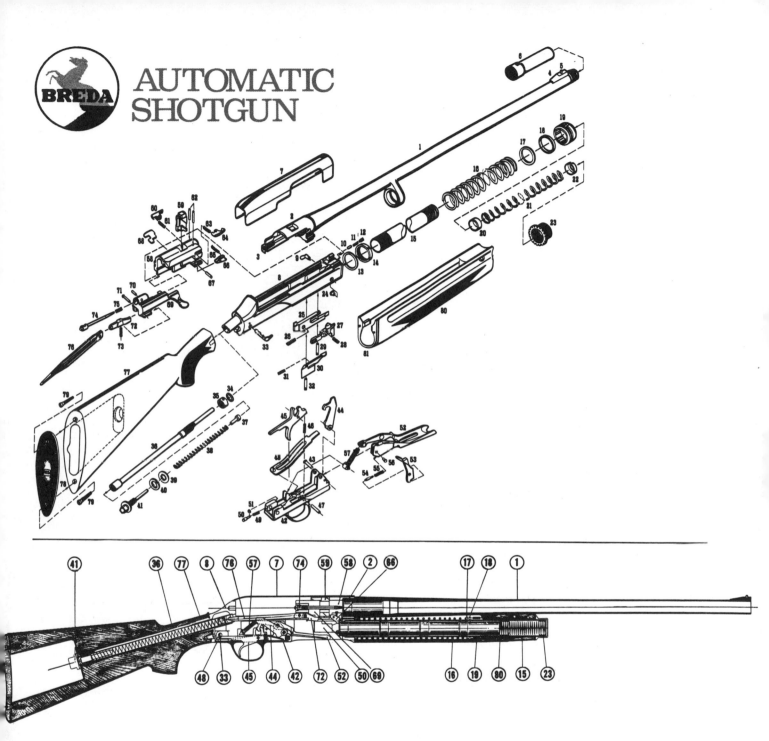

AUTOMATIC SHOTGUN

**Text and Photos
Siegfried F. Hübner**

1 *P 9 standard version (hammer down), Cartridges: 1) 9 mm Luger, 2) 9 mm Luger armour piercing, 3) 9 mm Luger Hollow Point*

1

The P 9 by Heckler & Koch is sensational in both performance and design. After I completed a 5-month fatigue test with this pistol, and had fired off over 1000 rounds without a jam, it was my opinion that the P 9 is the best mass-produced combat pistol around. Indicative of its worth is the fact that all my colleagues who tried the P 9 at the range wanted to buy one immediately. This pistol's accuracy, as well as low recoil, was the reason for their enthusiasm. Without a doubt, this 9 mm (Luger) pistol sets new standards for combat weapons!

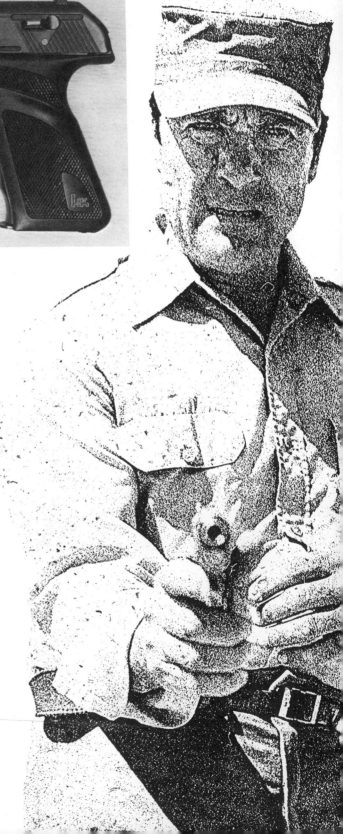

The Heckler & Koch
Combat Pistol P 9

2 *P 9 standard version (cocked), right side*
3 *P 9 with trigger stop swung out. With adjustable rear sight*
4 *P 9 with trigger stop swung out, right side. With adjustable rear sight*

This pistol possesses so many new features that a few of them must be mentioned right from the start. The P 9 has a polygon barrel, breech locking rollers, a side cocking lever, a concealed hammer, etc., and operates with a double action. More important for accuracy, the barrel is positively locked to the receiver. Only the breech locking rollers and slide are mobile. The polygon rifling of the barrel has been swaged with extraordinary care, which makes for precise shooting, apart from excellent penetration power. The standard trigger has a pull of only 3 lbs. Even when firing double action, the pull is only 8 lbs., which is good when compared with most other pistols. The breech locking rollers cut down on recoil tremendously.

From a technical point of view, it is interesting to know that the P 9 is made from non-cut metal parts with visible grain. The re-

5

6

7

ceiver and trigger guard are of nigh unbreakable plastic. Moreover, the P 9 does not have sharp edges, and on account of its compactness you can well believe that it would go on shooting, even after being confronted with a dollop of mud.

Heckler & Koch offers the P 9 in various versions, so virtually every pet requirement has been taken into account. If the would-be P 9 owner wants an accurate, hard-hitting defense weapon, then he should acquire the stan-dard P 9 S as illustrated in Figs. 3 and 4. He will have in his possession a 9-shot handgun, the high accuracy, shattering penetration and low recoil of which will amaze him.

Fig. 5 shows 9 shots I fired at 27 yards. When a pistol delivers such tight groupings, I can only assume that the P 9 will eventually be adopted by the German Armed Forces and the Border Patrol. Even the German police, who today are only armed with plinking .32 auto pistols, will have to take a long look at the P 9.

The P 9 is also available with target sights, trigger stop and wooden grips, which makes it ideal for range shooting. Furthermore, the P 9 is chambered for .45 ACP. A double-action .45 combat pistol with extra low recoil must interest a number of professional groups. See Figs. 6 and 7. The .45 cartridge has double the stopping power of the 9 mm Luger (namely 60 vs. 30 rsp). In other words, the P 9 should greatly interest the American police who are gradually going over to large-calibre pistols.

For target fans the P 9 can be had in single action (without cocking lever), as shown in Figs. 8 and 9. Here I would recommend a trigger stop, and a 5.5 in. polygon barrel. Figs. 10 and 11 illustrate the P 9 dressed up in target grips. If full-jacketed bullets are prohibited at the shooting range you frequent, you can use the 9 mm lead projectile by Dr. Weigel (Fig. 10) which can be inexpensively moulded and loaded in the Alzey reloading tool. For target-shooting purposes, the P 9 can be fed with low-power cartridges containing 3.85 grains of Norma R 1 powder. Accuracy is actually better, owing to reduced muzzle velocity and recoil.

Of course, for the .22 L.R. fans H & K can offer an insert barrel.

At the moment, I don't want to say too much about the military version, but I can disclose that it has a 20-shot magazine, a low cyclic rate of automatic fire, a graduated rear sight, and a shoulder stock attachment. The evolution of modern military small arms is branching out in two directions. The assault rifles G 3, Ak 47 and M 16 follow the one path. Low cyclic rate machine pistols (not machine guns) with shoulder stock attachment, like the Stechkin, Beretta and the P 9, follow the other.

The design features of the P 9 are best gleaned from the cross sectional drawings of Figs. 12 and 13. With the magazine withdrawn and safety applied, slight pressure on the catch in front of the trigger will release the slide. Pull slide forward, and up and away. The barrel will lift out of the slide when pushed forward. Figs. 14 and 15 show the P 9 field stripped. The plastic grip is of one piece, but is held by two screws. Two screws also hold the plastic trigger guard. The pitch of the handle grip is less favourable for combat

8

9

10

11

5 *Free hand grouping at 27 yards*
6 *.45 ACP P 9*
7 *.45 ACP P 9, right side, Cartridges: 1) .45 ACP, 2) .45 ACP Target, 3) .45 ACP Hollow Point*
8 *P 9 with single-action trigger, trigger stop, and adjustable rear sight*
9 *P 9 with single-action trigger (right side). Reduced energy 9 mm Luger cartridge by Dr. Weigel*
10 *P 9 with anatomical target grips by Franz König, Plüderhausen, West Germany, 5.5 in. barrel with muzzle weight*
11 *P 9 right view*

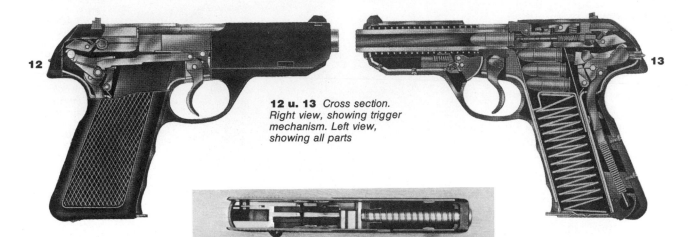

12 • 13

12 u. 13 *Cross section. Right view, showing trigger mechanism. Left view, showing all parts*

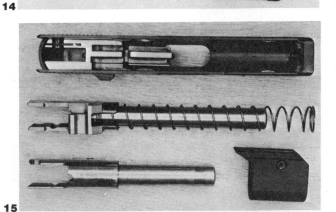

14

15

16

14 *Field stripped*
15 *Slide and barrels*
16 *Experimental wooden grips*

shooting, for it is too upright for instinctive pointing. The flat handle of the P 9 is just right for attaching a shoulder stock, but not for holding in the hand. Only the Luger had an anatomical handle. However, H & K will, in time, probably do a wee bit of redesigning here. At the moment, I can warmly recommend the H & K wooden grips (Figs. 16 and 17) which fill your hands, and are kindly disposed to instinctive shooting. The P 9 looks smarter, too, with wooden grips. The large-size extractor (Fig. 18) tells you immediately whether or not a cartridge is chambered. Regrettably, the empty cases fly into your hair. The angle of ejection should be changed.

The trigger stop can be swung out at a moment's notice, as illustrated in Fig. 19. When firing double action, the trigger continues to travel after the shot has been fired. A trigger stop puts an end to that.

The side cocking lever cocks and decocks the inside hammer. It also releases the slide when a fresh

17 Right side of experimental wooden grips
18 The extractor appreciably rises when a cartridge is in the chamber. Hence, it serves as a fair warning
19 The barrel mounting. Trigger stop swings up when magazine is empty
20 Pin indicating that hammer is cocked
21 The side cocking lever
22 View of the double action trigger. Trigger stop in action

magazine has been inserted. The magazine catch is at the bottom of the magazine well. When the hammer is cocked, an indicator pin protrudes through the rear of the receiver (Fig. 20).

If a cartridge is in the firing chamber its presence is read off by the raised extractor. In order to decock the hammer, the side cocking lever is depressed, and the trigger pulled. By releasing the side cocking lever before the trigger, the hammer is decocked, which is shown by the disappearance of the indicator pin. An automatic safety device engages if your thumb should slip off the cocking lever, while lowering the hammer. If the user wishes to take pin-point aim, and take advantage of the lighter single action trigger pull, he need only lift the hammer with the side cocking lever. If the safety is applied when the hammer is cocked (white dot visible), the trigger bar is disengaged and the firing pin is blocked. That is, the hammer of the P 9 is not lowered

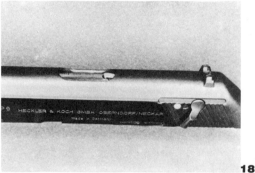

18

19

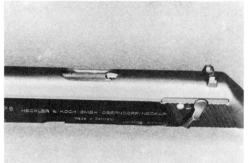

20

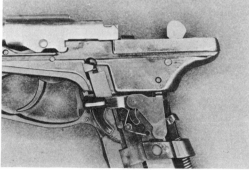

21

22

23 *The P 9 fits squarely in the hand*
24 *P 9 being tested in a sand swirling chamber*
25 *The magazine holds 9 rounds. One in the chamber makes 10*

26 *Adjustable rear sight*
27 *Breech face and ejector*
28 *This part drops out when the grips are removed. Should be remedied.*

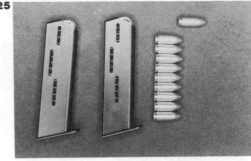

25

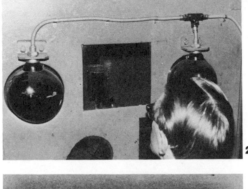

23

24

27

26

when the safety is applied, as is that of the P 38. This is a decisive advantage for a combat pistol. The P 9 can also be loaded, unloaded or cocked with the safety applied.

Weight with 9 cartridges is approx. 2 lbs. 1 oz. Hence, the P 9 is not too heavy for a holster weapon, and not too light for accurate shooting, considering the low recoil. An inside hammer has definite advantages when the user is in dusty or mucky terrain. Fig. 24 shows the P 9 being tested in a sand-swirling chamber. It is unlikely that grit will enter the P 9 and jam the action. Since the P 9 does not have a magazine safety, single shots without a magazine can be fired. Sight radius is 5.8 in., and the front sight is .1 in. wide, which makes it quick to line up. An adjustable rear sight is also available, as is depicted in Fig.

28

26. The large grips that cover the metal parts are comforting in hot and cold weather.

A definite plus would be a plastic finger extension on the ends of the magazine (cf. Walther PP, etc.).

As a service pistol the P 9 would need a lanyard ring. Fig. 27 shows the breech face and the powerful extractor, and the bifurcation in which the locking rollers are housed. One fault I discovered when removing the grips. Unfortunately, a part falls out when they are lifted off (Fig. 28). Here simplicity has gone too far, and H&K will doubtless remedy this defect. For target shooters, who like to change grips, won't appreciate this loose bit . . .

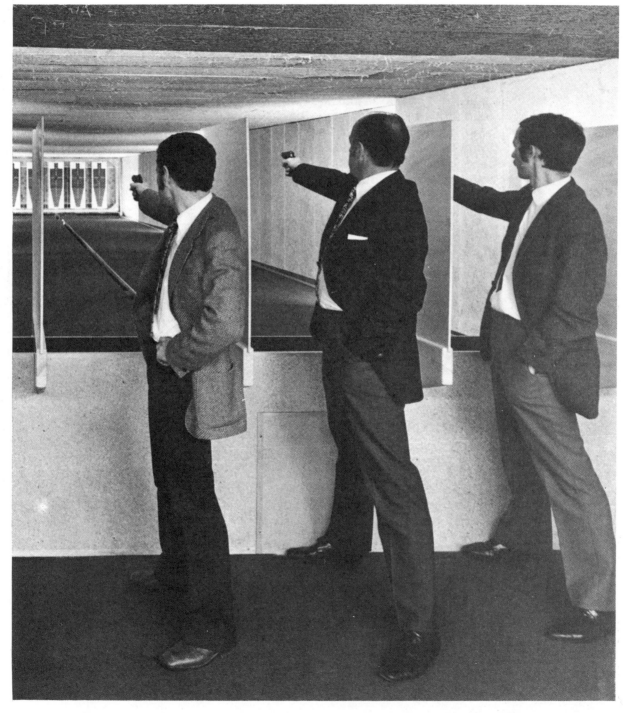

Gerhard Seifert

Sword hilts are made up of two main elements, grip and guard, the sub-elements of which can be quite numerous depending upon the age of the weapon, apart from developmental tendencies during specific eras – especially in the case of military weapons. Sabre hilts, therefore, were also subject to evolution, although the hilts of some sabres do not seem to have followed this fashion. As a group they are known as "sabres sans knuckle-guard," and the Caucasian shashka, the best-known representative of this group, remained a military weapon until quite recently.

Books specializing in edged weapons do not treat "guardless" sabres with much detail. No reliable explanation can be found anywhere as to why such swords were used without knuckle-guards. The opinion that these swords were the weapons of primitive peoples who did not wish to forsake old traditions cannot be verified. Expediency has always conquered conservatism in the end! One can only assume that the warriors who fought with this type of sword did not deem it necessary to have a knuckle-guard. A guard is superfluous when the sword is used for attack, but not for defense. Sur-

prise attacks and quick retreats is the way these "guardless" sabres were used. Of course, this explanation does not offer unquestionable proof that that was the case, but other interpretations are not more credible. Let us now, after this short introduction to the problem, take a look at some of these sabres sans knuckle-guard.

In the 3rd edition of "Die Kriegswaffen", 1891, August Demmin illustrates what he calls a "Dacian sabre after Trajan's victory column" (Fig. 1).

This weapon closely resembles the Abyssinian shotel (Fig. 2). The Zanzibar sabre (Fig. 7) has a

Sabres Sans Knuckle-Guard

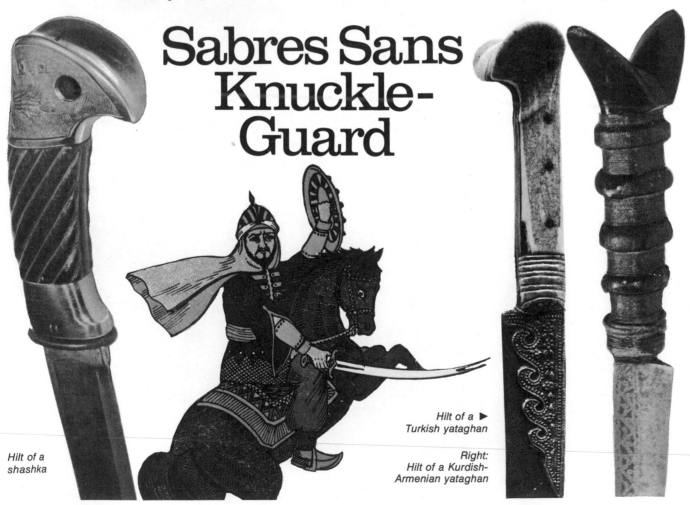

Hilt of a shashka

Hilt of a ▶ Turkish yataghan

Right:
Hilt of a Kurdish-Armenian yataghan

weaker curve in the blade. The pommel, quadangular in cross section, is of iron, and the grip is leather-covered. The Kurdish-Armenian yataghan (Fig. 3) must be viewed as the prototype of all the other types of yataghan. This double curved blade was incorporated into some of the "hewing" bayonets of European armies of the last century (Bavaria, France, England), although the original curve was straightened out a bit. A near relative of the yataghan, if not a direct descendant, is the Caucasian shashka. The shashka, used by mountain tribes, must have taken the enemy's fancy. How else cavalry units followed suit (Fig. 4). The Burmese dha (Fig. 8) is similar to the Japanese katana, but it has not got the guard or tsuba. The long grip is circular in cross section, and the blunt point restricts its use to hewing and cutting. A most interesting specimen of this group is the so-called kabylenflissa of northern Algeria (Fig. 6). It is classed as a sabre on account of the double curved blade. Finally, we come to the famed Turkish yataghan (Fig. 5), a sabre found in all Balkan states, by the way. The Turkish yataghan is the most lavishly decorated sabre sans knuckle-guard of them all. Even the most

1. Dacian sabre
   (after Demmin)
2. Abyssinian shotel
3. Kurdish-Armenian
   yataghan
4. Cossack shashka
5. Turkish yataghan

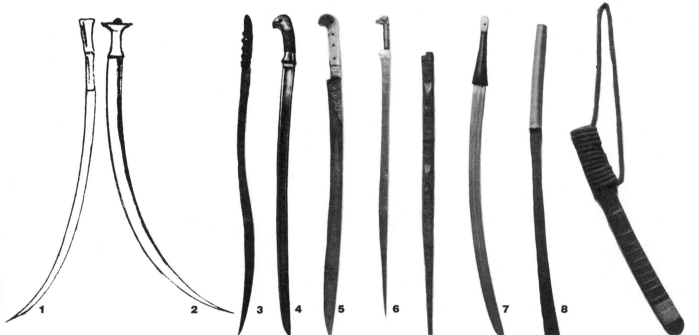

6. Algerian
   kabylenflissa
7. Zanzibar sabre
8. Burmese dha

can one explain its sudden popularity with the Cossacks at the end of the 18th century? Today the shashka is usually known as the Cossack sabre. However, not only the Cossacks carry this weapon, after World War I and II other Russian worthless specimen, if such a quality may be hung on an yataghan, at least has a damascened blade, usually with artistic inlay work. Precious and semi-precious stones, ivory, silver and gold adorn the hilt and blade of a full-bred yataghan, a sight uncommon on most other types of swords.

No effort has been made to describe these sabres with a flurry of details, that can be accomplished at another time.

THE HEGE PRÄSIDENT

Strength and long life of a gun with break-open action, especially of a drilling (S by S shotgun, rifle bbl. under) or an O/U sporting arm, hinges on its lock-up system. It is important to absorb at least two of the forces that build up when the cartridge explodes. The first of these attempts to tip the breech end of the barrel up, whereas the second aspires to blow the receiver away from the barrel assembly (pull-off moment).

Inventors have spared no pains to devise ways and means of counteracting the two forces just described, to extend the weapon's service life as long as possible; above all to make the lock-up system solid and free from wear.

**Text and Photos
Dr. Manfred Rosenberger**

Superposed Shotgun / Rifle Combination

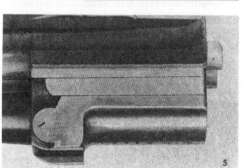

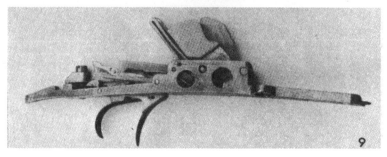

4 Traditional under lugs and hinge pin have been replaced by two hinge rolls that are mounted on lower barrel.

5 These rolls are easily interchanged, or worked up.

6 Similar to the Purdey system, the bolt engages over . . .

7 . . . two extensions that project laterally from the face of the upper barrel and which mate in slotways of the standing breech.

8 The Präsident has the selfcocking Blitz-type lock. Trigger and lock mechanism are mounted . . .

9 . . . on the trigger plate.

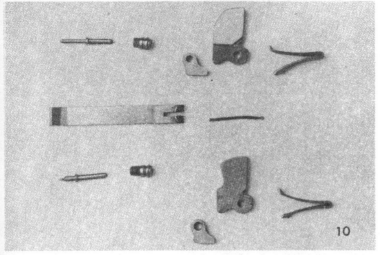

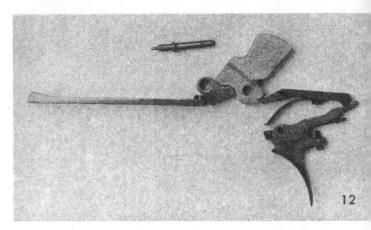

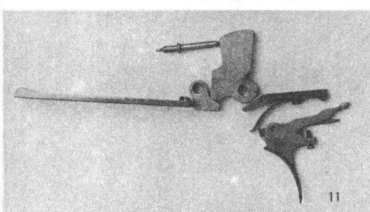

As a rule, the axis of the pitching moment in a break-open weapon lies under the barrels. Hence, the parts offering resistance, namely the breech bolt and the matching extensions on either side of the top barrel or the barrel rib, are exposed to heavy strain and in the long run wear to the point where the barrel facing no longer aligns with the standing breech. Most of the break-open breech systems developed in the past, strangely enough, were designed with an eye to counteracting these forces, not to abolishing them. Take, for example, the Greener, Kersten, Purdey and Flanken bolts. Very few people have attempted to transfer the point of rotation (normally the axis of the hinge pin) to the top end of the receiver, in order to cut out the pitching moment, or at least substantially reduce it.

The Hege (pronounced: hay-ga) can be reckoned among these rare exceptions.

Characteristic of the Präsident is its two-roll hinge system situated on either side of the lower barrel, substituting the conventional hinge pin. However, not only is the hinge pin missing, the under-lugs have disappeared, too. Of course, at this point I must inform the reader that break-open shotguns without under-lugs are not entirely new. The idea can be traced back to the last century. Pidault tinkered at this concept in 1885, and was followed by Beesley and Purdey. In 1930 Schüler introduced the first "lugless" superposed shotgun, with a Herkules lock. Semper & Krieghoff and Rempt (Remo lock) followed suit some time later. During the developing phase of the Hege lock, the works engineers incorported all the positive aspects of earlier models in a present-day design.

The two absolutely unorthodox side rolls of the Hege lock offer a series of considerable advantages. To begin with, the bearing surfaces of the two rolls within the flanks of the receiver are considerably larger than that of the hinge pin.

10 *The firing mechanism consists of: Firing pins, firing-pin bushings, leverage plates, hammers, hammer springs; centre: cocking iron and cocking-iron spring.*

11 *When breaking the barrels, a stud in the forearm forces the cocking iron rearwards. This action . . .*

12 *. . . rotates the leverage plates, which, in turn, tip the hammers back far enough to engage in the sear.*

13 *When a trigger is pulled, the corresponding sear loses contact with the bent. The hammer is driven forward under spring pressure, against the firing pin.*

14 *The firing-pin bushings are screwed in from the rear of the breechblock face.*

15 *The trigger assembly consists of (top) set-trigger spring, (left) sear and rear trigger, (right) sear, centre arm, front trigger, set-trigger arrester and spring.*

16 *French set trigger in "activated condition."*

Ergo, the compressive load is absorbed by a larger surface area with the effect that there is much less of a chance of the barrels moving than is the case with the under-lug system. Therefore, it can be claimed that the Hege can be subjected to higher loads, or, expressed reversely, the Hege has a longer service life than that of a gun with under-lugs. See illustration 4.

Still, the large-surface rolls of the Hege bolting system are just a side effect. The "prima novatio" is the upward transference of the point of rotation.

The two hinge rolls are so mounted that their centre points are barely 6 mm beneath the axis of the bore of the lower barrel. This means that pitching moment is virtually eliminated when firing the under barrel. See illustration 5. Apart from such physi-

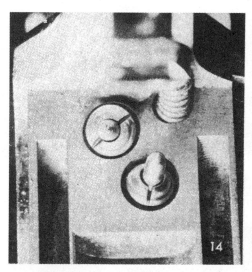

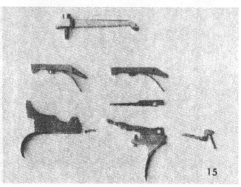

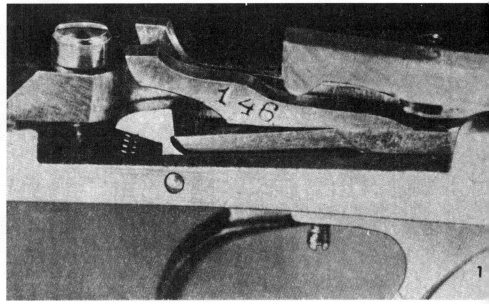

cal aspects, the nature of the Hege system also has practical significance. When fitting interchangeable barrels, no changes have to be made to the receiver or old barrel. This does away with a decided disadvantage, for the subsequent fitting of barrels usually requires extensive work, and is expensive. Furthermore, the hinge rolls of the Hege system can be interchanged without difficulty, or worked up. A bolt, similar to the Purdey system, engages over two extensions that laterally project from the face of the upper barrel (illustrations 8 and 9) and mate in slotways of the standing breech. The Präsident has a

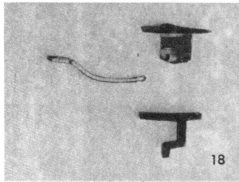

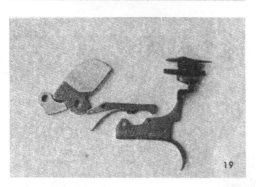

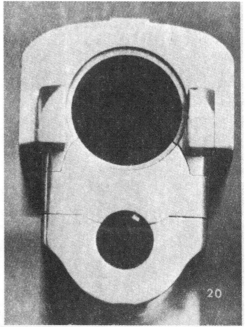

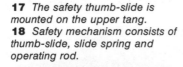

17 The safety thumb-slide is mounted on the upper tang.
18 Safety mechanism consists of thumb-slide, slide spring and operating rod.

19 When the safety is engaged, the flat head of the operating rod lies on the trigger leaves, preventing sears being jarred out of the hammer bents.

20 The Monoblock barrel union offers a relatively large breech face.

21 The receiver of the Präsident and the dummy side plates ...

22 ... are elegantly engraved (below).

self-cocking Blitz-type action, that is, trigger and lock mechanism are mounted together on the trigger plate. See illustrations 8 and 9.

The firing mechanism consists of two hammers, hammer springs, leverage plates, cocking iron, firing pins, and firing-pin bushings (illus. 10). An interesting feature is the small leverage plates, which are activated by the cocking iron, in lieu of conventional cocking levers. When the breech is opened the cocking iron is forced backwards via a stud in the forearm shoe, against the two leverage plates. These plates now revolve around their axes and hence lift the

the safety mechanism presses its flat head against the shoulders of the two trigger leaves (illus. 19), preventing the sears from being jarred out of the hammer bents.

Both barrels are of chrome-nickel steel, and joined together by the monobloc method, that is, the breech end of the barrels are brazed to the centre block. This is a long-lasting union and today this method is used by numerous gun-makers. Moreover, this block system offers a relatively large face around the chambers (illus. 20), hence pressure can be absorbed by a larger area. Otherwise, the barrels are soft soldered

23 The conventional sights are the U folding-leaf . . . **24** and a ramp-mounted post front. **25** As with other modern weapons with two-piece stocking, the receiver of the Präsident is anchored by a butt-stock bolt.

hammers far enough back to engage in the nose of the sears (illus. 11 and 12). Without a doubt, this design has advantages. Cocking is not so strenuous and neither of the leverage plates can bend or break. When a trigger is pulled, the sear is lifted away from the hammer bent and the hammer strikes against the firing pin (illus. 13).

The firing-pin bushings are screwed into the back of the breechblock face, not into the front (illus. 14).

The trigger mechanism is conventional. It consists of two triggers, two sears, a centre arm, a set-trigger arrester, an arrester spring, rear trigger spring and set-trigger spring (illus. 15). The set trigger (at front) is of the conventional type (illus. 16).

The Präsident's safety thumb-slide is mounted on the upper tang in usual fashion. See illus. 17. The parts are: thumb-slide, slide spring and operating rod (illus. 18). When engaged, the operating rod of

to the ribs and blued by brush application. Polish is pretty good. The steel receiver together with the dummy side plates are elegantly engraved (illus. 21 and 22), which greatly attributes to the Präsident's pleasing appearance.

Both post front sight and U folding-leaf rear sight are ramp mounted (illu. 23 and 24).

As with other modern weapons with interrupted stocking, a buttstock bolt is used to help anchor the receiver (illus. 25). This has an advantage over the tang screw, as the stock bolt runs in the same direction as the wood grain. Bolt holes running across the grain tend to be detrimental to tight fitting in the long run, owing to extra strain. The buttstock has a so-called German cheekpiece, it is also slightly hog-backed. The black plastic buttplate is underlaid with a white-line spacer (illus. 26). The wrist flows into a pistol grip whose pitch is neither too steep nor

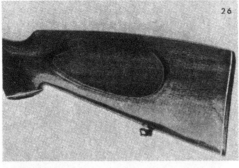

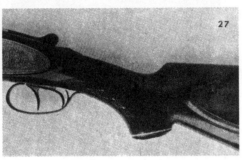

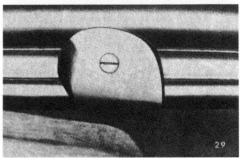

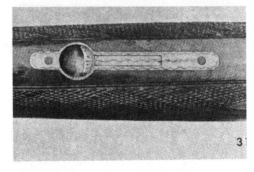

Manufacturer	Hege GmbH & Co, Schwäbisch Hall, West Germany
Designation	Präsident
Type	Superposed shotgun/rifle combination Self-cocking
Finish	De Luxe
Bolting	Lugless with hinge rolls in lieu of hinge pin; top bolting after Purdey (but two-sided)
Ignition	Blitz system, firing pins
Triggers	Front trigger for rifle barrel, rear for shotshell barrel. Front trigger French set type
Trigger pulls	Rifle trigger: 1.8 kg (no slack) Shotgun trigger: 1.6 kg (no slack)
Safety	Thumb slide on tang
Overall length	103 cm
Weight	3 kg (220/16 x 70)
Barrel length	61 cm
Barrel	Chrome-nickel steel
Choke	Full choke
Length of twist	35.5 cm
Direction of twist	Right hand
Grooves	6
Cartridges & Shotshells	.222 Rem., .222 Rem. Mag., .220 Swift, 6.5 x 57 R, 7 x 57 R, 7 x 65 R, .308 Win., .30–06 Springfield (illus. 37) 12 x 70 ga., 16 x 70 ga., 20 Mag.
Sights	Front post; U folding leaf
Distance between sights	45 cm
Stocking	Waltnut, lacquered; German cheeckpiece; Scotch checkering on pistol grip and forearm; buttplate and pistolgrip cap of black plastic

26 The buttstock is of conventional design, boasting a slight hog back and so-called German cheeckpiece.

27 The pitch of the pistol grip is neither too steep nor too flat, taking into account requirements of both rifleman and shotgunner.

28 High-walled, beavertailed forearm.

29 ... rests against a plastic "saddle" which is screwed to the middle rib.

30 By means of this "saddle," the forearm is not suspended in mid air.

31 Forearm is provided with a patent catch.

32 The base of the riflescope mount is soldered to the sighting rib and held by three screws.

33 The riflescope is simply slipped into the recesses of the mount and locked by tightening up two setscrews with a coin.

34 The .222 Rem. cartridges that were tested. Left to right: Norma, Winchester, Sako, DWM, Remington.

Table I
Performance of the rifle barrel .222 Rem.

Distance (m)	100	200
Cartridge	dispersion	(cm)*
Norma	3.5	7.5
Winchester	2.2	5.9
Sako	3.4	7.8
DWM	3.0	6.4
Remington	2.1	5.4

Note: Firing position was sitting with gun resting on sand bags. *) These results are based on an arithmetical mean of eight 5-shot series apiece. There was a 10-minute interval between each series.

Table II
Performance of the rifle barrel .222 Swift

Distance (m)	100	200
Cartridge	dispersion	(cm)*
Winchester	2.1	5.0
Remington	2.6	5.8
Norma (TM)	2.5	5.8
Norma (VM) hand loaded	2.8	6.0
Power Lokt	2.0	5.1

Note: Firing position was sitting with gun resting on sand bags. *) These results are based on an arithmetical mean of eight 5-shot series apiece. There was a 10-minute interval between each series.

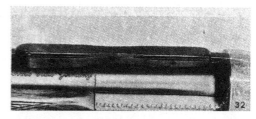

Table III
Ballistic data of the various .222 Rem. loads used

Make		Norma	Win.	Sako	DWM	Rem.
Bullet weight in grains		50	50	50	50	50
Bullet 's shape		Or	CS	Or	Or	Or
Bullet type		SJ	SJ	SJ	SJ	SJ
	Distance (m)					
Velocity m.p.sec.	0	975	975	950	974	975
	100	823	815	786	812	798
	200	684	675	635	673	634
	300	560	552	500	550	505
Energy mkg	0	157	157	149	157	155
	100	112	110	102	109	118
	200	77	75	66	75	66
	300	52	50	41	50	42
Trajectory ceiling in cm	100	1.3	1.3	1.7	1.3	1.5
	200	6.1	6.6	7.2	6.6	7.2
	300	19.1	19.4	21.0	19.5	20.9

Abbreviations: Or = ogival; CS = conical, spitzer; SJ = semi-jacketed
Source: Gun Digest 20/66; Ballistics of DWM sporting cartridges 1963; Sako Patruunat

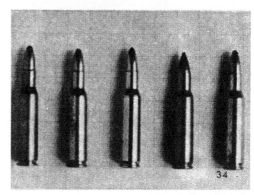

too flat, taking into account the requirements of both the rifleman and the shotgunner (illus. 27). The butt-stock as well as the forearm are beautifully decorated with "Scotch checkering." The forearm is beavertailed (illus. 28). Of particular interest, however, is that the front end of the forearm rests against a two-piece plastic "saddle" that is screwed to the rib, and is not suspended in mid air as is so often the case (illus. 29 and 30). Hence, no dirt or foliage can find entrance between barrel and forearm. Barrel or forearm expansion is hindered in no way. Furthermore, the forearm is provided with a patent catch (illus. 31).

Another novel feature is the way the riflescope is mounted. The scope mount and rail are soldered to the massive sighting rib, and additionally clamped with three screws. See illus. 32. The foot of the mount can now be easily slipped into the recesses in the rail and locked in place by tightening up two setscrews with a coin (illus. 33). The only drawback is that the barrels have to be dropped when mounting the riflescope.

Two Präsidents were sent in for test purposes. The first was chambered for the .222 Rem. cartridge and a 16 x 70 ga. shotshell (Serial No. 37113). The second for the .220 Swift and a 16 x 70 ga. shell (Serial No. 36925).

Rating

Workmanship	2
Functional safety	1
Performance	1
Finish	1
Design	0
Sights	2
Balance	2
Pointing qualities	2
Stocking	1
Total	**12**

Faults:
Slots in screwheads too shallow for most screwdrivers.
Note: The higher the number, the lower the rating.

Table IV
Ballistic data of the various .220 Swift loads used

Make		Win.	Rem.	Norma	Norma	Hand Loaded **)
Bullet weight in grains		48	48	50	50	50
Bullet's shape		CS	Or	Or	Or	Or/HP
Bullet type		SJ	SJ	SJ	FJ	FJ
	Distance in yds					
Velocity m.p.sec.	0	1240	1240	1253	1253	1261
	100	1070	1070	1100	1050	1013
	200	895	895	952	863	960
	300	742	742	817	694	826
Energy in mkg	0	250	250	259	259	262
	100	182	182	202	185	204
	200	127	127	153	126	158
	300	88	88	110	81	117
Trajectory ceiling in cm	100	0.7	0.7	0.9	0.9	0.9
	200	3.6	3.6	3.0	3.6	3.0
	300	9.7	9.7	9.4	9.9	9.3

Abbreviations: CS = conical, spitzer; Or = ogival; Or/HP = ogival hollow point. **) 50 gr. Rem. bullet Power Lokt; Load 41.7 grains Norma 203 powder; Remington primer
Source: Gun Digest 20/66; Norma Ballistic Table No. 61

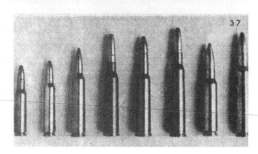

35 *The .220 Swift loads tested.*

36 *The shotshell loads tested.*

37 *The Präsident is chambered for the following cartridges: Left to right: .222 Rem., .222 Rem. Mag., Swift 6.5x57 R, 7x57 R, 7x65 R, .308 Win. and .30-06 Springfield.*

During our test, 60 shots apiece were fired from the shotgun barrels (full choke) of the two candidates, using four different loads (illus. 36). Representative differences in performance between the two guns couldn't be ascertained. Based on the results obtained at 30, 40 and 50 metres, employing the Wannsee Rating Formulae, both guns received, after eliminating load influence, the mark: "Excellent for normal purposes." On average, effective maximum range was limited to 38 metres. The shotgun barrels of both weapons shot a trifle high, and point of impact and point of aim coincided at 37 metres with the first weapon, and at 41 metres with the second. As one might have expected, the results obtained with the rifled barrels deviated considerably from each other. The explanation offered points a finger at "brand dispersion", on the one hand, and "cartridge dispersion", on the other. Cf. Tables I and II. Two hundred rounds were fired through the .222 Rem. barrel, that is, five different loads times 40 (illus. 34). Down the .220 Swift barrel went 100 cartridges, this time five different loads grouped in 20s. See illus. 35. Worthy of note is the fact that the Swift-chambered barrel, on average, outmanoeuvred its Remington-chambered counterpart. This is really astounding, since both barrels have 35.5 cm length of twist. However, mention must be made that the Swift-chambered barrel was prophylacticly thoroughly cleaned with a solvent after the 54th shot.

The results achieved, especially with the often not-too-respected .220 Swift cartridge, speak well for the Präsident. Let it also be said that the last 20 shots of the .220 Swift remained constant in performance. Recently someone falsely maintained that "the barrel would be discardable after 100 rounds." Changes in headspace could not be observed.

The Swift produces a gas pressure of 3600 at. against 3300 at. of the 7 x 64 Brenneke with 6.7 gram. bullet. In total, only three primers (Winchester) were conspicuously pancaked.

Apart from one solitary instance where the centre arm, on account of defective material, got bent, no problems cropped up during testing. Stripping, on the other hand, is difficult even for a gunsmith, since the screw slots are so shallow that most turnscrews (screwdrivers) refuse to fit.

The Präsident is by all means dignified in appearance. It is a nicely designed and nicely made workaday gun. Balance and pointing qualities though are somewhat impaired on account of the relatively heavy steel receiver. Still, this is only noticeable when rapidly swinging the shotgun barrel. Otherwise, the Präsident rests squarely in the hand. Its singular advantage is the lock-up system used, which guarantees longevity, heavy-duty wear, and savings in adapting interchangeable barrels. And such features are well worthwhile ...

Hans Frömming
Photos R. Triebel

The Arms of the German Imperial Troops in South-West Africa

Generally speaking, very little is known about the arms used by the German imperial troops in Africa. After two World Wars, German archives are devoid of information.
This article is based on eye-witness accounts and some official material, and describes conditions in the ex-colony of Deutsch-Südwest-Afrika only. The rifle issued to the imperial troops differs considerably from the standard 98 in a number of points, and will therefore be of especial interest to gun historians.

Shoulder arms

The Gewehr Mod. 71 in 11.2 mm was in service between 1884 and 1889. However, the Jägerbüchse Mod. 71 was also issued to the troops. Some of these Jägerbüchsen were fitted with a magazine that was pushed up into the receiver from below, and curved around the stock to the right. Olsen illustrates a refitted Jägerbüchse 71 in his book, "Mauser Bolt Rifles". We do not know whether other specimens of this "pilot job" are still around. This after-thought magazine must not be confused with the tube magazine of the Gewehr 71/84.

Starting 1889, the German colonial troops were armed with the Gewehr 88 and the Karabiner 88 in 8 mm, and were used to quell the rebellions of the 1890s. The 88s were again used to suppress the large-scale uprisings between 1903 and 1908. In 1904 the imperial troops received the first of the Gewehre 98, which were chambered for the cartridge 88/8 and boasted a straight bolt handle. In the autumn of 1908

the 98 was converted to accept the S cartridge. This change-over was completed on 1st April, 1909.

The "erste Batterie" (first company), formed in 1894, was equipped with the Karabiner 88. The machine-gun detachments and artillery reserves that left for Africa between 1904 and 1905 were accompanied by various models of the Karabiner 98. These had a 17 inch barrel and were chambered for the cartridge 88.

The artillery and MG platoons were armed with the short Karabiner 98. Late in 1908, the colonial troops conducted experiments with the S cartridge and the "lengthened" Karabiner 98. This long Karabiner 98, if successful, was to be issued to all the troops. With a 29 inch barrel this model became known as the 98 a. After further tests it was adopted as the Schutztruppengewehr 98 (colonial troops rifle 98).

Colonial troops rifle 98

This specialized rifle for the German colonies in South-West Africa was chambered for the S cartridge, and had a 29 inch barrel. Its triangular front sight was standard issue. The lowest graduation of 400 metres was whittled down to 200 metres on the rear sight for fighting in wooded territory. Maximum sight range was 2000 metres, with intermediate 100-metre adjustments. This feature is overlooked in other gun books.

The bolt handle described a downward curve like that of the Karabiner, and the bolt knob was flattened on one side and serrated. The stock was that of the Gewehr 98 with a depression under the bolt knob for better handling. As with the Gewehr 98, the sling was mounted under the belly, not along the side as in the case of the Karabiner, as the colonial troops were basically cavalry soldiers. A metal plate in the stock bore the initials "KS" and the number of the unit. An extra "S" signified that the rifle was chambered for the S cartridge. The South-West troops wore a special cartridge belt with braces. This was not usual in

▲ The grip sported a beak-like pommel.

◀ Bayonet with toothed rear edge, made in Erfurt.

◀ *An ox rider armed with the Gewehr 88.*

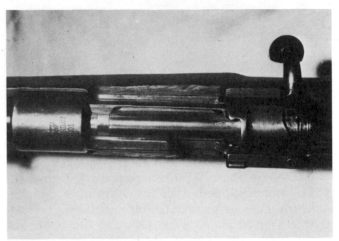

▼ *Curved bolt handle of the Gewehr 98 for South-West Africa.*

German ▶ signpost with eagle, indicating the border of their Protectorate.

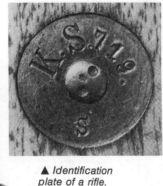

▲ *Identification plate of a rifle.*

Gewehr 98 ▶

the German Armed forces, but as this belt had 12 pockets for 120 cartridges weight was formidable. A bayonet hung from the left side and rings held the canteen plus digging utensils on the right. The belt itself was of stout leather. A buckle was at the back.

Edged weapons

The M 71/84 bayonet was standard issue between 1884 and 1904. Fresh reserves from Germany brought the 98 (long) bayonet with them, a model that was issued to all troops from 1909 onwards. It was just under 10 inches long and sported a toothed rear edge. The grip was of hard leather, serrated and fastened by 3 pins. Furthermore, the metal pommel was shaped like a bird's beak.

Fifty bamboo lances dating back to 1894/95 were still being warehoused by 1914. The troops frowned on such weapons for modern warfare, and hence did not use them. A hundred Bowie knives, lying around in depots, were also turned down.

Revolvers and pistols

Originally, the Reichs revolver 83 saw service. In 1914 about 500 of the 83s were still in storage. The Luger in 9 mm with 6 inch barrel and shoulder stock was then issued in 1904, during a period of rebellion. In 1910 the 4-inch barrel Luger in 9 mm was adopted.

The Mauser Broomhandle in 7.63 mm and the Browning 7.65 mm Modell 1900, the latter extremely popular in the officers corps, were usually handguns that had been bought privately.

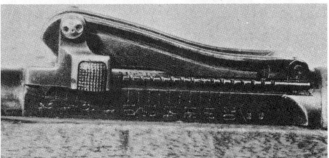

Machine guns

The first machine gun to reach the troops in South-West Africa was chambered for an 11.2 mm cartridge, and it arrived in 1894.

It was probably sent to Africa to undergo a thorough testing in the native uprisings. No information is available regarding make, type and length of service. The only photo of this weapon (see below) was lent us by an ex-trooper, who assures us that his unit made good use of the contraption. Other bits of information that trickled in verify the calibre of 11.2 mm. Whether this cartridge was the Mauser M 71 or 71/84 is anybody's guess.

According to authentic reports, SMS Habicht sailed to South-West Africa with 1 MG on board. Another 17 MGs were shipped to Africa with fresh troops. After 1909, all MGs had been re-chambered for the S cartridge.

Field guns

The South-West troops possessed 5 light cannon, 4 rapid-fire 5.7 cm guns and 5 mountain 6 cm guns. During the native uprising, the SMS Habicht brought 3 revolving cannon 3.7 cm, 8 machine cannon 3.7 cm (borrowed from the Marine-Expeditionskorps), 2 field cannon 91/93 (taken from the German troops in Cameroon), 30 field cannon 96, 4 field howitzers 98 (not used) and 6 mountain guns 7 cm.

In 1908, the 7.5 cm mountain gun with recoiling barrel, the Erhardt, was taken into service. During the same year, 4 field cannon 96 were returned to Germany for a change-over to recoiling barrel. The Erhardts and the coverted 96s were provided with a front armour plate, too. The three remaining companies after 1st October, 1908, were equipped with 2 mountain guns and 1 field cannon.

Explanation: **Gewehr,** German for gun or musket. **Büchse,** German for gun with rifled barrel. However, today Gewehr and Büchse are attached pretty indiscriminately to one and the same thing: a rifle. **Jäger,** depending on the circumstances, may be translated as hunter, chasseur or rifleman. Germany also has a number of "Jäger" regiments that specialize in skiing, mountaineering, etc. **Karabiner,** short rifle or carbine.

◄ The first machine gun used by the Germans in South-West, in calibre 11.2 mm.

CPL Bell, A.

Philip Webley
1812–1888

WEBLEY HANDGUNS

The firm of Webley has existed for 130 years, and it delivered handguns to the British Armed Forces for more than 40 years. Webley was to Britain what Colt was to America, or Mauser to Germany.

The first Government Model was produced in 1886 in .442, .455 and .476

The factory premises in 1897

calibres. This was a hinged-frame revolver with double-action lockwork chambered for 6 rounds. In 1887, the British Army placed an order for 10,000 pieces, all of them for .455 ammunition. This particular version became know as the Government Model Mark I (GM Mk I). In 1894,

an improved model, the Mk III, was introduced. This, however, was followed by the Mk III in 1897.

Two years later, the Mk IV made its first appearance, the so-called Boer War Model. It was produced with 3, 4, 5 and 6 inch barrels, and some Mk IVs were converted to sub-calibre target revolvers.

In 1913, yet another improved model was adopted, the GM Mk V. Though ordinarily the Mk V was issued with a 4-inch barrel, models with a 6-inch barrel are seen occasionally.

The last of the Government Models, the Mk VI, was adopted in 1915. In contrast to the Mk V, the Mk VI was standard with a 6-inch barrel, although some of them had 4-inch barrels. After 1921, all Mk VIs were manufactured at the Royal Small Factory in Enfield. Nonetheless, the Mk VI was abandoned in 1929 and replaced by the Enfield No. 2 Mk I .380 pistol.

Webley went on to design a Pistol No. 2, but commissioned the Royal Small Arms Factory with its manufacture. The Webley No. 2 remained in service till 1957.

Today the British Armed Forces are armed with the Belgian 9 mm Hi Power Pistol.

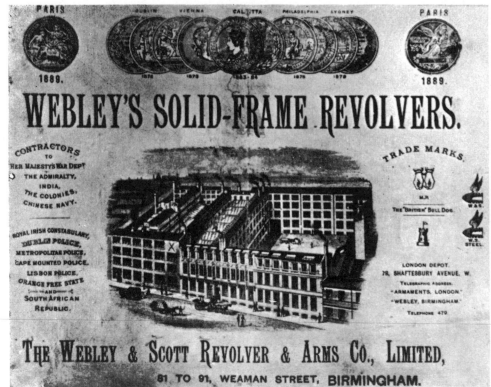

PARIS 1889. DUBLIN VIENNA CALCUTTA PHILADELPHIA SYDNEY PARIS 1889.

WEBLEY'S SOLID-FRAME REVOLVERS.

CONTRACTORS TO HER MAJESTY'S WAR DEPT THE ADMIRALTY, INDIA, THE COLONIES, CHINESE NAVY.

ROYAL IRISH CONSTABULARY, DUBLIN POLICE, METROPOLITAN POLICE, CAPE MOUNTED POLICE, LISBON POLICE, ORANGE FREE STATE AND SOUTH AFRICAN REPUBLIC.

TRADE MARKS.

M.R
THE "BRITISH" BULL DOG.

LONDON DEPOT.
78, SHAFTESBURY AVENUE, W.
TELEGRAPHIC ADDRESS:
"ARMAMENTS, LONDON."
"WEBLEY, BIRMINGHAM."
Telephone 479

THE WEBLEY & SCOTT REVOLVER & ARMS CO., LIMITED,
81 TO 91, WEAMAN STREET, BIRMINGHAM.

Technical data for Mk VI revolver (standard production)

Cylinder chambered for 6 rounds (right-hand rotation)	
Overall length	11.25 in.
Barrel length	6 in.
Accurate range	50 yds.
Maximum range	820 yds.
Muzzle energy	220 ft. pds.
Muzzle velocity	600 ft./sec.
Bullet weight	255 grains

1. *Webley GM Mk I, .455*
2. *Webley GM Mk IV, .455*
3. *Webley GM Mk V, .455*
4. *Webley PM Mk IV, .380.*
The GM Mk VI is identical with the PM Mk IV.
5. *Webley Pistol Mk I, .455 (1913)*
6. *Webley Very pistol*

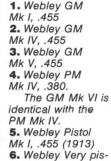

Webley
REGD
TRADE MARK

Webley also produced a scaled-down Government Model in .380 for police duties, the PM. This police version appeared as light-weight Mk IIs, Mk IIIs, and Mk IVs, with different barrel lengths and various grips. During the last war, these PMs were occasionally issued to the troops. But by and large the PMs remained mothballed for home defense, should the need arise.

Another Webley, which became the official hand-gun of the Royal Navy in 1913, was the .455 Self Loading Pistol, Mk I. The pilots of the Royal Flying Corps (the forerunner of the Royal Air Force) were armed with this model in 1915. However, manufacture of the Self Loading Pistol was stopped in 1916, as intricate hand-fitted parts proved too costly to assemble. Webley can also be associated with Very pistols, which were usually made of brass.

213

The Garrucha from the left.

A Brazilian Derringer

Weapons from Brazil are little known outside of South America, as few would normally wish to buy a South American pistol. Nevertheless, we want to acquaint our readers with the Garrucha, a double-barrelled .22 LR Derringer-type made by Metalúrgica e Munições Amadeo Rossi & Cie. in São Leopoldo, Rio Grande do Sul. In Brazil, this pistol costs about ten US dollars.

Both barrels were machined from a one-piece blank. The quality of the bore surface though was rough by our standards. Of course, it is far from simple to bore two 2¾ in. barrels parallel to each other. We had only to look down the barrels of our specimen to realize that each of the barrels had a different orientation, which explains its poor performance: At 5.5 yards, the left barrel printed a shot 3 inches to the right of the point of aim, and the right barrel managed to place its bullet 1½ inches to the left of the point of aim. Scoring couldn't be improved, even with practice. But that was not all, at this short range the groups were also 5 inches too high! Anyone unfamiliar with the "ballistics" of the Garrucha could not hit a man-size silhouette at 25 yards. Indeed, the bullets began to keyhole at just over 5 yards.

Sights consisted of a shotgun-type bead only which, for target purposes, makes the Garrucha use-

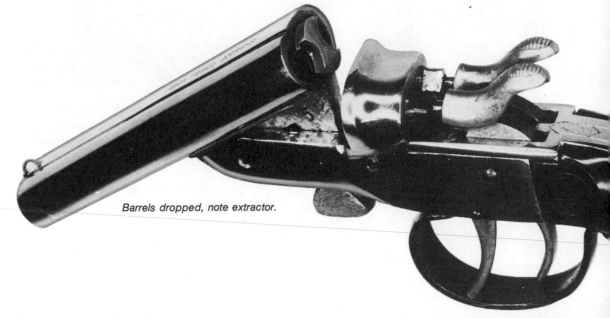

Barrels dropped, note extractor.

RUCHA

Text and photos Wolfgang Weigel

A view showing the two barrels.

less; still, it is small enough to conceal in one's sleeve, and two high-velocity .22s are sufficiently vicious to ward off any would-be assailant.

Receiver and handle frame were of one piece. The barrels are dropped by depressing a knob in front of the trigger guard. Extractors raise the cartridge cases high enough to get one's finger tip under the rims.

Both firing pins are kept rearwards via their recoil springs until hammer is activated. In other words, they are full length, not inertia firing pins. When at rest, the hammers lie a fraction of an inch behind the firing pins. When falling, they strike the pins and immediately rebound. A drop would be insufficient under normal circumstances to cause an accidental discharge, as the two mainsprings are pretty stiff. Although the triggers are confined to a smallish trigger guard, and the Garrucha can only be fired by the tips of one's fingers, trigger pull has been nicely balanced: 3 lbs. for one, and 3 lbs. 8 oz. for the other. The handle is petite, too. It is difficult to get more than one's middle finger around it. The Garrucha is nickel plated, apart from the hammers, triggers, trigger guard and barrel release knob. The stocks are of smooth black plastic, bearing the monogram ARC. Backstrap and trigger guard sport a bit of engraving. Once the stocks are removed, crude workmanship comes to light, however, the finis is not bad enough to influence the mechanics of the pistol.

Brazilian workers normally don't have the money to buy expensive guns, so the Garrucha has been tailored to the country's needs. Brazil, by the way, has a healthier gun-ownership law than we! Every citizen of Brazil with an honorable record may purchase a gun by simply producing his ID card. Moreover, he may carry a gun, or conceal one in his car. A criminal knows only too well that virtually everyone is armed. Hence, the crime rate with firearms is astoundingly low in Brazil . . .

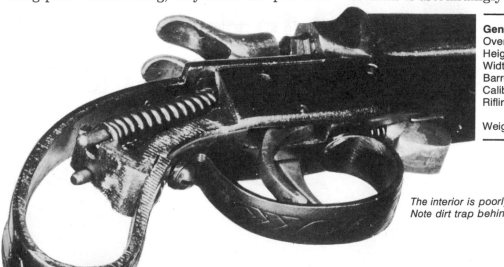

General data

Overall length	6.7 in.
Height	2.4 in.
Width	approx. 1 in.
Barrel length	2.75 in.
Calibre	.22 LR
Rifling	6 grooves, right-hand twist
Weight	11 oz.

The interior is poorly finished.
Note dirt trap behind barrel release knob.

Text
Richard Horlacher

Photos
Hans Kubach

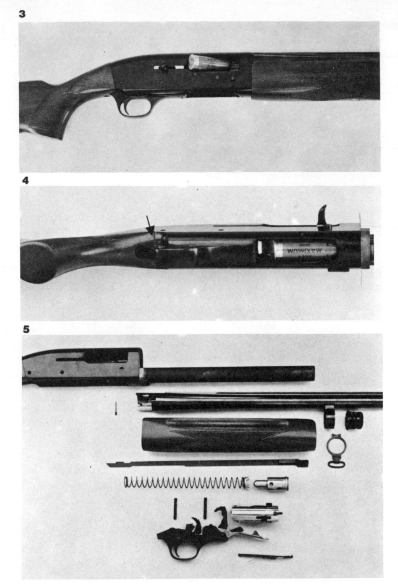

Manufrance Automatic Shotgun Model Perfex

German hunters view automatic shotguns with a measure of scepticism if they depart from traditional, well-known examples.

In another article we presented the Breda with moving barrel, here we are dealing with an automatic shotgun with a stationary barrel. The Perfex belongs to the lightest and most inexpensive models of its type. When holding the Perfex for the first time, everyone is amazed at its feathery weight and its good balance.

1 and **2** *The Manufrance automatic shotgun, showing both sides*
3 *Loading the chamber through the ejection port*
4 *Carrier being in the up position, 2 shotshells can be fed into the tube magazine (arrow: safety applied)*
5 *Receiver with tube magazine, barrel, forearm, plus the easily taken down bolt and trigger assembly*
6 *Forearm with swivel and magazine cap, which contains the gas regulator*
7 *Dismantled bolt*
8 *Locking block retracts when operating handle is pulled back*
9 *Locking block engages when operating handle is in the forward position*

6

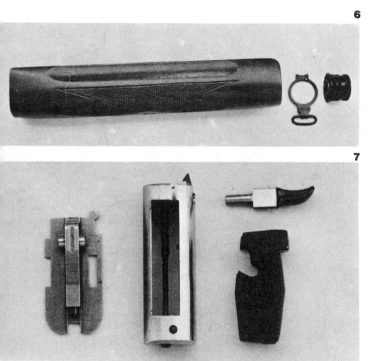

8

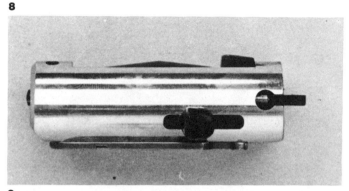

7

9

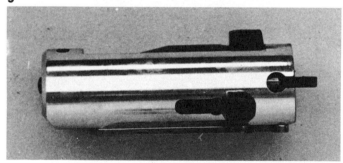

Loading and unloading

Apply the safety by pressing the button to the right and pull back bolt far enough for it to stay open. Now a shell can be chambered. The carrier latch lever is situated on the right side of the receiver, under the ejection port. By depressing this lever the bolt closes.

When loading the tube magazine, activate the carrier latch lever again. The carrier then tips into loading position and two shells can be loaded. The gas operated mechanism is located in the forward third of the tube, hence there is limited space for only two shells. After loading, touch the carrier latch lever again to tip up the carrier. By pressing the safety button to the left the Perfex is ready to fire.

If all three shells are to be fired off one after the other, turn the magazine cut-off lever forwards. A red dot is then visible. If only one shot is to be fired, turn the cut-off lever back. A white dot will now be visible. The shells in the magazine tube will not load and the action will remain open when the one shell has been fired. By pushing the cut-off lever forward again, the bolt will close.

The hammer of the Perfex, operated by a coil spring, strikes an inertia firing pin. This inertia firing pin is so short that it isn't forced directly against the primer. The hammer blow actually imparts momentum to the heavy firing pin, which flies forward to strike the primer. After the shot the reciprocating parts open and eject the empty hull.

When the bolt returns, it chambers the shell lying on the tipped up carrier. After the action has relocked itself the gun can be immediately fired; that is, if the trigger has been released. The trigger must

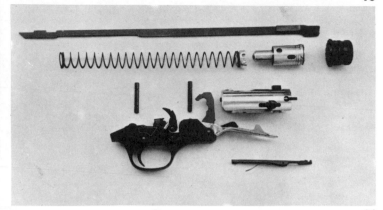

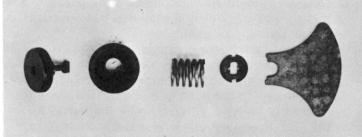

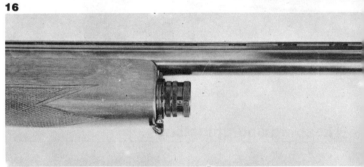

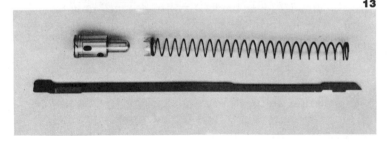

be released after each shot to re-set the disconnector. In this way there is no fear of doubling. The bolt of the Perfex remains open after the last shot. The gun is then re-loaded, as described.

To unload the gun, push carrier down to loading position and depress the bolt pawl (right side of receiver) to let the shells slide out. The shell in the chamber is removed by opening the action.

Adjusting the gas regulator

Adjustment should be made when using heavy or light loads to prevent excessive wear of parts. A gas

10 Trigger assembly, hammer, piston and gas regulator
11 Trigger assembly (light metal), hammer down, carrier in low position
12 Trigger assembly, hammer cocked, carrier in high positon
13 Piston, piston ring, spring, operating rod
14 Gas regulator/magazine cap dismantled. Note key
15 Dismantling the regulator
16 Regulator has nice grippy edges

regulator is built into the magazine cap which meters the amount of gas pressure reaching the piston.

The barrel is easily taken down for cleaning; it is simply drawn forward with the forearm, once the cap has been removed.

Workmanship and finish

The 70 cm chrome-lined barrel bears a silver bead virtually too fine for the job, and a ventilated rib. The black eloxal finished receiver is made of top-grade, lightweight special alloy. The bolt is well finished and partly polished. Trigger housing and trigger guard are also of light metal.

The stock is walnut with a long, rather weak pistol grip. Both the grip and forearm are checkered. The buttstock has no cheekpiece but this does not mar the picture for it is well proportioned.

Performance

Testing was subjected to the Wannsee procedure, but we did not test fire beyond 35 metres. The following loads and shot sizes were used:

Winchester Standard	2.9 mm
Win. Super Speed	2.9 mm
FN Legia Star (red)	3 mm
RWS Waidmannsheil	3 mm
RWS Tiger	3 mm
Remington Peters	3 mm
Eley Maximum	3 mm

The Perfex functioned perfectly with all loads, no duds or jamming were experienced.

TECHNICAL DATA

Manufacturer: Manufacture Française D'Armes et Cycles, de Saint Etienne

Designation: Manufrance, Model Perfex

Gauge: 12/70 (16/70); by adjusting the regulator in the magazine cap, 65 mm shells can also be used

Action: Locked

Safety: Push button in trigger guard (blocks trigger)

Trigger pull: 2.14 kg

Receiver: Alloy, black eloxal processed

Barrel: 70 cm long, chrome lined, ventilated rib, full choke

Magazine: Tube for 2 shells (12 or 16 ga.)

Stock: Lacquered walnut, no cheek piece. Pistol grip. Forearm well checkered. Swivels.

Stock measurements:

Trigger-Buttplate	=	35.5 cm
Drop at comb	=	3.5 cm
Drop at heel	=	5.2 cm
Pitch	=	6.0 cm

Weight: 2.95 kg

Guarantee: 5 years

17

17 *Shotshells we used*

Shotshell	Win. Super Speed	Win. Standard	RWS Waidmanns- heil	RWS Tiger	FN Legia Star red	Eley Maximum	Remington Peters
Shot size	2.9 mm	2.9 mm	3 mm	3 mm	3 mm	3 mm	3 mm
Number of pellets	258	214	196	208	223	202	188
Spread							
Inner circle	45	51	80	77	60	63	50
Outer circle	110	108	93	80	126	92	80
Whole target	155	159	173	157	186	155	130
Density	1:2.44	1:2.14	1:1.16	1:1.04	1:2.1	1:1.46	1:1.60
Percentage	60 %	74 %	89 %	74 %	83 %	77 %	70 %

Manufrance
Automatic Shotgun
Model Perfex

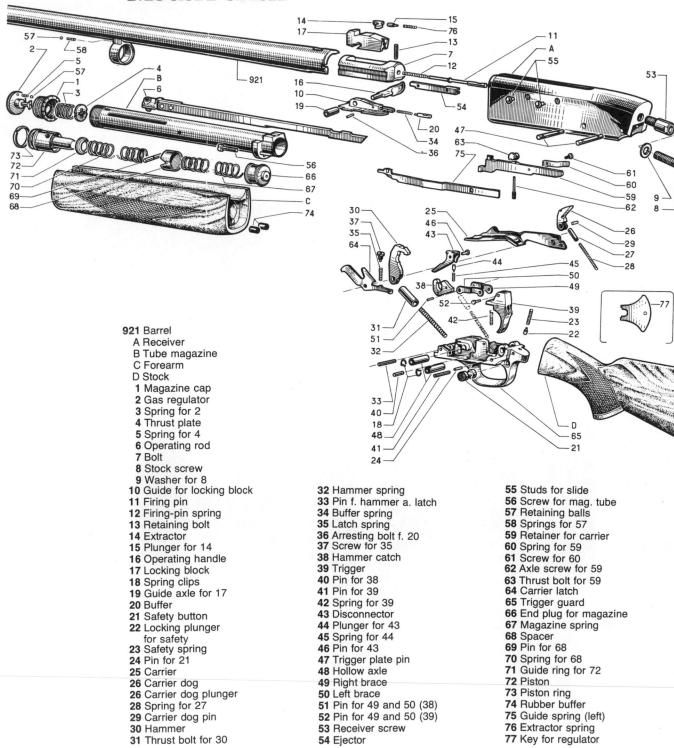

921 Barrel
A Receiver
B Tube magazine
C Forearm
D Stock
1 Magazine cap
2 Gas regulator
3 Spring for 2
4 Thrust plate
5 Spring for 4
6 Operating rod
7 Bolt
8 Stock screw
9 Washer for 8
10 Guide for locking block
11 Firing pin
12 Firing-pin spring
13 Retaining bolt
14 Extractor
15 Plunger for 14
16 Operating handle
17 Locking block
18 Spring clips
19 Guide axle for 17
20 Buffer
21 Safety button
22 Locking plunger
   for safety
23 Safety spring
24 Pin for 21
25 Carrier
26 Carrier dog
26 Carrier dog plunger
28 Spring for 27
29 Carrier dog pin
30 Hammer
31 Thrust bolt for 30

32 Hammer spring
33 Pin f. hammer a. latch
34 Buffer spring
35 Latch spring
36 Arresting bolt f. 20
37 Screw for 35
38 Hammer catch
39 Trigger
40 Pin for 38
41 Pin for 39
42 Spring for 39
43 Disconnector
44 Plunger for 43
45 Spring for 44
46 Pin for 43
47 Trigger plate pin
48 Hollow axle
49 Right brace
50 Left brace
51 Pin for 49 and 50 (38)
52 Pin for 49 and 50 (39)
53 Receiver screw
54 Ejector

55 Studs for slide
56 Screw for mag. tube
57 Retaining balls
58 Springs for 57
59 Retainer for carrier
60 Spring for 59
61 Screw for 60
62 Axle screw for 59
63 Thrust bolt for 59
64 Carrier latch
65 Trigger guard
66 End plug for magazine
67 Magazine spring
68 Spacer
69 Pin for 68
70 Spring for 68
71 Guide ring for 72
72 Piston
73 Piston ring
74 Rubber buffer
75 Guide spring (left)
76 Extractor spring
77 Key for regulator

YAN DARGENT

PINFIRE CAR

Jürgen Pirkl

1 A =metal cylinder   B =Cardboard cylinder

2 The biggest and the smallest of the pinfire revolver cartridges
C =ball   D =pellets

The invention of the pinfire cartridge coincides with the natal hour of modern industry and technology in the 1830s. This type of cartridge was still being made by some ammunition factories up to the Second World War. Proof enough for its popularity; for one would have thought that the pinfire cartridge had lost its right to exist when centre fire cartridges made their appearance round about 1860.

The main difference between the pinfire and the modern cartridge is the system of ignition. The hammer of the gun drops on a side pin, which, in turn, crushes a cap and sets off the fulminate. The "firing pin", therefore, was a part of the cartridge, and not a part of the gun, as is the custom today. The propellant usually consisted of black powder.

The pinfire cartridge is erroneously attributed to Lefaucheux, a Parisian gunsmith, who in fact did have the gun and ammunition patented in 1836. All the same, he cannot be regarded as the inventor of the pinfire system. Since this contention of mine does not fit in with the accepted view, let me clarify a couple of points:

The origin of the pinfire system is undoubtedly to be found in France. Pottet was granted a patent in 1829 (Vol. 39, No. 3.930) for a cartridge with removable head in which the primer was accommodated. A pin stuck out to the rear of the head. In 1832 Lepage placed the pin to one side of a cartridge sporting a metal head and a cardboard cylinder. In volume 48, one finds the patent entered under the the No. 5.468.

Lefaucheux was granted his patent in 1836, and Jarre Fils followed in 1840 with a metal cylinder and lateral pin.

Nobody had given gas sealing between pin and cartridge case much thought, apart from Houllier who designed a double wall, whereby the inner wall was squashed by the pin to cause the explosion. This invention was patented in 1846 under the No. 1.936 (vol. 7). Chaudun was granted a similar patent in 1847 for a type-metal gas seal. Less expensive systems used cardboard props. Lefaucheux's patent of 1850 (No. 4.839, vol. 17) does not give mention to sealing problems, although it describes a removable head . . . 21 years after Pottet's patent!

Calling the pinfire cartridge the Lefaucheux can only be interpreted as a salute to a remarkable gun-

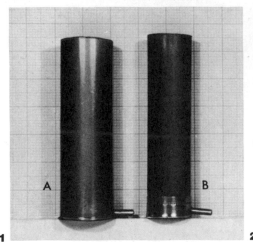

1

2

3 Berloque pistolette
. . . as small as they come

TRIDGES

mith, nothing more. Of course, Lefaucheux did much to popularize the pinfire system, as his weapons were famous for their high quality, and they always attracted large crowds at exhibitions and trade fairs. In 1863 the French Army adopted a Lefaucheux revolver.

The pinfire system was very successfully used by sharpshooters and hunters. Indeed, some old trappers in the outback still bemoan the demise of pinfire shotguns. Still, the only advantage to this system is that the pin indicates that the firing chamber is loaded. It is not fair to degrade the pinfire revolver cartridges. The weapon, not the cartridge, is at fault. Thousands of revolvers dumped on the market by French and Belgian cheapjacks gave the genuine Lefaucheux product a bad name. After all, not every revolver is a Colt, although it is difficult to drive this message home in some circles! As a noise-maker, the pinfire cartridge is still encountered today, combined with the Berloque pistolette (cf. illustration).

Editor's Note: I feel that this writer has fallen into the trap of rendering a decision on insufficient evidence. Many French gunmakers in the 1820s and 30s were furiously working to perfect the breechloading

gun and self contained cartridge following the pioneering efforts of Pauly about 1812. French patents dealing with these developments appear to have been issued to dozens of inventors almost on a weekly basis.

My own research into the history of the pinfire gun and cartridge turned up French patents of Lefaucheux clearly showing pinfire cartridges in 1835. The gunmaker Robert was the maker of excellent lift-up breech guns in the early 30s and is credited by some with having invented the pinfire cartridge. Correspondence with Gevelot, the French ammunition making firm, produced the information that they considered the pinfire to have been invented by Casimir Lefaucheux and that they, Gevelot, were manufacturing pinfire cartridges in various calibers by 1838. Had Robert, or any other gunmaker, a legitimate claim to the invention of the pinfire it is highly unlikely that Gevelot would have credited it to Lefaucheux within 2 or 3 years of its introduction.

Houllier has often been credited with inventing the pinfire in 1846 simply because he **improved** it with his patent for the base wad which rendered the pinfire case truly gas tight. The English firm of Eley was

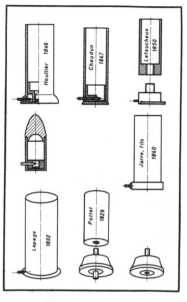

Drawings of 6 patents (taken from originals)

patenting pinfire improvements in the late 1850s and the 1860s.

The English gunmaker and historian W. W. Greener, who lived quite near in time to the invention of the pinfire cartridge, credits it to Lefaucheux.

The 1829–1832 French patents of LePage, Potet, Jarre, Beringer, et al, which superficially **look** like pinfires, were nothing more than cartridges with a **nipple** and an **external percussion cap.** Or a projecting tube filled with detonating compound. Blackmore, the very sound English firearms historian, documents this period in detail and credits Lefaucheux's patents of 1832 and 1835 as clearly establishing his claim to the invention of the pinfire. Those patents also persuaded me of that fact.

and Tokarev and Tokagypt Pistol

1 *Tokarev Mod. TT 30, right view*

3 *Tokagypt Mod. 58, right view*

The Tokarev self-loading pistol (single action with external hammer) and the 7.62 mm Tokarev cartridge originally made their appearance in or around 1930. In 1938 this pistol was officially adopted by the Red Army (Figs. 1 and 2). Experience gained in World War II emphatically proved that the Tokarev is more than a match for many other self-loading pistols on account of simplicity; and reliability due to this simplicity.

For a number of years now a Hungarian version, produced under the name of Tokagypt, has been available. Reportedly, this model was designed to fulfil, the wishes of the UAR (Egypt). See Figs. 3 and 4. When comparing the two weapons, certain differences become obvious that seem to speak in favour of the Tokagypt. Since both these arms are available on the commercial markets, we have taken the trouble of subjecting them to a series of tests.

Without a doubt, the Browning and Colt pistols acted as godparents to the Tokarev. The differences between the Russian and Hungarian versions limit themselves to calibre (Tokarev: 7.62 Tok./Tokagypt: 9 mm Luger), the safety catch, the shape of the grips, and the base of the magazine. All other parts are identical and interchangeable.

The dismounting of both weapons is very simple and no special tools are needed. An ordinary nail will suffice. Withdraw the magazine, then draw the slide back and check that there is no cartridge lodged in the firing chamber. With a nail, nose of a cartridge, or

2 *Tokarev, left view*

4 *Tokagypt, left view*

the tip of the magazine floorplate, press in the recoil-spring retainer, which is located under the muzzle of the barrel, and push aside the bushing (Figs. 5 and 6).

After the bushing has been carefully removed, pull out the spring clip located on the right side of the receiver (over the trigger) in order to release the slide stop. Now ease the slide stop (Fig. 7) out from the left side of the receiver. Barrel, slide and recoil spring can now be slid off the front of the receiver. Withdraw recoil spring and guide, and push the link forwards to remove barrel. The firing pin is held by a retaining split pin that is easily knocked out of the receiver. Make sure, however, that the firing pin does not suddenly fly out to the rear. The extractor pin is drifted out by tapping against the end that is inside the slide. At first sight it would seem that the grips are riveted to the receiver. That is not the case, however. Reach into the magazine well with a nail or similar instrument, and press against the latch of

5

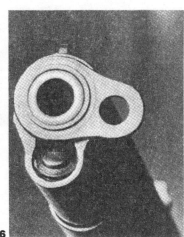

6

7

5 *To remove barrel and receiver, press in the recoil-spring retainer . . .*

6 *. . . and turn the barrel bushing 180 degrees, and lift free of the slide*

7 *The stem of the slide stop passes through the barrel link*

8 *Slide, recoil spring and guide, barrel and slide stop*

9 *To remove the grips, use a screwdriver to push over the latch inside the magazine well (arrow)*

10 *Once the left grip has been removed, the latch for the right grip (arrow) can be reached*

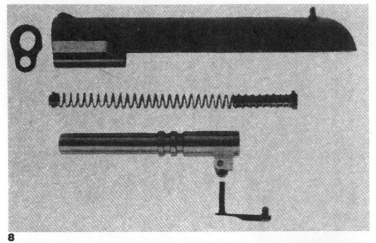

8

9

10

11 *Such grips are easily mounted*

12 *This sub-assembly which guides the cartridges from magazine into firing chamber also contains the hammer mechanism. It is lifted from the receiver as one unit*

13 *Sub-assembly stripped. 1 = disconnector, 2 = sear, 3 = hammer, 4 = mainspring*

11

12

13

the left-hand grip. The left grip can now be removed by pressing up against the inside surface. The latch of the other grip is then activated in the same way (Figs. 8, 9 and 10). The trigger may now be squeezed back and withdrawn through the magazine well. Punching the split-pin magazine release catch through from the right-hand side of the receiver will bring it out with its return spring, permitting removal of the bushing in which it is housed. The safety catch of the Tokagypt is dismantled by extracting its spring clip. As the hammer group is accommodated in its own sub-assembly, it may be lifted directly out of the receiver without tools. This sub-assembly is easy to strip: Knock out sear pin, and remove the sear, pull out the disconnector, then displace hammer pin, hammer and mainspring (Figs. 11 and 12). However, due to extremely strong spring tension, difficulty will probably be encountered in reassembling the mainspring. Hence, the sub-assembly ought not to be meddled with, unless absolutely necessary.

A superficial comparison of the Tokarev and Tokagypt, when fully stripped, shows that, technically, important differences do not exist. See Figs. 14 and 15.

Of interest is the way the breech is locked at the moment of firing. The system devised by the Russians is virtually identical with that used by the Americans in their Colt Government Model 1911, .45 ACP. When the slide is in its forward, home position, two barrel ribs engage in corresponding recesses on the inside of the slide (Fig. 16). As the cartridge is fired, barrel and slide, firmly locked together, begin their journey rearwards for about 6 mm (.236 in.). At this point, the barrel link, which is anchored to the slide-stop pin, pulls the barrel down out of engagement with the afore-mentioned recesses in the slide. Though the barrel comes to a stop, the slide continues to open. See Figs. 17, 18 and 19.

The hammer mechanism is ingeniously straightforward. Contrary to the Colt or Browning designs, a short coil spring fits into a hole in the hammer (Fig. 13). The hammer can be set at half cock, so the pistol can be safely carried with a round in the firing chamber. When the trigger is activated its drawbar forces the sear out of the hammer bent and the hammer drops on the firing pin. The opening slide, powered by the explosion of the cartridge, drives the hammer back and depresses the disconnector (Colt type). As the sear is mounted on the same pin as the disconnector, this downward movement of the disconnector

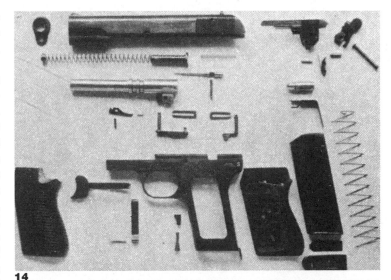

14

15

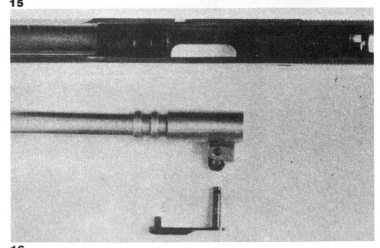

16

14 *Component parts of the Tokagypt 58*

15 *Component parts of the Tokarev TT30*

16 *At the moment of firing, the two ribs in the barrel engage in the corresponding recesses in the slide*

227

17

18

19

carries the sear down with it. This break in the linkage between trigger and hammer prevents the hammer from dropping until the trigger has been released and pulled again deliberately. When the slide closes, under the influence of the recoil spring, the hammer remains cocked for the next shot. If, however, the hammer has been lowered to half cock, the sear engages in a different bent and cannot be reached by the drawbar of the trigger. In theory, the hammer cannot accidentally be jolted out of half cock, nor released by the trigger. In practice, though, the half-cock bent often becomes worn, so this system is not a hundred per cent safe. That is why, pre-

sumably, the Tokagypt has been provided with a separate safety catch (Fig. 20). When applied, the safety mechanism blocks the sear in such a way that the sear cannot be freed from the hammer bent. Ergo: the safety functions when the hammer is at full or half cock. Here the Tokagypt has a definite advantage over the Tokarev. Of course, the safety cannot be applied when the hammer is resting against the firing pin. And the hammer cannot be cocked when the safety has been applied.

The sub-assembly that houses the hammer group is provided with two arms of unequal length, the one on the left being longer. The inside surfaces of these two

Tokarev and Tokagypt Pistol

TABLE I

	Tokarev	Tokagypt
Country of origin	USSR	Hungary
Calibre	7.62 Tok. 7.63 Mauser	9 mm Luger
Weight (empty)	1 lb 14 oz.	1 lb 15 oz.
Overall length	7.64 in.	7.64 in.
Height	4.64 in.	4.88 in.
Barrel length	4.96 in.	4.96 in.
Twist	1 in 9 in.	1 in 14 in.
Rifling	4 grooves, r.h.	6 grooves, r.h.
Action	Locked breech, single action	
Safety	—	Blocks sear
Trigger pull	5 lb 12 oz.	5 lb 5 oz.
Sights	U-notch and front post	
Sight radius	6.22 in.	6.30 in.
Magazine	Box type for 8 rounds	

20

17 The gases force barrel an slide, locked together, about 6 mm (.0236 in.) to the rear

18 The barrel link, which is anchored to the stem of the slide stop, then draws the barrel down out of engagement with the recesses in the slide . . .

19 . . . and the slide continues on its rearward journey alone

20 The Tokagypt is provided with a safety catch (arrow), not so the Tokarev

arms serve as cartridge guides to facilitate accurate feeding into the firing chamber (Fig. 21). This is a very important feature. Normally, self-loading pistols depend on the folded-over lips of inherently weak magazines to guide cartridges into the firing chamber; one of the main reasons for auto pistol jams. As the magazines of the Tokarev and Tokagypt have been exempted from this duty, their lips are particularly low and narrow. No stoppages were experienced during our tests. Furthermore, these magazines can be quickly disassembled and cleaned, a feature not shared by all magazines. Regrettably! The component parts of the Tokarev and Tokagypt magazines are the few that are not interchangeable. The shell of the Tokagypt magazine has the same dimensions as its Russian brother, but a rib was inserted in the Hungarian magazine to bridge the shorter length of the 9 mm Luger cartridge. See Fig. 22. The 7.62 mm Tok. measures 24.7 mm, whereas the 9 mm Luger cartridge only measures 19.1 mm. The magazine spring of the Tokarev is longer and broader than that of the Tokagypt (Fig. 23).

Moreover, the base of the Tokagypt magazine is fitted with a plastic finger rest, which was a wise decision, for the pistol lies better in the hand. The grips of the Tokagypt, also of plastic, wrap around the handle and really fill one's hand.

The sighting arrangement of both pistols is iden-

21

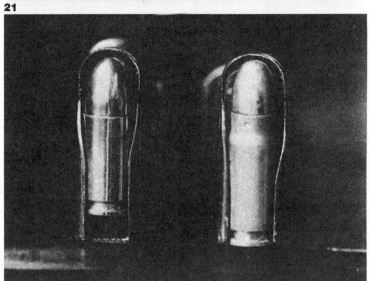

22

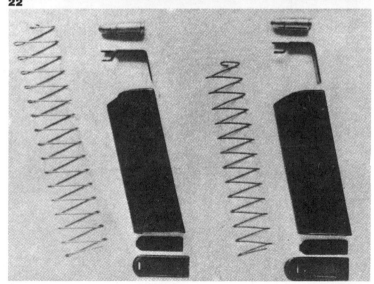

23

21 *The two arms of the hammer unit reliably guide the cartridge into the firing chamber*

22 *A backbone has been inserted into the magazine of the Tokagypt, since the 9 mm round is shorter than the 7.62 mm one*

23 *On the other hand, the spring of the Tokarev magazine is longer and stronger than that of the Tokagypt magazine*

tical. Though the front sight is integral with the slide, the U-notch rear sight can be laterally adjusted. See Figs. 25 and 26.

Apart from the safety catch, the hand-filling grips and the finger rest on the magazine, another, more important difference exists between the To-kagype and Tokarev: the cartridge. While the To-karev is chambered for the 7.62 mm Tok. (muzzle velocity = 1378 fps; muzzle energy = 369 ft.pds.), the Tokagypt is chambered for the 9 mm Luger cartridge (muzzle velocity = 1083 fps; muzzle energy = 322 ft.pds). Despite lower mathematics at the muzzle, the 9 mm bullet, owing to diameter, has much better stopping power. Why else do most of the armed forces of the world pack 9 mm or even .45 pistols? That's reason enough to opt for the

Toyagypt. By the way, the Mauser 7.63 mm cartridge can be fired in the Tokarev. The Russian round has a 0.5 mm (.019 in.) longer case. See Fig. 28 and Table II.

Both the Tokarev (No. 2908/1950) and the To-kagypt (No. 12627/1958) shot about equally well. See Table III. Each pistol was fed with 100 rounds. No stoppages, which might be ascribed to the misfunc-tioning of the pistols, oc-

24 *The Tokagypt magazine is provided with a finger rest*

25 *A conventional U-notch rear sight*

26 *Low post front sight*

27 *Left to right: .380 ACP, 9 mm Luger (old type), 9 mm Luger, 9 mm Mauser*

28 *The 7.62 mm Tok. (left) has a case that is 5 mm (.019 in.) shorter than that of the 7.63 mm Mauser*

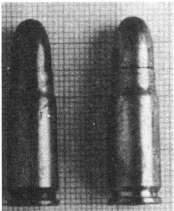

TABLE II

Ballistic data

	7.62 Tok.	7.63 Mauser	9 mm Luger	9 mm Luger (o/t)
Make	Russian	Kynoch	Geco	Western
Case length in inch	.953	.973	.752	.752
Weight of bullet in grains	86	85	123	116
Bullet's shape	OR	OR	OR	CF
Bullet type	FJ	FJ	FJ	FJ
Bullet's diameter in inch	.30	.30	.35	.35
Muzzle velocity	1377	1443	1082	1043
Muzzle energy	369	398	321	289

Key: OR = ogival, round head, CF = conical, flattened, FJ = fully jacketed
Source: Gun Digest 1964, Metallic Cartridges ICI 1960

TABLE III

Averaged dispersion in inches at 27 yards

	7.62 Tok.	7.63 Mauser	9 mm Luger	9 mm Luger (o/t)
Tokarev	2.28	1.58	—	—
Tokagypt	—	—	1.73	2.04

curred. Of 50 rounds 7.62 Tok., 7 were duds. This, however, is not surprising, as this ammunition was made in 1940, and little if anything is known about its storage during these long years. The component parts of the two pistols were fully interchangeable, apart from the grips and parts of the magazines. This is a marvel, since spare parts usually have to undergo a certain degree of hand fitting.

Both pistols share the disadvantage of being single action, though external hammers make for more safety when handling a pistol than the hammerless system does. As far as reliability is concerned, the Tokarev and Tokagypt can be thoroughly recommended, without hesitation, as simple, yet dependable handguns. Although, as we have seen, the Tokagypt has a slight edge on the Tokarev, the serious collector will ignore such practical arguments. He will have a place for both of them in his collection!

Text
and Photos
Günter Frères

During the long course of technical development of handguns from the match-lock to today's automatic rifles, military arms have influenced the design of sporting guns. Exceptions to this are the hinge-frame sporting weapons, and the automatic shotgun that appeared at the beginning of this century. Although automatic shotguns became relatively foolproof many years ago, the Browning auto shotgun of 1904, for example, difficulties are still being experienced with many automatic rifles.

BROWNING FN BAR AUTOMATIC RIFLE

In most autoloading pistols, shotguns and sporting rifles the force or energy of recoil is used to open the action. When the gas-operated Garand M1 rifle was adopted by the US Army in 1937, the news of such a move caused quite a sensation in other armies. During WW2 the effectiveness of the Garand M1 was amply proved in many theatres of war, and German soldiers rapidly developed respect for it. The M14 rifle is a further development of the Garand M1, although it is chambered for the NATO 7.62 mm round.

Also during the 1930s, the firm of Sempert & Krieghoff in Suhl, Germany, introduced a gas-operated rifle. Production of this well-designed semi-automatic weapon did not get under way, however, on account of the outbreak of war, and of the bombed out Krieghoff premises after the war. You might well say, "oh, what a pity," for now autoloading sporting rifles are winning favour among sportsmen. Remington introduced the "Woodsmaster," and Winchester followed up with the "Model 100." Both rifles have been available in a number of calibres.

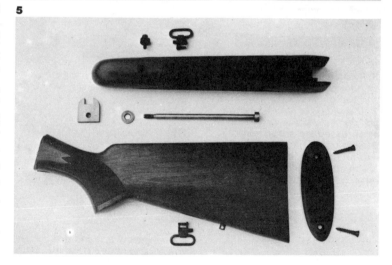

3 *View of receiver with action closed.*
4 *The receiver with action open. Bolt carrier is held back by the magazine follower.*
5 *Forearm and buttstock with swivels, screws, bolt and bearing plate, etc.*

Still, it will be a long haul before all Europeans will accept auto rifles, or auto shotguns, for that matter. When these die-hards are asked what they have against modern weapons, they go all out to substantiate the claim that "pom-pom" shooting just isn't sportsmanlike. The spirit of fairness depends on the hunter himself, not on the speed at which he can shoot.

The clicking of a bolt-action rifle chambering a second cartridge has often scared off wounded or other animals in a herd, which did not bolt when the initial

6 Forearm removed, showing gas cylinder assembly, action spring and two guide rails.

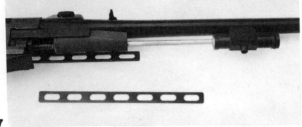

7 The slide has forced back the bolt carrier, via side bars, and has compressed the action spring.

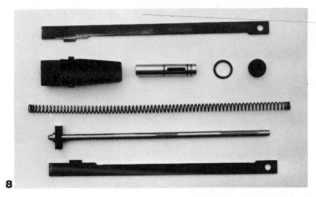

8 Side bar, slide, cylinder, washer, cylinder cap with nozzle, action spring, guide rod with slide buffer, left side bar.

shot was fired. An automatic reloads within the bang, so the hunter has a better chance of putting in the second shot. However, it is really a matter of personal taste whether you like automatic firearms, or whether you think they are too "machiny." In Germany automatic rifles and shotguns are seldom encountered in the field, and only foreigners seem to use them, usually American makes. However, across the border in Belgium where the FN plant is producing the BAR auto rifle, the scene is a little different, for FN is famous for its quality, and these BARs are chiefly exported to America. For our test, we chose a BAR chambered for the .308 Win. cartridge (Illus. 1 and 2).

Description

Two basic versions of the BAR are available. The standard model has a 22 in. barrel, a 4-shot magazine, and a plastic buttplate. It is chambered for .243 Win., .270 Win., .308 Win., or .30–06 Springfield. The Magnum version is available in 7 mm Remington Magnum, .300 Win. Magnum, and .338 Win. Magnum. Barrel length is 24 in. As the Magnum model fires belted cartridges, the magazine holds 3 shots only, and the butt is adorned with a rubber recoil pad. Otherwise, apart from minor differences in the breech assembly, both rifles are identical.

Remarkable is the fact that an automatic rifle has been built around Magnum

9

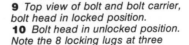

10

9 Top view of bolt and bolt carrier, bolt head in locked position.
10 Bolt head in unlocked position. Note the 8 locking lugs at three levels.

11

12

11 Bolt head and bolt carrier seen obliquely from below. A finger in the carrier rides in a camway in the bolt, hence the bolt can rotate in and out of the recesses in the barrel. The breech face is sunk into the bolt head, where extractor and ejector pin are mounted.
12 Carrier and bolt, in which the firing pin is housed. Below, cover plate and operating handle.

cartridges that can develop a pressure level of up to approx. 56.000 lbs.sq. in. The most powerful cartridges fired hitherto in automatic rifles were the .270 Win. and the .30–06 Springfield, with a pressure level of about 54.000 lbs.sq. in. Nonetheless, the two American rifles we are referring to did not function properly at this pressure, since blown primers and extraction troubles were often experienced. The BAR seems to have overcome these problems, which is good news for hunters; for a jammed autoloading gun can at best be used as a single-shot rifle in the field.

The BARs are made with crisp, single-stage shotgun-type trigger only, and the one on test has a trigger pull weighing 3.2 lbs. This trigger pull is favourable for shooting at running game, and is expedient when working with beaters. Of course, for long-distance shooting double-set triggers are preferable.

The BAR has a modern appearance, it has a hand-filling forearm, full pistol grip, and lacquered stock. However, for field use, I would thoroughly recommend an oil-finished stock. FN must also be praised for the sharp, hand-cut checkering. In the US these days, checkering is often stamped on to the wood, and blunt and broken lines are the result, in many cases. Receiver and barrel,

13

14

15

13 *Trigger plate, hammer (down) with two springs, sear arm and disconnector. Crossbolt safety button is behind the trigger, and magazine latch in front of trigger guard.*
14 *Hammer cocked and retained by sear arm.*
15 *Trigger plate seen obliquely from above. Note the dual coil springs for hammer. This is an unusual feature.*

both deep black finished, have been beautifully mated to the wood in the BAR we are examining. The whole gun, in fact, reflects excellent workmanship.

When handling the BAR, you immediately notice that it is muzzle heavy. This is due to the centre of balance being 7.6 in. ahead of the trigger. The only way to overcome this awkwardness is to grab the forearm up front when swinging or shouldering the gun. Before long, you get used to the new "hold," that is, if you don't shoot with a number of guns.

With a weight of approx. 8.5 lbs. (7.5 lbs. for non-Magnum calibres) and an overall length of 45.4 in. (43.4 in. for non-Magnums), the BAR is not exactly undersized. For many of us the BAR might be a little too bulky to trek across mountains with, or to deerstalk in woodland country.

However, the only true fault was the forward swivel eyelet which bruised the hand on recoil. If this were repositioned, the gun would be easier to carry, too. The BAR we shouldered with a lanyard sat so high that the muzzle rustled

16 *The crossbolt safety button. When pressed to the right it blocks the trigger.*

17 *When the safety button is pushed to the left a red ring warns the user that the safety has been disengaged.*

18 *Magazine detached with two cartridges. The cartridges are held at the shoulder and cannot slip out of alignment, and only one cartridge at a time can leave the magazine.*

19 *The BAR trapdoor magazine.*
20 *The adjustable rear sight seen from the front.*

the leaves of the lower tree branches. But since the swivel eyelet is also the forearm screw, engaging in the forearm stud under the barrel, the BAR owner himself cannot alter the position of the swivel. This is a re-think job for the FN people at Herstal.

The BAR shoulders nicely and snuggles against one's face. Still, the front sight comes up a little too high, which seems to indicate that the stock is too straight. Shortening length of pull might also improve matters. If using a scope, it would be unwise to reduce the height of the comb, as a high comb is an excellent cushion to lean against when peering down an optical sight. No stock is ideal for scope and open sights. For those hunters who like taking their animals "on the dash" and need open sights for a double-quick line-up, it is preferable to adjust the stock

BROWNING FN BAR AUTOMATIC RIFLE

accordingly and make allowances when using the scope. On the other hand, for those hunters who pinpoint game over long distances and need a scope, the comb of the BAR is just right. The BAR has good pointing qualities, even if it does not class with a double shotgun or hinge-frame rifle.

How the BAR functions

This FN rifle is gas operated. In other words, gas pressure behind the bullet reaches its maximum when the bullet has travelled a certain distance down the barrel.

After the peak, as the bullet travels farther from the chamber, gas pressure begins to subside on account of increased volumetric capacity, whereas the speed of the bullet increases. In the BAR, gas is bled off through a small port in the barrel wall 9.25 in. from the chamber. At this point, gas pressure has dropped to between 21,330 and 28,440 lbs./sq. in., according to the type of ammunition used. The gas enters an auxiliary chamber where it exerts force on a piston to unlock and open the action. The piston travels .59 in. rearwards, and pushes the bolt carrier against the action spring, via two side bars (illus. 6, 7 and 8). During the firing phase, the rotating, multiple-lug breech bolt is

21 *Dovetailed bead front sight, hood removed.*
22 *The 1.5 x Hensoldt scope that came with the BAR had a crosshair reticle with centre dot. Note the Suhl hook-in mount.*

21

22

TECHNICAL DATA

Manufacturer: Fabrique Nationale D'Armes des Guerre S. A., Herstal, Belgium.

Model: BAR (Browning Automatic Rifle).

Calibres: .308 Win., .243 Win., .270 Win., 7 mm Rem. Magnum, .30–06 Springfield, .300 Win. Magnum or .338 Win. Magnum.

Action: Gas operated, rotating bolt with 8 locking lugs.

Safety: Crossbolt type in trigger guard, blocks trigger.

Magazine: Trapdoor, swing-down type for 4 cartridges, or 3 Magnums.

Trigger: Crisp shotgun, single-stage type. Pull 3.2 lbs.

Barrel: Special barrel steel in 22 or 24 in. Button swaged rifling.

Sights: Adjustable, folding leaf rear. Front sight bead dovetailed into hooded ramp.

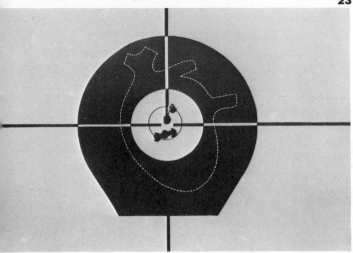

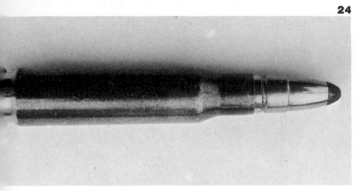

23 *The cartridge we used for the test. DWM .308 Win. with 180 gr. TUG bullet.*
24 *Our grouping at 55 yds. with scope mounted, in machine rest. Dispersion 1.06 in.*

locked in recesses in the rear of the barrel. See illus. 3 and 9. To lock or unlock, the bolt rotates about 60 degrees, when moved longitudinally over .59 in. (illus. 10, 11 and 12). Hence, the distance the bolt requires to unlock coincides with that travelled by the piston. Although the piston only travels .59 in., to unlock the bolt, the momentum imparted to the bolt carrier opens the action still further to extract and eject the empty cartridge case. On the return travel, occasioned by the action spring, the bolt assembly strips the top cartridge out of the magazine and chambers it; then,

during the last .59 in., the bolt rotates into the recesses in the barrel and locks the action.

Impact on the piston differs with each type of cartridge, of course. The .308 Win. has a relatively rapid powder, while the .300 Win. Mag. has a very progressive one. In the first example, when using the .308 Win., impact on the piston is less. Gas flow is regulated in the cylinder cap. Excess pressure is let off between forearm and barrel, and the shooter espies a puff of smoke at the side of his gun. Another point to mention is that the action stays open after the last shot (illus. 4).

The supporting element is the receiver, into which the barrel is screwed.

On the right side is the ejection port, through which the bolt operating handle protrudes. In the belly is the trap-door magazine. The magazine can be removed from its hinge, or simply swung down for loading. See illus. 18 and 19. The trigger plate contains the sear, disconnector, and the hammer, etc. See illus. 13 and 14. Unique is that this model uses two hammer springs (illus. 15). When the trigger is pulled, the disconnector pushes the sear forwards to drop the hammer on the firing pin in the bolt. The hammer is re-cocked when struck by the bolt assembly during the opening phase, whereby the disconnector is removed from the sear. The hammer, therefore, engages in the sear, and remains at full cock. The BAR can be fired in quick succession, provi-

ded the trigger is released between each shot. The crossbolt-type safety is accommodated in the trigger guard, behind the trigger. By pressing the safety button to the right, the trigger cannot be pulled. However, when this button is pushed over to the left (red ring visible), a shot can be fired (illus. 16 and 17).

The receiver is mounted on the buttstock and fastened by a stock bolt that screws into a stock bearing plate. The forearm is screwed on to the gas cylinder bulge. Stripping is simple. After removing the buttplate and undoing the stock bolt, the buttstock, stock bearing plate and trigger plate can be taken down. Then, once the operating handle has been removed, the bolt carrier is pressed downwards out of its seating. By removing the forearm and gas cylinder cap, the piston and slide bars will easily lift out. Further dismantling is not necessary for cleaning, yet any handyman can take the BAR completely to pieces with screwdriver and appropriate spanners.

Sighting and performance

The BAR comes with an adjustable, folding leaf rear sight (illus. 20). The front sight is a bead dovetailed into a hooded ramp (illus. 21). Our gun was fitted with a 1.5 x Hensoldt scope, clipped into a Suhl detachable mount (illus. 22). The scope had a crosshair reticle with centre dot which is detrimental to lining up with black bullseyes for testing purposes.

At approx. 55 yds this dot concealed the bullseye of a DJV-A2 target sheet. As this reticle is designed for quick-response shooting at large moving objects, and not for target practice with small bullseyes, we clamped our BAR in a machine rest (type Preuss) for our 55 yards trials. We used DWM .308 Win. ammunition, with 180 gr. TUG bullet (illus. 23). Dispersion was 1.06 in. with 5 shots (illus. 24), which would mean approximately 2.12 in. at 109.4 yds. Considering the fact that automatic rifles are never as accurate as good bolt-action rifles, the performance of the BAR was acceptable . . .

1 Barrel unit
2 Washer for gas cylinder cap
3 Gas cylinder cap
4 Front sight
5 Hood
6 Rear sight
7 Piston
8 Cylinder guide pin
9 Slide
10 Slide buffer
11 Buffer plates (2)
12 Side bars (2) **13** Guide rails (2) for side bars
14 Action spring guide
15 Action spring
16 Receiver **17** Closure screws for scope mount holes
18 Hinged magazine floorplate
19 Magazine retaining bar
20 Crosspin
21 Retaining springs
22 Crosspin for retaining springs
23 Bearing plate
24 Cover plate
25 Bolt carrier
26 Carrier stop dog
27 Pin for carrier stop dog
28 Extractor
29 Extractor spring
30 Bolt operating handle
31 Operating handle retaining feather
32 Operating handle arrester
33 Operating handle arrester pin
34 Bolt
35 Locking block
36 Ejector
37 Ejector spring
38 Ejector pin
39 Trigger plate and guard
40 Trigger

41 Trigger pin
42 Sear
43 Sear pin
44 Plunger connecting sear and disconnector
45 Spring for plunger
46 Hammer
47 Hammer axle
48 Hammer springs (2)
49 Hammer spring guides
50 Hammer spring yoke, top
51 Hammer spring yoke, bottom
52 Firing pin
53 Firing-pin spring
54 Firing-pin retainer
55 Safety button
56 Safety button plunger
57 Safety button plunger spring
58 Spring retaining pin
59 Magazine latch
60 Magazine latch spring
61 Retaining pin for magazine latch spring
62 Magazine spring guide
63 Disconnector
64 Disconnector pin
65 Magazine housing
66 Buttstock
67 Stock bolt
68 Washer for stock bolt
69 Eyelet for rear swivel
70 Buttplate
71 Buttplate screws (2)
72 Forearm
73 Forearm bushing
74 Forearm screw
75 Nut for forearm screw.

The BAR automatic rifle showed, for a mass production gun, fine workmanship. Performance and reliability should meet all requirements during the hunt. With enough practice, swinging and shouldering can be mastered, despite some muzzle heaviness. The front swivel should be repositioned, to avoid bruising one's hand while firing.

25 Exploded view of the BAR rifle.

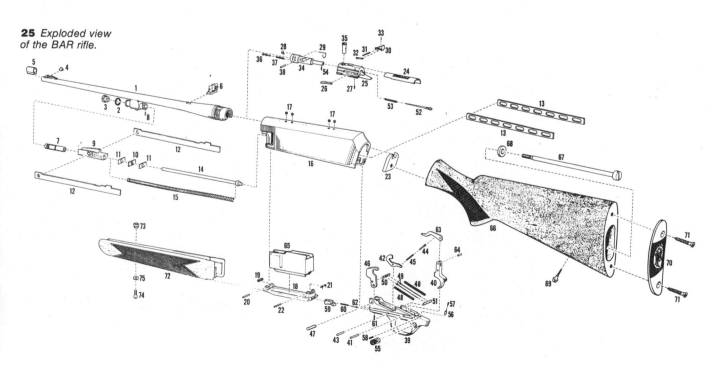

> **The nomenclature of British military rifles is a little puzzling.**

British .303 Rifle No. 4 Mark I

Before WWI they were classified by a "Mark", followed by a Roman numeral. For example, Mark I or Mark II. An exception to this rule was Model 13, which later became Model 14. Between the two World Wars these Lee-Enfield rifles were coded with Marks and Numbers. Due to this change-over, the Mark III SMLE was rechristened Rifle No. 1 Mark III SMLE, for instance. However, towards the end of WW2 both groups were expressed in Arabic numerals. In addition, an asterisk was occasionally placed behind the designation, in order to denote that that particular rifle deviated from the norm.

Rifle No. 4 Mark I was introduced in 1931. By and

large, it was the same as the No. 1 Mark VI. In 1939, when Britain desperately needed great quantities of rifles, the No. 4 Mark I underwent simplification to meet mass production requirements. It became the standard rifle of the British armed forces and it saw service in all theatres of war. Manufacturing techniques were simplified wherever possible. The No. 4 Mark I, for example, was made with four different patterns of rear sights varying from precision adjustable leaf to simple L types. The metal fittings, once hammered and properly fitted, were replaced by cheap stampings.

More than five million No. 4 Mark I's were produced during the 1939–45 war in England, Canada, USA and India. Australia, however, continued to produce the No. 1 Mark III.

All British bolt-action military rifles were derived from the American Lee-Metford of 1888. The design of the No. 4 Mark I corresponds to the Lee-Enfield version of 1895. About 14 changes were incorporated, of which not all are said to have been improvements!

Characteristic of the Lee-Enfield bolt is its movable breechbolt head. Cocking is done on the forward stroke, not on the opening one. Furthermore, the bolt is not too simple to disassemble. The Lee-Enfields have a 10-round magazine, but single cartridges can be loaded quite easily.

The No. 4 Mark I's made in USA bear an asterisk, hence they differ from the norm. They sport one-piece stocks, and the trigger is pivoted to the receiver, not to the trigger guard. The Canadian version will fire rifle grenades. Ch. Sch.

2 L-type sight with peep-hole
3 Action open. The safety catch is on the left of the receiver, which turns 180 degrees.
4/5 In some models cord was entwined around the forearm, by the factory. This was to give the British Tommy a firm grip when jabbing at the enemy with a bayonet.

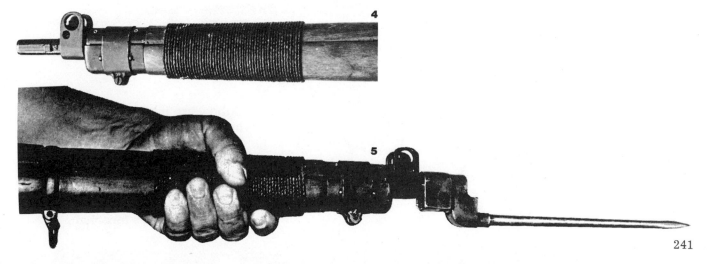

Klaus Nocher

Reck Single-Action Revolver R 14

The firm of RECK, West Germany, has introduced the caliber 4 mm (.157 in.) R 14 revolver for indoor (or outdoor) range shooting. The R 14 is by no means a plaything for young "Cowboys and Indians" for 4 mm cartridges are still dangerous enough to be taken seriously. See Figs. 1 and 2.

The R 14 resembles in appearance and size the Ruger "Black Hawk", although a fundamental difference between the two exists:– The R 14 is, in part, made of pressure-cast zinc alloy. Certainly, you must look twice to detect this difference as the alloy casting is not noticeable as such.

The use of zinc alloy pressure castings for handguns has now become accepted, for by means of this system of manufacture prices can be kept down. In Germany, the R 14 can be had for DM 124, whereas other revolvers cost three or four times this price.

Subcalibre tubes for cheaper ammunition have been on the market for years. Unfortunately, the shooter is faced with installing the insert barrel every time he wants to practise, so after a few weeks these tubes usually end up in a drawer and are forgotten.

General

The R 14 is a 6-shot single-action revolver, chambered for 4 mm rim-fire cartridges. Apart from the frame, handle, barrel rib, gate, and the front section of the ejector rod, all parts are of steel. The lockwork is similar to that of the Colt SAA, with the exception that the firing pin is not on the hammer but screwed into the frame (Fig. 3).

Barrel

The 5.9 in. barrel is screwed and pinned in the receiver and the 10 rifling grooves have a twist rate of 1 in 9.9 in. The button rifling is within the tolerance of 4/100 mm.

The junction slope has been bored at an angle of 2 degrees and the gasket (Fig. 4) functions as a labyrinth seal, which enhances accuracy. The gap between cylinder and rear end of barrel, that is, gasket, measures only approx. 7/100 mm.

By the way, it is not advisable to clean the barrel with the brass brush delivered by the company. I use this brush to clean the cylinder only. Still, the barrel must be mopped out immediately after use, since 4 mm cartridges produce a lot of fouling. Tow should be passed through the eyelet of an aluminium or brass rod, and powder solvent should not be spared.

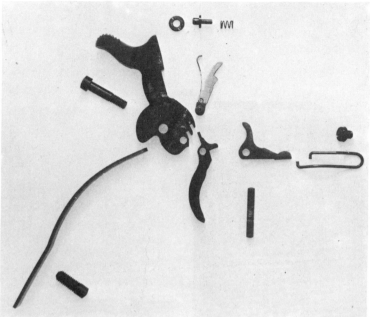

1 *R 14, left view*
2 *R 14, Right view*
3 *The lockwork*
4 *The gasket*
5 *Cylinder, three chambers loaded*
6 *Rear sight dismantled*
7 *Firing pin is screwed into the standing breech. Gate open*

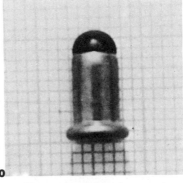

8 *The "face" of the R 14*
9 *The impress of approval*
10 *4 mm cartridge, No. 7 ball*
11 *Three balls: flattened, soft landed, box trapped*

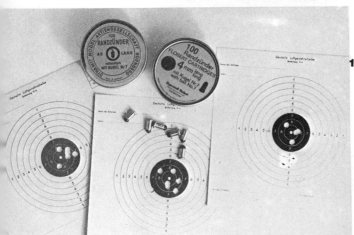

12 *Groupings at 11 yds*
13 *The firm's emblem in the grip plate*
14 *R 14 dismantled*

TECHNICAL DATA

Manufacturer: Reck Sportwaffen, Lauf, W. Germany **No.** 150091	
Action: Single	
Overall length: 11.4 in.	
Height: 5.1 in.	
Barrel: 5.9 in.	
Rifling: 10 grooves, right-hand twist (1 in 10 in.)	
Calibre: 4 mm rimfire	
Weight: Approx. 2 lbs. 3 oz.	
Trigger pull: Approx. 3 lbs **Mag. Capacity:** 6 rounds	
Stocks: Walnut, oil finished, emblem	
Finish: Black	

Cylinder

The cylinder rotates to the right. The chambers are countersunk to safeguard the shooter should a cartridge case split. Like the SA revolvers, the R 14 cylinder is mounted on a central pin and retained via a sprung screw. The ratchet is very carefully machined and no signs of wear and tear were evident after 300 shots.

Sights

The sights of the R 14 would do honour to an expensive target pistol. So beautifully aligned are the sights that it is a joy to use them. The rear sight (Figs. 6 and 7) is exceedingly rugged and is click adjusted for windage and elevation. Fig. 8 shows the front sight which is integral with the top rib. It is serrated to help avoid reflected light. The barrel rib, the overlap of which holds the ejector rod, has a small pin at its rear end (Fig. 14) that fits into the frame. At its front end it wraps around the muzzle and is fastened with a screw.

The law

According to German law, Section 22 of the Federal Firearms Act, handguns chambered under 5 mm (.197 in.) diameter and under 15 mm (.591 in.) in length are not subject to proof in the normal sense of the word.

However the Physikalisch-Technische Bundesanstalt, known generally as the PTB, have been entrusted with the task of checking safety, reliability, durability and design of such handguns. Their impress of approval is stamped on the side of the frame (Fig. 9).

Ballistics

The purpose, of course, behind this sub-calibre revolver is to give modern man the chance to shoot within his own 4 walls, now that civilization has clamped down with all sorts of restrictions outside his home. Despite the pipsqueak load, accuracy has not been overly impaired. When firing the first shots the user is surprised at the lack of recoil and probably thinks he is playing with a toy. A glance down the following table will refute this.

Muzzle velocity = 1086 fps
At 5.5 yards = 991 fps
At 11 yards = 909 fps
At 16.5 yards = 840 fps

These figures are for an 8 in. barrel. As a means of comparison, a .22 L.R. cartridge (standard) has a muzzle velocity of approx. 1145 fps. The 4 mm cartridges, on account of their light weight, travel only about 360 yards.

At short distances, the 4 mm cartridges can be dangerous, as illustrated in Fig. 11. As you can see, the left ball is as flat as a pancake, after hitting a piece of metal at 11 yards.

Performance

Fig. 12 shows groupings at 11 yards. An average dispersion of .5 in. is good shooting. The firm of Reck showed me a grouping with only .35 in. dispersion. At 11 yards all 5 shots should be within the inner circle of a long-playing record.

Conclusion

Is a sub-calibre revolver a good idea? I say "yes," for there are numbers of shooters who would like to practise in attic or cellar who otherwise would not have the chance to do so.

There is only one recommendation I should like to make to the manufacturer: Please weaken the mainspring. My thumb is so sore that I can't cock the hammer anymore.

14

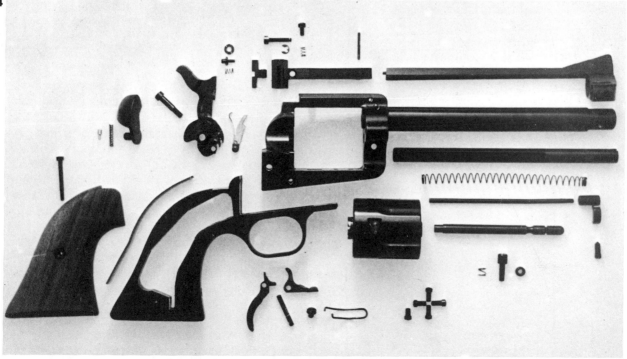

SODIA-ANSON

Shotgun/Rifle Combination Model 1954 AD

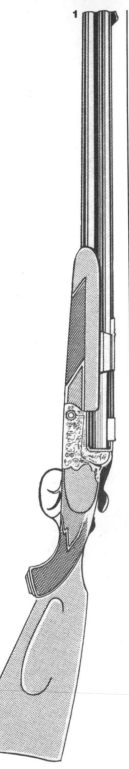

Manufacturer:	Sodia (Ferlach, Carinthia, Austria)
Designation:	Model 1954 AD
Type:	Hammerless superposed combination gun
Grade:	Standard
Bolting:	Kersten type combined with double under lugs
Ignition:	Anson-Deeley system, separate firing pins, however.
Safety:	Automatic, tang thumb-slide
Triggers:	Front: set trigger with slack (pull: approx. 2 kg) Rear: for shotshell barrel (pull: approx. 1.7 kg)
Overall length:	103 cm
Weight:	3.2 kg
Barrels:	Shotshell: Full choke, Böhler Blitz steel Rifle: Böhler special steel Ventilated top rib
Barrel length:	60 cm
Rate of twist:	22 cm Direction of twist: clockwise
Number of grooves:	4
Cartridges:	.22 Hornet, .22 Savage HP, 6.5 x 57 R, 7 x 57 R, 7 x 65 R, 8 x 57 IRS, .222 Rem., .270 Win. .30–06, Springfield, 7 x 75 R
Shotshell:	20 x 70, 16 x 70, 12 x 70
Sights:	Silver bead, Folding U leaf
Distance between sights:	43 cm
Stocking:	Walnut, polished; German-type stocking; Checkering on forearm and pistol grip; Buttplate and grip cap of black plastic
Length of stocking:	In total 70 cm; 35 cm up to front trigger, 32.5 cm up to rear trigger. Drop at comb 4 cm, drop at heel 7.3 cm

2

The manufacture of weapons employing the drop-down opening system is subject to a large amount of technical know-how. For a reliable, sturdy lock-up between barrel(s) and action is dependent on the skills of a master gunsmith. This, of course, contributes substantially to the fact that genuine top-grade guns of this type, irrespective of whether they are superposed shotguns, drillings, double barrelled shotguns or combination guns, etc., are usually produced in family-run workshops that have existed for generations. In Austria, namely in the gun-making town of Ferlach, there still exists today more such gunsmithing families who make truly high-grade, individually styled weapons, than in any other European country. The firm of Franz Sodia, Sporting Gun Factory, Ferlach, Carinthia, Austria, produces guns that have been known for many decades on both sides of the Atlantic, and appreciated

DR. MANFRED ROSENBERGER

by sportsmen for their beauty and quality. Although Sodia can no longer claim to produce solely hand-made guns (with 130 employees this firm is the largest and most modern family-run gunsmithing business in Austria), the quality of their quantity-production firearms is superb. The Sodia-Anson superposed shotgun/rifle combination 1954 AD (illus. 1) amply proves this statement.

This standard-type weapon comes with a Kersten action, double under lugs, Anson Deeley lock system and trigger-blocking safety mechanism. The most important requisite of a break-open gun is a rock solid lock-up between barrel(s) and action.

toughest and most durable lock-up in break-open guns. This system will even withstand heaviest loads, repeatedly. This cannot be said of all other lock-up types.

The locking mechanism consists of top snap, top-snap lever, double headed cross bolt, double wedged flat bolt, top-snap shaft, top-snap spring, and top-snap screw (illus. 2). The topside locking arrangement is of the Kersten type, whereby the double headed cross bolt engages in the barrel extensions that fit into the slotways in the face of the standing breech when the weapon is closed (illus. 3 and 4). When the gun is opened or closed, the rotation of the

3

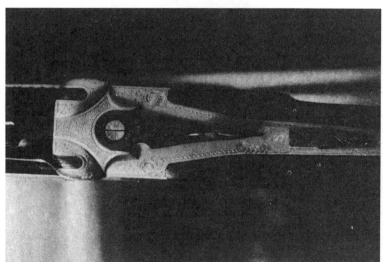

4

This lock-up has two different functions when a shot is fired. On the one hand, it counteracts the pivoting moment which is caused by the hinge pin not being on the same plane as the forces of recoil. On the other, the lock-up can reduce the strain on the breech face of the receiver, against which the forces of recoil batter. Continuous exposure to heavy strain leads to material expansion, and sooner or later to a non-alignment between barrel(s) and breech face. Just how long a shotgun will remain tightly fitted depends on the strength of the standing breech and on the quality of the lock-up system; along with proper use and the quality of the material the gun is made of. The larger the area of surface resistance, the greater is the distribution of forces of recoil. Strain is reduced, so too is the danger of deformation.

Combining the Kersten action (also known as dou-ble Greener) with double under lugs represents the

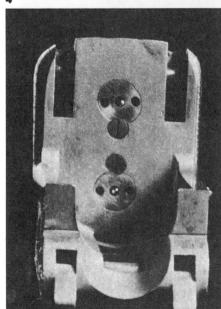

1 Sodia-Anson combination gun Mod. 1954 AD.
2 Top snap (with screw), double headed cross bolt, top-snap lever, dou-ble wedged flat bolt, top-snap, shaft, top-snap spring.
3 The double headed cross bolt engages in barrel extensions . . .
4 . . . that fit into slotways in the stand-ing breech when the weapon is closed . . .
5 . . . and the flat bolt engages in the double under-lugs.

5

247

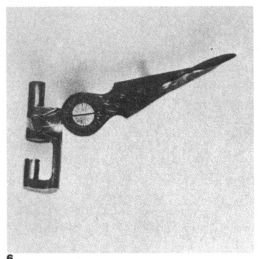

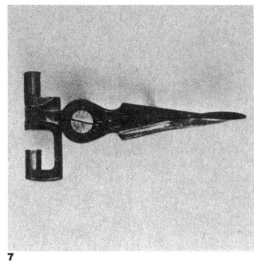

6

7

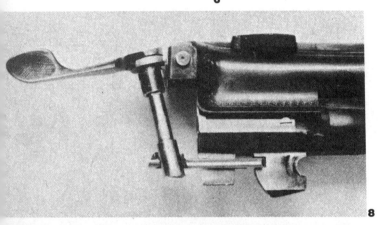

8

9

top snap is transferred to the top-snap lever, which, in turn, operates the cross bolt (illus. 6 and 7).

This upper bolt first and foremost counteracts the pivoting of the barrels immediately upon discharge.

The double wedged flat bolt engages in the cutouts of the under lugs of the lower barrel. The flat bolt is connected with the top snap via the shaft (illus. 2, 8, 9). This second bolt also counteracts pivoting, whereas the hinge pin, the two lugs and the surface area of the breech face help nullify the so-called pull-off moment.

It need not be over-emphasized that the double bolting system of this gun is greatly dependent on fine workmanship, allowing all the parts to fit perfectly in each other without tolerances. Only then can there exist a guarantee that headspacing between the surface at the rear of the chambers and the face of the breechblock will remain constant. When combining the Kersten lock-up with double lugs, the flat bolt must be accurately fitted, more so than with other systems. Perfect interfitting of parts is heavily dependent on smooth surfaces. A requirement not always fulfilled in many cheap guns.

The Sodia-Anson's durability may also be ascribed to the strong surface area around the chambers (illus. 4). Hence, the union between barrels and action is better, and recoil is more widely distributed, owing to larger area of resistance. In addition, the receiver is reinforced, between horizontal and vertical sections.

The extractor is conventional. When opening the action, the shell (case) is withdrawn about 11 mm out of the chamber (illus. 10). Its two side arms run in slots on the outer surfaces of the rifle barrel. Another excellent feature of this gun is its Anson-Deeley lock system. The hammers are embedded in the receiver, contrary to those of the Blitz system (illus. 11 and 12).

6 The movement of the top snap . . .
7 . . . is transferred to the cross bolt via the lever.
8 The lower flat bolt that engages in the under-lugs is steered by the top snap, via the shaft.
9 The wedges of the flat bolt can be seen through the windows in the floor of the receiver (into which the under lugs fit), and hinge pin, far right.

SODIA-ANSON

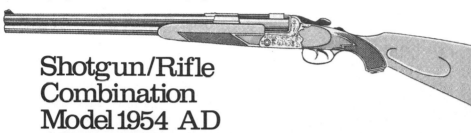

Shotgun/Rifle Combination Model 1954 AD

10 The extractor is of traditional design, and lifts the hulls/cases just far enough from the chambers for the fingers to grasp.
11 The hammers are let into the receiver (arrow) . . .
12 . . . so they are independent of each other, and take up little space.
13 Firing mechanism (right-hand side). Bushing, firing pin, sear arm (with spring), hammer, cocking lever.

10

11

12

This arrangement allows the triggers to lie nearer the muzzle. And their action is softer into the bargain. Doubling (the firing of two barrels inadvertently at the same time) is also out of the question, although not so with the Blitz system. Morever, the tie-in between buttstock and action is much stronger than in other systems, as less wood is removed when fitting.

The Anson-Deeley lockwork consists of the following pairs: hammers, hammer springs, sears, sear springs, and cocking levers (illus. 13 and 14). When the breech is opened, the forearm rotates the cocking levers around their axles, which, in turn, cock the hammers. As the hammers are pushed backwards, the nose of the sears engages in the hammer bents, and keeps the hammers at full cock. See illus. 15 and 16. The sears are suspended high in the receiver and

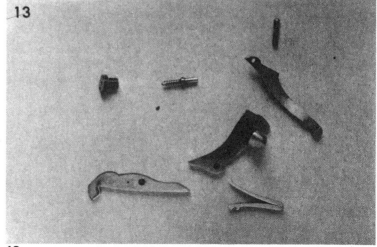

13

13

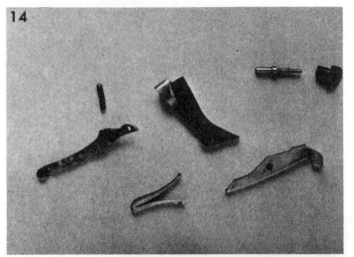

14

rest against the blades of the triggers, under influence of the sear spring (illus. 12). When one of the triggers is activated, the sear is drawn out of the bent to let the hammer fly forward against the firing pin. Suspending the sears is conducive to a soft let-off. And owing to the length of the sears, less energy is needed to lift them from the hammers.

Normally, in the Anson-Deeley system the firing pins are mounted in, or integral with the hammers. The Sodia-Anson model, however, as all guns made in Ferlach, has separate firing pins, which, together with the bushings, are screwed into the breech face from the front. See illus. 5, 12 and 13. Separate firing pins have a softer impact and are less subject to general wear and tear. Furthermore, firing pins let into the front of the breech face safeguard against blown

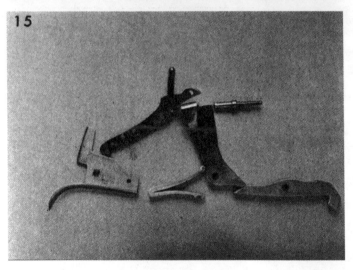

15

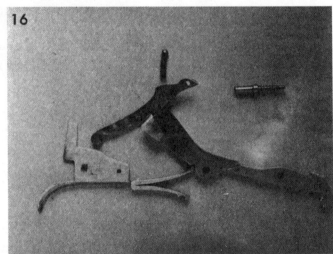

16

SODIA-ANSON Shotgun/Rifle Combination Model 1954 AD

primers, since the rearward flowing gases cannot propel the firing pin into the buttstock so as to injure the user. The angle of impact of the firing pins can be reset by changing the bushings, if the firing pins are separate, that is.

The trigger mechanism (set trigger at front) consists of two triggers, the centre arm, set-trigger arrester and springs.

These parts are installed on the trigger plate, as is usual. The set-trigger spring and the arrester spring are held by one and the same screw (illus. 19). While the shotgun trigger is not directly controlled by its own spring (it is tensioned by light pressure from the sear arm), the rifle trigger has a powerful spring (illus. 19) that steps into action when the set trigger is applied. In other words, it is more a set-trigger spring than a trigger spring. To activate the set trigger, the front trigger is pushed far enough forwards for the centre arm to engage in the arrester (illus. 17 and 18).

The safety mechanism blocks the triggers. When the top snap is activated, the safety automatically engages. The parts are thumb-slide, safety lever, top-snap plunger, and spring (illus.). When the safety catch is applied, the safety lever rests on the trigger blades, preventing the triggers being pulled and the sears being jarred out of the hammer bents (illus. 21 and 22). The thumb-slide is mounted on the tang.

The shotgun barrel is of Böhler Blitz steel, the rifle barrel of Böhler special steel. They are soft soldered and blued by brush application. The ventilated top rib is doubly high at front and rear sights. The top

barrel is mounted on the lower one at the chamber end. Again, the relatively large face around the chambers is a fine bastion for resisting the effects of recoil. Traditional sighting of the 1954 AD Model consists of a bead (illus. 24 and 25) and a simple folding-leaf rear sight (U type), the mount of which is let into the top rib (illus. 26).

Stocking comes in dark walnut, polished, not lacquered. Polished stocks can get wet without the wood coating cracking or splitting. Moreover, scratches are particularly ugly on lacquered woodwork, not quite so much on polished. The buttstock is of the general pistol-grip type (illus. 27) and the buttplate is of black plastic.

The receiver is fastened with a crossbolt (illus. 28). Its rear wall is undulated, to fit better with the stock.

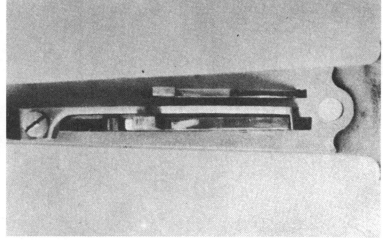

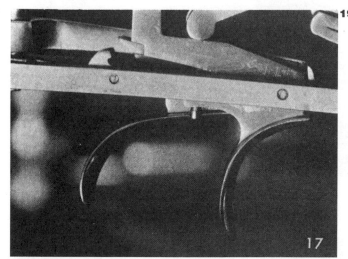

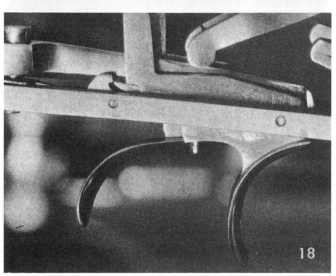

14 Firing mechanism (left-hand side).
15 Left firing mechanism in down position.
16 Right firing mechanism cocked. Note that the full-cock bent of the hammer is now engaged.
17 The set trigger is conventional. By pressing it forward . . .
18 . . . the centre arm engages in the arrester.
19 The triggers seen from above. Note the set-trigger spring.

20

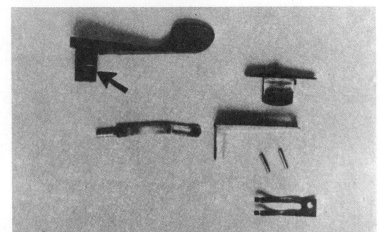

SODIA-ANSON
Shotgun/Rifle
Combination
Model 1954 AD

21

22

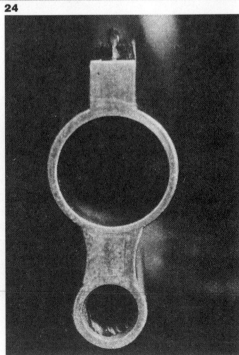

20 *The safety mechanism: top snap (note recess for plunger-arrow), thumb-slide, top-snap plunger, lever, arresting pin, spring.*
21 *If the thumb-slide is pushed forwards, the safety lever moves away from the trigger blades . . .*
22 *. . . if it is pushed back, the trigger blades are blocked.*
23 *There is a large surface area around the chambers.*
24 *The sight is mounted on the raised top rib . . .*

23

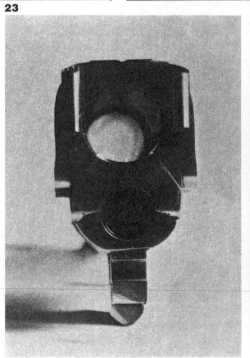

24

The relatively long wrist flows into a low-line pistol grip (illus. 29), especially practical for fast, smooth pointing when shotgunning. The forearm slopes and its tip has a strong slanting plane (illus. 30) which bestows a pleasing appearance. It is fastened with a patent catch (illus. 31).

Collectively, one can say that the Sodia-Anson 1954 AD is a handsome gun. The nicely engraved receiver (illus. 32 and 33), the increased area surface around the chambers, the receiver reinforcement and the eye-catching forearm all contribute to its good looks. However, the excellent workmanship is even more prominent. It's a real joy to examine the polished "innards" of this gun.

All moving parts interplay so perfectly that no harsh noises are heard, everything functions velvety-soft. Opening and closing the breech causes only a whisper, the safety slide rides back noiselessly. In addition, the action is extraordinarily rugged. When one considers that the 1954 AD is a standard weapon, it is not hard to understand the high reputation the Sodia people enjoy.

For testing, we chose the 7 x 57 R cartridge and 16 x 70 shotshells (serial No. 13 005). No misfunctioning of any kind showed up. Balance and pointing qualities were excellent. Stocking was a little short for the average-length arm (from front trigger 35 cm, from rear 32.5 cm), however.

25

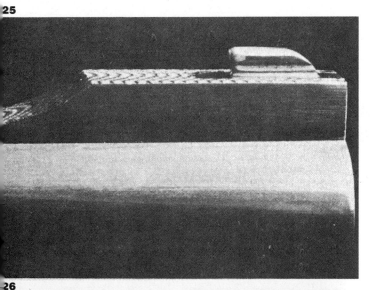

26

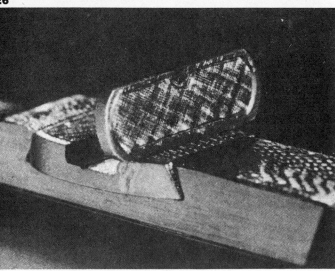

27

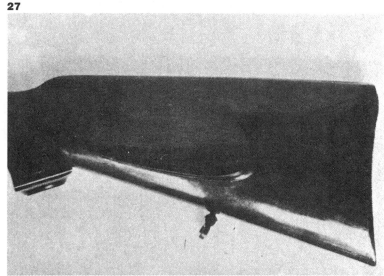

28

25 . . . and has a sliver bead.
26 The folding-leaf rear sight is mounted on a rail.

27 The buttstock is of traditional shape . . .
28 . . . and is held to the receiver via a crossbolt.

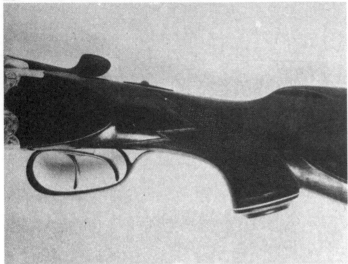

29

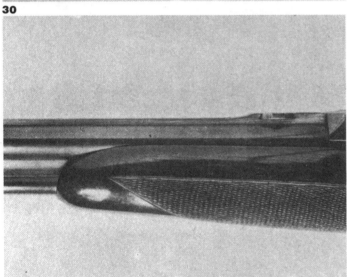

30

Four different cartridges and four different shot-shells were tried out in the 1954 AD (illus. 35 and 36). The results were as follows:

a) Rifle barrel (length of twist 22 cm)

Average dispersion at 100 metres, 5 shots fired from each of the following types of cartridge:

DWM 103 grs. PSP (tombac)	4.6 cm
DWM 154 grs. Solid jacket (tombac)	2.8 cm
DWM 162 grs. TIG	3.8 cm
RWS 173 grs. Partition bu.	3.7 cm

Measured against the old test norms, these are really good results. The greater dispersion of the 103 grs. bullet can probably be put down to the short rate of twist (22 cm) of this barrel for such a short bullet.

b) Shotgun barrel (full choke)

The various brands of shotshells (shot size 2½ mm) did not pattern uniformly, as expected. After eliminating these cartridge type influences, we achieved the following at 35 metres:

Regularity from shot to shot – good

Evenness of pattern – excellent

Density – 1:1.68

Maximum effective range was 41 metres. Point of aim and point of impact (concerning vertical deviation) coincided at 35 metres. These results are likewise quite satisfactory. This combination gun sported natural pointing qualities when used against flying targets. However, the stocking has been designed more for the shotgun than for the rifle.

The Sodia-Anson Model 1954 AD is the silver lining among standard-type guns for it is extremely well made, it is a good looker, and it shoots well.

31

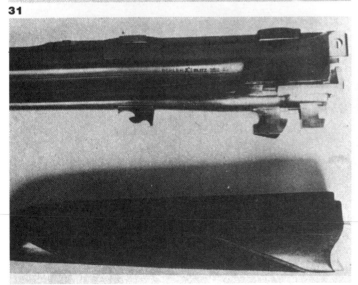

32

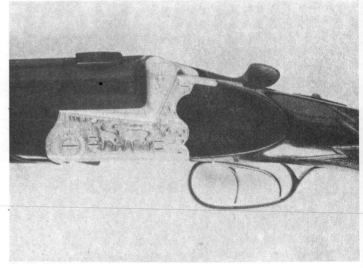

Rating

Workmanship	1
Functional safety	1
Performance	2
Finish	1
Design	0
Sighting	2
Balance	1
Pointing qualities	1
Stocking	2
Total	10

The lower the number, the higher the rating.

Ballistic data of the 7x57 R cartridges used during testing

Brand		DWM	DWM	DWM	RWS
Bullet weight		103	154	162	173 grains
Bullet's shape		CS/tt	Or/f	Or/tt	Or/bt
Bullet type		SJ/sp	SJ/sm	SJ/TIG	SJ/par.
Distance (m)					
Velocity mps	0	992	826	770	770
	100	844	733	694	714
	200	706	661	633	664
	300	578	601	583	620
Energy mkg	0	336	365	302	339
	100	243	288	246	291
	200	170	234	204	252
	300	114	193	173	219
Trajectory ceiling in cm	100	1.9	2.5	2.8	2.7
	200	6.4	8.4	9.5	9.0
	300	17.4	22.0	24.2	22.3

Abbreviations:
CS = conical, spitzer, tt = tapered tail, Or = ogive, bt = boat tail, f = flat point, SJ = semi-jacketed, sp = soft point, sm = solid mantle, TIG = torpedo, par. = partition bu.

3

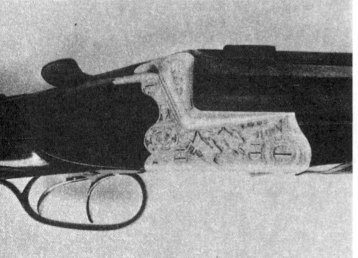

34

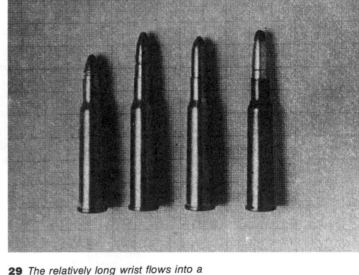

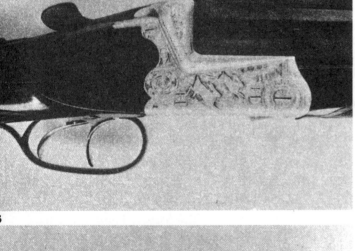

29 The relatively long wrist flows into a low-line pistol grip.
30 The front of the forearm is slanted.
31 The forearm is fastened to the barrels with a patent catch.
32 The side walls are nicely decorated . . .
33 . . . and the receiver is attractively designed.
34 DWM 103 grs. PSP, DWM 154 grs. Solid Jacket, DWM 162 grs. TIG, RWS 173 grs. Partition bullet.
35 Shotshells used during testing.

Text and Photos   E. Brunnthaler

The .44 S&W Russian of 1870

When self-contained cartridges appeared, the problem of removing the empty metallic cases from the firing chambers appeared simultaneously, irrespective of wheter the arm was designed for pinfire (Lefaucheux), rimfire or centrefire cartridges. Revolvers with non-swing out cylinders were awkward to unload in that each case had to be individually poked back past the loading gate by means of an ejector rod. This procedure was both time-consuming and awkward.

In the case of the very first Smith & Wesson revolvers (and other makes of similar design), the cylinder had to be lifted from its mounting and each chamber had to be slid over the forward end of the base pin to push out the empty cases.

Only in revolvers provided with swing-out cylinders (as in modern revolvers) or top-break frames can all the spent cases be ejected at one and the same time. Here, of course, such revolvers as the Ghaye, Galand, Merwin & Hulbert, etc., which had to be axially pulled apart to load and unload, are disregarded, since they rapidly disappeared from the market anyway.

One of the first, and at the same time one of the best top-break revolvers with automatic ratchet-type ejector was the .44 S & W Russian that saw service with the Russian cavalry between 1870 and 1895 under the czars Alexander II and III, and which is a choice collector's piece today. This Russian model was evolved from the S & W 1869, and differs only in respect of the bow guard with fingerpiece for third finger, slightly different-shaped handle, smooth grips, and a few other insignificant items. Smith & Wesson of Springfield, USA, and Ludwig Loewe of Berlin, Germany, produced this model for the Russians. Workmanship and quality of materials are truly excellent. S & W delivered 250 000 pieces, although some authorities still speak of 200 000. The Turkish army adopted a similar model, the S & W .44 rimfire. This so-called Russian version was very popular up to World War I as a target revolver, on account of its excellent balance. This popularity might also be credited to the fact that hammer and trigger had separate springs; thus trigger pull could be reasonably well adjusted, with a bit of skill. A number of other models were derived from the S & W Russian, in various calibres. Other gun makers followed suit, especially in Belgium. However,

S & W quality was seldom if ever achieved.

Figures 1 and 2 show a specimen made in Berlin in 1874. Name of manufacturer and place of manufacture are stamped in Cyrillic on the barrel strap, as well

as a double-eagle-with-crown proofmark. The year of manufacture is stamped on the left side of the frame.

Figure 3 exemplifies a patent drawing in cross section. The barrel assembly (1) is swivel mounted to the

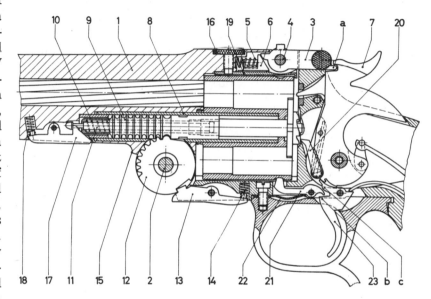

Main data of .44 S & W Russian Calibre .44
Barrel length 6.5 in.
Rifling 5 grooves Right-hand twist Grooves and lands of equal width
Overall length Approx. 12 in.
Number of chambers 6
Outside diameter of cylinder 1.67 in.
Weight, without ammunition 2 lb. 9 oz.
Finish blue (hammer and screw-heads bright/yellow tempered)
Source: Jaroslav Lugs, Handfeuerwaffen, Vol. 1 H. W. Bowman, Antique Guns

frame via a hinge screw (2), and both parts are locked together by means of the T-shaped barrel catch (3) that is screwed to the rear of the barrel. Spring (5) and slide (6) exert pressure on the barrel catch to prevent it inadvertently opening. Nonetheless, this T-shaped barrel catch is the weakest feature of this otherwise superb revolver. When a shot is fired, gas pressure tends to pull the barrel assembly away from the frame, so the barrel catch and screw (4) are subjected to terrific strain. Unfortunately, this catch is sharp edged where it engages with the locking post of the frame, which reduces the ultimate breaking limit. Care should be taken when using modern ammunition, even weak loads, in these S & W Russians. The hammer (7) is provided with a small lip that partially enshrouds the protrusion (a) of the barrel catch just before the striker nose explodes the primer. If the revolver is not properly closed, the falling hammer will strike against this protrusion (a) and tip down the barrel assembly. Then again, the striker cannot reach the cartridge if the barrel catch is not fully engaged.

Extractor (9) and extractor spring (10) are housed in the extractor well (8). The racked section of the extractor stem engages in the pinion (12), which, in turn, is positioned by the spring (14), via the arm (13). When the hammer is placed at half cock, the barrel catch is pulled up between thumb and forefinger of the left hand, to cause the barrel assembly to swivel around its hinge pin. The pinion (12) drives the extractor out of the face of the cylinder, and

throws out the empty cases. Just before the angle of traverse is completed, the leading edge (15) abuts against arm (13); an action that frees the pinion (12). Spring (10) draws the extractor back into its well and rotates the pinion to its starting position, since the latter is geared to the extractor stem.

When the revolver is closed again, arm (13) re-engages in the cutout of the pinion (12). If the cylinder is to be removed, the knurled screw (16) is simply loosened and the latch (17) is pressed against its spring (18) when the revolver is open. Once the drawbar (11) is liberated from latch (17), cylinder and ejector may be pulled out of the ejector well (8). The sprung retaining hook (19) is also withdrawn a short distance, until it disengages from the top edge of the cylinder. Once the cylinder is re-fitted, the retaining hook is snapped over the edge and the knurled screw is tightened again. The latch (17), driven by the spring (18) automatically

re-engages in the drawbar (11).

The .44 S & W Russian is single action only. Thanks to the outstanding quality of all mechanical parts, working action is velvety smooth. When a shot is being fired, the cylinder is not locked by the pawl (20) and a stop stud mounted on the trigger, as in virtually every other revolver. This model has its own cylinder stop (21), which engages in the stop notches placed around the cylinder wall. This cylinder stop is held by a small flat spring (22) that is housed in the trigger guard. When the hammer is put at half cock, the shoulder (b) of the trigger pushes the cylinder stop out of contact with the cylinder. The cylinder then freely rotates. On pulling back the trigger, the protrusion (c) forces the cylinder stop up hard into the stop notch, making sure that the chamber about to be fired is kept in line with the barrel.

The rear sight sits atop of the T-shaped barrel catch. The front sight is integral with the barrel, and not adjustable either. The smooth grips, of oiled walnut, are held by a grip screw. In addition, they are pinned near the butt and positioned by the horseshoe curve of the frame at the top.

A lanyard ring is riveted into the butt. Figure 4 shows the S & W stripped. In conclusion, it must be said that this model was exceptionally well designed and painstakingly made. At the International Exhibition in Moscow in 1872 the Smith & Wessen Russian was awarded a gold medal.

▼ The S & W Russian broken down into its component parts.

SIG P 210

Text and Photos Georg von Stavenhagen

SWISS SERVICE PISTOL

The SIG pistol is manufactured in various versions by the Schweizerische Industrie-Gesellschaft at Neuhausen/Rheinfall. It has made a reputable name for itself on account of quality, finish and performance. The SIG design traces its ancestry back to the auto pistols of C. G. Petter, although, of course, in conception the SIG is an outgrowth of John Browning's ingenuity. I don't intend to describe how this pistol works, or name every minute part, in detail. The beginner can find all this sort of information in prospectuses, and the old hands would find such details boring. There is a number of interesting things about handguns that cannot be found in the normal firearms encyclopedias.

chambered for
9 mm, 7.65 or .22 LR

1 *SIG P 210-6, 9 mm target model with plastic grips*
2 *Do. Left view showing slide stop and safety catch*
3 *Do. in .22 L.R.*
4 *Remington Rand M 1911 .45 ACP with sub-calibre conversion unit. Note floating chamber peeking out of ejection port*
5 *Do. with slightly reduced target sights*
6 *Colt National Match .45 ACP with Elliason rear sight and trigger stop*

SIG P 210

The SIG P 210 was adopted by the Swiss Army in 1948.

When handling this pistol for the first time, one cannot help but notice a feeling of ruggedness and top-grade quality. The slide operates with watchmaker precision, for the guide rails are long and exactingly machined. Very few pistols had longer guide rails, the ones that did were the Colt 1902 Sporting or Military and the Model 1905 chambered for .45 ACP, both pioneered by John Browning.

The hammer thumbs back easily, especially from the half-cock position, so there is no problem for small hands. As with other external hammer pistols, the spur is mounted too high, the newer ones being no exception. Anyone not knowing the SIG can get a fright when the hammer at half cock drops, when the trigger is lightly pressed. However, the cartridge cannot be ignited, as hammer drop is too short to activate the inertia firing pin fitted.

This half cock, therefore, is in reality only an interceptor that blocks the falling hammer, should it slip from under one's fingers. In this respect, the SIG can be carried with a round chambered and the hammer in the fully down position, since the firing pin's nose does not protrude through the breechface. This pistol allows the chambering of a round whether the safety is on or off. The manual safety blocks the sear, and, in turn, the trigger itself. The SIG also (regrettably) comes equipped with a magazine safety. When the magazine is removed the sear arm is pressed downwards, so in no way can the hammer be released. Much the same situation is created when the slide

7 Hole for the hammer-housing screw in SIG P 210-6
8 Slides and barrels for the various calibres (9 mm, 7.65 mm, .22 L.R.)
9 9 mm magazine (with loader), do. 7.65 mm, do. .22 L.R.

7

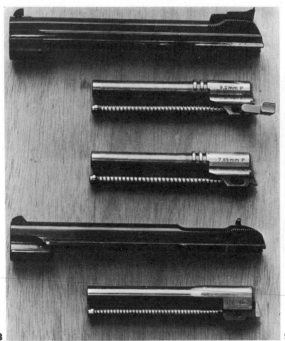

8

9

does not quite close. As soon as the action is locked, barrel and slide move backwards somewhat in a straight line, more so than in pistols using a barrel link, such as Colt 1911, Tokarev, or S & W 1939. This means unlocking begins later, "long after" the bullet has left the barrel.

The SIG balances nicely in the hand; still, some handgunners prefer to remove the hump over the backstrap. If the stocks are of wood, this is but a simple task, as the stocks cover the recessed metal frame, as they also do on the P 38.

In the target version, the trigger is better shaped than in the military one. Nonetheless, the SIG trigger is a little unorthodox, for pull is divided into three stages. The first "gear" takes up about 1 mm (.0394 in.), the second "gear" about 4 mm (.1576 in.), up to the pre-letoff point, and the third "gear" requires another 2 mm (.0788 in.) to drop the hammer. Weight of pull for the first phase is just under 11 ozs., for the second about 1 lb. 8 oz., and for the third phase about 1 lb. 10 ozs. In other words, trigger pull is about 3 lb. 13 oz., but it could be reduced to about 3 lb., if desired.

The front surface of the trigger is unfortunately slippery-smooth, but in return the front strap of the handle is evenly serrated, that is, on the target model. The crisp-working hammer mechanism is encapsulated in its own housing, similar to that of the Tokarev, which is readily removed. In the target version, the hammer mechanism housing is additionally anchored by means of a small screw. In early models, this screw was located under the hand grip, in later **10**

10 *Grouping printed by SIG target model .22 L.R. at 33 yds from a machine rest. Dispersion 22x44 mm (6 shots)*
11 *Grouping printed by SIG 7.65 at 55 yds from a machine rest. Dispersion 57x47 mm (8 shots)*
12 *Grouping printed by SIG 9 mm at 55 yds from a machine rest. Dispersion 33x48 mm (10 shots)*

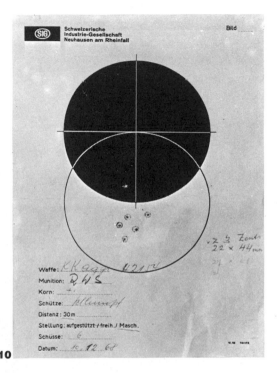

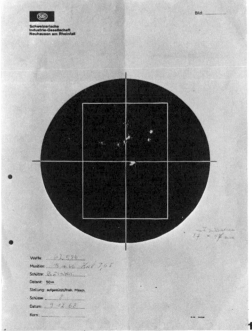

11 **12**

263

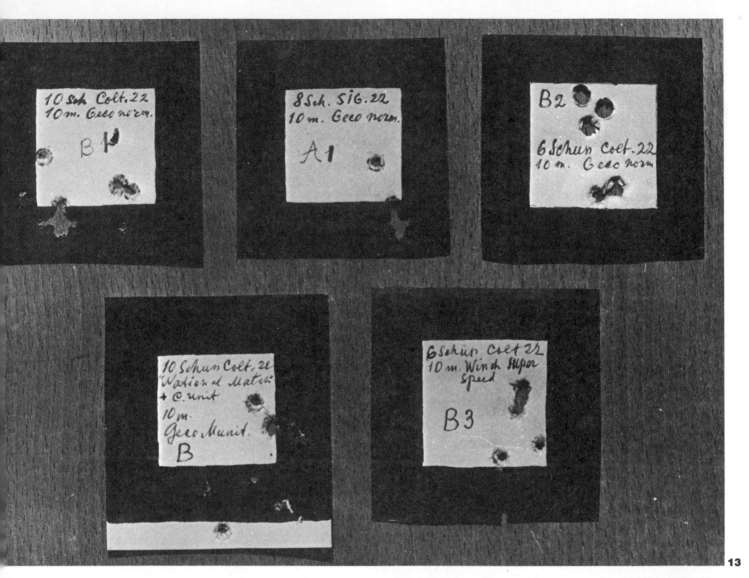

models it will be found, freely accessible, under the backstrap of the hammer. I don't feel this screw makes the SIG any more elegant, but today target pistols are degenerating into "target machines," and it therefore does not much matter what the pistol looks like, provided Match Regulations are not infringed.

Both the safety lever and the slide stop of the SIG can only be manipulated by a big hand, or by a long flexible thumb. The safety lever over-engages in its bents. It slides nicely between the two, but the lever is difficult to move once it has engaged in either of the end positions. The SIG to my mind does not fulfil the requirements of a "one-hand" gun. For loading and unloading two hands are needed, of course, but for cocking the hammer, thumbing over the safety catch, and operating the slide stop, one hand only ought to suffice.

The magazine latch is in the butt, which is the right place for it. Although some American authorities dislike this arrangement, the new Walther TPH has followed suit. The SIG magazine catch greatly resembles that of the Mauser 1934 (Pocket Mauser), and that of the Czech Mauser 1922/24. This catch consists of a flat spring that is folded at its lower end to form the clasp. Durable, practical, simple and cheap. But is makes a "cheap" impression, too.

The recoil spring is mounted on a guide, it is fastened at one end by a ring and at the other by an eyelet. This arrangement facilitates stripping and reassembling. To take off the spring, knock out the pin and remove the head of the guide.

The sights are good on all models; but the rear sight of the army version is a little too narrow, although it does match the gun. On the other hand, the sights on the target models stand out like a sore thumb and the pistol does not have uniform lines. At this point, however, it is fair to say that virtually all

14 *Remington Rand M 1911 .45 ACP with .22 L.R. Colt Conversion Unit. Note floating chamber and extractor*

15 *National Match .45 ACP with conversion unit and standard barrel and slide (left). Cartridges: Colt .45 ACP from Geco, Remington, Winchester and .455 Eley. Conversion unit (.22 L.R.) can be used in Colt 1911 .455 model*

16 *SIG P 210-6 for .22 L.R. shooting, 3 different calibre magazines, 7.65 barrel and recoil spring, slide for 7.65 and 9 mm version, cartridge loader. Cross section of P 210-1 or 210-2.*

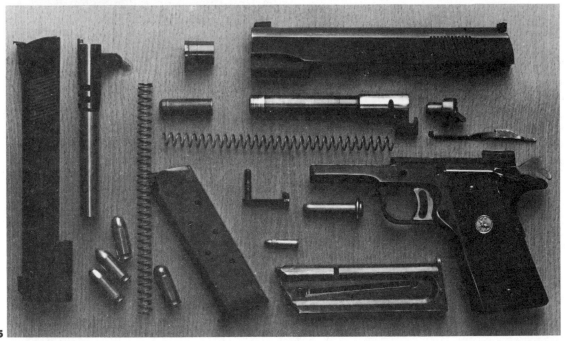

target weapons have protruding contraptions placed on top of them. I admit my criticism cannot be considered constructive, as I cannot propose any improvements, other than to emphasize the fact that all S & W revolvers can be provided with a target sight not higher than 2 mm (.0788 in.). I have yet another complaint to air: today a ventilated top rib is a must for pistols and revolvers, especially for the big ones. Otherwise there exists the danger of burning one's hand on the hot barrel, above which the air scintil-

lates so disturbingly! For all that, every beginner must know that the round barrel shoots best, as it can freely vibrate. The rear sight of the SIG 210-5 and 210-6 is placed so far back (to increase sight radius?) that it is a little difficult to cock the hammer, unless it is thumbed back from half cock. Still, I was favourably impressed by the absence of the ventilated rib, the roughened section behind the rear sight being adequate to break up any unwanted reflection.

The SIG P 210 not only leads in quality, at the same

265

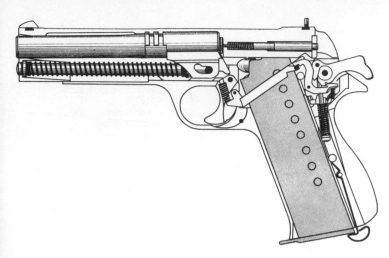

time it is the most awkward army pistol to load! Even the old Luger was less exasperating to load, despite the acute angle of its handle. Furthermore, the SIG magazine lacks the thumb stud, so it is more convenient to load via a plastic loading tool. Such antics can only be tolerated by an army that has no fear of ever having to fight a war . . .

The P 210 is heavier and larger than, say, the FN 1935. Measured across the grips, though, the FN is 3 mm (.118 in.) broader. However, the grip of the FN can be reduced to give the pistol a slimmer appearance, the frame of the handle being only 25 mm (.985 in.) in width. Despite the fact that trigger pull of the FN is more than 8 lb. 13 oz., and its sights are a vestige of the last century (also those of the FN pocket pistol), it still sells well. Fourteen rounds (13 in the magazine and 1 up the spout) is a splendid sales ar-

gument! The staggered box magazine is not more prone to jamming than the ordinary single-line magazine, and the FN High Power does not weigh too much either. With 9 cartridges, the SIG P 210 weights 2 lb. 9 oz., whereas with 14 cartridges the FN weighs 2 lb. 7 oz.

SIG pistols don't cost much more than other service pistols, but one does have to pay for quality just the same. Still, I feel the disadvantages of the SIG are considerable. For example, I was disconcerted to discover that the .22 L.R. magazine, designed for 8 cartridges, only accepted 7 rounds. And that was not all, not by any means. To load this magazine I was obliged to drop the rounds in vertically, by pressing the follower down farther than normal, and then to tip them on to their sides. On top of that, the magazine lips shaved off lead from the nose of the bullets. That old magazine from the Colt Conversion Unit .22, which I have lying around, "absorbed" 9 rounds without resorting to subterfuges. I mention this for the sake of comparison. However, when practising with the SIG .22 L.R. and the .22 L.R. Colt Conversion Unit (placed on a Remington Rand .45 ACP receiver), both pistols functioned perfectly. At 10 m (10.9 yds.) I juggled up the grouping under Al with the SIG. The Colt was not so accurate: cf. grouping under Bl.

Well, of course, trigger pull of the SIG beats that of the Remington Rand, so I then placed my conversion unit on a Colt National Match 45 for the sake of fairness, and the pistol jammed 3 times within ten shots. The results can be viewed under B.

So as not to be defeated, I put the conversion unit

back on to the Remington, and installed the barrel bushing and plug of the National Match into the Remington, too. With Geco ammunition, I printed the grouping under B 2, and with Win. Super Speed the grouping under B 3. Trigger pull of the National Match weighed 3 lb. 13 oz., that of the Remington Rand (improved) 4 lb. 7 oz., and that of the SIG, as mentioned before, 3 lb 13 oz.

The Colt Conversion Unit .22 utilizes a floating chamber to simulate the high recoil of a .45 pistol. Furthermore, the slide oft the conversion unit weighs .353 oz. more than that of the National Match 45 and .353 oz. less than that of the Remington Rand. The floating chamber can reciprocate 1.8 mm (.070 in.), and is bayonet mounted. For the sake of comparison, here a table of weights of Colt, SIG and FN pistols.

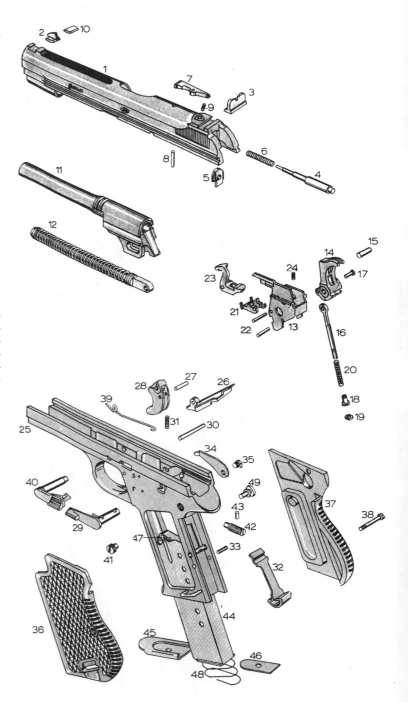

Weight (unloaded)			Slides	
Colt Army .45	2 lb.	7 oz.	Colt Army .45	13 oz.
National Match .45	2 lb.	5 oz.	National Match .45	12½ oz.
National Match .22 L.R.			National Match .22 L.R.	13 oz.
	2 lb.	10 oz.	SIG P 210 target .22 L.R.	6½ oz.
SIG P 210 target .22 L.R.			SIG P 210 9 mm	11 oz.
	2 lb.	1 oz.	FN High Power 9 mm	11 oz.
SIG P 210 9 mm	2 lb.	5 oz.		
FN High Power 9 mm		2 lb.		

He who appreciates precision shooting should consider the SIG, although it has some drawbacks. Its performance outweighs the disadvantages. As an incorrigible perfectionist I shall put a SIG on my "wish list" for Christmas, but one with double action trigger, and chambered for .45 ACP, 9 mm Luger or .22 L.R.! That would be a nice present from that little country of watches, chocolate, dairy cows, peace and commonsense . . .

TECHNICAL DATA

Type	Calibre	Overall length	Barrel length	Rate of twist	Number of grooves	Weight without mag.	Weight of mag.	Muzzle vel.	Weight of pull at let-off point	Magazine capacity	Sight radius
	mm	in.	in.	in.		lb	oz.	fps	lb		in.
P 210-1/-2	9	8.47	4.73	9.85	6	2 lb	3	1099	4 lb 15 oz.*	8	6.46
P 210-1/-2	7.65	8.47	4.73	9.85	4	2 lb	3	1263	4 lb 15 oz.*	8	6.46
P 210-1	.22 L.R.	8.47	4.73	17.73	6	1 lb 14 oz.	3	1083	4 lb 15 oz.*	8	6.46
P 210-5	9	9.65	5.91	9.85	6	2 lb 2 oz.	3	1132	3 lb 14 oz.*	8	7.96
P 210-6	9	8.47	4.73	9.85	6	2 lb 1 oz.	3	1099	3 lb 14 oz.*	8	6.93
P 210-5	7.65	9.65	5.91	9.85	4	2 lb 3 oz.	3	1296	3 lb 14 oz.*	8	7.96
P 210-6	7.65	8.47	4.73	9.85	4	2 lb 1 oz.	3	1263	3 lb 14 oz.*	8	6.93

*± 9 oz.

A NEW GERMAN

1

3

Text and Photos B. Romanski

TARGET PISTOL

This pistol was designed to combine the advantages of an auto pistol with those of a revolver, in reference to the trigger. Since the author (and inventor) was in a position to build the handgun he had in mind himself, there was nothing to prevent him realizing his idea. The German patent has the number 1280089. This pistol has been subjected to German proof, and it corresponds with international UIT specifications. Trigger pull of many of the auto pistols on the world market is stepmotherly, at best. The short, crisp let-off of a high-quality revolver is never reached. With an eye to remedying the universal creepy, heavy trigger pull in auto pistols, I set about designing the Romanski (Illus. 2).

I trust you will be interested in the result of many leisure hours. Basing my pistol on the old Mauser C 96 (military or broomhandle Mauser), which is still a masterpiece of engineering in anybody's language, design and balance somewhat resemble that old-timer. The Romanski has intentionally been made muzzle heavy to prevent high shots. One of the latest Walther models now also employs this principle. The trigger of the Romanski does not have to be interchanged for various

A NEW GERMAN TARGET PISTOL

4

5

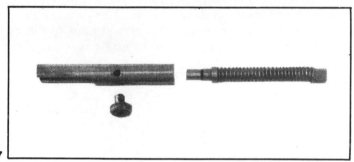

7

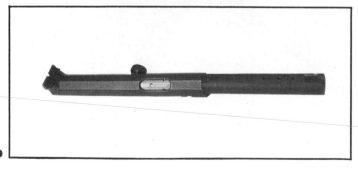

styles of shooting, for trigger pull is easily adjusted. It is blowback operated and has an external hammer. The parts of the pistol are: barrel and barrel extension, receiver, breech bolt and trigger mechanism (Illus. 3). Furthermore, it is chambered for .22 L.R. Sight radius is 8.7 in. The front mount for the sight is soft soldered to the barrel. Rear sight is adjustable for elevation and windage. The breech bolt is (hand) operated via the handle on the left side (Illus. 4). The hammer has been so designed that it cannot strike the rear sight, or the user's hand.

The breech bolt does not ride back beyond the rear section of the pistol during its rearward journey, hence centre of balance is not upset. The safety lever is over the trigger, on the left side of the receiver; the red dot meaning "fire," the white

8

9

"safe." A 5-shot magazine is situated Mauser-fashion in front of the trigger guard. Loading a 6th shot is not possible. Barrel length is 5.31 in., and the right-hand twist rifling has 8 grooves. Barrel and barrel extension are dovetailed to the receiver and held via a clamp lever (Illus. 5). By rotating this clamp lever forwards through 180 degrees, barrel and extension can be lifted away from the receiver (Illus. 6).

The breech bolt accommodates firing pin and recoil spring. The firing pin is activated when the hammer strikes the intermediate connecting rod (Illus. 7), which lies within the bolt housing. The receiver is of light metal and the mainspring is housed in the handle. The trigger, which is separately mounted, can be exactly adjusted to 2.2 and 3 lbs pulls. Moreover, by altering the amount of pre-travel, a trigger pull of only .33 lbs is possible. Extra light trigger pull is important for quick-fire shooting, and for this requirement a special .22 short barrel (Illus. 9) can be mounted. Fig. 10 shows the Romanski with .22 short barrel and appropriate magazine.

TECHNICAL DATA

Action: Blowback, with external hammer
Calibre: .22 L.R.
Twist: Right, 8 grooves
Lengt of barrel with chamber: 5.31 in.
Receiver: Light metal
Overall length: 13 in.
Height: 5.4 in.
Width: 1,85 in.
Sight radius: 8.7 in.
Weight with full magazine: 2. lbs 3 oz.
Angle of handle: 60 degrees

Trigger pull: .33, 2.2 and 3 lbs

The quick-fire pistol
Calibre: .22 short
Twist: Right, 8 grooves
Length of barrel with chamber: 5 in.
Overall length: 12.4 in.
Height: 5.2 in.
Width: 1.85 in.
Sight radius: 9.4 in.
Weight with full magazine: 2 lbs 2 oz.

Text and Photos G. Frères

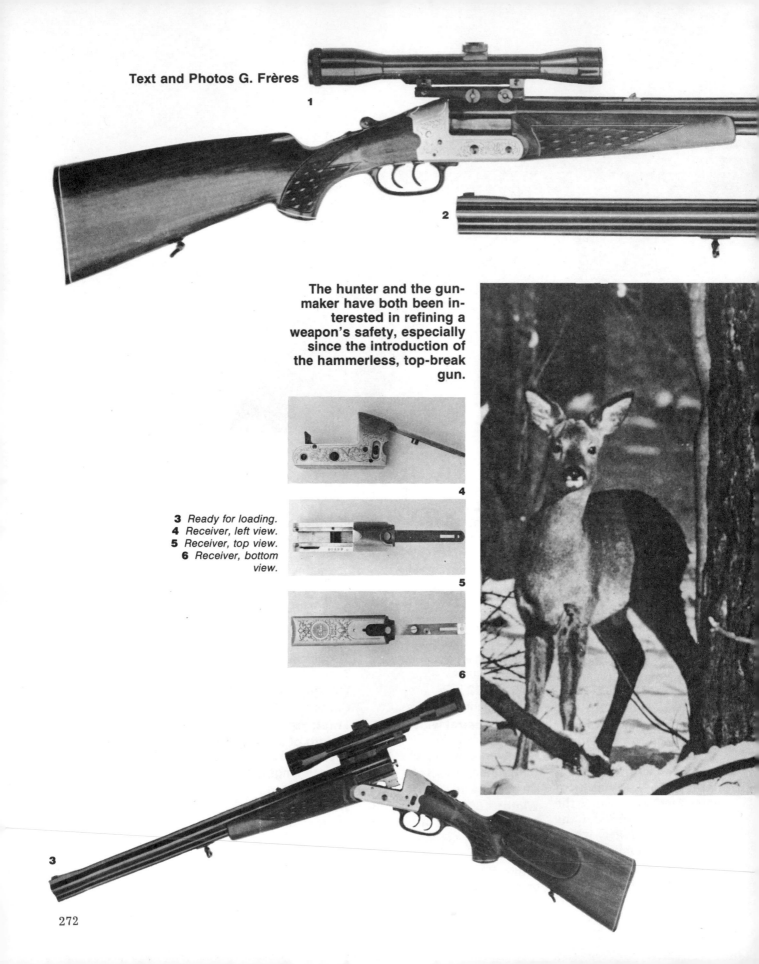

The hunter and the gun-maker have both been interested in refining a weapon's safety, especially since the introduction of the hammerless, top-break gun.

3 *Ready for loading.*
4 *Receiver, left view.*
5 *Receiver, top view.*
6 *Receiver, bottom view.*

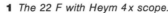

1 *The 22 F with Heym 4x scope.*
2 *The Heym safety rifle/shotgun combination 22 F.*

HEYM SAFETY RIFLE/ SHOTGUN COMBINATION MODEL 22 F

The Mauser 98 feature of locking the firing pin by flipping over a safety catch, frequently copied by other manufacturers, really does offer a high degree of safety. However, today there is a tendency with makers of bolt-action rifles to forsake this well-tried practice.

Top-break weapons are fitted out with all sorts of safety devices, some block only the trigger, others the sear or even the firing pin. When these devices are located in the receiver or sideplate, the measure of safety offered is excellent. Still, a completely different course has been followed by those firms who have concluded from their deliberations that an uncocked gun is surely the safest gun of all.

So-called external cockers were evolved before WWII, whereby a lever was depressed to lift the hammer(s) back to full bent, just prior to the gun being fired. A hunter possessing a gun of this type could scramble over the tallest fence with impunity, in spite of the round in the chamber.

The firm of Friedrich Wilhelm Heym, ex-Suhl gunmakers who today are domiciled in Münnerstadt, have taken another step forward with their safety top-break gun programme 22. These weapons are cocked by pulling back on the rear trigger, an action that also "hair" sets the first. The best known representative of this series is the rifle/shotgun combination 22 F, which is popular among sportsmen requiring a light, rugged, inexpensive all-season longarm.

Here are the details

The Heym Safety Rifle/Shotgun Combination Model 22 F (Figs. 1, 2 and 3) is elegantly designed and tastefully finished, despite its low price. Its light alloy receiver is decorated with arabesque scrollwork (Figs. 4, 5 and 6). Thumb safety slide and top snap are mounted on the tang, but the change-over lever for the barrels is located on the left side of the receiver. The cold-swaged barrels are made of KRUPP SPECIAL GUN STEEL and are black finished. A fine, ventilated rib sits atop the shotgun barrel, forming the base for a post front sight and a folding-leaf rear sight. Forearm and buttstock are of dark-stained walnut, and I must say that those of the test gun were most beautifully figured. The buttstock sports a pistol grip, a cheekpiece, and is slightly hog-backed.

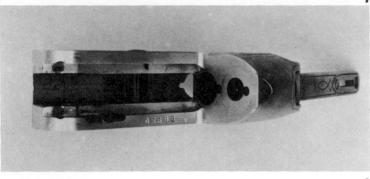

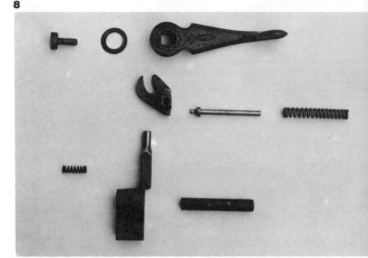

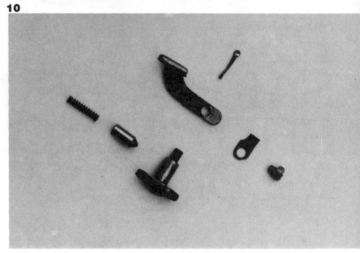

7 Standing breech, showing firing-pin bushings.
8 Top snap with washer and screw cam, guide and spring.
Locking bolt, axle and spring.
9 Safety thumb slide. Push rod with spring and screw.
Fastening and arresting screw.
10 Change-over mechanism. Transfer bar with split pin, guide
spring and screw coil spring, plunger, and thumbpiece.

Checkering is nice, and of the type known as Scotch checkering here in Germany.

When the 22 F is resting in your hands, its low weight of 5 lb 8 oz and its excellent pointing qualities will immediately strike you. Light-weight materials have been used, but thickness of barrel walls and receiver readily compensate for this. Its fine pointing qualities may be attributed to a well dimensioned pistol grip (corresponding a medium sized hand) and backset comb that does not collide with the ball of the thumb.

The forearm harmonizes well with the rest of the gun, but it might be made a little longer and stouter for even better pointing qualities. As it stands, one's hand could easily slide off the forearm and fly against the front swivel, especially when firing the shotgun barrel. At 4 in. in front of the trigger, the point of balance is very favourable. However, this is reduced to 3 ¾ in. when the light-weight scope is mounted. Furthermore, the 22 F lines up well with one's face when quickly shouldered. Both sights align beautifully, as pitch and buttstock measurements are meticulously calculated. The fullness of the buttstock and the slight hog back are ideal when using a scope, there is no need to break your neck while seeking proper eye relief. On the other hand, the 22 F is so constructed that aiming through open sights is a pleasure, too. Thanks to the relative shortness of this model (overall length: 39.2 in., barrel length: 23.5 in.), pointing qualities are truly excellent, as said before.

At the time of writing this article, I had already owned a 22 F for 18 months, and had been very successful against closed-season targets as well as against black grouse all the way up to roebuck, either by stalking or sitting in a hide in a tree. Indeed, I am now so used to this rifle/shotgun combination that it accompanies me on most of my rounds. Believe me, it is very reassuring to know that both chambers are loaded, yet nothing can make the gun go off. I leave my 22 F loaded in the back of the car when I am on duty. But I still have time to cock the hammers and

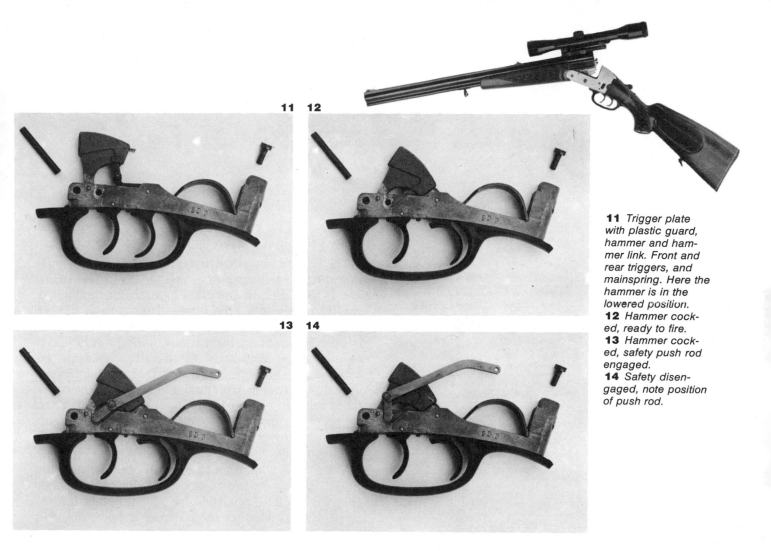

11 *Trigger plate with plastic guard, hammer and hammer link. Front and rear triggers, and mainspring. Here the hammer is in the lowered position.*
12 *Hammer cocked, ready to fire.*
13 *Hammer cocked, safety push rod engaged.*
14 *Safety disengaged, note position of push rod.*

let fly at some troublesome varmint before that critter has become aware of the danger. Normally, I wouldn't have time to load the gun and get a shot in at a magpie, or crow, or wild cat. They don't hang around when they see the gleam of gun metal! As you probably realize by now, I fight shy of selfcocking guns with loaded chambers, even with the safety applied.

How the 22 F functions

When the top snap is pushed over to the right, a cam withdraws the flatbolt (Fig. 8) from the notch in the under lump, and the action can be opened. Many of my readers will be accustomed to the Greener crossbolt and double lump locking, or to the Kersten system, or to a system of additional double lump locking. In these guns, the flatbolt, if any, runs parallel to the axis of the bore. In the 22 F, only one bolt and one under lump have been fitted. It is of some interest to learn that this bolt swivels at an angle of ap-

proximately 45 degrees to the axis of the bore. At the outset, this strange looking bolt does not inspire one with much confidence. However, it did not take long to realize that this type of bolting was more than sufficient to counteract the effects of pitching moment. When a shot is fired, the barrel tends to break out of the receiver. In the 22 F, the bolt does not show a tendency to slip out of the under lump, as one might have thought, on the contrary: this bolt is so designed that it is actually drawn into the notch of the under lump when the weapon is fired. The Heym lock-up system might be likened to a trestlework, that is, the higher the pitching moment is on the one hand, the stronger the action of the bolt is on the other. Furthermore, the pull-off motion generated by the shot, which is additional to the pitching moment, is countered by a very powerful hinge pin and fixed crossbolt, against which the massive under lump rests when the action is closed. Viewed collectively, this is truly an ingenious system.

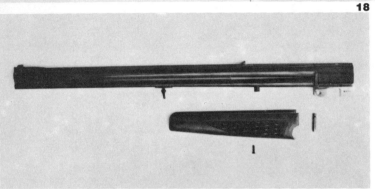

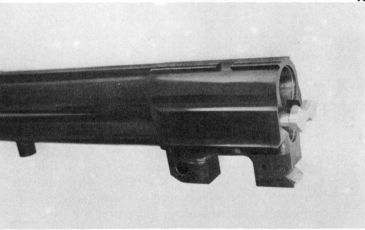

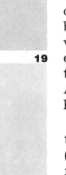

15 *Lowered hammer, safety disengaged, rifled barrel selected.*
16 *Cocked hammer, safety engaged, rifled barrel selected.*
17 *Cocked hammer, safety disengaged, shotgun barrel selected.*
18 *Barrels, forearm with screw, note loose hinge pin.*
19 *Round forward stump anchors the forearm, hinge-pin block and locking under lump. Note V block for scope, and extractors.*
20 *Looking down the business end.*

As stated at the beginning of this account, the lockwork is not cocked by breaking the action.

The hammer can be lifted back to full bent by pulling the rear trigger only (Figs. 11, 12, 13, 14, 15, 16 and 17), which is linked to the hammer via a swivel. A small projection on the blade of the second trigger engages in its counterpart on the blade of the front trigger, hence at the same time creating a double set, or hair trigger. Actual weight of pull can be adjusted by rotating a set screw, in the normal manner. By reversing the procedure, the hammer can be de-cocked, if the hunter decides not to shoot after all. Then the second trigger is held back by your middle finger. And then slowly let forward, once the front trigger has been released.

Via a push rod and a shaft with one side flat, the thumb safety on the tang blocks the front trigger (Fig. 9). The 22 F can, therefore, be put on "safe" irrespective of whether the hammer is up or down.

The change-over slide for the upper and lower barrels is located on the left side of the receiver (Fig. 10). An anvil or transfer bar is flicked over in front of the firing pin selected for the next shot. In other words, when the hammer falls it will drive both the transfer bar and the firing pin forward to ignite the primer. When the change-over slide is down, the rifled barrel will fire; when it is up it is the shotgun barrel that is ready for action. Both firing pins are inserted from the front into the breechface (Fig. 7), a system that does not weaken the firing-pin seating in the breechblock.

The trigger plate is fastened to the receiver by a pin at its front end and by a cylindrical head screw at its rear end. At the same time, the rear, curved section of the trigger plate helps to secure the buttstock by means of a socket head screw. White-line spacers are sandwiched under the pistol grip cap buttplate (Figs. 23 and 24).

The two barrels are brazed into a monobloc, which carries out a number of functions (Figs. 18 and 19). Its forward under lump accepts the hinge pin, allowing the barrels to be removed from the receiver only after the hinge pin has been slid out sideways. And the rear (locking) under lump, described earlier in this discourse, accepts the flatbolt. Moreover, this block also accommodates the extractor, activated by a tongue on the left side of the receiver when the gun is opened. On its top edge a V-block has been machined for a slip-on scope mount. The shotgun barrel is crowned with a ventilated rib that serves as a base for the front sight ramp and folding leaf rear sight (Fig. 20).

The front swivel is soft soldered to the rifled barrel, whereas the stump for the forearm is brazed. This stump serves as a base for a slotted screw. A slip-on wedge scope mount (Fig. 22) is pushed on from the front, and tightened by means of the knurled knobs. These mounts are available with clamp rings for steel scopes, or with grooves for light-metal scopes (Fig. 21). Not all scopes have double reticle adjustment, so for those that don't these mounts have been designed to adjust laterally. Although these scope mounts look tough, they are regrettably rather massive, too. Of course, the slip-on scope mount is not as fast and easy to manipulate as the Suhler claw mounts are. But the slip-on version costs less.

Performance

We tested the Heym 22 F with a 4 x Heym light-metal scope on top. Most hunters using a slip-on mount rarely remove the scope, as there is little time to do so during the chase, so it is important to know the point of impact of the shotgun barrel when using the scope. You must remember that scopes on combination guns are usually sighted in for the rifled barrel, as the spread of the shotgun barrel is less precise.

Nonetheless, in most cases the shotgun barrel will not produce patterns that align with the centre of the reticle.

The rifled barrel is chambered for the DWM 5.6 x 50 R Magnum. This cartridge, marketed for the first time in 1968, was designed to counter difficulties experienced with rimless rounds in top-break weapons, and to give the sportsman a pepped-up load to kill small game as well as deer. The efficiency of this relatively new round is higher than that of such cartridges as .222 Remington and .222 Remington Magnum. An interesting feature is that barrels for the Remington .222 cartridges can be rechambered for the 5.6 x 50 R, since the dimensions of the grooves, lands and twist are identical. Reloaders will be happy to learn that these DWM cases are Boxer primed.

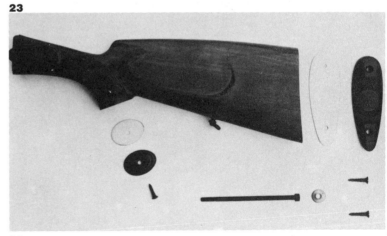

21 Heym 4 x 36 scope with slip-on mount.
22 Bottom view of slip-on mount, showing wedges.
23 Buttstock and appurtenances.
24 Buttstock with receiver.

Firing from a Preuss machine rest, dispersion was just under an inch when using soft-nosed bullets at 109 yards (Fig. 27), and 1.18 inches when using fully jacketed bullets. As seen from the illustrations, a series of 5 shots was fired on both occasions. I find this tight grouping excellent, and could imagine the disposing of a fox or crow at a greater distance.

Three German shotshells were chosen for the second test: ROTTWEIL/STERN (No. 7 ½ shot), ROTTWEIL EXPRESS (No. 5), and WALD-MANNSHEIL (No. 3), as can be seen in Fig. 25. Of each brand 5 shotshells were fired at a 16-field German hunting target, over a distance of 38.3 yards. The results, based on the booklet, "Der Schrotschuß,"*) are shown in Table I.

Taken as a whole, the performance of the rifled barrel was excellent, and that of the shotgun barrel was very suitable for normal hunting conditions. The point of impact for the shotgun barrel was about 6 inches under the centre of the scope reticle. This means that the target would have to be covered up by the main post of the reticle when firing the shotgun barrel.

*) Der Schrotschuß, by Herbert von Wissmann, Verlag Paul Parey, Berlin and Hamburg.

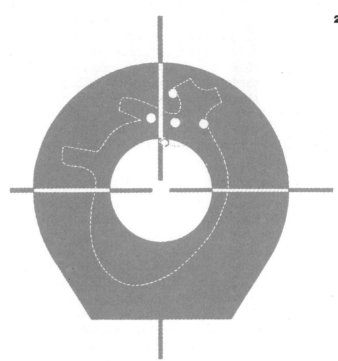

27

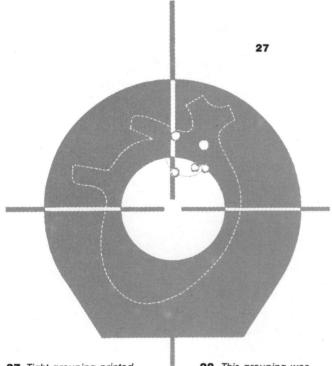

27 *Tight grouping printed by DWM 5.6 x 50 R Magnum with 49.9 gr. soft-point bullet and 29.3 gr. special powder. Five shots fired at 109 yds, dispersion 0.98 in.*

28 *This grouping was created with a 49.9 gr. fully jacketed bullet and 29.3 gr. special powder. Five shots fired at 109 yds, dispersion 1.18 in.*

Manufacturer: Gun Factory Friedrich Wilhelm Heym, Münnerstadt/Ufr., West Germany.

Designation: Safety Rifle/shotgun Combination 22 F.

Calibre: 5.6 x 50 R Magnum and 16/70 ga. Shotshell. Also available in .222 Rem. and .222 Rem. Mag, plus 20/70 ga. Shotshell.

Action: Hammer cocked via second trigger. Front can only be used as hair trigger. Changeover lever on left side for selecting barrel. Locked via under lump and rotating bolt.

Safety: Tang mounted thumb slide, blocks trigger.

Receiver: Light metal, matt grey, with simple arabesque scroll.

Barrel joining: Brazed into a monobloc, reinforced with side bands.

Rifled barrel: Krupp Special Gun Steel, hammer forged rifling, length: 23.5 in. Diamter across grooves: 0.225 in. (5.71 mm). Diameter across lands: 0.219 in. (5.57 mm). Length of twist: 1 in. 14. 93 in. (379 mm).

Shotgun barrel: Krupp Special Gun Steel, hammer forged, length: 23.5 in. Ventilated top rib.

Sights: Ramp-mounted silver bead. Folding-leaf rear sight with fine and coarse notch.

Stock: Walnut, stained, with cheekpiece, pistol grip, slightly hog backed. Checkering on forearm and pistol grip. Dimensions: Length of pull 14 in. Drop at comb 1.65 in. Drop at heel 3 in. Pitch 1.3 in.

Overall length: 39.2 in.

Weight: 5 lb 8 oz. With scope 6 lb 8 oz.

 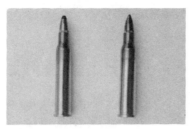

25 *Shotshells used for testing.*
26 *Cal. 5.6 x 50 R Magnum soft nosed and fully jacketed rounds.*

TABLE I Results obtained with 2.5 (No. 7), 3 (No. 5) and 3.5 mm (No. 3) shot at 38.3 yards	Rottweil Stern 16/70 ga. 338 pellets / 1.02 ozs. Batch No. MG 26 R 17 2.5 mm	Rottweil Express 16/70 ga. 188 pellets / 1.08 ozs. Batch No. MN 13 N 14 3 mm	Waldmannsheil 16/70 ga. 123 pellets / 1.06 ozs. Batch No. AP 14 N 16 3.5 mm
Number of hits			
Inner circle	89	43	30
Outer circle	142	79	43
Whole target	231	122	73
Density	1:1.88	1:1.63	1:2.09
Regularity (Mean deviation of a 5-shot series)	15.0 = satisfactory	6.0 = good	10.8 = unsatisfactory
Covered fields (geared to number of hits)	10.0 = good	12.0 = satisfactory	9.8 = excellent
Extreme variation of effective hits			
Diameter	24 in.	–	22.85 in.
At distance	33.9 yds.	–	43.7 yds.
Max. effective range	46 yds.	42.6 yds.	52.5 yds.
Rating	Good for normal pupuses	Satisfactory for normal purposes	Satisfactory for normal purposes
Pattern in percentage	68.3 %	64.9 %	59.3 %
16/70 = 2 ¾ cases			

Jürgen Pirkl

Mannlicher Selfloading Carbine M/1901 and Carbine Pistol M/1901

Both the Selfloading Carbine M/1901 and the Carbine Pistol M/1901 designed by Ferdinand Ritter von Mannlicher are as interesting as they are rare. The idea of creating a short, light weapon for firing pistol ammunition still ties in with our conceptions today. Just think of the many assault rifles and automatic carbines that have been designed since WW 2! The reader must remember that von Mannlicher was well ahead of his time, as in 1901 not even the machine gun had been accepted by military circles. Only minor differences exist between the carbine and the pistol, mainly length, so both weapons can be described together. The M/1901 is a semiautomatic weapon in which barrel and bolt are locked together at the moment of firing. The thrust of the powder gases forces the receiver (3) with screwed-in barrel (1) and the bolt (5) in unison to the rear, for approximately 4 mm. At this junction, the locking block (14) automatically disengages, whereby the bolt continues its rearward journey alone. During this opening phase, the spent cartridge case in extracted from the firing chamber and ejected out of the gun. Furthermore, the hammer (23) is re-cocked and held cocked by the sear arm (31).

Mannlicher Carbine Pistol M/1901 with Holster-cum-Shoulder Stock.

Pressure exercised by the compressed bolt spring (9) then thrusts the bolt forward again. During this closing phase, the boltface strips the top cartridge from the magazine and guides it into the firing chamber. Just before the bolt returns to battery, the receiver with screwed-in barrel joins it to go forward together with the bolt. The locking block then re-engages. The weapon will fire again immediately. Once the last round has been fired, the follower (42) rides up to prevent the bolt returning to battery, so the user knows that the weapon is empty. The safety catch (33) protrudes out of the frame behind the (sliding) receiver. It engages in the collar of the hammer axle and operates irrespective of whether the hammer is cocked or not.

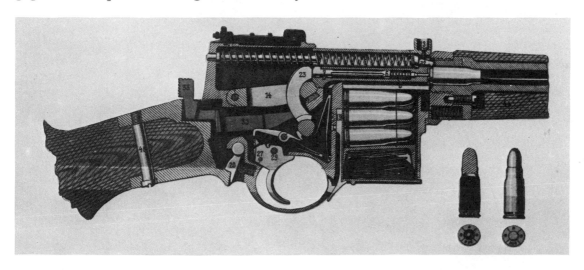

Parts Legend

1 Barrel	11 Bolt spring guide	22 Latch screw	35 Rear sight screw
2 Setscrew for barrel	12 Extractor	23 Hammer	36 Rear sight spring
3 Receiver	13 Extractor screw	24 Mainspring	37 Screw for rear sight spring
4 Barrel spring	14 Locking block	25 Trigger	38 Slide plate
5 Bolt	15 Locking block pin	26 Drag link	39 Slide plate screw
6 Firing pin	16 Frame	27 Drag link pin	40 Magazine
7 Retaining pin	17 Lockwork and magazine housing	28 Drag link spring	41 Floorplate
8 Firing pin spring	18 Magazine retaining spring	29 Trigger pin	42 Follower
9 Bolt spring	19 Screw for magazine retaining spring	30 Trigger spring	43 Magazine spring
10 Bolt spring cap	20 Latch	31 Sear arm	44 Forearm
	21 Latch spring	32 Sear arm pin	
		33 Safety catch	
		34 Rear sight	

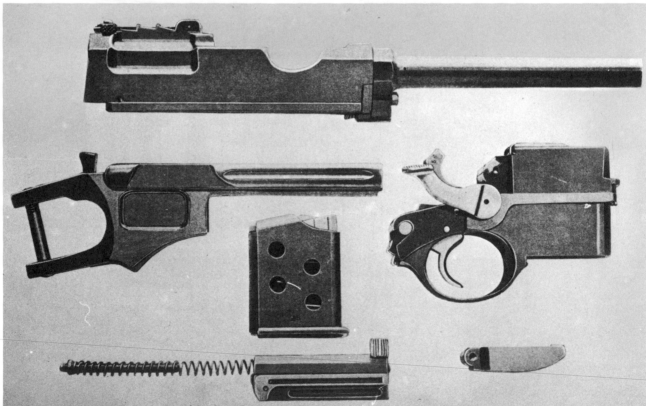

The M/1901 may be loaded by inserting a magazine from below, or by stripping cartridges down through the breech. Some models were designed for 6, others for 7 cartridges. The Mannlicher-Pieper ammunition clip holds the cartridges pincer-like at both ends. When the clip is put into its feed grooves, slanting surfaces deactivate the claws and the cartridges can be readily thumbed into the magazine.

A novel feature is the external cocking piece, integral with the hammer that lies flush against the lockwork and magazine housing (17). Hence, the hammer can be easily cocked without any part of the bolt or breech mechanism flying back into the firer's face.

The M/1901 is field stripped by depressing catch (20). Lockwork and magazine housing (17) is then slid off the frame (16, followed by barrel (1) and receiver (3). As the forearm reciprocates with the barrel, although only 4 mm, von Mannlicher advised users to grasp the magazine housing with one's left hand. The carbine weighs only 3 lb 14 oz, or 4 lb when loaded.

The pistol lacks the forearm, and the frame is shaped to accept a grip, in lieu of the buttstock. A holster could be clipped to this handle, following the example set by the Broomhandle Mauser (C 96), Borchardt, M 53, M 82 and M 59 handguns. This carbine pistol was available with a 119 mm or 152 mm barrel. It handled superbly, as centre of balance was in the magazine. As the M/1901s were manufactured by the Austrian Steyr-Werke, material and quality is excellent.

The cartridge is known as the 7.65 mm M 1901, and can only be differentiated from the 7.65 mm Borchardt, 7.63 mm Mauser or 7.62 mm Tokarev by its headstamp (Hirtenberg, Keller & Co., G. Roth). Of course, the cartridge box may also be referred to! It is extremely difficult to detect differences in dimensions. However, ballistically the 7.65 mm Mannlicher is the weakest of this related group, the 7.62 mm Tokarev the strongest.

Model	Length of		Weight		Grooves				Dispersion		
	Gun	Barrel	Loaded	Unloaded	Number	Direction	MV	ME	lat.	verl.	
Selfloading Carbine M/1901	29 in.	12 in.	4 lb	3 lb 14 oz	4	right	1476 fps	413 ft/pds	11 in.	11.8 in.	
Carbine Pistol M/1901											109yds
Long barrel	12 in.	6 in.	2 lb 7 oz	2 lb 5 oz	4	right	1230 fps	286 ft/pds	14 in.	16 in.	
									9 in.	11.8 in.	54.7 yds
Short barrel	10.5 in.	4.7 in.	2 lb 5 oz	2 lb 3 oz	4	right	1181 fps	265 ft/pds	–	–	

Text and Photos
G. Wirnsberger

The RÖHM RG30 Revolver

Every gun fan picks out the weapon he thinks is ideal. Mr. A. has absolute confidence in the reliable revolver, while Mr. B. prefers the faster autoloading pistol. Which gentleman is right cannot be clarified here, for even the experts are still debating the question. This report deals with a revolver that is exceedingly interesting, if not remarkable in some respects.

The creator of this revolver is the firm of Röhm in Sontheim an der Brenz, West Germany. It is available in .22 L.R., .22 Win. Magnum, and .32 S & W long. The Röhm RG 30 has double action and a swing-out cylinder, and can be ordered with large target grips. It is also available as a combo set with both .22 L.R. and .22 Mag. cylinders. Considering that the RG 30 costs less than $ 50, it seems to give excellent value in its price range. It is elegantly designed and well made, and is dependably rugged.

Technical description

The 6-shot cylinder opens to the left. The lockwork is, by and large, a copy of the Smith & Wesson (Fig. 3). The barrel, which is embedded in a die-cast sleeve, is button rifled with 8 grooves and 8 lands. The barrel is pinned to the receiver. Top rib is .43 in. wide, ventilated, and sports lengthwise flutes (Fig. 1). The frame is also die-cast.

However, the face of the standing breech is reinforced with steel (Fig. 6), which guarantees a longer working life. When removing the sideplate, which is held by three screws, the lockwork mechanism is accessible, revealing typical S & W features (Figs. 7, 8 and 9).

When the sideplate is lifted away from the receiver, the plunger for the hand (Fig. 10) can easily drop out. So great care should be taken not to let the plunger fall on the floor, otherwise a lot of creeping around on your hands and knees will be unavoidable. Let's hope this plunger will

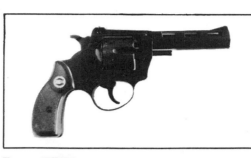

1 *RG 30 with target grips*
2 *RG 30 with normal grips*

A Revolver among many?

be retained in the sideplate in future models. When re-seating the sideplate, the best plan is to press the plunger back and hold it in place by passing a thin punch through a hole already in the sideplate (Fig. 11). A thin nail or a straightened out paper clip will also do the trick. Spiral springs have been used throughout the gun, which have an advantage over flat springs.

Hammer and trigger are section moulded. By pushing the thumbpiece forward (Fig. 12) the cylinder swings out to the left. Unfortunately, the ejector rod is not sprung mounted, so if the

3 *The lockwork*
4 *Steel barrel visible in die-cast jacket*
5 *Good sighting*
6 *Standing breech is steel reinforced*
7 *Hammer cocked*

The RÖHM RG 30 Revolver

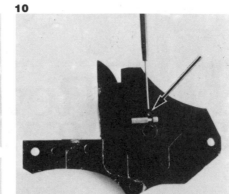

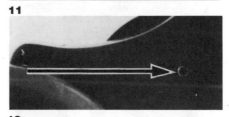

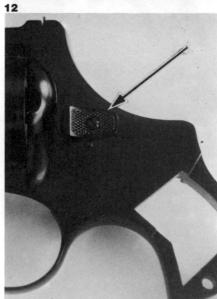

muzzle of the revolver is pointing upwards the cylinder will not close. The revolver has to be pointed down again to close the cylinder, to retract the extractor, which otherwise hits against the frame. Grooves in the cylinder prevent the extractor from rotating out of position (Fig. 13). Small guide pins also act as positioners. The

8 Hammer engaged in trigger sear
9 Hammer down, trigger under hammer sear
10 Inside view of sideplate. Loose hand plunger
11 Hole for punch or similar instrument
12 Thumbpiece, for releasing the cylinder
13 Guide groove for the ejector
14 Cylinder face, ratchet in centre
15 Yoke retaining screw
16 Bulge of safety arm out of recess
17 Bulge of safety arm in recess. Hammer can strike the firing pin
18 Position of mainspring rod causes hammer to rebound after the shot
19 Grouping fired at 27.3 yards, with RWS standard .22 L.R. cartridges.

ejector head, by the way, is beautifully fitted to the cylinder (Fig. 14). If a combo cylinder is to be inserted, the yoke retaining screw (Fig. 15) is undone and the cylinder unit removed as a whole. The yoke is then pressed into the other cylinder. In Figs. 3, 7, 16 and 17, the safety arm can be seen. When the hammer is triggered back, the bulge of the safety arm snuggles into a recess in the hammer (Fig. 17) and the hammer can strike the firing pin. The mainspring rod (Fig. 18) is so positioned that the hammer automatically rebounds after the

shot and the bulge of the safety rod moves out of its recess (Fig. 16), once the trigger is released. If your thumb were to slip while cocking the hammer (single action), the bulge of the safety arm prevents the hammer from falling on the firing pin.

The Röhm RG 30 has a fixed front sight and a rear sight adjustable for windage. These sights permit quick-draw practice from a holster. There is no adjustment for elevation. However, a bit of filing at front or rear sight will help the alignment, if necessary.

Figs. 1 and 2 show the

checkered plastic grips. The target grips bestow the gun a good balance. Still, I think a thumb rest, as seen on other revolvers, would be a splendid idea.

Barrel and frame are of black finish, the cylinder is blued. However, nickel finish is available.

Performance. We fired RWS Standard, Remington Standard, Eley Rifle Club, Pobeda, RWS-HV and Remington HV through the .22 L.R. model that was sent to us. The Röhm RG 30 functioned to our full satisfaction and all empty cases were easy to remove from the cylinder.

Technical data

Calibre:	.22 L.R., .22 Win. Magnum, .32 S&W long
Capacity:	6 shots
Trigger pull:	Single Action: 3 lbs, Double Action: 13 lbs
Total weight:	Approx. 1 lbs. 15 oz.
Overall length:	with normal grips 8.47 in., target grips 8.86 in.
Width:	with normal grips 4.53 in., target grips 5.4 in.
Barrel:	4 in.
Total thickness:	1.4 in.
Model:	RG 30
Features:	Black or nickel finish
Manufacturer:	Röhm GmbH (Sontheim/Brenz), West Germany

15

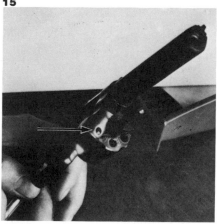

16

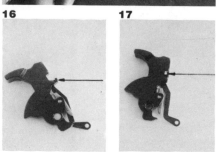

17

18

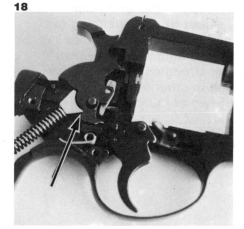

19

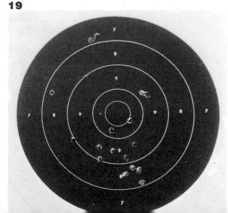

Dr. Manfred Rosenberger

THE BRNO ZP47 DOUBLE BARRELLED SHOTGUN WITH SIDELOCKS

Despite all the superposed shotguns, the drillings and self-loaders, the classic smoothbore with side by side barrels remains the favorite of the European sportsman. Probably no one can offer a simple explanation for this. Although the European's preference, of course, is undoubtedly linked with tradition. A host of different types of locks and bolting is available, the better known ones being the Greener, Kersten, Purdey, Flanken, Exzenter, Holland & Holland, Blitz and Anson Deeley. Apart from influencing the service life of the gun, all these different systems have their own particular strengths and weaknesses, which is often reflected in the selling price of the piece.

3 Slotway and top bolt can be seen in the face plate of the standing breech. Note that the firing pins and bushings are inserted from the front.

4 The two under lugs and the barrel extension are split pairs, each half being integral with its own barrel.

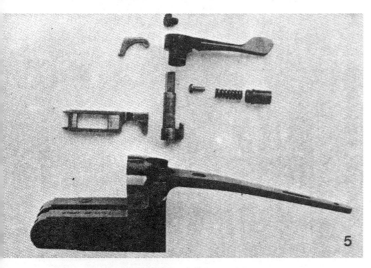

The double barrelled BRNO ZP (illus. 1 and 2), made in the well-known gun town of the same name in Czechoslovakia, sports the following features. It comes with a Purdey-type bolt, double under-lugs, and side locks. This gun also has an auto safety and a self-cocking action.

A Purdey top bolt is fitted along with a small extension situated just under the sighting rib, at the rear of the barrel. In turn, this fits into a slotway in the face of the standing breech, and is locked by the bolt. See illustrations 3 and 4. The extension is a part of the barrel itself, not a part of the sighting rib. When compared with the Greener system, the Purdey top bolt has the advantage that the slotway in the face of the breech cannot be seen when the gun is closed. The surface of the receiver appears, therefore, smoother and more streamlined.

A conventional flat under bolt moves to and fro in the floor of the BRNO ZP, and engages in the rear cutouts of the under lugs. This double-wedged under bolt is coupled with the top-lever shaft, and hence with the top bolt and top lever, too. When thumbing

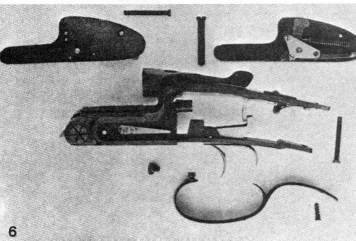

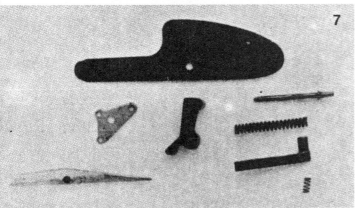

5 Top: Top lever and top bolt; below: double-wedged flat bolt, top-lever shaft, top-lever spring with bushing and guide.

6 Receiver with side plates off.

7 Stripped side plate. Left: cocking lever, bridle, hammer, sear, hammer spring with guide.

BRNO ZP47

the top lever to the right, both top and under bolt become actuated and the breech can be opened. For a look at the breech mechanism, see illus. 5. The moment the breech is closed, the top-lever shaft returns to its home position, assisted by its spring, with top and bottom bolts snapping home again.

One of the charms of the ZP 47 is the side looks (illus. 6). They are rugged, work completely independently of each other, and take up little space. Furthermore, they are easily dismantled and cleaned, so repairs are not too expensive. Without exaggerating, the side-plate lock is the oldest and most trusty ignition mechanism there is. Top grade shotguns bear side locks. Those of the ZP 47 are conventional in design. Each lock consists of side plate, bridle, hammer, sear, hammer spring and spring guide (illus. 7).

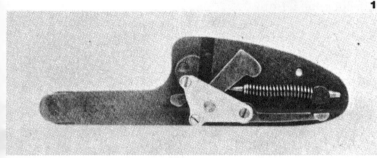

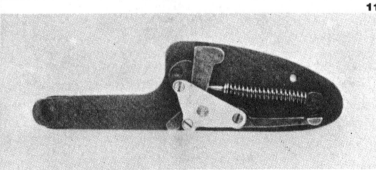

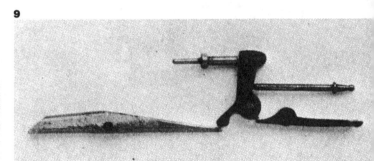

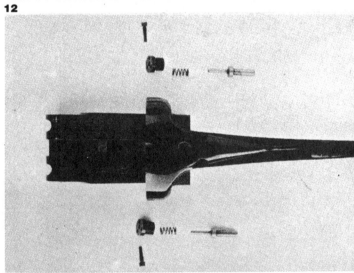

8 Hammer in full-cock position.

9 Hammer has just struck firing pin.

10 Right plate, hammer cocked.

11 Right plate, hammer forward.

12 Both firing pins are inserted into the standing breech from the face end, as are the bushings. Retaining screws fit in sideways.

13 Only the twin triggers adorn the trigger plate.

When the barrels are broken, the cocking lever, activated by an abutment in the forearm, raises the hammer far enough back to engage in the tip of the sear. Conversely, when a trigger is pulled, the sear is lifted out of engagement with the hammer notch – and the hammer swings down on the firing pin (illus. 8–9). Both cocking levers are embedded in the flanks of the receiver, according to well-established principles.

The firing pins of the ZP 47 are let in at the front of the breech face, as are the bushings (illus. 3), which are fastened by side screws (illus. 12). This arrangement safeguards against blown primers, since the backward streaming gases cannot propel the firing pin into the innards of the receiver.

Personally, I find it amazing that some manufacturers still insert the firing pins from behind the breech face. The twin triggers of the ZP 47 are axle-mounted in the trigger plate (illus. 13). When the two retaining screws have been removed, which also fasten the receiver to the stock, the trigger plate is easily lifted out. The tang-mounted safety button is conventional for this type of weapon. The safety lever operating rod engages in a recess in the left-hand side of the top-lever shaft (cf. illus. 15). Once the top lever is activated, therefore, the safety lever is forced over the trigger blades, and so automatically blocks them (illus. 14, 15, 16).

The barrels of the ZP 47 are made of poli-electro steel and joined by means of the demiblock process, which uses brass brazing. This is a very efficient way of mating the barrels, for the under lugs and barrel extension consist of split pairs, the sides of which are integral with the left and right barrels. The under lugs and extension are brazed together, as are the barrels (cf. illus. 4). Strain on the surface area around the chamber is hence evenly distributed. Top and bottom ribs are soft soldered (illus. 17). The bead is not soldered, it is screwed into the top rib and can therefore be interchanged. The right barrel has modified choke, the left one full choke.

The ZP 47 is available with extractor (illus. 4), or if preferred, with an ejector. The tapered forearm is fastened to the underbarrel forearm hook by means of a press-button Anson-Purdey unit (illus. 18, 19, 20). The metal parts are made of wrought iron. The relatively short wrist flows into a low pistol grip with a pitch that is not too steep.

The comb of the buttstock is straight and the buttstock itself has a small cheekpiece (German stocking). See illus. 22. Forearm and pistol grip sport a

14

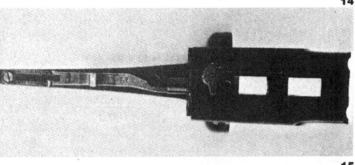

15

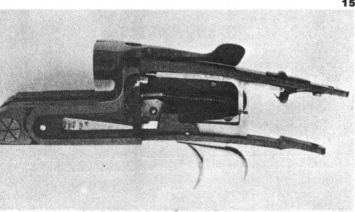

16

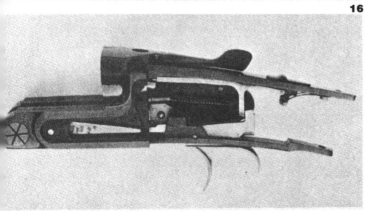

14 *The safety lever operating rod fits into a recess in the top-lever shaft, in order that the safety mechanism is automatically applied when the gun is broken.*

15 *The safety lever, integral with the safety lever operating rod, is forced . . .*

16 *. . . over the trigger blades to block them.*

BRNO ZP 47

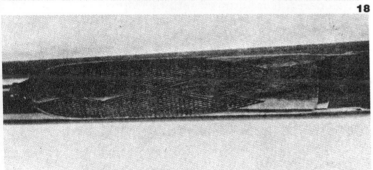

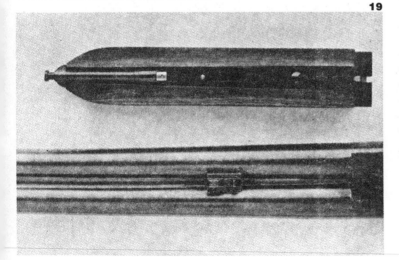

version has designs decorating the edges of the side plates, whereas the C version is completely bedecked with ornametation and bold scrolls.

The Brno ZP 47 is chambered for 16 x 70 ga. and 12 x 70 ga. The following versions are available:
ZP 45 = 16 ga. with extractor ZP 50 = 16 ga. with ejector
ZP 47 = 12 ga. with extractor ZP 49 = 12 ga. with ejector
Additional
P = German-type stock
A = English-type stock
H = No engraving
P = Edge engraving
C= Full engraving

For testing purposes, we were presented with a ZP 47 -PH (illus. 1 and 2) with a 72 cm barrel (Serial No. 47 098). As can be deduced from the list above, this was a 12 ga. gun, no engraving, fitted with ordinary extractor, and German stocking. We fired 150 shot-

Manufacturer:	Gun Works Brno, Czechoslovakia
Importer:	Continental Arms Corp, 697 Fifth Ave., New York
Exporter:	Omnipol, Prague, Czechoslovakia
Type:	S by S shotgun, self-cocking (internal hammers)
Designation:	BRNO ZP
Grade:	Standard
Bolting:	Purdey-type, double under lugs
Breech:	Break-open action
Ignition:	Sidelocks
Triggers:	Shotgun type
Trigger pull:	Front: approx. 1.9 kg, rear: approx. 1.7 kg
Safety:	Automatic, tang button
Overal length:	114 cm (72 cm barrels), 112 cm (70 cm barrels)
Weight:	3 kg to 3.2 kg, according to barrels and gauge
Barrels:	Special poldi-electro steel
Unison of bbls.:	Demiblock, brass brazing
Barrel lengths:	70 cm and 72 cm
Choke:	Full and Modified
Gauges:	16x70 and 12x70
Sight:	Silver bead, interchangeable
Receiver:	Special steel. Angle of standing breech not reinforced. Obtainable with and without engraving
Stocking:	Walnut. Checkered forearm and pistol grip. Plastic buttplate and grip cap. English-type stocking available.
Length of stocking:	In total 68 cm, 36 cm in regard to front trigger, 34 cm in regard to rear trigger, drop at comb 4.5 cm, drop at heel 7.3 cm, pitch 3 cm
Finish:	All metal parts blackened (barrels by brush application, receiver by dipping)
Accessories:	Lanyard swivels

17 *The two barrel ribs are soft soldered in place.*

18 *The tapered forearm ...*

19 *... is secured to the under-barrel forearm hook ...*

shells: Waidmannsheil, Alphamax and Hubertus (illus. 23). Average effective maximum range for the right barrel (modified) was 43 metres, and for the left (full choke) 45 metres.

The average difference between the three makes of shotshells came to about 9 metres. At 35 metres point of aim and point of impact more or less coincided, for both barrels. The density of pattern for the left barrel averaged 1:1.61. Regularity from shot to shot was "excellent" for the left barrel, and "good" for the right one. General performance of both barrels was "excellent," so for everyday purposes the ZP 47 can be thoroughly recommended. When analysing these very satisfactory results, we must point out that we intentionally used "normal" shotshells. So these results can be viewed as "standard conditions."

The test gun was well balanced, and had good pointing qualities. It shouldered easily and quickly, although the buttstock was a little too short.

The Brno's eyecatching lines match the fine workmanship of the internal parts, and the quality of the material used. Headspacing was in perfect order, and the action opened and closed smoothly. Trigger pull (approx. 1.9 kg) might have been a little lighter. In regard of fittings, workmanship and performance, the Brno ZP 47 double barrelled shotgun can be thoroughly recommended as a trusty pack-horse for all occasions, and at a very reasonable price, too ...

Rating

Workmanship	1
Functional safety	1
Performance	1
Finish	1
Design	1
Sighting	0
Balance	1
Pointing qualities	1
Length of stock	2
Total	**9**

Faults:

The weapon under test was approx. 1.5 cm too short in stocking. The front-trigger pull was too heavy.

23

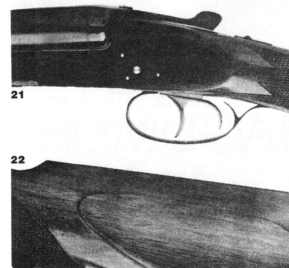

21

22

20

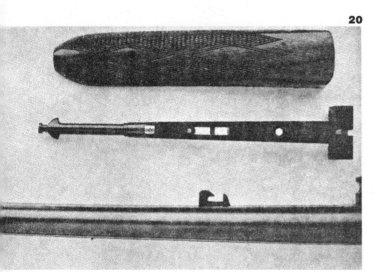

20 ... by means of a press-button Anson-Purdey unit.

21 The relatively short wrist flows into a low pistol grip that is not too steep.

22 Straight comb and small cheekpiece

23 Shotshells used

Christian Schenk

The JAGDMUSEUM in Munich

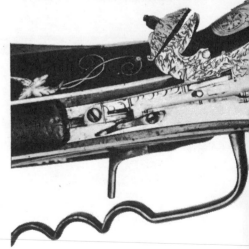

Photos by courtesy of Deutsches Jagdmuseum, Munich, West Germany.

Not only the Hofbräuhaus exists in Munich. In the heart of the city, not far from the main railway station where everyday life is pulsating noisily, stands the former Augustin Church and later custom-house. Here the Deutsches Jagdmuseum or German Hunting Museum has found a new home.

The Jagdmuseum has a fine collection of arms. Only a few important items were lost during the war, for most of the collection was stored away at Ast Castle for safe keeping. The original Jagdmuseum was inaugurated in October, 1938, and arms that remained at the museum during the war were stolen by plunderers. Today, the Jagdmuseum displays rows of boar spears from the 16th and 18th centuries, hunting and boar swords, crossbows, match-lock muskets, wheel-locks and flintlocks, cutlasses, misericords, daggers, and powder flasks, etc. Of course, sporting arms only make up a part of the whole. This, museum purports to foster interest in hunting lore and the many facets of woodsmanship, and the Stif-

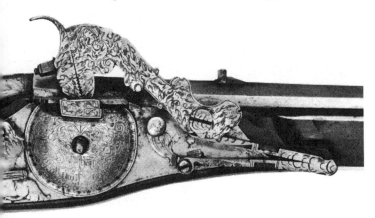

This wheel-lock gun was made by the famous Vienese master gunsmith Wolf Paumgartner in 1568. The lock bears the hall-mark IG, and the fire-gilded wheel cap displays the coat of arms of one Johann Jakob Khuen (archbishop of Salzburg 1560–1586). The German-type stock is of choice mahogany and is inlaid with engraved ivory.

terverband für Jagdwissenschaften e. V. (an association of benefactors) was called into being to promote scientific research in the fields of veterinary medicine, anatomy, kynology (dogs and dog breeding), the history of hunting, and the preservation of forests, fisheries, and wildlife in general, etc. It is hoped that the museum will create a bridge between town citizens and outdoor life.

There is an excellent menagerie of mounted red deer, fallow deer, roe deer, bears, boars, moufflons, winter and summer chamois, lynx, wild cats, foxes, badgers, sheep, small rodents, and big-game animals from Africa and America.

The world of ornithology is well represented, too, as there are 1500 dressed skins to choose from! The diorama (a painted background against which models are blended) is a breathtaking creation, and is in no way stuffy or museum-like. Each animal has a place in its natural habitat.

Furthermore, the trophies of the chase, built up around the collection of Count Maximillian of Arco-Zinneberg, cannot even be surpassed by the famous collections housed at Erbach and Moritzburg. For the Jagdmuseum was fortunate enough to purchase the Count's collections both at Munich and Berchtesgaden. The visitor is confronted with a three-horned chamois that has been proved to be genuine through x-ray photos provided by the Munich Röntgeninstitut of the University Clinics. In addition, there are heads and horns of animals from many parts of the world.

Of especial interest is a varied collection of baroque, rococo, and Empire style sleighs. Numerous paintings and drawings portray, more or less by way of factual reporting, many aspects of hunting and the adventuresome life of the hunter; including the capture of "Bavarian Hiesel," a German-type Robin Hood who made the great forests of Bavaria unsafe with his band of (merry) followers during the 18th century, but who was loved by the peasants just the same.

Last but not least, the ethnological department of the Jagdmuseum must be mentioned. Some of the items of this collection are described in Karl Sälzle's book, "Tier und Mensch – Gottheit und Dämon," which might be translated as "Animals and Man-

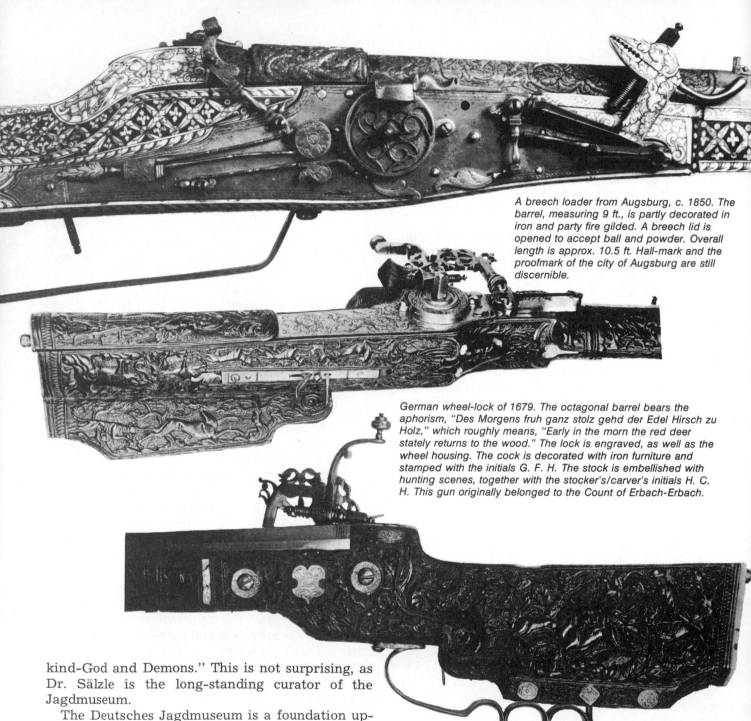

A breech loader from Augsburg, c. 1850. The barrel, measuring 9 ft., is partly decorated in iron and party fire gilded. A breech lid is opened to accept ball and powder. Overall length is approx. 10.5 ft. Hall-mark and the proofmark of the city of Augsburg are still discernible.

German wheel-lock of 1679. The octagonal barrel bears the aphorism, "Des Morgens fruh ganz stolz gehd der Edel Hirsch zu Holz," which roughly means, "Early in the morn the red deer stately returns to the wood." The lock is engraved, as well as the wheel housing. The cock is decorated with iron furniture and stamped with the initials G. F. H. The stock is embellished with hunting scenes, together with the stocker's/carver's initials H. C. H. This gun originally belonged to the Count of Erbach-Erbach.

kind–God and Demons." This is not surprising, as Dr. Sälzle is the long-standing curator of the Jagdmuseum.

The Deutsches Jagdmuseum is a foundation upheld by the Free State of Bavaria; Munich, the Bavarian capital; the Deutscher Jagdschutz-Verband; the Bayerischer Jagdschutz-Verband; and the Stifterverband für Jagdwissenschaften.

Although these benefactors help financially wherever possible, there is never enough money to go round. The "Verein der Freunde des Deutschen Jagdmuseums e. V." has been founded so that private individuals or clubs can make donations if they want to. Basic yearly fees are not exorbitant: full members DM 10, professional hunters and forest wardens DM

5, clubs and private firms DM 50. In Germany, such donations can be presented to the inland-revenue department for a deduction in income-tax. Possibly, a similar regulation also applies in other countries. Anyone interested in supporting the Deutsches Jagdmuseum might like to contact the Verein der Freunde des Deutschen Jagdmuseums e. V., Theatinerstraße 38, 8000 München 2, West Germany.

VAP Hunting Match Rifle

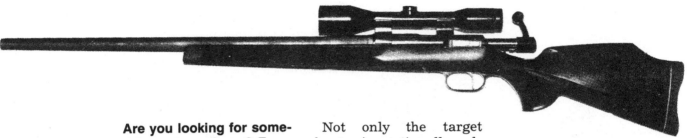

Are you looking for something extraordinary? For hunting wild goats in the Rocky Mountains or gazelles and antelopes in the vast savannahs of Africa, the Vapenspecialists AB (VAP) of Stockholm have evolved their "hunting match rifle." Our man in Stockholm, Mr. Wiegard, has been putting this VAP through its paces.

Lothar K.-H. Wiegard

Not only the target shooter is continually calling for better equipment, the hunter is also demanding his share of technological spin-off.

For hunting goats in America or gazelles and antelopes in Africa you need a rifle offering the following features:
– minimum dispersion at long distances
– flat trajectory
– effective killing power at long distances

In view of the general scarcity of game these days, and of the hunter's humane attitude towards the issue of "clean" kills, having the right tool to do the job is an essential prerequisite. Man can no longer afford to butcher his animals thoughtlessly. In some countries, the authorities even go so far as to heavily fine hunters for lost wounded animals. Taking today's situation into account, the firm of Vapenspecialists AB, Stockholm/Sweden, has de-

veloped a match-type rifle for the big-game hunter.

The VAP Hunting Match Rifle is a bolt-operated, single-shot weapon, whereby bolt and receiver are machined from high-quality Bofors steel, and barrel is of rustless material.

The trigger, available as one or two-stage, can be adjusted from 1.8 oz. to 3.3 lbs. The tang safety blocks trigger bar and bolt. There are no iron sights, since the VAP comes fitted with a scope that is soldered in place to prevent a change in point of impact.

As the performance of this VAP rifle depends largely on caliber and load, we pre-tested the caliber suitable for our purpose. Before long we ascertained that the Norma .308 Magnum was by far the best, as even factory loads printed within 2.4 inches at 328 yards, when firing a string of 5 shots.

VAP Hunting Match Rifle

A proficient marksman, therefore, just cannot miss the target, even at 550 yards. The stock is made to measure with a free-floating barrel. The contours of the pistol grip are no less important; so it is wise to have the grip formed to the size and shape of one's hand. For your trigger finger must contact the trigger at the right point to assure smooth let-off. Moreover, a swelling on the right-hand side of the pistol grip helps prevent the hand slipping forward on recoil, which normally results in a bruised middle finger.

The buttcap is of the ventilated rubber type, and the swivels can be easily removed. The VAP trigger guard has a sort of basket weave around the edges, to reduce sharpness. And all screws have Allen-key heads.

Of course, this rifle is custom made only.

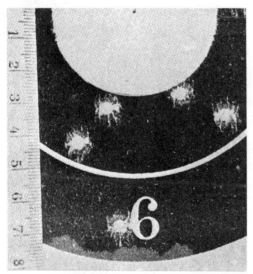

5-shot grouping at 328 yards

Hand Loading Table

Bullet weight in grains	Load	Charge Norma No.	Quantity in grains	Muzzle vel. fps.	Muzzle energy ft.p.
129.6	max.	204	78.7	3559	3645
	medium	204	74.9	3359	3247
	min.	203	64.4	3159	2871
149.7	max.	204	77.3	3349	3725
	medium	204	74.8	3149	3327
	min.	204	71.8	2949	2893
179	max.	205	76.7	3100	3819
	medium	204	71.8	2900	3341
	min.	204	69.9	2700	2893
219.1	max.	204	69.0	2811	3848
	medium	204	65.7	2611	3319
	min.	204	63.0	2414	2835

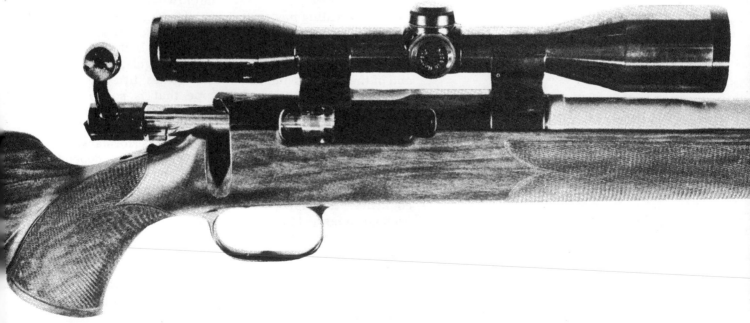

Modell: VAP Hunting Match Rifle

Action: Single shot, bolt has two locking lugs

Trigger: Match type, fully adjustable

Barrel material: Rustless Bofors steel

Barrel length: 27.6 in.

Twist: 1 in 10 in.

Grooves: 6

Caliber: .308 Norma Magnum

Sighting: Scope (top quality)

Stock: Custom made, oiled walnut with special insulation, Monte Carlo comb, swollen pistol grip, fine checkering

Finish: Receiver, bolt sleeve, bolt handle and trigger guard are blued, barrel is pickeled grey, and all other parts are polished

.308 Norma Magnum
Case: 7.62x65 mm Mag. belted
Bullet: Norma No. 578, 179 gr., Dual Core
Charge: Norma No. 205, 76.7 gr.
Pressure: 49,926 psi (mean)

V muzzle	V 100 yds.	V 200 yds.	V 300 yds.
3100	2880	2668	2464 fps.
E muzzle	E 100 yds.	E 200 yds.	E 300 yds.
3842	3318	2846	2427 ft.p.

Max. height of trajectory in inches

100 yds.	200 yds.	300 yds.
.60	1.6	4.6

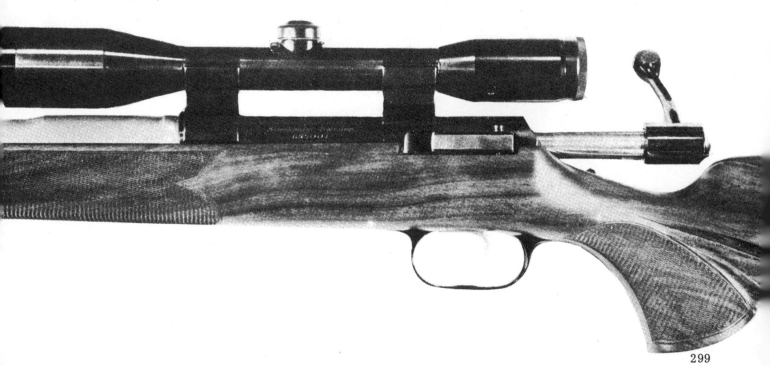